Fairness in Selecting Employees

Second Edition

Richard D. Arvey
UNIVERSITY OF MINNESOTA

Robert H. Faley
KENT STATE UNIVERSITY

 ADDISON-WESLEY PUBLISHING COMPANY

Reading, Massachusetts   Menlo Park, California   New York
Don Mills, Ontario   Wokingham, England   Amsterdam   Bonn
Sydney   Singapore   Tokyo   Madrid   San Juan

To Marvin Dunnette,
Winifred and Henry

THE ADDISON-WESLEY SERIES ON MANAGING HUMAN RESOURCES
Series Editor: John P. Wanous, *Michigan State University*

Fairness in Selecting Employees, Second Edition
Richard D. Arvey, *University of Minnesota,* and Robert H. Faley, *Kent State University*

Managing Organizational Conflict
Dave Brown, *Case Western Reserve University*

Performance Appraisal and Goal Setting
Gary P. Latham, *University of Washington,* and Kenneth N. Wexley, *University of Akron*

Managing Careers
Manuel London, *AT&T,* and Stephen A. Stumpf, *New York University*

Organizational Entry: Recruitment, Selection, and Socialization of Newcomers
John P. Wanous, *Michigan State University*

Library of Congress Cataloging-in-Publication Data

Arvey, Richard D.
    Fairness in selecting employees/Richard D. Arvey, Robert H.
Faley.—2nd ed.
        p.   cm.—(Addison-Wesley series on managing human resources)
    Includes bibliographies and indexes.
    ISBN 0-201-00078-4
    1. Employee selection—United States.   2. Discrimination in
employment—United States.   3. Employee selection—Law and
legislation—United States.   4. Discrimination in employment—Law
and legislation—United States.   I. Faley, Robert H.   II. Title.
III. Series.
HF5549.5.S38A78   1988   87-22173
658.3'112—dc19   CIP

ABCDEFGHIJ-DO-898

Foreword

In 1979, the first edition of Richard Arvey's *Fairness in Selecting Employees* initiated the Managing Human Resources Series. It has been highly successful, receiving critical acclaim from the reviewers and popular acclaim from students and teachers alike. This text is the standard to which others are compared.

The field of personnel selection is probably the most dynamic area within the larger field of human resources. The specific topic of fairness in selection has been particularly volatile due to the constant flow of court decisions. This second edition updates legal developments and psychological measurement improvements made in the 1980s.

The continuing primary objective of the Addison-Wesley Managing Human Resources Series is to articulate new solutions to chronic human relations problems. As the Series Editor, I have sought out authors who are recognized as the top experts in a particular human resource specialty. The authors are charged with the difficult assignment of writing a book that is equally relevant to human resource professionals, students, and fellow academics. Richard Arvey is such a person; his first edition was such a book; this second edition, co-authored by Robert H. Faley, continues the tradition.

John P. Wanous
Series Editor

Preface

Almost ten years ago, the first edition of *Fairness in Selecting Employees* was written to examine the complex issues of fairness in selection contexts. The task was difficult because no one before had coherently combined the diverse research, case law, and principles to guide researchers and practitioners in this area. The first edition successfully accomplished its goals by providing guidance to those interested in fairness issues.

At that time, the topic of fairness in selecting employees was achieving growing recognition and importance. Vast numbers of minority and nonminority job candidates have been and still are being affected by legal decisions in this area as well as by the psychological research being conducted around specific issues of "unfair discrimination." However, prior to 1979, the few treatments of the issues associated with fairness in selecting employees had focused predominantly on whether employment *tests* were fair or unfair with regard to minority black job applicants. Also, previous reviews only lightly examined the legal aspects of unfair discrimination. The first edition of this text provided a broader perspective by dealing with the fairness of the *full range* of decision-making devices in selecting employees—e.g., the interview, height and weight requirements, and so forth. Furthermore, it provided a review of the fairness of these selection "devices" as they affected blacks, females, the elderly, and the handicapped. Finally, the first edition, which gave considerable attention to the legal aspects of unfair discrimination in selection, integrated psychological and research-oriented literature. Thus, the initial edition considerably broadened and expanded prior treatments of this topic area.

In the past ten years there has been a steady growth in case law in the area of selection fairness as well as many new important developments in the research literature. Because of this growth, much of the material in the first edition needed to be updated. This second edition includes current research literature and recent case law citations. In addition, we expanded our treatment of several statistical concepts and related models.

Finally, we tried to elucidate more clearly the kinds of standards and procedures followed by the courts in their review of fairness/bias issues. There has been considerable expansion and clarification of these legal principles and standards in the last ten years. We have tried, however, not to make this a legal treatise, but instead have attempted to provide the basic framework around which courts evaluate fairness issues.

We wish to extend thanks to those who have provided support and encouragement during the revision process. We also wish to extend our support and encouragement to all those people in the real world who are struggling with their own personal fairness issues.

Minneapolis, Minnesota   R.D.A.
Kent, Ohio   R.H.F.

Contents

Introduction

1

In recent years, the selection and promotion practices used by organizations have been challenged in courts of law. Consider, for example, the following cases:

- In June 1976, a federal class-action suit was brought against Merrill Lynch, Pierce, Fenner, and Smith, Inc., charging the company with employing sex and race discrimination policies. A major contention was that the employment-aptitude test battery was based on "traits of majority males." In the settlement, Merrill Lynch agreed to spend $1.3 million to recruit women and minorities, to pay $1.9 million in compensation to hundreds of persons denied jobs since 1971, to hire one woman for every ten persons hired, and to meet other requirements.

- In 1973, American Telephone and Telegraph agreed to pay $15 million in back wages to some 15,000 women and minority-group males against whom it had allegedly discriminated in job assignments and promotions (Wallace, 1976).

- In 1979, the revenue-sharing funds of the city of Chicago were impounded by a federal district court because the city failed to take affirmative action to end discrimination in its police department, and the department had failed to eliminate purposeful sex discrimination. Among the issues in this case were the employment-testing requirements and the minimum height requirements used in selecting and promoting police officers.

- In 1983, General Motors agreed to pay 45.3 million dollars to settle a class action lawsuit, and in 1984 Burlington Northern, Inc. reached a $60 million settlement with the Equal Employment Opportunity Commission (EEOC) related to allegations of racial discrimination.

The challenges to traditional employment practices, the resulting lawsuits, and the various governmental guidelines and directives are confusing and bewildering to many managers—and no wonder. Much of this activity has been aimed directly toward the eradication of minority-group discrimination in employment and the implementation of affirmative action. On the other hand, a variety of cases alleging "reverse discrimination" have been filed against male Caucasians. In *Reeves* v. *Eaves* (1977), for example, the court ordered a police department to stop hiring less-qualified minorities simply because of their race. Subsequently, in *U.S. Steelworkers* v. *Weber* (1979), the Supreme Court articulated standards for determining when a system of voluntary preferential treatment is valid under the law (see Chapter 9).

The proliferation of lawsuits and the progression of case law have discouraged many from "keeping on top" of employment discrimination issues. This has happened for two reasons. First, the complexity of the issues has increased. As lawyers and judges become more sophisticated in case law, the complexities of the lawsuits naturally increase. Similarly, as psychological research becomes more sophisticated, so do the statistical models developed and the research methods used to deal with issues of employment discrimination. Second, there are many inconsistencies: The courts hand down differing opinions dealing with similar facts and circumstances. In addition, guidelines issued by the various governmental agencies differ in emphasis. Employment practices that may satisfy one agency's set of guidelines may not satisfy those issued by another agency.

In light of the burgeoning legislation and lawsuits, personnel managers often just don't know how to go about selecting individuals for jobs. Questions such as the following often occur: Should we use an aptitude test to select applicants? Is the interview "safe" from lawsuits? May we use height and weight requirements?

PURPOSE

This book addresses these employment concerns. It focuses primarily on issues associated with alleged discrimination occurring in the selection of employees and will provide perspectives on the following four aspects of these issues: (1) Some *historical background* concerning the development of legislation, litigation, and research in the area; (2) *practical knowledge* concerning which employee selection procedures are currently considered legally acceptable; (3) a *conceptual framework* concerning "unfair" discrimination from both a legalistic and a psychological framework; and (4) *directions and trends* for both the law and future psychological research.

A final purpose of this book is to describe how to use scientific methods to ensure that *all* employees in organizations are treated fairly and used wisely.

Our discussion will be presented through an integration of three literature sources. First, existing statutes, laws, and governmental guidelines which serve as basic sources of authority are examined as they provide a crucial understanding of the development of case law in the area. Second, the legal literature is cited frequently, and illustrations are drawn to document and develop the necessary principles and concepts. One need not be an expert in law, however, to understand the cases discussed here. Comprehensive legal reviews are not a part of this book; instead, the most relevant leading cases are summarized. Third, research articles found in psychological and business journals are cited in an effort to present *both* supporting and conflicting research results of selection discrimination.

We believe that a better understanding of the issues in discrimination can be achieved by integrating these three literature sources. The reader should be aware, however, that the field of employment discrimination is changing rapidly. New cases are being filed, Supreme Court decisions are being made, and new research methodologies and findings are constantly appearing. Nevertheless, we believe that it is important to provide clarity in this area for nonexperts *now* and that, armed with this knowledge, individuals will be better prepared to follow future directions and trends and to know how to examine their own particular selection procedures for fairness.

INTENDED AUDIENCE

This book is directed toward several audiences. The concepts and issues it presents should provide insights useful to managers making selection decisions in businesses and educational administrators facing lawsuits dealing with issues of discrimination in academic promotion policies. Graduate students and professionals in industrial and organizational psychology and law also should find the text useful. It is somewhat surprising that so few formal courses concern *both* psychological and legal perspectives of fairness in selection.

Although one need not be an expert in statistics to read this book, several chapters and sections require an understanding of basic statistical concepts. A review is provided in Chapter 2, but it would be very helpful for readers to be acquainted with the basic principles of statistical inference, correlation and regression analyses, and statistical significance. In addition, readers would be well advised to have read basic books on personnel selection and the basic models involved in selection techniques and practices, such as those by Dunnette (1966), Guion (1965), and Schneider and Schmitt (1986).

It is not entirely necessary, however, for the reader to have had previous exposure to all of the concepts and principles discussed here. Some chapters (such as Chapters 5 and 6, which deal almost exclusively with employment tests) require more understanding of statistics than others.

"FOCAL" POPULATIONS

Throughout the book, four groups of minorities are considered: blacks, females, the elderly, and the handicapped. We focus on these groups for three reasons. First, the research and litigation are generally presented in terms of these groups. Even so, little research is available in some situations concerning discrimination against even these basic subgroups. For example, relevant research demonstrating bias against the handicapped in interview situations is very scarce. Second, many of the principles and methodologies used to investigate discrimination generalize to other groups. Third, the legal principles that have evolved based on these four minority groups will almost certainly apply to other subgroups as well. Thus, focus on these four groups will provide sufficient knowledge concerning the research methodology and legal principles to be used for other subgroups. Finally, space limitations curtail comprehensive coverage of other minority groups.

We hasten to emphasize, however, that the principles developed here should ensure fairness for *all* employees. The "theme" of this book is the importance of making wise and fair selection decisions for the *total* organization.

SELECTION PROCESS

It is important at the outset to clarify what we mean by the "selection process." Typically, when an organization hires new employees, it uses one or more of several selection procedures. An essential ingredient in each of these procedures is to obtain information to be used in making selection decisions. Figure 1.1 provides a diagram of these various information-gathering procedures.

Not every organization will use all of the strategies specified. For example, small organizations may employ only an interview and an application blank, whereas large organizations may use all the procedures.

This book deals with issues, concepts, and cases involved in the components of the selection process outlined in Fig. 1.1. The research and legal literature reviewed throughout the book is mostly limited to the selection of individuals in entry-level jobs, rather than management-executive positions. While the concepts may generalize to these higher positions, little data are currently available concerning selection fairness for higher level positions. While we will not deal directly with promotion, transfer, or salary decisions, many of the issues discussed will be relevant to those kinds of employment decisions as well. A complete review of the total employment process is beyond the scope of this book.

Likewise, we will not deal with the area of *self*-selection. How individuals decide to apply for particular jobs and choose organizations is a process that is outside the scope of this book. However, self-selection

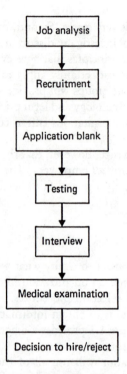

Figure 1.1 *The se-lection process.*

is an important topic indeed, and those readers interested in it and in the area of organizational entry may want to consult another book in this series, *Organizational Entry* (1980), by John P. Wanous.

DISCRIMINATION AND BIAS

It is also important to define as carefully as possible the meaning of "discrimination" and "bias," or "unfairness." This is difficult because there are several factors that cloud definitions and discussions of employment discrimination—particularly when dealing with selection processes.

The basic objective in selection is *to discriminate*—that is, to provide a means by which some individuals may be selected and others rejected.

A selection system that does not elicit variability among job candidates provides little or no information with which to make a decision. What is crucial is whether the discriminations are "fair" or "unfair." Perhaps another way of putting it is to ask whether the decisions made about employees are biased or unbiased. We will use the terms "fair" and "unbiased" interchangeably.

Unfortunately, it is not altogether clear what is meant by the terms "fair" versus "unfair" discrimination. There are several definitions of these concepts, all of which make some sense, but at present, there is no universally accepted definition of "unfair" or "biased" discrimination. However, in order to provide a foundation for the reader, we would like to offer a working definition and modify this definition as we proceed:

> *Unfair discrimination or bias is said to exist when members of a minority group have lower probabilities of being selected for a job when, in fact, if they had been selected, their probabilities of performing successfully in a job would have been equal to those of nonminority group members.*

To provide a simple illustration, suppose a merchandising firm decided to adopt a requirement that applicants must be at least 5 feet 6 inches tall in order to be hired as sales clerk? Because females are shorter than males on the average, a much larger proportion of women would be excluded from this position. However, it is certainly possible that if short women were hired, they could perform just as adequately as tall men in this job, which would prove that height actually makes no difference whatsoever in performance for either male or female employees. Under these circumstances, unfair discrimination or bias would be said to exist against female job applicants.

This illustration is, of course, a simplification. The definition is also simple, compared to more complex statistical models of unfair discrimination. However, many important elements found in the more complex models may be found within this definition.

ORGANIZATION OF THE BOOK

The remaining material in this book is divided into eight chapters. Chapter 2 provides a basic summary and review of statistical and validational principles needed for comprehending some of the later chapters. Chapter

3 reviews the major legislative acts and governmental directives which prohibit discrimination against blacks, females, the elderly, and the handicapped.

Chapters 4, 5, and 6 contain materials dealing with employment testing. Chapter 4 presents a historical and legal perspective involved in employment testing. Because the litigation involving testing has developed the most rapidly and also because it serves as the major authority for decisions involving other selection processes, these materials are presented early. Chapter 5 deals with the statistical issues involving unfair testing and the various research findings surrounding this controversy, and Chapter 6 treats topics and issues involved in unfair testing.

Chapter 7 reviews research regarding the employment interview and unfair discrimination, and Chapter 8 presents material regarding other components of the selection process and possible discrimination. Finally, Chapter 9 provides a summary of previous chapters as well as a forecast of future trends.

REFERENCES

Bakke v. *Regents of California,* 17 FEP 1000 (1978).

Dunnette, M. D. (1966). *Personnel Selection and Placement.* Belmont, Calif.: Wadsworth.

Griggs v. *Duke Power,* 3 FEP 175 (1971).

Guion, R. M. (1965). *Personnel Testing.* New York: McGraw-Hill.

Reeves v. Eaves, 15 FEP 441 (1977).

Schneider, B., and Schmitt, N. (1986). *Staffing Organizations.* Glenview, Ill.: Scott, Foresman.

U.S. Steelworkers v. *Weber,* 20 FEP 1 (1979).

Wallace, P. A. (1976). *Equal Employment Opportunity and the AT & T Case.* Cambridge, Mass.: M.I.T. Press.

Wanous, J. P. (1979). *Organizational Entry.* Menlo Park, Calif.: Cummings Publishing Company.

Statistical Concepts and Validation Principles: A Short Review

2

Much of the evolution in both the legal and statistical perspectives in unfair discrimination and Title VII litigation has its origin in psychological testing. Several of the early major legal decisions, e.g., the *Griggs* v. *Duke Power* (1971) and the *Albemarle* v. *Moody* (1975) Supreme Court cases, concerned the use of tests in employment settings. The principles that emerged from these cases have served as precedents for deciding cases concerning other selection devices, such as height and weight requirements and educational requirements. Because of this, it is vital that the reader achieve a good understanding of the progression of case law and the development of the statistical issues and models associated with employment testing and test validation.

In order to achieve this understanding, however, the reader must have some familiarity with many of the basic concepts and statistical principles involved in the test-validation process. As mentioned earlier, it would be helpful if readers had some exposure to texts such as those written by Guion (1965), Dunnette (1966), or Schneider and Schmitt (1986). Moreover, readers should have a working knowledge of descriptive and inferential statistics, such as provided by Hayes (1981), Guilford and Fruchter (1973), or Runyon and Haber (1976). The following pages provide an explanation of most of the concepts and statistics used in the remaining chapters. Those who have a working knowledge of these principles may want only to review these pages briefly or even to skip them entirely. It should be stressed, however, that this section is not intended to provide in-depth coverage of these concepts or to educate readers in any comprehensive sense with regard to statistics. Other sources should be consulted for more in-depth exposure to these materials.

SOME BASIC STATISTICS

The Mean

Possibly the most frequently encountered statistical index in psychological research is the mean or the average. The mean of a series of scores consists of simply adding up the scores to form a total and dividing this sum by the number of scores. Operationally, the mean is calculated by the following formula:

$$\bar{x} = \frac{\Sigma x}{n},$$

where

$\bar{x}$ = the mean;
x = a particular score;
Σ = the sum of the scores;
n = the number of scores.

For example, suppose a manager had the following test scores for ten employees: 21, 26, 23, 15, 21, 17, 18, 19, 21, and 24. The mean or average of this distribution of scores is calculated to be

$$\bar{x} = \frac{205}{10} = 20.5$$

The mean is a statistic that summarizes a distribution of scores into the single most representative value.

Standard Deviation

Distribution of scores often tends to fall into a particular shape, sometimes referred to as a "bell-shaped" (because the distribution resembles a bell) or normal curve. Figure 2.1 illustrates two such curves. While each of these two distributions demonstrates "properties" of a normal curve

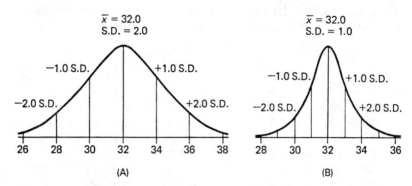

Figure 2.1 *Two distributions with same means but different standard deviations.*

(e.g., the distribution "peaks" at the mean; the shape of each curve is not disproportionate), the two distributions differ in that one has a greater "spread" than the other. Distribution A in Fig. 2.1 has scores that are more dispersed than the scores in distribution B. A useful statistic that helps to summarize a distribution of scores is the standard deviation. The standard deviation is an index of the amount of spread or dispersion among a set of scores. When a standard deviation is used to summarize the amount of spread among scores in a *sample,* it is represented by the letters S.D. (When the standard deviation is computed for a total *population* of scores, it is typically represented by the Greek symbol σ). For two distributions with the same mean, the distribution with the larger standard deviation (S.D.) will have relatively more spread, or variability, around the mean.

One may use the standard deviation to calculate the interval within which most of the scores will lie. Specifically, the interval $\bar{x} \pm 1$ S.D. will contain approximately 68 percent of the scores and the interval $\bar{x} \pm 2$ S.D. will contain approximately 95 percent of the scores. Thus, for distribution A in Fig. 2.1, 95 percent of the scores will fall between $\bar{x} \pm 2$ S.D. $= 32 \pm 2(2.0)$, or 28.0 to 36.0.

The formula for calculating the standard deviation is as follows:

$$\text{S.D.} = \sqrt{\frac{\Sigma(x - \bar{x})^2}{n}}.$$

Thus, the standard deviation of the test scores for the ten employees given above would be calculated in the following way:

$x - \bar{x}$		$(x - \bar{x})^2$	
$21 - 20.5 =$	$.5$	$(\ \ .5) =$	$.25$
$26 - 20.5 =$	5.5	$(\ \ 5.5) =$	30.25
$23 - 20.5 =$	2.5	$(\ \ 2.5) -$	6.25
$15 - 20.5 =$	-5.5	$(-5.5) =$	30.25
$21 - 20.5 =$	$.5$	$(\ \ .5) -$	$.25$
$17 - 20.5 =$	-3.5	$(-3.5) =$	12.25
$18 - 20.5 =$	2.5	$(\ \ 2.5) =$	6.25
$19 - 20.5 =$	-1.5	$(-1.5) -$	2.25
$21 - 20.5 =$	$.5$	$(\ \ .5) =$	$.25$
$24 - 20.5 =$	3.5	$(\ \ 3.5) =$	12.25

$$\Sigma(x - \bar{x})^2 = 100.5$$

$$\text{S.D.} = \sqrt{\frac{\Sigma(x - \bar{x})^2}{n}} = 3.17.$$

The t-Test

Researchers using statistics often are interested in making inferences about the population from which samples have been drawn. For example, suppose a researcher had administered an employment test to ten male and ten female applicants. The researcher might have asked the following question: Are the means of the population from which these samples were drawn equal or unequal? The classical statistical procedure for a researcher to follow is to start by proposing *no* differences between the population means. This is commonly referred to as stating the *null hypothesis*. The *alternative hypothesis* states that there is, indeed, a difference between the means of the two populations. The next step is to review the data to determine if the empirical results support one or the other of these two hypotheses. Based on the sample data, if the two means are very different from each other, researchers typically reject the null hypothesis and indicate that the observed data are more consistent with the alternative hypothesis; that is, the observed difference between the means is so great as to be considered essentially true in general, rather than a chance occurrence, or "fluke." Researchers will typically reject the null hypothesis when the odds are less than 5 out of 100 that the results obtained were due to chance factors and accept that the difference between the two groups is real. This cut-off point is known as the .05 significance level. When a researcher reports that the difference between the means of two groups is significantly different, this is a way of expressing that the probability is less than 5 chances out of 100 that the sample means would be this different from each other purely by chance, *if* the null hypothesis were indeed true and the two population means are equal. Researchers will also adopt a significance level of .01 indicating that the odds of finding such data solely by chance (if the null hypothesis were true) are less than 1 out of 100.

A statistic commonly employed in detecting whether the means are different is the *t*-test (although the *t*-test is used frequently in other applications). To illustrate this test using the example above, suppose the researcher found that the ten males and ten females who took the employment test displayed the following means and standard deviations:*

Males	Females
$\bar{x}_1 = 26.7$	$\bar{x}_2 = 35.4$
S.D. = 1.7	S.D. = 1.4
$N_1 = 10$	$N_2 = 10$

where the subscripts 1 and 2 indicate from which group the statistical indices were derived (1 = males, 2 = females). If the two distributions have similar spread or variability around their means (technically, this is known as homogeneous or equal variances), a *t*-test may be computed according to the following formula:

$$t\text{-value} = \frac{\bar{x}_1 - \bar{x}_2}{\sqrt{\left[\frac{(N_1 - 1)\text{S.D.}^2 \, (N_2 - 1)\text{S.D.}^2}{N_1 + N_2 - 2}\right] \cdot \left[\frac{1}{N_1} + \frac{1}{N_2}\right]}} .$$

---

* When a standard deviation is computed in situations where its values will be used to estimate the standard deviations of the population from which the sample was drawn, the formula for its calculation is

$$\text{S.D.} = \sqrt{\frac{\Sigma(x - \bar{x})^2}{N - 1}}$$

Following this formula, the computation of the t-value based on the data given above for the male and female employees is as follows:

$$t\text{-value} = \frac{26.7 - 35.4}{\sqrt{\left[\frac{(10-1)(1.7)^2 + (10-1)(1.4)^2}{10 + 10 - 2}\right] \cdot \left[\frac{1}{10} + \frac{1}{10}\right]}}$$

$$= \frac{-8.7}{\sqrt{\left[\frac{26.01 + 17.64}{18}\right] \cdot [.2]}} = \frac{-8.7}{\sqrt{.485}} = \frac{-8.7}{.696}$$

$$= -12.5.$$

After the t-value is calculated, it is compared to a theoretical distribution (technically known as the t-distribution) which allows the researcher to determine the probability of obtaining a mean difference of this observed magnitude if, in fact, there is no difference between the population means of the two groups. In the present example, the probability of finding a difference of this magnitude by chance is less than .001, or 1 time in 1,000. Thus, the researcher would reject the null hypothesis of no difference between the two population means and assert that there is a difference between them.

It should be noted, however, that one must *not* always adhere to this .05 convention. One could instead reject the null hypothesis if the probability (also called the p-value) is less than .10 or .15 (or any p-value, for that matter). The decision depends on the researcher's notion of what constitutes a relatively rare event. But, in almost all court cases that deal with research associated with discrimination issues, the .05 level of significance is adopted as the basic indicator of a statistical difference.

A further concept that should be explored in t-tests is the idea of one- versus two-tailed tests. Without going into great detail, when a researcher has no prior knowledge concerning which group might exhibit the larger mean value, a *two*-tailed t-test is conducted. However, if specific differences are expected (e.g., if one suspects that a particular group will score higher), then a *one*-tailed t-test is conducted. A two-tailed test is sensitive to significant differences in either direction, greater *and* less. The one-tailed test is sensitive to differences in only one direction, greater *or* less. A researcher should employ a one-tailed test only when the direction in which the difference will occur can be specified ahead of time. An advantage of using a one-tailed test is that it is relatively easier to find statistical significance compared to a two-tailed test.

Type I Error, Type II Error, and Power

Researchers use statistics in order to make "best guesses" about the true state of affairs when incomplete data or measurement error exists. These best guesses may either be true or false. A framework for examining the accuracy of the inferences drawn is provided in most statistics texts under the rubric of Type I and Type II errors.

As we have noted above, researchers employ a procedure in which a null hypothesis and an alternative hypothesis are stated. They then collect data, conduct a specific statistical test (e.g., the t-test), and make a decision about which hypothesis is correct based on the results of the statistical test. For example, a researcher will make a decision concerning whether the null hypothesis is true or false. In actuality, the situation will be either one of these alternatives: The null hypothesis will be true or it will be false. In other words, the two groups actually may not differ, except by chance, or they may indeed differ. Thus, there are four possible outcomes when a researcher makes an inference or a decision based on a statistical study.

1. The researcher could reject the null hypothesis when it is in fact true. This error in the researcher's decision is called a Type I error and is represented by the Greek letter α. It is also referred to as alpha or the probability of rejecting the null hypothesis when it is actually true.

2. The researcher could fail to reject the null hypothesis when it is actually false. This is referred to as a Type II error and is represented by the Greek letter β. This value corresponds to the probability of accepting the null hypothesis when it is *not* true.

3. The researcher may decide that the null hypothesis is true when it does, in fact, represent the actual state of affairs. This, of course, would be a correct decision. It is often symbolized as $1-\alpha$.

4. The researcher may decide that the null hypothesis is false when, in fact, the alternative hypothesis is true. This too would be a correct decision. It is often referred to as the *power* of a statistical test. It

represents the probability that a researcher will detect a difference when it exists and is often symbolized by $1-\beta$.

We might represent these four outcomes as shown in Table 2.1.

Researchers are most interested in the fourth outcome, *statistical power*. They want their tests to have as much power as possible, so that if the null hypothesis is false, they are able to detect it. The power of a test is affected by essentially three variables:

1. Sample size—the larger the sample, the greater the statistical power.
2. Degree of actual differences—the larger the differences among the means of the groups, the greater the power to detect these differences.
3. Stated alpha level—researchers who use a .01 significance level will have less power than those who use a larger (e.g., .05) alpha level.

Thus researchers can increase the power of their statistical tests by increasing sample sizes in their studies and by less stringent significance levels. More will be said about power in a later chapter.

Correlation Coefficient

Another statistic frequently encountered in psychological research is the correlation coefficient. This statistic summarizes the degree of *linear association* between two variables. Consider a situation in which a group of 15 employees were administered a psychological test. Suppose further

Table 2.1
Types of errors made as a function of the true status of the null hypothesis.

		NULL HYPOTHESIS TRUE	NULL HYPOTHESIS FALSE
Researcher's decision (based on data from a sample of the population)	Accept null hypothesis	$1-\alpha$	Type II error (β)
	Reject null hypothesis	Type I error (α)	Power $(1-\beta)$

that their supervisor also rated each employee's "overall" performance using a 10-point scale (1 = poor performance, 10 = superior performance). In order to examine the relationship between the test score and the job-performance rating, these data would be plotted on a graph such as that shown in Fig. 2.2. Each point represents a single individual. Thus,

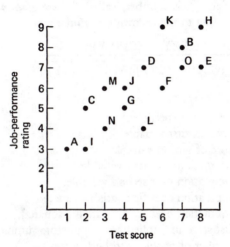

Employee	Test score	Job-performance rating
A	1	3
B	7	8
C	2	5
D	5	7
E	8	7
F	6	6
G	4	5
H	8	9
I	2	3
J	4	6
K	6	9
L	5	4
M	3	6
N	3	4
O	7	7

Figure 2.2 *Scatterplot for test scores and job-performance ratings based on 15 employees.*

employee A had a test score of 1 and had a job-performance rating of 3. The coordinates of point A on the graph represent these two scores for this individual. A graph of this sort is commonly referred to as a "scatterplot."

While this graph is a good *visual* representation of the degree of relationship, it would also be useful to have a number that would summarize those data. This number, called the *correlation coefficient*, is computed according to the following formula:

$$r_{XY} = \frac{N\Sigma XY - (\Sigma S)(\Sigma Y)}{\sqrt{[N\Sigma X^2 - (\Sigma X)^2][N\Sigma Y^2 - (\Sigma Y)^2]}}.$$

where

r_{XY} = correlation coefficient,
X = score on first variable,
Y = score of second variable,
ΣX = summation over first variable,
ΣY = summation over second variable,
ΣX^2 = summation over first variable squared,
ΣY^2 = summation over second variable squared,
ΣXY = first score multiplied by second score summed over people,
N = number of people with both scores.

The correlation coefficient for the data presented in Fig. 2.2 is calculated as follows:

Employee	X	X²	Y	Y²	XY
A	1	1	3	9	3
B	7	49	8	64	56
C	2	4	5	25	10
D	5	25	7	49	35
E	8	64	7	49	56
F	6	36	6	36	36
G	4	16	5	25	20
H	8	64	9	81	72
I	2	4	3	9	6
J	4	16	6	36	24
K	6	36	9	81	54

Employee	X	X²	Y	Y²	XY
L	5	25	4	16	20
M	3	9	6	36	18
N	3	9	4	16	12
O	7	49	7	49	49
	$\Sigma X = 71$	$\Sigma X^2 = 407$	$\Sigma Y = 89$	$\Sigma Y^2 = 581$	$\Sigma XY = 471$

The resulting r_{XY} is .82. The values of a correlation coefficient range between $+1.00$ and -1.00. A correlation of $+1.00$ represents a perfect positive relationship and indicates that if you know the value of one variable, the exact value of the other variable can be determined. A correlation of zero indicates that no relationship exists, and a correlation of -1.00 represents a perfect negative correlation between two variables. Obviously, there are a great many relationships that are less than perfect, and the correlation calculated here using the employee data given in Fig. 2.2 is just one example. Our correlation here of .82 indicates that if one knows the particular test score of an employee, one may fairly accurately predict his or her job-performance rating. In other words, a person with a high test score is more than likely to receive a high job-performance rating.

Additional types of relationships are shown in Fig. 2.3. Part (a) depicts a high positive relationship between the variables X and Y. Part (b) shows a high negative relationship. Part (c) depicts a situation where there is essentially no relationship. Part (d) shows the same thing as (a)—a high positive correlation—by means of an *ellipse diagram*. Frequently, instead of plotting each individual point, an ellipse is used to show the relationship.

The correlation coefficient may also be tested for statistical significance in order to determine whether the correlation is "real" or whether it was simply a chance finding and the "true" correlation or relationship in the population is zero.

It is possible to determine the probability of achieving a particular correlation in a sample of people purely by chance if the population was actually zero. Most frequently, if the probability is equal to or less than .05, the correlation is considered to be statistically significant—that is, the "real" relationship is *not* likely to be zero.

In order to determine if the correlation is statistically significant, one

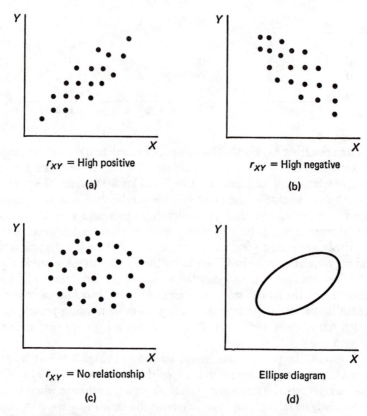

Figure 2.3 *Several kinds of correlational relationships.*

must consult a table of the minimum correlation needed to achieve significance (sometimes called the critical value). There is a different critical value for each sample size used, as shown in Table 2.2. The magnitude of the obtained correlation is compared with the correlation needed to be significant (as derived from Table 2.2 or any statistics text). If the observed correlation equals or exceeds the value in the table, it is said to have reached the level of statistical significance.

For example, given a sample size of 15, one would need a correlation of .51 to be significant at the .05 level. The correlation computed in the example was .82. Referring to Table 2.2, this computed or obtained value

Table 2.2
Magnitude of correlations needed to achieve significance for various sample sizes.

SAMPLE SIZE	.05 LEVEL	.01 LEVEL
3	.98	1.00
4	.95	.99
5	.88	.96
6	.81	.92
7	.75	.87
8	.71	.83
9	.66	.80
10	.63	.76
11	.60	.73
12	.57	.71
13	.55	.68
14	.53	.66
15	.51	.64
20	.44	.56
25	.40	.50
30	.36	.46
35	.33	.43
40	.31	.40
50	.27	.36
70	.23	.30
100	.19	.25

(.82) is higher than either .51 or .64. Thus, we may say that the correlation is significant beyond the .01 level. This is often communicated symbolically by $p < .01$.

It is worthwhile here to point out the special relationship between sample size and the magnitude of the correlation needed to achieve significance. In general, the smaller the sample size, the larger the size of the correlation needed to reach significance. For example, a correlation of .35 based on a sample of 20 people is not large enough to be considered significant. But, if the same correlation of .35 were found based on a sample of 50, the correlation *would* be considered significant. This is due simply to the fact that correlations computed on smaller samples tend to fluctuate more than correlations based on larger samples.

Another fact to keep in mind is that the correlation coefficient is based on variables assumed to have a linear (that is, a straight-line) relationship. When two variables are related in a nonlinear fashion, as in Fig. 2.4, the correlation coefficient *under*estimates the true relationship.

Regression Equations

On many occasions, researchers would like to be able to predict one variable from knowledge about another. For example, a personnel manager may wish to predict a prospective employee's job performance on the basis of his or her score on an employment test. A method of analysis that permits these predictions is called *regression analysis*. Figure 2.5 illustrates the situation discussed earlier in which a manager had available both the test scores and the job-performance ratings for 15 employees. In this instance, a way of summarizing these data is through the use of a "straight" line, usually called a regression line. This line has been statistically derived so that its path represents the best possible "fit" to the data (that is, the distance from the regression line to the various data points is at a minimum).

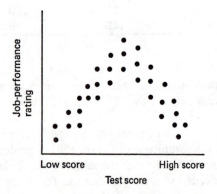

Figure 2.4 *A nonlinear relationship between Test X and job-performance rating.*

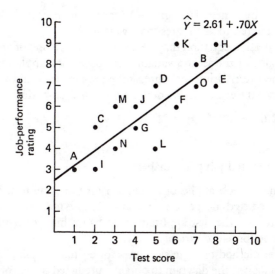

Figure 2.5 *Regression line based on test scores and job-performance data.*

Some readers will recall from an early course in algebra that any straight line may be represented mathematically by the formula

$$Y = a + bX,$$

where

Y = score on the Y-variable,
a = intercept value,
b = slope of regression line,
X = score on the X-variable.

For example, the regression line depicted in Fig. 2.5 is summarized by the regression equation: $\hat{Y} = 2.61 + .70\,(X)$, where $\hat{Y}$ = predicted job performance. The intercept value (2.61) is the distance from the zero point on the Y-axis to the point where the regression line crosses the Y-axis. The slope value (.70) indicates the amount of change in the Y-variable that occurs with every unit of change in the X-variable. That is, for every one-unit increase in test score, one should expect a .70 increase in the Y-value. It is also possible to derive a negative slope, which would be indicated by a negative sign (−) for the slope value. These slope values are referred to as "regression" weights.*

The regression equation may be used to predict scores of one variable from the value of the second variable. Suppose a job applicant scored 8 on a selection test. Using the regression equation, we could incorporate this value into the equation and derive a *predicted* job-performance value:

$$\hat{Y} = 2.61 + .70(8) = 8.21,$$

where

$$\hat{Y} = \text{predicted job performance.}$$

Suppose another job applicant scored a 3 on the same test. Using the equation, predicted job performance is 4.71. The manager would probably want to hire the first applicant, who had a higher predicted score on the job-performance variable.

Another method of regression lines for estimating job performance is simply to look at the diagram to obtain a predicted score. For example, Fig. 2.6 presents a regression line of the formula $\hat{Y} = 2.61 + .70(X)$. Suppose again we are interested in knowing the predicted Y-value for an individual with a test score of 8. Using the diagram, one would find 8 on the X-axis, look up from this score to the regression line, and then follow the dotted line to the Y-axis. The predicted Y-value is 8.21.

It should be obvious that the predictions based on regression-line equations are not perfect. In fact, while some of the data points in Fig. 2.5 fall close to the regression line, only a few points fall exactly on the line. A way of summarizing the degree of error in prediction is through the use of a statistic known as the *standard error of estimate*. This statistic is computed according to the formula

$$\sigma_{Y \cdot X} = \sigma_Y \sqrt{1 - r_{xy}^2}$$

where

$$\sigma_{Y \cdot X} = \text{standard error of estimate,}$$
$$\sigma_Y = \text{standard deviation of } Y,$$
$$r_{XY} = \text{correlation between } X\text{- and } Y\text{-variables.}$$

---

* Occasionally, these weights are calculated in a different fashion (according to a procedure using "standardized scores"), and are called "Beta weights."

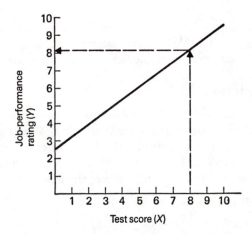

Figure 2.6 *Finding predicted* Y-value *by visually using regression-line diagram.*

The standard error of estimate may be treated as a standard deviation of the errors made in predicting Y from X. We expect about two-thirds (68 percent) of the observed Y-values to lie within the limits of plus and minus one standard error of estimate from the predicted value of Y. The standard error of estimate for the data shown in Fig. 2.5 is 1.31. Theoretically, about 68 percent of those who score 8 on the test will be expected to receive performance ratings within the limits of 8.21 ± 1.31, or between 6.90 and 9.52.

Finally, it should be noted that it is also possible to construct a regression equation predicting X from a knowledge of Y, e.g., $X = a + bY$. In most situations in this text, however, the variable predicted (Y) will be some form of *job performance* (which we call the *dependent* variable) and the variables used to make the predictions (X) will frequently be some form of *test score,* or other standard used in making selection decisions (which we generally call the *independent* variable).

A question which often arises is why should one want to make predictions about some Y-variable (e.g., job performance) when one already has knowledge about these scores. The answer is simply that these data points are used to determine whether a relationship exists and to describe the relationship. Then the equation derived can be used to make predictions *in the future* for prospective employees for whom job-performance data are *not* available. A basic assumption is that the relationship found among one group of employees will hold up in the future.

Multiple Regression

Occasionally researchers want to make predictions about one variable from knowledge based on *more* than one other variable. When there are more than one independent or predictor variables in the equation, researchers use a method of analysis known as *multiple regression*. In general form, the multiple-regression equation looks like the following:

$$\hat{Y} = a + b_1 X_1 + b_2 X_2 + \ldots + b_N X_N,$$

where

$$\hat{Y} = \text{predicted value of the } Y\text{-variable,}$$
$$b_1, b_2, \ldots, b_N = \text{regression weights associated with the various predictors,}$$
$$X_1, X_2, \ldots, X_N = \text{scores on the various predictors,}$$
$$a = \text{intercept value.}$$

Similarly, a multiple-correlation coefficient may be calculated by correlating the *observed* values of Y with the *predicted* values of Y ($\hat{Y}$) across the number of individuals.

For example, suppose a personnel manager had two tests (Test X and Test Z) which were positively correlated with job performance. The manager might calculate* the regression equation to be as follows:

$$\hat{Y} = .75 + .41(\text{Test X}) + .24(\text{Test Z}).$$

For an applicant with a score of 5 on Test X and a score of 7 on Test Z, the predicted Y-score would be

$$Y = .75 + .41(5) + .24(7) = 3.36.$$

It should be noted that the same applicant might have achieved nearly this same predicted Y-score in a different fashion. That is, if his or her score on Test X was 3 and score on Test Z was 9, the predicted Y-

---

* Methods for calculating multiple-regression equations are given in Guilford and Fruchter (1965) and other standard statistics texts.

score would have still been 3.41, which is quite close to the previous predicted value. The regression model has been called *compensatory* because high scores on one of the predictor variables will sometimes compensate for low scores on the other predictor(s).

RELIABILITY OF MEASUREMENT

As we will see, the *reliability* of specific measuring instruments is critical when evaluating them for evidence of potential bias. Thus, it is important to define reliability in some detail for use in later chapters.

Reliability concerns the consistency of measurement. When we measure the same thing twice, do we obtain the same scores? Of particular concern is whether selection tests and job-performance measures demonstrate consistency. Suppose we administered an employment test on one day and subsequently readministered the same test the following day. We would not be too surprised if the scores were highly correlated; however, we would have grave doubts about the potential usefulness of the test if the correlation was low! If a test does not correlate well with itself, how can we expect it to demonstrate a relationship with some other variable?

Many psychologists have dealt with reliability by representing the variation among people's scores on a selection test as being composed of two components: (1) variation due to the individuals' "true" scores (that is, the scores that accurately represent the characteristics of the individuals) and (2) variation due to "error." That is,

$$\sigma_x^2 = \sigma_t^2 + \sigma_e^2,$$

where

σ_x^2 = observed score variation,
σ_t^2 = variation due to "true" scores,
σ_e^2 = variation due to "error."

To the extent that there is relatively little error in the measuring system, reliability will be high. Thus, one definition of reliability is

$$r_{tt} = 1 - \frac{\sigma_e^2}{\sigma_x^2},$$

where r_{tt} = reliability of the test (or correlation of the test with itself).

The error component may have a variety of sources. Dunnette (1966) has described four sources of error in psychological measurement:

1. *Errors due to inadequate sampling of content.* The correlation between two tests designed to measure the same thing may not be perfect (+ 1.00) due to the fact that the test items for the two exams may have been slightly different.

2. *Errors due to chance response tendencies.* Occasionally, individuals will simply guess on test items, or answer at random the test items that seem to be meaningless. Any tendencies toward guessing or random responding contribute to error.

3. *Errors due to changes in testing environment.* Physical conditions such as the lighting, music level, temperature, or time of day, may affect test scores. Similarly, the particular manner in which a test is administered may contribute to error in test scores.

4. *Errors due to changes in the person taking the test.* An individual could score differently on a test given on different occasions due to factors peculiar to the individual. For example, health factors, fatigue, and mood shifts may contribute to error. In addition, individuals may actually develop new competence in the same area being measured, but this is not considered measurement error.

There are various ways of estimating the reliability (r_{tt}) of measurement. A common method is to obtain a remeasure after a period of time. For example, employees might be asked to retake an employment test after a month or so, or supervisors might be asked to rerate their employees on job performance. The scores over these two administrations are then correlated. This procedure is commonly referred to as computing a *test-retest reliability coefficient,* or an estimate of *stability.* There is one major factor which inflates this estimate of reliability: People tend to recall the test questions and their answers to them, and they tend to repeat their answers. Similarly, supervisors remember how they rated employees from one rating to the next.

Another way to measure reliability is to correlate one *part* of the test with some other part of the test. If the test is measuring the same ability or aptitude reliably, it should do so throughout the entire test. For example, in a 40-item test of mechanical ability, the scores individuals receive on the first 20 items of the test can be correlated with their scores on the second 20 items. This practice is referred to as computing a *split-half reliability*. Alternatively, a score for each individual based on all the *even*-numbered items of the test can be correlated with a score based on all the *odd*-numbered items. This is called an *odd-even reliability coefficient*.

When a researcher computes an odd-even or split-half reliability coefficient, the coefficients are computed based on a test half the length of the original test. In a sense, half the items on the test have to be "folded back" to correlate with the other half of the test in order to establish the reliability of the test. It is possible, however, to estimate what the reliability of the test would be if it were at "full strength" with *all* the items. The Spearman-Brown formula provides this estimate:

$$r_{tt} = \frac{2r_{xx}}{1 + r_{xx}},$$

where

r_{tt} = reliability of a total test estimated from the reliability of one of its halves,

r_{xx} = correlation between halves of a test.

For example, suppose a personnel manager administered a 100-item test to 200 employees and calculated a split-half reliability coefficient of .45. He wished to determine what the reliability would be for the full-length test. Using the Spearman-Brown formula, the estimate would be

$$r_{tt} = \frac{2(.45)}{1 + .45} = .62.$$

An additional method of correlating the parts of a test with one another is to correlate each test item with every other item. These are usually referred to as *internal-consistency* measures of reliability, and several formulas for calculating estimates along these lines may be found in Guilford (1965).

A method of establishing reliability through the construction of different forms of a test is called *equivalent-forms* reliability. Employees are again asked to take two tests, except that the two tests differ in the specific items contained in the tests. An advantage of this method is that it eliminates the problem of memory effects found in the test-retest method.

However, the construction of equivalent forms of the same test is quite difficult and expensive, and thus is not frequently used.

A method of establishing the reliability of *supervisory ratings* of job performance (versus *test* scores) is to obtain independent ratings or measurements from two or more supervisors on each employee. While it is likely that different supervisors appraise employee behavior differently, it is usually desirable that some degree of agreement be achieved among the raters.

Standard Error of Measurement

A statistic that indicates the amount of error in a measurement system is called the *standard error of measurement*. One way to understand this concept is to consider a situation where a person is measured and tested repeatedly. If we were able to secure a large number of measurements on an individual, we would expect to find the scores distributed in a normal-curve fashion. The mean of this distribution is considered to be the individual's "true score"—or error-free score, as discussed earlier. The standard deviation of this distribution represents the degree of error in the measuring system. About 68 percent of the scores fall within plus or minus one standard deviation. This standard deviation is referred to as the standard error of measurement and may be estimated by the following:

$$\text{S.E.M.} = \sigma_x \sqrt{1 - r_{xx}},$$

where

$$\text{S.E.M.} = \text{standard error of measurement,}$$
$$\sigma_x = \text{standard deviation of test,}$$
$$r_{xx} = \text{reliability of test.}$$

This statistic is helpful in estimating a person's "true score" when we are able to test that person only once. For example, if a person is administered a test and obtains a score of 89 and the S.E.M. of the test is 3.0, we can conclude with fair confidence that the individual's true or error-free score is somewhere between 86 and 92 (89 ± 3.0).

In fact, there may be occasions in which we wish to directly estimate the "true score" for a number of individuals in a distribution. This "estimated true score'' may be a more precise estimate of each individual's standing on the construct being measured. The relevant formula is

Estimated true score $= r_{xx}(X - \overline{X}) + \overline{X}$.

VALIDITY: A REVIEW OF THE BASIC CONCEPTS

While reliability has to do with the stability and consistency of measurement, validity involves whether a test or measuring instrument is measuring what it is supposed to measure. One could have an extremely reliable measuring instrument but be using it to measure the wrong attribute. For example, a ruler, which is an extremely reliable instrument, would not be a valid measuring device for the assessment of I.Q. Dunnette (1966) defines validation as the process of learning more about the meaning of a measuring device.

Because the concept of validity is so important in the context of the present text, the basic strategies and principles of validity are reviewed. However, we will not be able to provide in-depth coverage of all the various strategies; readers might also consult other standard texts in selection. A particularly important guide to validation principles was issued in 1975 and revised in 1980 and again in 1987 by the Society for Industrial-Organizational Psychology (American Psychological Association, 1987). Entitled *Principles for the Validation and Use of Personnel Selection Procedures,* this booklet details the various validation methods and considerations. In addition, the reader is advised to consult *Standards for Educational and Pyschological Testing* (1985), the most recent document representing a consensus among testing experts on important testing issues.

It is at this point, however, that we want to emphasize that when one talks of validity and determining the meaning of a test or test scores, one is really referring to the kinds of inferences or decisions that may be made based on the test scores. For example, when we say that an employment test is ''valid,'' we are suggesting that the employer or decision-maker has a degree of confidence that, for example, high scores on the test are helpful in determining who will do well on the job. The amount of confidence on the part of the decision-maker has to do with the kinds of evidence that may be gathered to substantiate these inferences. Decision-makers using a test with ''high'' validity may be more confident than decision-makers using a test with relatively low validity. However, validity has to do with the kinds of inferences drawn and the correctness of the decisions made. It may be based on a variety of evidence,—for example, evidence that a test is correlated with job performance. As Guion (1980) has argued, validity is based not only on a set of scores or a correlation, but also on the accuracy of the inferences made.

Thus validity may be inferred and one's confidence in the accuracy of the decisions made may be based on a variety of evidence. Whether a test is valid or not may indeed depend on a careful review of the *totality* of evidence concerning the test. For example, a psychologist may assess a test for its reliability, the kind and degree of its correlation with performance, whether different groups exhibit differences on the test when the groups are known to differ on what the test is supposed to measure, and even the adequacy of the job analysis on which the test may have been developed or chosen. Focusing on any single element for the assessment of validity may be too narrow. A careful review and assessment of all the evidence associated with a test is needed for a decision-maker to determine whether a test is valid and may be used in an employment setting.

The following section summarizes several accepted and frequently used validation strategies.

Criterion-Related Strategies

This form of evidence is widely used. In fact, it was given almost a "preferred" status in the 1970 EEOC testing guidelines and in court decisions. Criterion-related validity means that a *predictor* (or "test") is associated (correlated) with a *criterion* (a measure of job performance). The most frequent example is the correlation of employee test scores with supervisory ratings of job performance. There are two basic variations of this strategy: predictive and concurrent validity. In predictive validity, individuals are tested at one point in time, after which some measurement of job performance is gathered and correlated with the test scores. Guion and Cranny (1982) presented five variations on this specific design:

1. Applicants are tested, and selection is based on a random selection of the applicants; test scores are later correlated with subsequently collected criterion data.

2. Applicants are tested, and selection is based on whatever selection procedures are now in effect; test scores are correlated with subsequently collected criterion data.

3. Applicants are tested and then selected on the basis of the test. Later the test scores are correlated with job-performance measures. Note that individuals with low test scores would not be selected.

4. Applicants are hired and placed on the payroll; they are subsequently tested (e.g., during an orientation or training program), and the scores are correlated with job-performance data collected at a still later time.

5. Applicants are hired, and their personnel records contain information such as education, experience, and even test scores (e.g., Graduate Record Examination scores). At some subsequent time, job-performance measures are correlated with the information contained in the personnel records.

Often, an organization simply does not have the time or resources to conduct a longitudinal predictive study. Sometimes it is necessary, especially under court pressure, to obtain an estimate of a test's correlation with job performance as soon as possible.

Another problem is that organizations (e.g., the civil sevice) are sometimes required by law to make decisions on the basis of tests. Thus it would be difficult, if not impossible, for such an organization suddenly to forego testing and use other devices for selection. For example, in *U.S. v. City of St. Louis* (1976), the court ruled that a predictive design was inappropriate because the length of time that would be required to conduct such a study was in conflict with the legal duty of the organization to establish a valid selection procedure immediately.

As noted above, one variation is to use actual test scores in making selection decisions (for example, by establishing a cutoff score), and to collect job performance data at a later time. Measures of association between the test and job performance are then computed. A problem is that the correlation *under*estimates the true test-performance relationship because of the *restriction of range* on the test, as shown in Fig. 2.7. Suppose that the true relationship between a test and job performance is represented by the scatterplot in Fig. 2.7(a). The data portray a reasonably high relationship, say $r = .50$. Suppose, also that the organization had been using a cutoff score at point A to select employees and

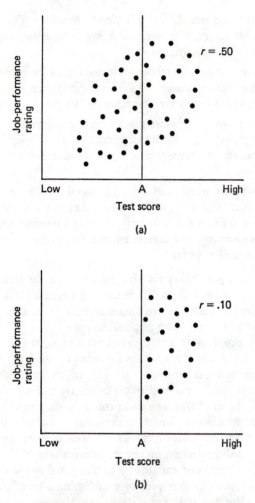

Figure 2.7 *Illustration of restriction-of-range phenomena.*

that only individuals who had scored above that point on the test had been hired. Now, if the organization decided to conduct a validation study, the only individuals for whom data would be available are those represented in Fig. 2.7(b). It is easy to see that a correlation computed on these subjects would be considerably reduced due to less variation on scores in this sample, e.g., $r = .10$. This phenomenon is known as a reduction in the correlation due to *restriction of range on the predictor.* There is also a reduced range of scores on the measure of job performance. Thus restriction of range on the *criterion* may also occur at the same time.

It is common practice now to make statistical corrections when restriction of range occurs (Olson and Becker, 1983). This correction is an effort to estimate what the true correlation would be if no restriction had occurred. The formula for estimating the true correlation when restriction of range has occurred on the predictor* is given by Thorndike (1982) as

$$r_{est} = \frac{r_{OB} \left(\dfrac{\text{S.D. total}}{\text{S.D. current}} \right)}{\sqrt{1 - r_{OB}^2 + r_{OB}^2 \left(\dfrac{\text{S.D. total}}{\text{S.D. current}} \right)^2}} \, ,$$

where

r_{est} = estimated true score;

r_{OB} = observed correlation between predictor & criterion;

S.D.$_{total}$ = standard deviation of predictor based on total or unrestricted sample;

S.D.$_{current}$ = standard deviation of predictor based on restricted sample.

Note that it is necessary to have knowledge of an estimate of the standard deviation of the total group or population. These values might be obtained by calculating the standard deviation based on all applicants or on normative data (usually provided in a test manual).

The use of the concurrent design, where presently employed individuals are tested, presents an additional set of problems to consider. Concurrent validity has to do with gathering the test and job information from current employees at the same point in time and correlating the two sets of scores.

---

* It is also possible to correct for restriction of range on the criterion or to correct simultaneously for restriction on both the predictor criterion variables.

This design has been criticized on several counts:

1. Because test scores are obtained from individuals already employed in the job, the results may not apply to others. Individuals tend to move into jobs for which they are best qualified and in which they will be satisfied. Their particular skills and personality patterns may fit the job, while individuals who leave the job may not have found such a good "fit" between the job and their own needs. Thus, the test-score range for the employee pool may be more homogeneous (restricted) than the range for job applicants. For this reason, it is important to collect information on job applicants and compare their test scores with those of job incumbents to determine whether any differences exist between the two groups.

2. It is possible that current employees change by developing particular skills necessary for success on the job. For example, a job that requires a certain amount of arithmetic is bound to have an effect of "sharpening up" the arithmetic skills of employees who may have let those skills get rusty prior to employment.

3. Job incumbents may also respond differently while taking the tests than job applicants. That is, incumbents may be less likely to "fake" tests than individuals who are applying for jobs. Again, to determine whether this could be the case, test scores of job applicants should be compared to the test scores of current employees. When performing concurrent validation studies, subjects should be asked to adopt an applicant "mental set" and be encouraged to do as well as they can on the tests.

A provocative article by Barrett, Phillips, and Alexander (1981) suggests that these criticisms may not be as damaging as once believed. For example, these authors suggest that the impact of an individual leaving a position because of termination or promotion is simply a special case of the restriction-of-range problem (leading to less variability on the predictor or criterion) and can be corrected for through statistical means. Similarly, they argue that the potential motivational differences between present employees and applicants and the impact on resulting correlations are not well known at present and we must await further research in this area. Finally, they argue that it is possible to statistically control for differential experience levels (which might operate to increase the test or performance scores of individuals) among the employee sample chosen for the validation study.

However, a clear advantage of the present employee design is that it is more expedient and less costly than predictive designs. It remains the most commonly used procedure to gather evidence concerning the criterion-related validity of a test.

Correction for Unreliability. More recent research methods in the validation arena use techniques that correct for unreliability in the test (and job performance) measures. We know that a test's ability to correlate with some external criterion such as job performance is influenced by its reliability. The lower the reliability of a test, the less capable it is of correlating with a different measure. In fact, the correlation of a test with itself (its reliability) sets the upper limit of its ability to correlate with some different measure. Theoretically, a test cannot correlate any better with a different measure than with itself.

Researchers use a statistical method called *correction for attenuation* to estimate what the true correlation would be between two measures if they have been perfectly measured (that is, if they were perfectly reliable). The relevant formula is

$$r_{xy\ est} = \frac{r_{xy\ observed}}{\sqrt{r_{xx}}\ \sqrt{r_{yy}}} ,$$

where

$r_{xy\ est}$ = estimated true correlation;
$r_{xy\ observed}$ = observed correlation;
r_{xy} = reliability of predictor;
r_{xy} = reliability of criterion.

For example, suppose a researcher conducted a study in which it was found that the reliability of the test used was .80, the reliability of the job performance measure used was .70, and the observed correlation between the test and the job-performance measure was .30. If the correction for attenuation formula is used, the estimated true correlation is .40. Note, however, that this is an estimation and can sometimes lead to values greater than 1.0 when incorrect reliability estimates are used. Nonetheless, this kind of statistical estimation procedure is well-accepted and used in validation strategies. The intent of these kinds of corrections is to estimate the true correlation value as best as possible given the data available.

An additional issue encountered when dealing with *either* concurrent or predictive validity strategies is that the estimated correlation (particularly correlations generated when using multiple regression procedures) may be biased due to several types of errors. Suppose, for example, that a researcher conducts a validation study with a sample of 100 employees from a population of 1000 currently employed individuals. Multiple regression procedures are used to estimate the relationship between two tests and job performance (the multiple correlation) as well as to calculate the relative contribution of each test in predicting job performance (the beta weights). However, the multiple correlation and beta weights may be inaccurate for two reasons:

1. *Statistical overfitting*—Finding an inflated relationship between the tests and the job performance measure due to the use of a statistical procedure that capitalizes on chance as it attempts to find the "best" solution in developing the estimates. This has to do with chance error found within the sample chosen.

2. *Sampling error*—Finding incorrect estimates because the sample chosen was not representative of the population as a whole. This may take the form of random sampling error where there are simply chance differences that occur between the sample and the population. Alternatively, it may take the form of systematic non-random error when the sample was drawn non-randomly (for example, if one chooses a sample that has been preselected via the individual test scores of the incumbents).

Researchers in this area suggest that various formulas be used when attempting to estimate the impact of random sampling error (Schmitt, Coyle, and Rauschenberger, 1977). That is, it is possible to correct for some of these biases by using statistical formulas (sometimes referred to as *correction for shrinkage*). In addition, *empirical cross-validation* might be a preferable estimation procedure when non-random sampling errors may operate. Empirical cross-validation procedures involve a variety of strategies. For example, a sample is divided into two parts. The correlational estimates and beta weights are developed on one part and the regression equation is applied to the second part to determine if the estimates "hold-up." Similarly, many samples might be drawn and the estimates derived based on one sample applied to the others.

There is a current debate regarding which type of estimation procedure—the use of statistical formulas or empirical cross-validation—is more accurate. Since we cannot provide details here, we refer the reader to Murphy (1983) and Schmitt *et al.* (1977) for more information. However, the major point to be made is that criterion-related validation procedures and the estimates derived from these methods need to be examined for potential sources of error and appropriate statistical corrections should be made when possible.

Content-Oriented Strategies

The term content-oriented validation generally refers to the adequacy of a test in *sampling* the relevant and critical behaviors, knowledge, and skills necessary for job performance. The inference of the adequacy of a test depends greatly on how well the items on the test directly reflect observed behaviors, skills, and knowledge considered essential, critical, or important for adequate job performance. The classic example of a test that uses this strategy is a typing test, which directly samples the skills presumably necessary for the job of "typist". However, even a typing test might be somewhat misleading because it measures speed as well as basic typing skills; a job may not require a typing speed of 85 words per minute.)

When evaluating a test that uses a content-oriented strategy, the emphasis is on the *development* of the test or the adequacy of the procedures used to develop the test. There is no single correlation index to assess the "validity" of the test. Instead, the degree of rigor or thoroughness in the development of the test is examined.

There are several steps usually considered necessary when developing a test that uses a content-oriented strategy. First, a *job analysis* is conducted to describe the basic tasks, duties, and responsibilities as well as the knowledge, skills, and abilities (KSAs) necessary for job performance. The job analysis should reveal all factors—behaviors, tasks, knowledge etc.—that are critical for successful job performance. Second, test items are written or work samples developed that reflect tasks, behaviors, knowledge, skills, or abilities outlined in the job analysis. Third, experts who are familiar with the job (e.g., supervisors, job incumbents) are asked to evaluate the test items (or work samples) to determine if they are an accurate reflection of the job. These subject matter experts should also be able to identify items that are irrelevant to the job in question. Lawshe (1975) provides a relatively simple quantitative method for assessing which items survive rater judgment. In addition, more recent case law suggests that job experts should also be asked to judge whether the knowledge, skills, and abilities identified in the job analysis are indeed related to the tasks and behaviors involved in a job. That is, these experts should provide judgments concerning the *linkages* between the behaviors and the KSAs involved in a job.

A content-oriented strategy is inappropriate for validating ability, intelligence, interest, and other abstract tests. The basic logic behind content-oriented validation is to build tests that reflect *directly* the behaviors and skills involved in the job rather than the aptitudes or underlying abilities *presumed* to be involved in the job. "Simply stated, a content-valid selection procedure should sample the job for the applicant and give the applicant a fair chance to demonstrate his or her competence to perform the job" (Sharf, 1976, p. 6).

Content-oriented validity is often confused with "face validity." A test which appears to the test taker as if it is related to a job is said to be "face valid." A content-valid test will almost always demonstrate "face" validity; however, a test with face validity may *not* have content-oriented validity.

The Outcomes of Predictions

It is not enough to obtain a significant validity coefficient and pronounce a test useful. There are other factors that influence the relative value of a selection test.

Suppose a personnel manager was able to collect test-score data on 100 employees who were eventually hired and that at a later date, he or she was able to collect job-performance data on all of these individuals using a 1–5 rating scale. Assume that the correlation between the test scores and job-performance ratings was calculated to be .70. The ellipse diagram in Figure 2.8 depicts this relationship graphically. Assume that the horizontal line in the diagram represents a dividing line: Those individuals rated at or above this line were considered successful in the job by their supervisor; those rated below the line were considered not successful.

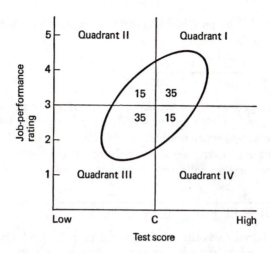

Figure 2.8 *Quadrant analysis to help determine utility of a test.*

The vertical line represents the cutting point (C) on the test: Individuals scoring at or above this point would be selected (in the future) and those scoring below the point would be rejected. The horizontal and vertical lines allow the division of the diagram into four quadrants.

1. *Quadrant I* (true positive) represents those individuals for whom success was predicted, and who were indeed successful.

2. *Quadrant II* (false negative) represents those individuals for whom success was not predicted, but who actually would succeed if hired.

3. *Quadrant III* (true negative) represents those individuals for whom success was not predicted, and who actually did not succeed in the job.

4. *Quadrant IV* (false positive) represents those individuals for whom success was predicted, but who did not succeed in the job.

Figure 2.8 also illustrates the number of individuals falling into the different quadrants. For example, the number of individuals for whom job success was predicted and who actually were successful (Quadrant I) is 35.

The first question we might ask is "How accurate were the predictions made by the test?'' This could be calculated by applying the following formula:

$$\frac{I + III}{I + II + III + IV} = \frac{70}{100} = .70.$$

That is, 70 percent of the predictions made using the test were correct. This seems to be fairly impressive evidence in favor of the test. However, a second question which must be asked in evaluating a predictor is "How accurate would I have been if no predictor was used?" This may be calculated by using the following formula:

$$\frac{I + II}{I + II + III + IV} = \frac{35 + 15}{35 + 15 + 35 + 15} = .50.$$

This is referred to as the *base rate*—the proportion of applicants who would succeed on the job if tests were not used to select them. In the example given, the accuracy of the predictions made using the test was .70 compared to a base rate of .50. Thus the use of the selection system represents greater accuracy of predictions made than would be found if no selection test were used.

It should be noted that as the base rate increases, it becomes relatively more difficult for a selection system to show improvement. For example, if 95 percent of employees selected are successful, it becomes difficult to improve on the current system.*

A further concept which is important in evaluating a selection device is the notion of the *selection ratio*.** The selection ratio is defined as the proportion of individuals actually hired to those who applied. For example, there may be 200 applicants and only 10 individuals are hired. This would represent a selection ratio of 10/200 or .05 percent. Generally speaking, a selection system has greater value when the selection ratio is small—that is, when there are many more applicants than jobs. Taylor and Russell (1939) provide methods for estimating the practical effectiveness of tests given different selection ratios.

---

* Wiggins (1973) has pointed out that a test with greater than zero validity will be better than random selection, no matter what the base rate.

** For a more extended discussion of the selection ratio as well as hiring rates see Alexander, Barnett, and Doverspike (1983).

To summarize, the value of a prediction system varies as a function of three basic variables:

1. *The magnitude of the validity coefficient*—As validity increases, so does the value of the system.

2. *The base rate*—As the base rate approaches 50 percent, the selection system demonstrates greater value.

3. *The selection ratio*—As selection ratios become smaller, the value of a selection system increases.

THE CONCEPT OF UTILITY

Utility refers to the *overall* usefulness of a selection system. The concept includes the accuracy of the decisions made but also concerns a consideration of the costs of using the selection system and the costs associated with the *errors* in the decisions made. Wiggins (1973), Cronbach and Gleser (1965), and Dunnette (1966) have shown how these costs may be considered in evaluating a selection system. The kinds of costs must first be made explicit and estimated. Dunnette (1966) groups the different kinds of costs into actual and potential costs:

1. *Actual costs* are those expenses incurred when an applicant is hired. These would include costs related to recruitment and testing, orientation programs, and training.

2. *Potential costs* involve those expenses associated with incorrect selection decisions. These are of two types: (a) Costs associated with hiring an individual who subsequently fails (false positives). These costs may involve termination costs, costs of undesirable job behavior (e.g., damaged equipment, accidents, loss of customers) and may represent one of the major personnel costs to an organization. Traditionally, managers have focused on these kinds of costs. (b) Costs associated with rejecting a person who could have been successful on the job (false negatives). While these costs are typically indirect, they may eventually come back to affect the organization. For example, minority-group applicants rejected during the selection process but who could actually do the job if hired, may eventually become passive, frustrated, and hostile. Such feelings may eventually erupt in actions against specific organizations or society in general.

The estimation of costs is, according to Cronbach and Gleser (1965), the "Achilles heel" of utility in personnel decision making. Dunnette (1966) and Wiggins (1973) provide excellent examples of how utility estimates, although clearly subjective in nature, may be made. Each specific outcome (e.g., false positive, valid negative, etc.) is assigned a "utility value" that indicates the relative worth or favorableness of an outcome for an institution. Similarly, Cascio (1987) provides an extremely useful framework and series of examples for costing the impact of various human resource-related decisions and interventions in organizations.

More recently articulated utility models have been receiving a good deal of research attention. Schmidt, Hunter, McKenzie, and Muldrow (1979) presented a model of estimating the net gain in dollar figures that could be realized by implementing valid selection devices. Their model includes the following factors in the calculation of such estimates:

1. The correlation between the test and job performance;
2. Knowledge of the existing or desired selection ratio (p);
3. The standard deviation of performance in dollar terms (SD_y);
4. The average *test* score of those selected (based on p) in z-score form (z_x);
5. The cost of testing per applicant (c);
6. The number tested (N_t) and the number selected (N_s).

The formula, which estimates the expected net gain in utility by using a particular selection device compared to random selection is expressed as follows:

$$\text{Expected gain} = N_s\, r_{xy}\, SD_y\, z_x - N_t c.$$

For example, suppose that we wish to estimate the net gain in utility in a situation where the correlation between a test and a measure of job performance is .40. Also, suppose that 100 individuals are applicants for a specific target job and that the selection ratio is .10. That is, only 10 percent of the individuals applying will be selected for the position. If individuals are selected because of their test scores and the top 10 percent of the applicants are hired, the average test score for this group in z-score form will be 1.29.* Furthermore, suppose that we have estimated that the standard deviation in dollar terms for the job performance measure is $10,000. This value denotes that an individual who is one standard deviation above the mean on the job performance measure is "worth" $10,000 more than an individual whose peformance is at the mean. Finally, suppose that the cost of testing each employee is equal to $10. If we use the above formula, we obtain

$$\text{Expected gain} = 10\ (.40)\ (10{,}000)\ (1.29) - 100\ (10)$$
$$= \$50{,}600.$$

That is, the expected net gain that can be realized by using the test is $50,600, a sizeable figure. If the organization planned to use this particular testing device to select a total of 100 employees annually, it could expect (all factors remaining the same) a net gain of $506,000, a very sizeable amount. However, if the cost of testing were more, the expected gain would decrease. In addition, if the validity of the test were lower or the selection ratio greater, the net utility would decrease.

A number of researchers have provided demonstrations of the utility model across a number of jobs and testing situations (e.g., Hunter and Schmidt, 1982a, 1982b; Cascio and Silbey, 1979); others have assessed the utility of recruitment and organizational interventions (Boudreau and Berger, 1985; Cascio, 1987). One of the biggest problems regarding the estimation method is obtaining accurate estimates of the standard deviation of performance in dollar terms. The typical procedure is to ask supervisors, job incumbents, or others familiar with the job to provide dollar estimates of the yearly value to the organization of the output produced by individuals performing at various levels. These estimated values are then converted into standard deviation units. Research is proceeding to confirm these and other kinds of estimation procedures (e.g., Easton, Wing, and Mitchell, 1985 or Burke and Frederick, 1986). Moreover, recent research is beginning to address the problem of the standard error of utility estimates. For example, according to Alexander and Barrick (1987), since all variables in a utility analysis have some associated variability, it makes sense to determine the standard error of the overall

---

* This z-score value may be obtained in tables presented in other sources, such as Cascio (1987).

utility estimate itself. They provide a method for calculating the standard error of estimate of utility gains as well as a demonstration of its use.

We will have more to say about recent utility models in later chapters.

JOB ANALYSIS

Because job analysis procedures and outcomes are so important in selection and validation efforts, it is useful to review them briefly and also to review key issues concerning job analysis and selection. Job analysis has to do with the process of collecting information about all aspects of a job that are essential for effective performance: tasks, duties, responsibilities, and working conditions as well as knowledge, skills, abilities, and behaviors. Usually, the job-information collection process results in some type of formalized document—a job description and/or specification sheet.

Various job analysis procedures focus on different types of job-related information. One procedure, which focuses on collecting information about the tasks and duties of a position, is called *task-oriented* job-analysis. A second procedure, called *worker-oriented* job-analysis, collects information about how work is performed and the kinds of mental processes, decision-making aspects, information input, and so forth, that are involved in performing the job. A third procedure, called *ability-oriented* job-analysis, is concerned with collecting information about the abilities needed to perform the job; that is, this procedure focuses on collecting information about the general and specific knowledge, skills, and abilities that are required for effective performance. Although any specific job-analysis effort might involve using a mixture of these three types of procedures, the use to which the job analysis information will be put often results in certain procedures being emphasized more than others. For example, a particular kind of selection strategy might make a particular job-analysis method more advantageous. If one is constructing a work sample or other content-related test, it would be preferable to use a task-oriented rather than a worker-oriented job analysis approach. Similarly, an abilities-oriented job-analysis approach might be desirable if the development of a work sample was not feasible or the selection device was being developed for applicants who had no prior job exposure and the testing had to be based on their abilities and aptitudes rather than their performance of actual job behaviors.

Different methods for collecting job-analysis information also exist. While a detailed presentation of these methods is beyond the scope of this text, the following summarizes the most common techniques:

1. Interviewing individuals familiar with the job;

2. Observing the job being performed;

3. Surveying individuals familiar with the job;

4. Reviewing prior information (e.g., the *Dictionary of Occupational Titles*, prior job-analysis reports, etc.);

5. Actually performing the job.

Besides being useful for training, development, and performance appraisal purposes, the information gathered from job-analytic procedures can be useful for selection and staffing purposes in a number of ways:

Job-analysis information may be helpful in establishing minimum qualifications for job entry. For example, information about a job may reveal that job holders must drive a car. Thus a valid driver's license would be a legitimate qualification for job entry. Similarly, a job analysis may reveal that understanding and writing Fortran programs is an important feature of the job. This information might be translated into the establishment of a minimum level of Fortran knowledge required prior to job entry. One must be quite careful, however, to avoid the specification of minimum qualifications that are based on trivial aspects of the job or the specification of KSAs that might be gained through initial training in the position. Moreover, it is also crucial that minimum qualification levels not be inflated. Inflating minimum qualification levels often leads to discrimination charges (i.e., disparate impact) and also screens out many candidates who could successfully perform the duties of the job.

Job-analysis information also provides good clues about the kinds of tests or predictors that may be related to job performance. For example, a job analysis might reveal that job incumbents need to understand and interpret city codes and ordinances. A test might thus be developed that will incorporate the most commonly used ordinances and codes. Similarly, job-analysis methods might reveal that assertiveness with customers is important for effective job performance. There are a variety of personality inventories that tap dominance and assertiveness dimensions; these scales might be potential predictors in this instance. In short, job-analysis information provides insight that might be used to help build tests by directly tapping the tasks, duties, and KSAs involved in the job (content-oriented validation strategies) or by suggesting other kinds of tests that might correlate with job performance (criterion-related validation strategies).

There are a number of questions concerning job-analytic processes that are worth discussing here.

What is the appropriate number of individuals to *sample* when collecting job information? For example, is an interview with only *one* incumbent a sufficient sample to fully understand the job? By now it is recognized that greater representation is needed to provide more precise job information. But how many incumbents should be sampled? In some instances, complete populations are given inventories to collect information about the job. For example, in *Guardians* v. *Civil Service Commission* (1980) a job-analysis inventory was distributed to 5600 police officers and the responses of 2600 incumbents were analyzed to yield a ranking of 42 major tasks. Although our review of case law in this area suggests this is common practice, it represents over-sampling. Statistical theory indicates that reasonably precise estimates of means and standard deviations can be obtained with much smaller sample sizes. Obviously, efforts to comprehensively sample in this manner are also quite expensive in terms of efficiency and costs.

Is there a possibility of bias in collecting job-analysis information? There are several arguments regarding this issue. One hypothesis that has been extended is that there are systematic differences between minority and nonminority group members in job activities. Thus any job analysis based on representatives of only one group may be excluding aspects of the job performed by another group. For example, black police officers might be systematically assigned to ghetto neighborhoods, which would require them to exhibit more caution because they would be exposed to more crime and danger. Females might be assigned to the more clerical aspects of jobs than male incumbents would be. This is really another sampling issue. It is important to ensure that representatives from minority and nonminority groups be included in the collection of job analysis information in order to determine if systematic differences exist between these groups in terms of their job duties. To our knowledge, this hypothesis has not been substantiated. Moreover, where minor differences in job duties have been found to exist between minority and non-minority job incumbents, we have not seen these differences translate into substantially different KSA requirements or lead to different job descriptions.

Are job analysts themselves free from bias? For example, do white analysts lower their evaluations of a job when interviewing black incumbents? Similarly, is a male analyst's interpretation of the nature of a job influenced in some manner when he is interviewing a female incumbent? In a study investigating this issue, Arvey, Passino, and Lounsbury (1977) found little evidence that the sex of the incumbent influenced resulting job descriptions of job analysts. This issue may receive more attention because of recent developments in *comparable-worth* claims (e.g., Arvey, Maxwell, and Abrahams, 1985). However, the issue simply has not received much research support.

In the next few chapters, the critical importance of conducting job analyses when developing and using selection systems will be highlighted often. In fact, many court decisions dealing with the fairness of a particular selection device have been decided based on the adequacy of the job analysis on which the selection device was developed. An analysis of the case law in this area has revealed a number of important requirements concerning the job-analysis procedure and the data collected. These have been delineated by Thompson and Thompson (1982) and include the following:

1. A job analysis must be performed. Organizations cannot rely on informal knowledge about a job that "everybody" knows. One of the important elements a court will review is simply whether a job analysis was conducted or whether a selection test was developed or employed based on stereotyped notions of what the job involved and the presumed knowledge, skills, and abilities.

2. The job analysis must be well documented. That is, there should be some kind of written documentation concerning the job-analysis procedure and the results of the job analysis. It will not be sufficient for job analysts to simply carry around in their heads information concerning the job.

3. The job-analysis information should be collected from several up-to-

date sources. For example, sources such as the following should be used:

- Interviews with incumbents, supervisors, and administrators;
- Training manuals and other pertinent publications;
- Observed on-the-job performance;
- Questionnaires and checklists;

4. The data collected should have sufficient "sampling" properties to reflect the job domain.

5. The job analysis should reveal the important and critical aspects of the job. As mentioned in our discussion earlier, some courts have asked for a demonstration that the selection instrument components are linked to the important and critical aspects of the job.

6. Several court cases imply relevant KSAs may be derived only after the important and critical tasks are identified.

We will provide more information concerning the role of job analysis in subsequent chapters.

SUMMARY

This chapter was meant to provide sufficient information for the reader to pursue the topics developed in later chapters. Some of the statistical terms and concepts are obviously more sophisticated than others. For a more comprehensive treatment, the reader is advised to consult a standard statistics text. However, if the reader has grasped most of the principles developed here, the statistical analyses presented in later chapters should present few problems.

REFERENCES

Albermarle Paper Company v. *Moody*, 10 FEP 1181 (1975).

Alexander, R. A.; G. Y. Barrett; and D. Doverspike (1983). An explication of the selection ratio and its relationship to hiring rate. *Journal of Applied Psychology* 68: 342–344.

Alexander, R. A., and M. R. Barrick (1987). Estimating the standard error of projected dollar gains in utility analysis. *Journal of Applied Psychology* 72: 475–479.

American Psychological Association (1985). *Standards for Educational and Psychological Testing.* Washington, D.C.: APA.

Arvey, R. D.; S. E. Maxwell; and L. A. Abrahams (1985). Reliability artifacts in comparable worth procedures. *Journal of Applied Psychology* 70: 695–705.

Boudreau, J. W., and C. J. Berger (1985). Decision-theoretic utility analysis applied to employee separations and acquisitions. *Journal of Applied Psychology* 70: 581–612.

Burke, M. J., and J. T. Frederick (1986). A comparison of economic utility estimates for alternative SDy estimation procedures. *Journal of Applied Psychology* 71: 334–339.

Cascio, W. F. (1987). *Costing Human Resources: The Financial Impact of Behavior in Organizations.* Boston, MA: PWS-Kent.

Cascio, W. F., and V. Silbey (1979). Utility of the assessment center as a selection device. *Journal of Applied Psychology* 64: 107–118.

Cohen, J. (1977). *Statistical Power Analysis for the Behavioral Sciences.* New York: Academic Press.

Cronbach, L. J., and G. Gleser (1965). *Psychological Tests and Personnel Decisions.* Urbana: University of Illinois Press.

Dunnette, M. D. (1966). *Personnel Selection and Placement.* Belmont, Calif.: Wadsworth.

Eaton, N. K.; H. Wing; and K. J. Mitchell (1985). Alternate methods of estimating the dollar value of performance. *Personnel Psychology* 38: 27–40.

Griggs v. *Duke Power,* 3 FEP 175 (1971).

Guardians v. *Civil Service Commission,* 23 FEP 909 (1980).

Guilford, J. P. (1965). *Fundamental Statistics in Psychology and Education.* New York: McGraw-Hill.

Guilford, J. P., and B. Fruchter (1973). *Fundamental Statistics in Psychology and Education.* New York: McGraw-Hill.

Guion, R. M. (1965). *Personnel Testing.* New York: McGraw-Hill.

Hayes, W. L. (1981). *Statistics for the Social Sciences*. New York: Holt, Rinehart and Winston.

Hunter, J. E., and F. L. Schmidt (1982a). Ability tests; Economic benefits versus the issue of fairness. *Industrial Relations* 21: 293–308.

——(1982b). Fitting people to jobs: The impact of personnel selection on national productivity. In *Human Performance and Productivity*, M. D. Dunnette and E. A. Fleishman, eds. (vol. 1, pp. 233–284). Hillsdale, N.J.: Prentice-Hall.

Lawshe, C. H. (1975). A quantitative approach to content validity. *Personnel Psychology*, 28: 563–575.

Olson, C. A., and B. E. Becker (1983). A proposed technique for the treatment of restriction of range in selection validation. *Psychological Bulletin* 93: 137–148.

Murphy, K. R. (1983). Fooling yourself with cross-validation: single sample designs. *Personnel Psychology* 36: 111–118.

Runyon, R. P., and A. Haber (1976). *Fundamentals of Behavioral Statistics*. Reading, Mass.: Addison-Wesley.

Schmidt, F. L.; J. E. Hunter; R. C. McKenzie; and T. W. Muldrow (1979). Impact of valid selection procedures on work-force productivity. *Journal of Applied Psychology* 64: 609–626.

Schmitt, N.; B. Coyle; and J. A. Rauschenberger (1977). A Monte Carlo evaluation of three estimates of cross-validated multiple correlation. *Psychology Bulletin* 84: 751–758.

Schneider, B., and N. Schmitt (1986). *Staffing Organizations*. Glenview, Ill.: Scott, Foresman.

Sharf, S. (1976). The influence of lawyers, legal language, and legal thinking. *Personnel Psychology* 29: 541–554.

Society for Industrial-Organizational Psychology, American Psychological Association (1987). *Principles for the Validation and Use of Personnel Selection Procedures*. College Park, MD: Author.

Taylor, H. C., and J. T. Russell (1939). The relationship of validity coefficients to the practical effectiveness of tests in selection: discussion of tables. *Journal of Applied Psychology* 23: 565–578.

Thompson, D. E., and T. A. Thompson (1982). Court standards for job analysis in test validation. *Personnel Psychology* **35**: 865–874.

Thorndike, R. L. (1982). *Applied Psychometrics*. Boston: Houghton Mifflin.

Usery v. *Tamiami Trail Tours, Inc.*, 12 FEP 1233 (1976).

U. S. v. *City of St. Louis*, 14 FEP 1473 (1976).

Washington v. *Davis*, 12 FEP 1415 (1976).

Wiggins, J. S. (1973). *Personality and Prediction: Principles of Personality Assessment*. Reading, Mass.: Addison-Wesley.

Legal Authorities and Framework

3

In order to understand the issues of fair employment and discrimination, it is important first to become familiar with the major legislative acts and government directives that have provided the basis for legal action and to understand the changes that have taken place in employment practices over the past few years. The objectives of this chapter are twofold: (1) to present the major regulations concerning employment discrimination, and (2) to present a basic summary of how the legal process works.

By "regulations" we mean those rules against discriminatory employment practices that are based on a number and variety of congressional enactments and presidential executive orders as well as the U.S. Constitution. By regulations we also mean those guidelines issued by Administrative agencies of the federal government (e.g., EEOC, OFCCP) and collateral guidelines issued by professional societies (e.g., APA, AERA). Unlike statutes, the Constitution, and executive orders, guidelines are influential only to the extent they are given "great deference" by the courts.

Statutory laws are based on the congressional authority to regulate the practices of businesses involved in interstate commerce; executive orders are based on the authority of the President to place restrictions on employees of the federal government as well as businesses selling goods and services to the federal government.

Regardless of the type or basis of the regulations against employment discrimination, they are generally recognized as requiring that all persons (in most cases, U.S. citizens only) be given an *equal opportunity* for employment; they do not require equal conditions of employment or an equal share of the available jobs. Generally stated, personal characteristics protected by equal employment opportunity regulations are immutable ones. That is, protected characteristics are those resulting from forces beyond a person's control, such as race, sex, or age. Readily changeable personal characteristics (e.g., hair length or sexual preference) have generally been considered outside the scope of regulatory protection.

SOURCE MATERIALS

There are several important source materials covering the legal matters in employment discrimination. One excellent source is the Bureau of National Affairs, Inc. (1231 25th St. N.W., Washington, D.C.), a private firm which publishes *two* important sets of materials: (1) the texts of federal and state laws along with editorial explanations of these laws; texts of the governmental directives and agencies' guidelines, and other relevant materials which are kept current and updated every two weeks; (2) a case law book, *Fair Employment Practices* (FEP), in which the full texts and opinions of federal and state court rulings pertaining to employment discrimination are published. These materials are also updated every two weeks. Both sets of materials greatly facilitate an understanding of the area.

Throughout this text the majority of court decisions will be cited using the Fair Employment Practices case law book as the source. For example, the citation 14 FEP 1066 (1977) indicates that the decision was made in 1977 and may be found on page 1066 in Volume 14 of *Fair Employment Practices*.

Another frequently cited source of various court decisions is a publication issued by the Commerce Clearing House (4025 W. Petersen Ave., Chicago, Ill.) entitled *Employment Practices Decisions* (EPD). For example, the citation 11 EPD 10,604 (1975) indicates that the decision was made in 1975 and may be found in Volume 11 of that book, case number 10,604. (We will follow the practice of not providing specific page references when quoting from these cases.)

MAJOR STATUTORY LAWS

Title VII of the Civil Rights Act of 1964

In 1964, President Johnson signed the Civil Rights Act, Public Law 88-352,* which was amended in 1972. This law included several "titles" which essentially forbid discrimination in various sectors of our society, such as education, federally assisted programs, and the right to vote. Title VII deals specifically with discrimination in employment, making it illegal for an organization to do the following:

1. To fail, refuse to hire, discharge any individual, or otherwise to discriminate against any individual with respect to his compensation, terms, conditions, or privileges of employment because of the individual's race, color, religion, sex, or national origin; or

2. To limit, segregate, or classify employees or applicants for employment in any way which would deprive, or tend to deprive, any individual of employment opportunities or otherwise adversely affect his stature as an employee because of such individual's race, color, religion, sex, or national origin.

Title VII applies to all employers with more than 15 employees, to labor unions engaged in an "industry affecting commerce," and to employment agencies that serve such industries. The 1972 amendment broadened this coverage to state and governmental agencies and to educational institutions.

In terms of legislative history, it is interesting to note several aspects of Title VII. First, the category of sex was added in an attempt to prevent passage of the law. Today litigation concerning sex discrimination is overwhelming the court systems. Second, Sec. 703(a) of Title VII was reinterpreted over the years. Originally, it seemed to permit exemptions on the basis of sex, national origin, age, or religious convictions in those instances where these factors provide "a bona fide occupational qualification (BFOQ) reasonably necessary to the normal operation of that particular business or enterprise." However, as case law progressed, the

---

* The text of this Act may be found in Volume 42 of the United States Code 200e, Stat. 253.

BFOQ requirement was construed "narrowly" so that now only in rare instances are jobs found where only a person of a particular sex, national origin, age, or religion may perform the job (e.g., sperm donor and wet nurse). Third, the categories of the aged and the handicapped were not included in this particular Act.

The agency charged with the enforcement of Title VII is the Equal Employment Opportunity Commission (EEOC). Originally limited to investigating and attempting to bring about conciliation between parties, the 1972 amendment extended the authority of EEOC to bring direct action in U.S. district courts against organizations. This had the effect of putting real "teeth" into Title VII and the enforcement agency.

In addition, the EEOC has published sets of guidelines that deal with EEO-related matters, including guidelines that concern discrimination based on sex and religion, recruitment and advertising practices, affirmative action, preemployment inquiries, as well as record-keeping and reporting practices.

The 1972 amendment to the Civil Rights Act of 1964 also provided for the establishment of an Equal Employment Opportunity Coordinating Council, which was composed of the Secretary of Labor, the chairman of EEOC, the Attorney General (representing the Department of Justice), the chairman of the U.S. Civil Service Commission, and the chairman of the Civil Rights Commission (or their respective delegates). The charge given to this commission was to promote effectiveness among the various agencies responsible for the enforcement of the Equal Employment Opportunity legislation, orders, and policies.

In 1973, this council developed a set of uniform guidelines for employee selection procedures as one of its first priorities, and on November 23, 1976 the *Federal Executive Agency Guidelines on Employee Selection Procedures* were published in the Federal Register. However, this document represented the official position of only three members of the EEOCC—Justice, Labor, and Civil Service. The Civil Rights Commission and the EEOC both opposed these new guidelines on the grounds that they were substantially "weaker." The following day EEOC republished its previous set of guidelines. The various federal agencies resolved their differences in 1978 and published collaboratively the *Uniform Guidelines on Employee Selection Procedures*. In response to calls for updating the 1978 Guidelines, the EEOC voted in 1984 to begin a comprehensive review of the *Uniform Guidelines*. The 1978 *Uniform Guidelines* is reproduced in the Appendix to this book and will be discussed in detail in Chapter 4.

Under reorganization plans developed and implemented during the Carter administration, major responsibility for the enforcement of EEO legislation and executive orders (to be discussed below) was placed under the control of the EEOC. For example, the EEOC took over from the Civil Service Commission responsibility for ensuring equal employment opportunity for federal employees and from the Labor Department responsibility for enforcing the Equal Pay Act and the Age Discrimination in Employment Act.

Finally, it should be noted that in addition to the guidelines on EEO-related matters issued by federal regulatory agencies, professional societies have issued collateral guidelines that reflect the consensus of their memberships on some of these same matters. These include, among others, *Principles for the Validation and Use of Personnel Selection Procedures* (1987) issued by the Society for Industrial-Organizational Psychology of the American Psychological Association and *Standards for Educational and Psychological Testing* (1985) issued jointly by the American Educational Research Association, the American Psychological Association, and the National Council on Measurement in Education. As noted above, neither regulatory agency nor professional society guidelines have a statutory basis; they are influential only to the extent that they are recognized by the courts an instructive on an EEO-related matter.

Age Discrimination in Employment Act of 1967 (ADEA)

This Act in many respects parallels Title VII and originally prohibited job discrimination against workers aged 40 to 64. The Act was amended in 1978 to raise the upper age limit to 69. In addition, this amendment eliminated mandatory retirement for federal workers; a 1986 amendment extended this provision to private-sector employees. Except under a limited set of circumstances, mandatory retirement is a thing of the past in the United States. The Act does, however, provide that age may be used as a "bona fide occupational qualification" (e.g., an actor required to portray a youthful character for a role).

The provisions of the ADEA differ from Title VII and other statutes in three major ways. First, only a subset of the protected classification (i.e., older workers) are covered by the Act. One obvious consequence of this is that claims of so-called "reverse discrimination" by younger workers cannot be made under the ADEA. Thus, employers are *not* prohibited from discriminating against individuals on the basis on their youth (under 40).

Second, the body of ADEA case law overwhelming supports the fact that the Act was intended to prohibit *only* intentional discrimination. Thus, claims of age discrimination based on *prima facie* evidence of disparate impact are very likely not possible; natural occurrences often better explain statistical disparities where age is the implied discriminatory variable. For example, an examination of hiring or termination statistics would likely reveal significant age differences. However, there exists a natural tendency for people beginning their employment to be younger than those ending their employment. Evidence of disparate treatment, including a showing of discriminatory intent, is thus required to establish a *prima facie* claim under the ADEA.

Third, plaintiffs may request a trial before a jury, which is not the case under Title VII. This certainly increases the likelihood that a larger number of employers will lose ADEA rather than Title VII lawsuits. Furthermore, since the liabilities of employers are potentially greater under the ADEA (e.g., monetary awards can be doubled for "willful" violations), losing an ADEA suit can be even more prohibitive for an employer.

Equal Pay Act of 1963

This Act prohibits discrimination on account of sex in the payment of wages by employers engaged in commerce or the production of goods for commerce. Originally, the Department of Labor was in charge of administering the Equal Pay Act; under President Carter's reorganization that responsibility shifted to the EEOC. Employers are required to give equal compensation to employees who perform equal work involving substantially equal skill, effort, responsibility, and working conditions. In *Schultz* v. *Wheaton Glass Co.* (1970), the Supreme Court upheld the reasoning that "equal" work does not necessarily imply *identical* but rather "substantially similar" tasks, duties, and activities.

Individuals can also bring a lawsuit involving discrimination in wages based on Title VII. Prior to 1981, however, it was believed that the Bennett Amendment to the Civil Rights Act of 1964 limited Title VII cases involving wage discrimination to the "equal pay for equal work" standard included in the Equal Pay Act. In *County of Washington* v. *Gunther* (1981), the Supreme Court ruled that the Bennett Amendment meant that *only* the four affirmative defenses included in the EPA be included in Title VII.* This ruling opened the door to comparable worth suits under Title VII, although the Court did not specifically endorse this doctrine.

The doctrine of comparable worth states that jobs involving substantially *different* levels and/or combinations of skill, effort, responsibility, and working conditions must be paid similarly if the *overall* worth of the jobs is the same. Thus, many have applied this doctrine to sex discrimination in wages by arguing that the pay differentials between female- and male-dominated jobs is the result of the arbitrary undervaluing of the characteristics of women's jobs and not that women's jobs are inherently worth less to employers.

Although discrimination based on sex has been the focus of the majority of research and legal suits involving comparable worth, many have failed to make the distinction between the "theory" of comparable worth and those affected by its implications. For example, applying the doctrine of comparable worth to race discrimination, it is possible that the characteristics of jobs heavily populated by minorities have been arbitrarily undervalued because these jobs are dominated by minorities and not because they are worth less.

What is "comparable" work is easier to define operationally from the standpoint of internal as opposed to external pay-equity considerations: Internal pay-equity decisions have traditionally been based on standardized job evaluation methods. For example, in terms of internal equity, "comparable" (as opposed to "equal") work would mean that the *total* number of job evaluation points associated with two jobs was substantially similar even though the number of points associated with one or more of the factors for each job was substantially different. In other words, the point profiles of the two jobs across factors would substantially differ in terms of either or both shape and elevation, yet the overall point values would be substantially the same (see Fig. 3.1).

However, the use of standardized job evaluation methods to establish the relative value of jobs within an organization has been the subject

---

* The EPA includes four exceptions which allow pay differentials for work of substantially equal skill, effort, responsibility, and working conditions if the differentials occur due to 1) a seniority system; 2) a merit system; 3) a system which measures earnings by quantity or quality of production; or 4) a differential based on any factor other than sex.

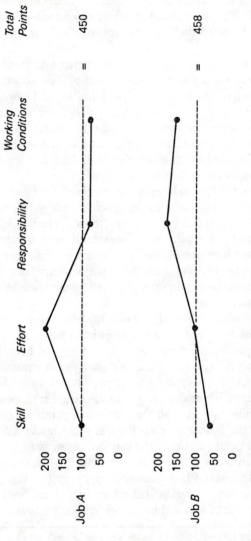

Figure 3.1 *Two different jobs with similar total point values.*

of much criticism by comparable worth advocates. For example, some researchers have expressed concerns about the potential for discriminatory bias in the judgments of raters using various job-evaluation methods (e.g., Gold, [1983]; Blumrosen, [1979]). Other researchers expressed concerns about the various technical problems associated with the underlying psychometric issues when using job-evaluation information to help establish wage discrimination claims (Arvey, Maxwell, and Abraham, 1985). Moreover, issues related to external pay-equity considerations (such as the influence of market factors related to labor supply and demand on wage rates) have also contributed to problems involved in the comparable worth debate.

Until generally acceptable methods for determining the "worth" of jobs can be developed and implemented, the issue of comparable worth will remain unresolved. However, the problem is not likely to go away because of this obstacle: In 1984 alone the EEOC investigated more than 250 comparable worth complaints involving discrimination in wages based on sex. Moreover, at least 21 states are now involved in comparable worth studies affecting state employees; another five had bills pending that would apply comparable worth to the private sector. These facts, among others, should spur organizations to assess their compensation practices for any vestiges of discrimination (especially sex discrimination).

Vocational Rehabilitation Act of 1973

Even though the Rehabilitation Act is a law enacted by Congress, it is much like Executive Order 11246 (to be discussed below) in that it applies only to government contractors and it *requires* these employers to take affirmative action. Although it does not require the hiring of unqualified handicapped workers, the Rehabilitation Act explicitly requires that plans for the handicapped include steps to *accommodate* workers with disabilities so they may perform jobs they otherwise could not. Accommodations might include job redesign, retraining, transfer to jobs requiring different skills, removal of impediments to access, etc. In addition, Section 504 of the Act prohibits discrimination against qualified handicapped individuals solely on the basis of their handicap:

> *No otherwise qualified individual in the United States . . . shall, solely by reason of his handicap, be excluded from the participation in, be denied the benefits of or be subjected to discrimina-*

tion under any program or activity receiving Federal financial assistance. (Sec. 504)

This Act is, for handicapped individuals, the counterpart to Title VII. The agencies charged with ensuring compliance to the Rehabilitation Act are the Departments of Labor (OFCCP) and Health, Education, and Welfare.

Although the term "handicap" is usually associated with physical impairments, the Rehabilitation Act also applies to individuals with mental problems; alcoholism and other forms of drug dependency are also covered. The Act defines a handicapped individual as a person who

(1) has a physical or mental impairment which substantially limits one or more of such person's major life activities, (2) has a record of such an impairment, or (3) is regarded as having such an impairment. For purposes of sections 503 and 504 as such sections relate to employment, such term does not include any individual who is an alcoholic or drug abuser whose current use of alcohol or drugs prevents such individual from performing the duties of the job in question or whose employment, by reason of such current alcohol or drug abuse, would constitute a direct threat to property or the safety of others. [29 U.S.C. § 706(7)(B) (Supp. III 1979)]

Although the Vocational Rehabilitation Act of 1973 applies primarily to affirmative-action programs of governmental contractors, courts have allowed individuals to sue employers under this Act. For example, in *Drennon* v. *Philadelphia General Hospital* (1977), a district court ruled that an epileptic job applicant who was rejected for a hospital job due to a policy of denying employment to epileptics, may sue the hospital under Section 504 of the Vocational Rehabilitation Act. In another case, (*Brown* v. *County of Genesee,* 1985), the court ruled an individual's failure to pass a preemployment physical exam because of her diabetes and history of diabetic coma was sufficient evidence that she suffered from an "impairment" as defined under the Act. The court also ruled the fact that the plaintiff had been gainfully employed for more than a year substantiated her claim that she was able to perform the work (i.e., she was a "qualified handicapped worker").

In a case with interesting implications (*Doe* v. *U.S. Postal Service,* 1985), the court ruled an individual's claim that her transsexualism was an impairment that substantially limited her ability to gain employment was potentially actionable under the Rehabilitation Act. As the judge noted, coverage under the Rehabilitation Act is *not* limited to traditionally recognizable disabilities.

Obviously, there appears to be a trend among the courts for broadening the definition of an "impairment" under the Rehabilitation Act. Employers should be aware that impairments will likely include more than those disabilities usually considered so. In the case of employment, at least, *any* mental or physical restriction that substantially limits an individual's ability to *gain* employment, yet does not perceptively affect the individual's ability to *perform* the job is likely to be actionable under the Act.

CONSTITUTIONAL LAWS

Fifth and Fourteenth Amendments

Many employment discrimination problems have been litigated on constitutional grounds, especially where statutory solutions prove unproductive or inappropriate. For example, employees have challenged selection procedures under the Fifth and Fourteenth Amendments to the Constitution. Under the "Equal Protection" clause of the Fourteenth Amendment, no state may deny any person within its jurisdiction the equal protection of the laws. The Fifth Amendment, which applies to the federal government, also imposes an equal-protection restriction. Both the Fifth and Fourteenth Amendments also contain "due process" clauses which state that no person shall be denied life, liberty, or property without due process of law. These due process clauses have occasionally been used by claimants as a basis for the remedy of discriminatory employment practices.

When analyzing a case using standards imposed by an equal-protection analysis, a discriminatory scheme or classification is unconstitutional if it bears no rational or reasonable relation to a legitimate purpose. Equal-protection analysis is not restricted to cases involving racial discrimination.

A person filing suit under Title VII need only demonstrate adverse impact; filing under an equal-protection analysis requires that the plaintiff establish discriminatory intent—which is much more difficult to establish. Thus when constitutional grounds are the basis for a lawsuit, only disparate treatment claims are possible; this fact was established by the Supreme Court in 1976 in *Washington* v. *Davis* (see Chapter 4). (More will be said about the meaning of adverse impact and disparate treatment below.)

Finally, it should be remembered that the Constitution and its Amendments are written in very broad and abstract language; they were not written with the intent to speak directly to *specific* issues (such as employment discrimination). For this reason, the courts prefer to defer to existing statutory laws when possible because of their greater specificity. Generally speaking, it seems preferable to bring suit on statutory rather than constitutional grounds.

EXECUTIVE ORDERS

Executive orders express the position of the executive branch of the government on a particular issue. They derive from the President's authority to institute rules and regulations for the executive branch as well as those doing business with the executive branch of the federal government. Since the U.S. government regularly enters into contracts with private organizations which amount to billions of dollars annually, the presidential right to impose certain conditions on the manner in which these businesses operate can have a substantial impact; noncompliance can be very expensive.

The most pervasive Executive Order in the area of equal employment opportunity is 11246, issued by Lyndon Johnson in 1965. It has been amended and superseded several times since. Generally speaking, it imposes obligations on contractors and subcontractors doing business with the government to ensure nondiscrimination along the lines of the provisions of Title VII:

> *The contractor will not discriminate against any employee or applicant for employment because of race, color, religion, sex, or national origin. The contractor will take affirmative action to ensure that applicants are employed, and that applicants are treated during employment, without regard to race, color, religion, sex, or national origin. [Sec. 202(1)]*

This directive covers all contractors and subcontractors whose business with the federal government exceeds a certain dollar value per year.

It should be noted that the directive does more than prohibit discrimination; for a large subset of the contractors and subcontractors it requires affirmative action efforts as well.

The agency initially responsible for the administration of the Order was the Office of Federal Contract Compliance (OFCC), located in the Department of Labor. In June 1975, the OFCC was merged with two other equal employment opportunity agencies to create the Office of Federal Contract Compliance Programs (OFCCP). Unlike the EEOC, investigators attached to the OFCCP proactively monitor compliance activities. They schedule unannounced compliance visits of employers; the EEOC must wait until a complaint is filed before it can begin an investigation.

The OFCCP has issued sets of guidelines on various EEO matters under its control. For example, in 1983 it issued guidelines published by BNA as *Affirmative Action Program Guidelines*. These parallel an earlier directive (Order #4) issued by the OFCC, which required that contractors develop specific affirmative action programs containing goals and time-tables of hiring commitments to relieve any "underutilization" of minorities. Underutilization occurs when an employer's work force does not reflect the availability of minorities and women in the relevant geographical population. Thus, the OFCCP has stressed the need for *positive* action to recruit and employ protected group members in contrast to the simple prohibition of discriminatory acts that Seligman (1973) has called passive nondiscrimination.

As most readers are aware, there has been a good deal of confusion regarding the differences between voluntary affirmative-action goals and court-ordered preferential hiring quotas. The legality of voluntary affirmative-action programs was confirmed by the Supreme Court in *U.S. Steelworkers* v. *Weber* (1979) and will be discussed in Chapter 9.

LEGAL FRAMEWORK

Many practicing industrial/organizational psychologists and personnel managers find that the courts are currently exerting serious influence on the direction of their profession. As Sharf (1976) says: "The standard to evaluate the psychologist's service may no longer be what the client organization will buy but what the court will 'buy'" (p. 546). In an excellent discussion of the influence of the legal process on professionals, Sharf argues that professionals have a role to play in educating and guiding the court concerning testing and validity issues. Indeed, it appears that psychologists and other professionals must become more aware of the legal process involved in Title VII litigation so they may meet this responsibility.

An example of what Sharf was talking about resulted from the court's ruling in *Brito* v. *Zia Co.* (1973). Here the court ruled in favor of the plaintiff, in most part, because the employer could not establish the criterion-related validity of a performance appraisal instrument used to make lay-off decisions. The *Brito* court's decision relied *heavily* on information in the *Uniform Guidelines* that the defendant must present evidence of a "test's" validity once adverse impact is established. In this instance, however, the information derived from the performance appraisal instrument was *not* used as a "test" (i.e., as a predictor), and thus it would have been *impossible* to establish the instrument's criterion-related validity.

As noted by Barrett and Kernan (1987), in most organizations the performance evaluation is the *only* standard by which an employee's performance can be assessed. Thus in *Brito,* the court demanded the impossible and no expert witness pointed this out. Unfortunately, the *Brito* decision is still cited by professionals (e.g., Banks and Roberson [1985] or Field and Holley [1982]) as a source of credible information about what constitutes a legally and technically sound appraisal instrument.

Obviously, information contained in court decisions has had a significant effect on EEO-related technical issues important to industrial-organizational psychologists and others used as expert witnesses. However, when professionals allow their expert recommendations to be based predominantly on court precedent without significant regard to more important theoretical considerations, they open themselves up to many problems—some potentially *very* embarrassing.

More realistically, the role of professionals should be to enlighten the courts as to how cases *should* be decided in light of empirical research knowledge for which there is a consensus. Where a consensus does not exist, expert witnesses should attempt to objectively summarize all sides of the issues. As noted by Kleiman and Faley (1985), professionals as expert witnesses have an ethical obligation to convey their expertise in a nonpartisan manner.

Although it is difficult to thoroughly educate the reader about the legal aspects of selection decisions, there are several principles that should prove useful. Prior to a discussion of these principles, we would like to note four important sources that may be consulted for a more complete understanding of the legal aspects of decisions. They are as follows:

1. *Fair Employment Practice Cases* (FEP). Mentioned earlier, this reference contains actual written decisions concerning employment discrimination cases. Published by the Bureau of National Affairs, Inc., it is updated every two weeks. Abbreviated FEP, it is a particularly common reference. (A very similar compilation of case law can be found in *Employment Practices Decisions* published by Commerce Clearing House. It is abbreviated EPD.)

2. *Fundamentals of Legal Research* by Jacobstein and Mersky (1973). Becoming acquainted with the legal citation system is frustrating and confusing for those unfamiliar with legal review. Two or three hours studying this book will allow the reader to understand the major systems of citations and sources, rudiments of how cases are summarized and reported, and cross-referencing systems.

3. *Employment Discrimination Law* by Schlei and Grossman (1983). The book is one of the most comprehensive texts on various aspects of employment discrimination. It presents a wide variety of case summaries as well as interpretations and analyses of current legal issues. A cumulative supplement published in 1985 is also available from the publisher (BNA). It contains information on the case law subsequent to publication of the main text.

4. *Lexis Nexis or Westlaw.* These are computerized case law data bases published by Mead Data Central and West Publishing Company, respectively. Both Lexis Nexis and Westlaw are more inclusive than either FEP or EPD because they contain *all* published and many unpublished federal and state court decisions as well as other related material. Moreover, like other computerized data bases, they provide for easy and fast retrieval of large quantities of information.

Generally speaking, most Title VII cases are tried in federal and state courts. Because so many cases are heard in the federal court system, the reader should understand the system in some detail. Figure 3.2 shows a structural outline of the system.

At the lowest level, the basic unit of jurisdiction is the district. Each district has a United States district court. There exist 91 district courts in the 50 states, plus one in the District of Columbia. Many states constitute

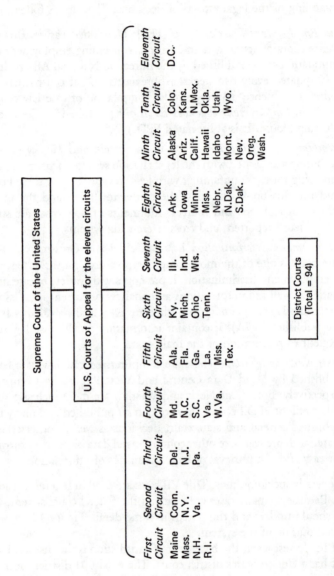

Figure 3.2 *Federal court system.*

a single district, but there are some states which are divided into two or more districts. Employment discrimination cases are tried and evidence is presented at this court level. In Title VII cases, there is no jury involved; arguments and briefs are presented before a federal judge who writes the decision.

Each district is part of a larger judicial area known as a circuit. There are eleven circuits, each covering groups of states and the District of Columbia and each served by a U.S. court of appeals. A major responsibility of each court of appeals is to hear appeals from the decisions of the district courts in its circuit. Decisions of the court of appeals are binding on the districts that belong within their jurisdiction. As might be expected, different case laws will evolve out of the various circuits. Thus, some circuits will have reputations of being more liberal or more conservative than others, and it is possible to have different circuit decisions based on similar case facts. The result is that the law may differ according to the particular geographical location in which a plaintiff or an employer resides.

Finally, the highest appeals court is the Supreme Court of the United States, whose nine justices sit in Washington. The Supreme Court considers only a limited number of cases that it regards as of particular importance to the legal system. Its decisions are binding across *all* appeals and district level courts. However, its decisions are not necessarily final; the Supreme Court can overturn its own or the decisions of earlier Courts. Moreover, if Congress does not agree with the Court's interpretation of its statutory enactments, Congress is free to pass new legislation (e.g., as it did when it passed the Pregnancy Disability Act of 1978 to change legislatively the Supreme Court's ruling in *General Electric Co. v. Gilbert*).

The Court Process

In typical discrimination suits, a person alleges that he or she is being, or has been, discriminated against due to an unlawful employment practice. The person filing the suit is called the *plaintiff*. The person and/or organization against whom the charge of discrimination is made is called the *defendant*.

It is the responsibility of the plaintiff(s) to establish that there is a good likelihood that a violation of EEO law has taken place; that is, the plaintiff must be able to establish a *prima facie* case of discrimination. This can be accomplished in either of two ways. First, plaintiffs may establish that a facially neutral employment practice (e.g., the requirement that all applicants possess a high school diploma) in reality has a significantly *disparate impact* (DI) on members of a protected group. (Disparate impact is also commonly referred to as adverse impact.) Subgroup differences in the *consequences* of an employment practice are important here; good intentions or the absence of discriminatory motive will not redeem employment practices with discriminatory consequences. For example, a plaintiff might demonstrate that out of 50 black and 50 white job applicants who participated in an interview, no blacks were hired, but 25 whites were placed in the job. This would be evidence of DI and a *prima facie* violation of Title VII would have been established.

Second, plaintiffs may establish that they were intentionally treated differently by an employer and that the reason for the *disparate treatment* (DT) was their race, sex, etc. Direct or inferential evidence of discriminatory *intent* is important here; a showing of subgroup differences in the consequences of an employment practice is not enough to establish a *prima facie* case under the doctrine of DT. Obvious examples of DT would include an outright refusal by an employer to consider blacks for a job, or the statement by an employer that employees over 40 were terminated solely because of their age.

The basic criteria for establishing a *prima facie* case of DI were outlined by the Supreme Court in *Griggs,* those for a DT claim in *McDonnell Douglas* v. *Green* (1973). Because a claim of DT requires evidence of discriminatory intent, it is substantially more difficult to establish a DT than a DI *prima facie* claim, and thus more DI than DT claims are brought before the courts.

Once a successful *prima facie* case has been made by the plaintiff, the "burden of going forward" (also called the "burden of persuasion") shifts to the defendant. Depending on whether the plaintiff's *prima facie* showing is based on the DI or DT doctrine, the defendant must either articulate a legitimate nondiscriminatory reason for the DT or establish the job-relatedness of the employment practice that resulted in the DI. In either instance, the "burden of proof" *always remains with the plaintiff* to establish that discrimination has taken place by either showing the articulated reason is a pretext for discrimination (DT) or that an equally valid, yet less discriminatory alternative employment practice exists (DI).

This shifting "burden of persuasion" model is applied to almost all suits filed in which there is a claim of employment discrimination. Figure 3.3 depicts the model graphically. The reader should become familiar with this model since most court judgments rest upon whether or not there has been a demonstration of (1) a *prima facie* violation and (2) the job-relatedness or validity of the employment practice. As one can imagine, a great deal of litigation has dealt with the determination of the disparate impact and job-relatedness of various selection procedures.

THE ROLE OF STATISTICS IN DETERMINING A *PRIMA FACIE* CASE

Disparate Impact Cases

Statistics have come to play an important and almost dominant role in employment discrimination cases. Heavy reliance on statistics has been the inevitable result of the *Griggs* v. *Duke Power Co.* (1971) case, noted earlier, which focused attention on "the consequences of employment practices." This focus on the *actual impact* of employment practices normally requires a careful assessment of the race/sex/ethnic composition of the persons who pass a test or other selection procedure, those who are eventually hired for a given job, and those who make up a given work force or general population. Such assessments and comparisons can be best expressed in statistical terms. In addition, reliance on statistical proof has also been encouraged because such data are sometimes the only available evidence since employers will seldom admit discrimination (Schlei and Grossman, 1983). As one court declared, "Statistics often tell much, and courts listen" (*United States* v. *Ironworkers, Local 86* [1971]).

Plaintiffs have used many kinds of statistical comparisons in an effort to establish a *prima facie* case of discrimination. Most can be subsumed under two broad categories:

1. *Flow Analysis Statistics*—The use of flow statistics is based on the assumption that differences in the proportions between/among protected groups related to various human resource activities should not exceed a certain percentage. For example, plaintiffs may offer statistical evidence showing that there exist different pass/fail rates of *actual* applicants for the job. This essentially involves a comparison of the following type:

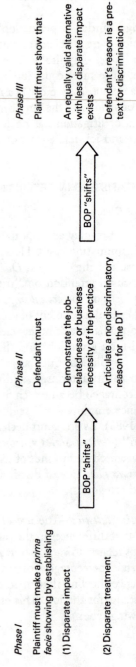

Figure 3.3 Shifting burden of persuasion (BOP).

Phase I

Plaintiff must make a *prima facie* showing by establishing

(1) Disparate impact

(2) Disparate treatment

BOP "shifts"

Phase II

Defendant must

Demonstrate the job-relatedness or business necessity of the practice

Articulate a nondiscriminatory reason for the DT

BOP "shifts"

Phase III

Plaintiff must show that

An equally valid alternative with less disparate impact exists

Defendant's reason is a pretext for discrimination

74

Number of successful minority applications		Number of successful nonminority applicants
————————	Compared to	————————
Total number of minority applicants		Total number of nonminority applicants

For example, in *Albemarle Paper Co. v. Moody* (1975), the plaintiffs established their *prima facie* case of disparate impact by showing considerable disparity between the percentage of *actual* black as opposed to white applicants who successfully passed a paper-and-pencil employment test. While it is not entirely clear "how much" of a disparity need be demonstrated to establish a *prima facie* case under the disparate impact doctrine, the *Uniform Guidelines* (1978) provides some guidance:

> *A selection rate for any racial, ethnic, or sex subgroup which is less than four-fifths (4/5) (or 80 percent) of the rate for the group with the highest rate will generally be regarded as evidence of adverse impact . . .*

For example, an employer may have had 200 applicants over a six-month period, 100 black and 100 white. Out of these 200 applicants, 100 individuals were hired, 80 whites and 20 blacks. Thus, the percentage of the whites hired is 80 percent (80/100) and the percentage of blacks hired is 20 percent (20/100). The passing rate for blacks is only one-fourth that of whites (20%/80%), and would thus be construed as adverse impact.*

A variation of this rule is based on the pass/fail rate of *potential* applicants for the job based on showing that the minority group in question possesses or does not possess some particular qualification or set of qualifications compared to nonminority members. For example, population norms may be used to establish that women are less likely to meet a 5 feet 7 inches height requirement, or that blacks are less likely to have high school diplomas, and thus, using these as job requirements will adversely impact women and blacks. The particular comparison in this situation can be shown as follows:

---

* It should be noted that these guidelines also caution about a strict adherence to this rule when sample sizes are small.

Number of minorities in relevant labor market with particular qualifications		Number of nonminorities in relevant labor market with particular qualifications
	Compared to	
Total number of minorities in relevant labor market		Total number of nonminorities in relevant labor market

In *Griggs* v. *Duke Power Co.* (1971), the plaintiffs made their case by showing that there was a substantial disparity between the percentage of black males in North Carolina who had a high school diploma (12 percent) and the percentage of white males in the same state who had a high school diploma (34 percent).

2. *Stock Analysis Statistics*—A second strategy plaintiffs have used to establish a *prima facie* case of disparate impact has been to offer statistical evidence comparing the race/sex/ethnic percentage of the general population in a particular geographical area with the race/sex/ethnic percentage of the employer's work force. The "relevant geographical area" is often based on the geographic scope of the employer's recruitment practices. For example, if recruitment took place nationwide, the courts would likely consider the relevant geographical area to be the entire country, and nationwide statistics would define the applicable comparison population for establishing a *prima facie* case. Population/work force comparisons involve the following:

Number of minorities employed		Number of nonminorities in relevant geographical area
	Compared to	
Total number of employees		Total number of people in relevant geographical area

In *United States* v. *Hayes International Corp.* (1972), for example, the court found evidence of a *prima facie* case of disparate impact because 30 percent of the general population was black, but only 6 of the employer's 624 employees (.65 percent) were black.

A variant on standard stock analysis statistics (sometimes called concentration statistics) has also been used to establish a *prima facie* case of discrimination. Concentration statistics are based on a showing that either there are significant differences between/among protected groups as they are distributed throughout the levels of the employer's organization or compared to how they are distributed in other similar organizations. For example, an employer may establish a lack of disparate impact based on other stock analysis statistics by showing that its work force composition reflects the minority composition in the relevant geographical area. However, the plaintiff may respond by showing, that although this is true, all minorities are concentrated in the lowest paying jobs within the organization. As further evidence, the plaintiff might produce concentration statistics from other similar organizations which show significantly greater concentrations of minorities in higher paying jobs or that the availability of minorities at various job levels based on general population statistics is significantly higher than their utilization by the defendant.

For example, in *O'Brien* v. *Sky Chefs, Inc.* (1982), the plaintiffs were able to establish a *prima facie* case of disparate impact by showing that there was a significant disparity between the representation of women in lower paying and higher paying jobs. Even though plaintiffs did not establish that women in lower level jobs were qualified for promotion, the court ruled the concentration disparities supported a *prima facie* claim since the organization had a policy of promotion from within and the jobs at issue did not require specialized supervisory skills. Moreover, in *Leisner* v. *New York Telephone Co.* (1973), female plaintiffs were able to establish that discrimination took place by showing that during the two-year period prior to trial only 6 percent of the participants in the organization's Management Development Program were women, although 38 percent of the company's management level employees were women.

Klinefelter and Thompkins (1976) have provided an overview of the particular strategies used to establish adverse impact. They indicate that stock analysis statistics are used primarily to bolster some other showing of adverse impact or when there is an absence of evidence based on flow analysis statistics. Morris (1977) and Baldus and Cole (1980) have also reviewed the role of statistics in determining disparate impact and provide an excellent overview of the complex issues involved.

What the use of these various statistics with potentially different results points to is that disparate impact is not a "hard fact" that does or does not exist; its existence, in part, depends on the statistics sanctioned by the court to establish disparate impact. This point is expressed well in *Dendy* v. *Washington Hospital Center* (1977):

> *The phrases "prima facie case" and "discriminatory effect" are terms of art without specific meaning. Lacking any pretense of scientific exactness, they merely serve as guideposts to assist in singling out employment practices for which it is appropriate to ask employers to offer justifications. The precise point at which statistical data casts sufficient suspicion on an employment practice to require explanation by an employer is not fixed by any rule of thumb.*

Disparate Treatment Cases

When disparate treatment is the basis of the *prima facie* case, plaintiffs must establish either directly or inferentially that they were *intentionally* treated less favorably than similarly situated majority group members. This requires that plaintiffs establish that the employer's motivation was discriminatory in nature. For example, direct evidence would include, among other things, statements of corporate policy that prohibit the hiring of blacks or women (e.g., "blacks need not apply" signs), letters that include reasons for termination or failure to hire which are discriminatory (e.g., "we don't hire anyone over 60"), or corroborated discriminatory statements by company employees involved in the disputed employment practice (e.g., "women can't handle managerial jobs" or "older people are incompetent").

Since such evidence is not easily obtainable, plaintiffs can also establish employer motivation based on inferential evidence of intent. To ease the difficult burden placed on plaintiffs in disparate treatment cases, as well as to establish reasonable criteria for inferring employer motivation, the Supreme Court articulated a sequence of steps plaintiffs could follow to establish inferentially a *prima facie* case under the disparate treatment doctrine. They include that plaintiffs show that

(i) they belong to a protected classification; (ii) they applied and were qualified for a job for which the employer was seeking applicants; (iii) despite their qualifications, they were rejected, and (iv) after their rejection, the position remained open and the employer continued to seek applicants from persons of complainants' qualifications (McDonnel Douglas Corp. v. Green, 1973).

In addition, plaintiffs often introduce evidence of subgroup differences to help bolster other inferential evidence of employer intent. Unlike such evidence in adverse impact cases, however, evidence of statistical disparities in subgroup results *alone* is not enough to establish a *prima facie* case under the disparate treatment doctrine.

As previously noted, once a *prima facie* case of discrimination has been demonstrated, the burden of persuasion shifts to the defendant. If the *prima facie* case has been established under the disparate treatment doctrine, the plaintiff must "articulate a nondiscriminatory reason for its actions." If the *prima facie* case is based on the disparate impact doctrine, the defendant must choose carefully among several options, which include, removing the disparate impact (e.g., by adjusting cutoff scores), finding an equally valid alternative employment practice with less disparate impact, or demonstrating the validity of the employment practice or its business necessity.

Generally speaking, the two concepts—validity and business necessity—are not exactly the same, although the lower courts often use them interchangeably. Establishing the validity of a practice generally involves correlational concepts and scientific principles. On the other hand, business necessity involves a broader context, with validity being just one method of proving business necessity. Organizations will use cost and economic data to defend the business necessity of a practice, plus an indication that no alternatives exist. Most of the concerns in this book will concern validity, rather than the broader concept of business necessity. Later chapters will focus more specifically on these validity issues.

MORE STATISTICS IN EMPLOYMENT DISCRIMINATION

The preceding sections have outlined the basic statistical procedures used by most courts in reviewing a case: percentages, means, standard deviations, and (perhaps) correlations. It appears, though, that more sophis-

ticated statistical procedures are being introduced into employment discrimination cases. For example, in *Ensley Branch NAACP* v. *Seibels*
(1977), a district court judge involved himself directly in many of the
statistical analyses involved in the case. Among other things, the judge

1. Calculated his own phi coefficients* to test for significant differences
   in minority/nonminority pass rates,

2. Discussed the determination of predictor reliability,

3. Performed a covariance analysis in dealing with fairness issues concerning slopes and intercepts of minority and nonminority regression
   lines,

4. Questioned the issue of utility and practical significance (the judge's
   decision being largely based on this issue).

Likewise, in a more recent decision (*EEOC* v. *Sears, Roebuck and
Co.*, 1986), the judge thoroughly immersed himself in many of the thorny
issues related to the statistical evidence presented by plaintiff and defendant. In *Sears*, the central issue was whether the defendant discriminated against women in hiring and promotion for commissioned sales
positions. The EEOC presented statistical evidence based on applicant
flow data to support its claim that Sears treated less favorably female
applicants for these positions. The district court judge showed a remarkable level of sophistication as he methodically reviewed the results of
studies based on univariate and multivariate, least squares and logit, and
multiple regression analyses. On the basis of his review, he rejected the
EEOC's claim that a *prima facie* case of disparate treatment existed against
Sears. This decision primarily rested on the judge's analysis that many
of the assumptions underlying the statistical procedures used by the EEOC
had not been met.

In short, courts, judges, and lawyers are now demonstrating considerable statistical sophistication in employment discrimination cases. As
we will see later, some of the directions indicated by the research and
thinking in the test "fairness" and validity generalization domains forecast even further statistical complexities in case law.

---

* A type of correlation coefficient where two variables are in a dichotomized form,
e.g., the relationship between white and black job candidates and whether or not they
held a high school diploma.

SUMMARY

This chapter summarized briefly the major rules and regulations that provide the legal foundation for employment discrimination cases and provided an overview of this legal process for those without any legal background. The specifics of this legal process are tremendously complex and it has been possible to present only the tip of the legal iceberg here.

REFERENCES

Albemarle Paper Co. v. *Moody,* 10 FEP 1181 (1975).

American Psychological Association (1985). *Standards for Educational and Psychological Testing.* Washington, D.C.: APA.

Arvey, R. D.; S. E. Maxwell; and L. M. Abraham (1985). Reliability artifacts in comparable worth procedures. *Journal of Applied Psychology* 70(4): 695–705.

Baldus, D.C., and J. W. L. Cole (1980). *Statistical Proof of Discrimination,* New York: McGraw-Hill.

Banks, C. G., and L. Roberson (1985). Performance appraisers as test developers. *Academy of Management Review* 10: 128–142.

Barrett, G. V., and M. C. Kernan (1987). Performance appraisal and terminations: A review of court decisions since Brito v. Zia with implications for personnel practices. *Personnel Psychology, 40,* 489–504.

Blumrosen, R. (1979). Wage discrimination, job segregation, and Title VII of the Civil Rights Act of 1964. 12 *U. Mich. J. L. Ref.* 397.

Brito v. *Zia Co.,* 5 FEP 1207 (1973).

Brown v. *County of Genesee,* 37 FEP 1596 (1985).

Bureau of National Affairs (1983). *Affirmative Action Program Guidelines.* Washington, D.C.

County of Washington v. *Gunther,* 25 FEP 1521 (1981).

Dendy v. *Washington Hospital Center,* 14 FEP 1773 (1977).

Doe v. *U.S. Postal Service,* 37 FEP 1867 (1985).

Drennon v. *Philadelphia General Hospital,* 14 FEP 1385 (1977).

EEOC v. *Sears, Roebuck and Co.,* 39 FEP 67 (1986).

Ensley Branch, NAACP v. *Seibels,* 14 FEP 670 (1977).

Equal Employment Opportunity Commission (1978). Uniform Guidelines on Employee Selection Procedures. *Federal Register* 43: 38290–38315.

Federal Executive Agency Guidelines on Employee Selection Procedures (1976). *Federal Register 41* (227).

Field, H. S., and W. H. Holley (1982). The relationship of performance appraisal characteristics to verdicts in selected employment discrimination cases. *Academy of Management Journal* 25. 392–406.

General Electric Co. v. *Gilbert,* 13 FEP 1657 (1976).

Gold, M. E. (1983). *A Dialogue on Comparable Worth.* Cornell University: ILR Press.

Griggs v. *Duke Power,* 3 FEP 175 (1971).

Jacobstein, J. M., and R. M. Mersky (1973). *Pollack's Fundamentals of Legal Research* (4th ed.). Mineola, N. Y.: Foundation Press.

Kleiman, L. S., and R. H. Faley (1985). The implications of professional and legal guidelines for court decisions involving criterion-related validity: A review and analysis. *Personnel Psychology* 38:803–833.

Klinefelter, J., and J. Thompkins (1976). Adverse impact in employee selection. *Public Personnel Management* 5: 199–204.

Leisner v. *New York Telephone Co.,* 5 FEP 732 (1973).

McDonnell Douglas Corp. v. *Green,* 5 FEP 965 (1973).

Morris, F. C. (1977). *Current Trends in the Use (and Misuse) of Statistics in Employment Discrimination Litigation.* Equal Employment Advisory Council, 1975 Pennsylvania Ave. N.W., Washington, D.C.

O'Brien v. *Sky Chefs, Inc.,* 28 FEP 661 (1982).

Schlei, B. L., and P. Grossman (1983). *Employment Discrimination Law.* Washington, D.C.: The Bureau of National Affairs.

Schultz v. *Wheaton Glass Co.*, 9 FEP 502 (1970).

Seligman, D. (1973). How "Equal Opportunity" turned into employment quotas. *Fortune*, March, 160–168.

Sharf, J. C. (1976). The influence of lawyers, legal language and legal thinking. *Personnel Psychology* **29**: 541–550.

Society for Industrial-Organizational Psychology, American Psychological Association. (1987). *Principles for the Validation and Use of Personnel Selection Procedures.* College Park, MD: Author

United States v. *Hayes International Corp.*, 4 FEP 411 (1972).

United States v. *Iron Workers, Local 86*, 4 FEP 37 (1971).

U.S. Steelworkers v. *Weber*, 20 FEP 1 (1979).

Washington v. *Davis*, 12 FEP 1415 (1976).

Unfair Test Discrimination: A Historical Perspective

4

The purpose of this chapter is two-fold. First, we will provide for the reader a perspective concerning the way courts are *currently* viewing testing practices by tracing the development of unfair test discrimination through a review of major court cases and seminal research articles. Second, we will summarize our views concerning future legal trends and directions in test discrimination.

EMPLOYMENT TESTING: A HISTORY

It may come as a surprise to the reader to realize that the history of the employment testing controversy is only around 20 years old. During this period there have been several court cases, governmental directives, and research articles which have provided major focal points around which other court decisions have been based and research conducted. Figure 4.1 is a visual representation of many of these "landmarks," starting with the *Myart* v. *Motorola* case through the 1978 Uniform Guidelines on testing and the issuance of the 1987 *Principles for the Validation and Use of Personnel Selection Procedures* by Division 14 of the American Psychological Association. We will also review here other cases and events not shown in this figure.

This chapter is organized along a time dimension. We feel it is im-

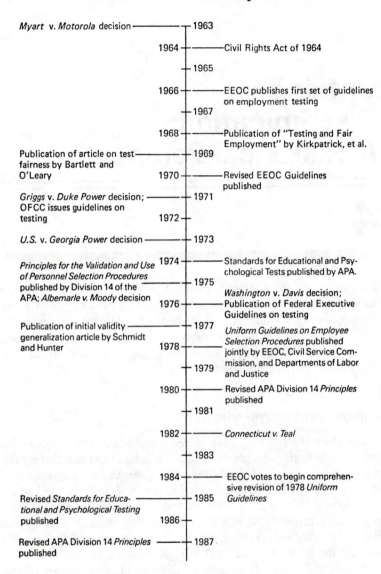

Figure 4.1 *Time chart indicating major events involving test discrimination.*

portant to retain the historical sequence of events and that this is the most logical approach to a very complex subject.

A Word About Tests

At the present time, there are thousands of published psychological tests which are sold and used in employment settings. Many tests are never used in employment settings and of those used for employment purposes, some are more prone to litigation than others. Generally speaking, tests may be divided into several broad categories:

1. *Aptitude and ability tests*—These tests are designed to reflect both general and specific capabilities or potentials of the individual. Tests of this sort are often designed to measure specific intellectual or motor functions, such as mechanical ability, numerical aptitude, finger dexterity, or perceptual accuracy. These tests are often subject to lawsuits, most often because of the adverse impact they have had on blacks.

2. *Achievement tests*—These tests are designed to measure the degree of mastery of specific material; that is, to assess whether an individual has profited from prior experience and has learned specific materials. Trade tests are examples of this type, since most of the items assess whether the individual possesses specific knowledge of concepts considered critical for a job. These tests are also subject to lawsuits, but less frequently than the ability and aptitude tests.

3. *Personality inventories*—These tests are usually designed to assess a person's *typical* behavioral traits and characteristics. Tests of this sort attempt to measure such traits as dominance, sociability, self-control, or introversion-extroversion. After a decline in their use following *Griggs* and *Albemarle* (see below), personality tests appear to be recently gaining renewed acceptance by employers.

4. *Interest inventories*—These tests are designed to predict job-choice behavior rather than job performance. These tests ascertain the occupational likes and dislikes of individuals, indicating the occupational areas most likely to be satisfying. While interest inventories have not been litigated per se, there are potential problems with regard to male-female differences, discussed later in Chapter 6.

Myart v. Motorola

Perhaps the first event signaling the involvement of the court system with the employment testing of job candidates was the 1964 *Myart* v. *Motorola* case. In 1963, Leon Myart, a black, was refused a job as a "television phaser and analyzer" at one of Motorola's plants because his score on a five-minute intelligence test was not high enough although he had previous job-related experience. Myart filed a complaint with the Illinois Fair Employment Practices Commission (IFEPC), charging that he had been racially discriminated against in his denial of the job by the company. At the hearing, the examiner of the Illinois commission directed that (1) Myart should be offered a job; (2) the particular test should no longer be used; and (3) every new test developed in its place should "take into account the environmental factors which contribute to cultural deprivation." Further, the examiner concluded that Myart's test scores had been compared with the scores of more "advantaged" groups and that the testing procedure adopted by Motorola did not lend itself to equal employment opportunity because it acted as a barrier against the "hitherto culturally deprived and disadvantaged groups." Many felt this implied that tests on which whites outperformed blacks could never be used for employment purpose regardless of the test's relationship to job-performance. The ruling was eventually overturned for lack of evidence by the Illinois State Supreme Court (French, 1965). However, it set the precedent to hear such complaints in the court systems (Cohen, 1974).

Civil Rights Act of 1964

While the Motorola case was being argued, Congress passed the Civil Rights Act of 1964. As noted in Chapter 3, Title VII of this Act deals directly with employment practices and prohibits employment discrimination on the basis of race, color, religion, sex, or national origin. Because of concern that employment testing, per se, might be construed as discriminatory, Senator John Tower of Texas proposed an amendment to avoid the kind of controversy surrounding the Motorola case. The so-called Tower Amendment (Section 703 (h)) reads as follows:

> . . . *nor shall it be an unlawful employment practice for an employer to give and to act upon the results of any professionally developed ability test, provided that such a test, its administration or*

action upon the result, is not designed, intended, or used to discriminate because of race, color, religion, sex, or national origin.

This amendment thus explicitly permitted the use of psychological tests, but was very ambiguous concerning the appropriateness of specific testing procedures for personnel decisions. The amendment also raised questions about the right of an organization to test applicants' "potential for development" (as opposed to specific job skills) and suggested the desirability of developing separate norms for different culture groups (Ash, 1966).

The governmental agency responsible for the enforcement of the Act, the Equal Employment Opportunity Commission (EEOC), first published a pamphlet in 1966 which gave some very general guidelines on testing procedures. These initial guidelines were considerably vague. However, one of the more significant features of these early guidelines was their interpretation of the language of the Tower Amendment as requiring that tests be valid (Holt, 1977).

EARLY RESEARCH

After the passage of the Civil Rights Act, several industrial psychologists began to consider the issues involved in unfair testing and published several articles which had a substantial effect on further developments in this area. Lopez (1966) conducted a study based on black and white female toll collectors in New York. A concurrent-validation strategy was employed in which four predictors (a written test, a clerical test, an interview check list, and a composite score) and three criterion measures (absences, tolls accuracy, and supervisors' ratings) were used. The result of this study suggested that the best method of predicting job performance for the white group of employees differed from the best method for the black employees. While the results of this study were clouded by statistical problems, it was one of the first published studies calling attention to the idea that tests might indeed be unfair to minority-group members.

Testing and Fair Employment by Kirkpatrick, *et al.* (1968) also had great influence. It reported the results of five studies involving minority and nonminority employees and concluded that there was no typical relationship between predictors and criteria for blacks and whites and that instances of unfair test discrimination among different ethnic groups were likely to occur. They recommended that tests be validated in the context in which they are used and on samples from the same populations from which applicants will be drawn.

Bartlett and O'Leary (1969) presented 11 models of possible test unfairness against minority-group members and drew illustrations from research literature to support each model. Their article was important for several reasons. First, it called attention to the wide variety of circumstances in which test unfairness could appear in employment settings. Second, it altered psychologists to differential validity (whether a test valid for one group is also valid for another group) and differential regression between minority and nonminority groups as factors contributing to test bias. Third, they addressed the issue of the legality of identifying and using race or sex in order to apply separate norms and perhaps different test batteries. They concluded that as long as the purpose was to improve the prediction of job performance rather than to discriminate, this kind of differential prediction appeared legal.

The results of the studies by Lopez (1966), Kirkpatrick, *et al.* (1968), and Bartlett and O'Leary (1969) were interpreted by some to indicate that

1. Unfair test discrimination did exist and the occurrences were not unusual, and

2. Unfair test discrimination might be thought of primarily in terms of differential validity.

These studies provided important preliminary findings for the EEOC committee to consider as it reformulated its earlier testing guidelines.

THE 1970 EEOC TESTING GUIDELINES

In 1970, a new version of the "EEOC Guidelines on Employee Selection Procedures" was published. Several aspects of these earlier guidelines that may be pointed out include as follows:

1. *Definition of test*—The term "test" is inclusive, referring not only to pencil-and-paper measures, but also to "all formal, scored, qualified, or standardized techniques of assessing job suitability; including . . . background requirements, educational or work history re-

quirements, scored interviews, biographical information blanks, interviewer's rating scales, scored application forms, etc.''

2. *Definition of discrimination*—The use of a test that adversely affects protected classes constitutes discrimination unless ''(a) The test has been validated and evidences a high degree of utility as herein described. (b) The person giving or acting upon the results of the particular test can demonstrate that alternative, suitable, hiring . . . procedures are unavailable for his use.'' A major point, then, is that an organization must justify the use of any assessment procedure that has an *adverse effect* on the hiring or promotion of minority workers.

3. *Rejection rates*—Related to (2) above, an adverse effect is suggested when there are *higher rates of rejection* of minority candidates for the same job, or when there is an underutilization of minority-group personnel among present employees in certain types of jobs.

4. *Differential validity*—The guidelines essentially emphasize the notion of differential validity as the basic concept of test bias and require that, when ''technically feasible, a test should be validated for each minority group with which it is used.'' The guidelines later state that ''a test which is differentially valid may be used in groups for which it is valid but not for those in which it is not valid.''

5. *Research standards*—The guidelines present minimum standards concerning the specific research approach to use in conducting a validation study. Specifically, the guidelines emphasize

   (a) The desirability of conducting a criterion-related validation strategy. The status of content and construct validity is somewhat uncertain, however, because of the following incongruous statement: ''Evidence of content validity or construct validity . . . may also be appropriate where criterion-related validity is not feasible'' (Section 1607.5 [a]). And later in the same paragraph, it appears as if any validation strategy is appropriate.

   (b) The need for representative samples of the typical candidates for the job or jobs in question.

   (c) The need for proper scoring and test-administration procedures.

   (d) That whatever criteria are used as part of the study, they ''must represent major or critical work behavior as revealed by careful job analysis.''

In addition, the guidelines indicate that supervisory ratings should be closely examined for evidence of bias.

In summary, the 1970 guidelines set highly demanding standards for the evidence needed to demonstrate that a test is valid. In consequence, they were the subject of much criticism. Ruch (1972) pointed to problems of a statistical, legal, and moral nature that they had not resolved. Glazer (1975) lamented that an analysis of these testing requirements by various authorities "led to the conclusion that just about no test that shows differential achievement really can be validated: The requirements are simply too stringent" (p. 52). Further, few organizations, even those able to provide sufficient evidence of validity, could provide evidence that alternative procedures did not exist which had less adverse impact.

As noted previously, the Office of Federal Contract Compliance (OFCC) issued a set of testing guidelines in 1971 very similar to the 1970 EEOC guidelines. The differences which existed between the two are minor.

FURTHER LEGAL DEVELOPMENTS

Griggs v. Duke Power Company

In 1971, the U.S. Supreme Court delivered a decision which shook all sectors concerned with fair-employment issues. The Duke Power Company had initially used a high school diploma requirement as a prerequisite for a transfer from its general labor pool to other departments in the organization. On the date Title VII became effective, the organization instituted several testing requirements in order to qualify interested individuals for placement in other departments. Several months later, the company began to permit employees who lacked a high school education to qualify for transfer by "passing the two tests"—the Wonderlic Personnel Test and the Bennett Mechanical Comprehension Test. The cutoff scores required approximated the national median for high school graduates. (The Court made note of the fact that these test standards were even more stringent than the high school requirement since they would screen out approximately half of all high school graduates.)

The district court and court of appeals found no violation of Title VII because the plaintiff had not demonstrated *discriminatory intent* in the adoption of the diploma and test requirements and the standards had been applied equally to whites and blacks.

The Supreme Court, however, reversed the lower court findings. As written by Chief Justice Burger, the Supreme Court ruled *against* the use of the tests in the organization without their validation. Several specific aspects of this decision should be noted:

1. The Court noted that the Civil Rights Act referred not only to overt discrimination, but also to practices that *appear* neutral but operate in a discriminatory fashion. "Congress directed the thrust of the Act to the consequences of employment practices, not simply the motivation."

2. The Court noted that "the touchstone was business necessity. If an employment practice which operates to exclude Negroes cannot be shown to be related to job performance, the practice is prohibited."

3. The Court indicated that the employer "has the burden of showing that any given requirement must have a manifest relationship to the employment in question."

4. The Court indicated that while tests and measuring devices are not to be disparaged and are useful, tests that are used should be used to measure the person for the job and not the person in the abstract. Going further, the Court felt that the facts of the case "demonstrate the inadequacy of broad and general testing devices as well as the inadequacy of using diplomas or degrees as fixed measures of capability."

5. Finally, the decision also included a strong note of confidence in the EEOC testing guidelines. The Court stated: "The administrative interpretation of the Act by the enforcing agency is entitled to great deference . . . Since the Act and its legislative history support the Commission's construction, this affords good reason to treat the guidelines as expressing the will of Congress."

The *Griggs* decision broke a judicial logjam which had been building at lower court levels concerning employment-testing cases. Perhaps the most important aspect of the case which extended across almost all fair-employment cases was the emphasis on the *consequences* of an employment practice and not just the intent factor in deciding whether discrimination may have occurred. It opened the door for statistical methods in reviewing the *consequential* effects of employment practices.

Byham and Spitzer (1971) noted that, nonetheless, the decision did not cover all parts of the guidelines and that additional significant questions remained unanswered. They speculated about how far the guidelines were going to be applied to nontest-selection techniques such as unscored or casual interviews, how the courts would deal with content validity, to what job in an organization a test should be related, and other issues. Quite clearly, the *Griggs* decision addressed broad issues of validity, but did little to clarify specific aspects of test usage and validation principles.

A substantial amount of litigation for the next four or five years was based largely on further refinements in what was considered necessary to fulfill the job-validity standards. However, it is clear that courts did not demand evidence of validity unless there was first a showing of adverse impact. Guion (1974) stated: "The law is clear and clearly interpreted; if there is an adverse impact, the employer (public or private) had better not go into court without competent evidence that the employment practice creating the effect is indeed valid" (p. 21).

The EEOC guidelines became almost a checklist used by the courts, where testimony would revolve around whether or not a particular validation study was in accord with the guidelines. While the guidelines were originally intended to provide a "workable set of standards for employees, unions, and employment agencies," they were perceived by some as written to reflect "ideals" for validation studies. However, these "ideals" were now seemingly being regarded as "minimum standards," and any deviation from these standards would be sufficient to compel a court to disallow the validity evidence.

A 1973 court case generated a good deal of attention. In fact, the Division of Industrial-Organizational Psychology of the American Psychological Association was sufficiently concerned with the direction in which the case was heading that it was going to write an *amicus curiae* brief (a document given to the court by a "friend of the court") in order to present its position. In *United States* v. *Georgia Power Co.* (1973), several tests had been implemented by the company for hiring and transfer decisions. After a finding of adverse impact against blacks was demonstrated, the company presented a validation study. The statistical technique used by the organization in conducting a concurrent-validity study was "multiple-discriminant analysis," a relatively sophisticated statistical procedure rarely used in validation studies. The court noted that the question at hand was "what comprises adequate demonstration that a company's testing program satisfies the *Griggs* requirement of job-relatedness?'' In addition, the court indicated that the EEOC guidelines, while not requiring compliance by every employer with each technical aspect of the validation procedures, still provided a valid framework for evaluating a validity study.

The validation evidence presented by the company was virtually destroyed when compared to the guidelines. Specifically, the court indicated as follows:

1. The company had not attempted to ascertain the existence of *differential validity* when adequate sample sizes were available and where it was "technically feasible" to perform such a study.

2. Statistical significance was achieved for only two of the six jobs that were studied. It is interesting to note what the court said about this point: "Were the only criticism of the validation procedure the fact that there was a significance factor of 1 out of every 15 or even 1 out of 10 instead of 1 out of 20, the employer might have better standing to complain that the guideline is arbitrary. We agree with the lower court that this, as well as other guidelines, must not be interpreted or applied so rigidly as to cease functioning as a guide and become an absolute mandate or proscription."

3. The study suffered from a considerable "restriction in range," since 40 percent of the total sample who took the test were not included in the validation sample (those low-scoring individuals who were not hired or transferred). Thus the sample on which the study was conducted was not representative of the applicants who would eventually take the test.

4. The company's testing conditions were not uniform.

5. The court concluded that the "discriminant-analysis" method of validation was not relevant to the actual way in which the tests were to be used.

This case represents a reasonably sophisticated attempt by a court to review a validation study. As can be seen, the court did apply the guidelines as standards, but allowed some flexibility.

Psychologists, by this time, were increasingly convinced that the courts were establishing and regulating professional standards and principles. Consider the following sample of cases:

- In *Boston Chapter, NAACP* v. *Beecher* (1974), a suit was brought against the Massachusetts Civil Service for its use of a multiple-choice fire-fighter exam. Adverse impact was established, and the U.S. Court of Appeals struck down the use of the test for several reasons: (1) the test was not "professionally developed"; that is, it was not developed by someone with professional training in psychological testing; (2) the cutoff score of 70 was derived in an arbitrary manner without reference to the actual or expected distribution of scores; and (3) the validation study found no correlation between the test and some overall measure of performance. Only minimal correlations between the test and two individual components of the job were found.

- In *United States* v. *Detroit Edison Co.* (1973), the court ruled that the test battery used for selection and transfer purposes was in violation of Title VII because of several factors:

  (1) Only one test battery was proved to be a valid predictor of job performance in accordance with EEOC's Guidelines on Employee Selection Procedures; (2) None of the test batteries was demonstrated to be administered with reasonable cutoff scores that screen out only those applicants likely to possess insufficient ability to perform on the job; and (3) Employer has not demonstrated differential validity for any of test batteries. (p. 613)

- In *Fowler* v. *Schwarzwalden* (1972) as well as in other cases, a civil service exam for fire fighters was attacked because of the inadequacy of the job-analysis phase of the validation process. Other cases (e.g., *Watkins* v. *Scott Paper* [1976] and *Association Against Discrimination* v. *City of Bridgeport* [1978]) indicate that the courts look carefully at the extensiveness of job analysis and its documentation.

- Two reviews, one by Guion (1974) and another by Sandman and Urban (1976), provide further details concerning legal developments in testing up until 1975.

If psychologists were still not convinced that the courts had their hands deep into the evaluation of validation strategies and methods, the decision reached in *Albemarle* v. *Moody* surely changed their minds.

Albemarle v. Moody

The Supreme Court decision in *Albemarle Paper Company* v. *Moody* (1975) concerned two basic questions:

1. What standards should a court follow in deciding to award back pay? (We will not deal with this issue here.)

2. What must an employer show to establish that preemployment tests that indeed have adverse impact, though not intentionally, are sufficiently "job-related" to survive challenge from Title VII?

The case involves a class-action suit brought against a paper mill company which had required applicants for employment into the skilled lines of progression* to have a high school diploma and to pass the revised Beta Examination (a measure of nonverbal intelligence) and the Wonderlic Test. On the eve of the trial, the company hired an industrial psychologist to study the "job-relatedness" of the testing program. The study, concurrent in nature, was one in which relationships between the test and supervisors' judgments of job performance were determined (using the phi coefficient†) in the job groupings selected from the middle and top of the plant's skilled lines of progression. (The tests were actually used in 13 different lines of progression in the company.) The jobs were grouped together solely by their proximity in the lines of progression; further, no attempt was made to analyze the jobs in terms of the particular skills they might require. The job-performance measures consisted of rankings by two supervisors with the following instructions: "Determine which ones (employees) they felt, irrespective of the job they were actually doing, but in their respective jobs, did a better job than the person they were rating against. . . . "

The company argued that the results of the study demonstrated the validity of the tests by showing a significant correlation in three job groupings for the Beta test, in seven job groupings for either Form A or Form B of the Wonderlic, and in two job groupings for the required battery of both tests.

The district court ruled that the organization had, indeed, met its burden of showing that the tests were valid. The court of appeals, however, reversed this decision and the case was appealed to the Supreme Court.

The Supreme Court rejected Albemarle's testing practices. The Court

---

* A line of progression is a set of jobs which are usually related in the type of tasks and skills required and in which individuals usually advance or "progress" from one job to another with corresponding salary increases. The most skilled jobs are usually those in the "top of the line."

† A type of correlation coefficient.

indicated that the EEOC had issued relevant guidelines which were entitled to "great deference." Measured against these guidelines, the Court found the Albemarle validation study "materially deficient" in several respects:

1. The tests were not validated for *all* of the skilled lines of progression for which the two tests were apparently being required. "Within some of the lines of progression, one form was found acceptable for some job groupings but not for others. Even if the study were otherwise reliable, the odd patchwork of results would not entitle Albemarle to impose its testing program within the Guidelines." Quoting from the guidelines themselves, the Court noted that a test may be used in jobs other than those for which it has been professionally validated only if there are "no significant differences" between them.

2. The study compared test scores with subjective supervisory rankings which were ambiguous. "There is no way of knowing precisely what criterion of job performance the supervisors were considering, whether each of the supervisors was considering the same criterion, or whether, indeed, any of the supervisors actually applied a focused and stable body of criteria of any kind."

3. The company's study focused on jobs near the top of the various lines of progression. Endorsing the EEOC guidelines, the Court went on to say: "The fact that the best of those employees working near the top of a line of progression score well on a test does not necessarily mean that that test, or some particular cutoff score on the test, is a permissible measure of the minimum qualification of new workers, entering lower level jobs."

4. There was no demonstration that it was actually unfeasible to determine whether "differential validity" was operating. The study "deals only with job experienced, white workers, but the tests themselves are given to new job applicants, who are younger, largely inexperienced, and in many instances nonwhite."

An additional element of the decision was the requirement that the complaining party—and not the employer—had the responsibility of showing that other tests or selection devices with less undesirable adverse impact were available. This was in contrast to the EEOC guidelines, which put this particular burden on the employer.

Chief Justice Burger cast a dissenting opinion regarding the Court's treatment of the testing issue. He indicated that the Court's analysis was based on a "wooden application" of the EEOC guidelines concerning test validation. These regulations, he noted, were not submitted to public comment and scrutiny, and he stated that "slavish adherence to the EEOC guidelines regarding test validation should not be required; those provisions are, as their title suggests, guides entitled to the same weight as other well-founded testimony by experts in the field of employment testing." Justice Blackman, too, expressed his view that absolute compliance with the EEOC testing guidelines was too rigid and left the employer little choice but to engage either in an extensive and complex validation study or in a subjective quota system of employment selection.

The implications of this case were far-reaching. The first and most obvious one stems from the majority's conclusion that the EEOC guidelines were entitled to so much "deference" that the Court proceeded to test the adequacy of the validity study by a point-by-point reference to particular provisions of the guidelines. According to Holt (1977), "The guidelines are the key. The *Albemarle* case has afforded them such a stature that from now on, as a practical matter, any testing program is going to have to be checked off against them point-by-point, whether you agree with the soundness of each point or not. Few judges have the time or the inclinations to become intimately familiar with the technical details of aptitude testing; they are going to use the Guidelines as a checklist, and the *Albemarle* decision blesses their doing so" (pp. 78–79). Holt went on to review the possible ramifications of the case. He worried that future litigation may outlaw the use of supervisory ratings of overall job performance, but he believed that, instead, the use of essentially irrelevant or marginally relevant criteria will be excluded. Further, he called attention to the fact that the Court adopted the EEOC guidelines requirement for differential validity in spite of more recent evidence (reviewed in Chapter 5) that this phenomenon may be a chance occurrence.

Washington v. Davis

Although it was a case brought on Fifth Amendment grounds, *Washington* v. *Davis* (1976) firmly established the degree to which Title VII standards could be used to adjudicate claims based on violations of constitutional law. Most earlier courts had relied heavily on Title VII standards to evaluate evidence in these cases.

Washington v. *Davis* involved a metropolitan police department that had been using a verbal-ability test—Test 21—for the selection of police recruits. Between 1968 and 1971, 57 percent of blacks failed this exam, compared to 13 percent of whites. As evidence that Test 21 was valid, the police department offered a study that demonstrated that the test was related to the average score recruits received on examinations given in the department's training academy, a 17-week course. Thus, the department claimed that their study was predictive of trainability, an acceptable criterion under the 1970 EEOC guidelines.*

The district court held for the department because of the department's affirmative-action program and because Test 21 had been shown to be job-related through its relationship to training academy performance. However, the court of appeals reversed the decision and found that (1) the lack of discriminatory intent in designing and administering Test 21 was irrelevant, since the test had clear adverse impact; (2) the recruitment efforts by the department were not relevant in this case; and (3) the department had not met the burden of demonstrating the job-relatedness of the test. This court ruled *against* the use of training success as a substitution for job performance.

The Supreme Court reversed the circuit court's decision. The Court ruled that, when a case is filed under a constitutional rule, a different standard of evidence is necessary to establish a *prima facie* case of discrimination; that is, there is a need to demonstrate *purposeful* or intentional discrimination (disparate treatment). For cases filed under Title VII, the court ruled that statistical evidence of adverse impact would suffice. Thus, the Court reaffirmed that evidence of adverse impact was sufficient in Title VII cases but refused to extend this standard to constitutional cases.

The Court went on to also rule on the job-relatedness issues in the case. It reversed the court of appeals, indicating that the use of training criteria was sufficient and that Test 21 was directly related to the requirements of the police-training program as shown by the validation study. Thus the Court essentially ruled in favor of the use of measures of training as legitimate criterion standards in validation studies.

---

* There have been criticisms of this type of criterion measurement because they often consist of pencil-and-paper tests. Thus it is not too surprising that pencil-and-paper employment tests will demonstrate a relationship with a pencil-and-paper measure of training.

Although at the time *Washington* v. *Davis* was thought to have potentially broad ramifications for Title VII cases, it never really did. However, it did have some effect on Title VII standards that concerned whether training performance could be a suitable criterion substitute for job performance in a criterion-related validity study. As noted by Kleiman and Faley (1985), Title VII court decisions regarding this issue have been mixed, depending on each court's interpretation of the applicability of *Washington* v. *Davis* to Title VII case law.

Although there is somewhat of a division among the courts on this issue, we would tend to agree with the conclusions of Russell (1984) that "the superior strategy is to validate training with job performance" (p. 266). Aside from being good business practice, this conclusion is also in keeping with recommendations in the 1978 *Uniform Guidelines* and testing principles of Division 14 of the American Psychological Association that training performance can be substituted only when it can be established that training performance is related to successful job performance (i.e., when it is job related).

THE UNIFORM GUIDELINES OF 1978

When the progression of case law indicated that courts were going to use the 1970 EEOC testing guidelines as a "checklist" to evaluate test validation, industrial psychologists (and organizations) became greatly concerned. Compliance with these guidelines had proven to be a particularly expensive process and there seemed to be no guarantee that even a well-designed and well-conducted validation study would "pass muster" under close review using these guidelines. In fact, Dr. William Enneis, the principal author of the EEOC's 1970 guidelines, testified in court that he was aware of only three or four criterion-related validation studies that met all of the 1970 EEOC guidelines. The only one of these cases whose cost he knew involved a sample of over 200 employees and cost $400,000.

Thus, there was grave concern on the part of industrial psychologists that these early guidelines were not being interpreted flexibly. In the brief submitted by the Division of Industrial and Organizational Psychology, American Psychological Association, to the Court in *Washington* v. *Davis* (1976), the Court was asked to recognize that both professional and governmental guidelines on test-validation methods were of "recent vintage." The brief also contended that judicial opinions often failed to recognize the need for flexibility and reasonableness in the application of professional standards developed for industrial psychologists. Certainly, the experience professional industrial psychologists were having in the courts created a pressure for revision of the guidelines. It was (and still is) clear that professional psychologists must take a more active part in deciding which standards are acceptable. As Schwartz (1976) explained, "Government intervention in psychological testing is here. . . . If we (psychologists) do not provide the guidance, the courts will. And, if they do, the guidance will be in terms of the law and not in terms of psychological principles and technical feasibility" (p. 524).

In other circles, another call for a revision to the guidelines had begun. The Equal Employment Opportunity Coordinating Council (EEOCC), created in 1972 in order to resolve the inefficiencies and conflicts of overlapping federal EEOC responsibilities, recognized the problems with the earlier guidelines. This council decided to develop a set of uniform guidelines on employee selection procedures to be used by all *federal* agencies having responsibility for fairness in employee selection. The attempt to develop a set of uniform guidelines began in early 1973 and went through several drafts, some of which were made public. Comments from public and private sectors were invited. An *ad hoc* industry group was formed in 1974 specifically to respond to these guidelines, and this group had substantial impact on the revision of these guidelines. On November 23, 1976, the new guidelines were published in the Federal Register. The document set forth the official position of three members of the EEOCC: the Department of Justice, the Department of Labor, and the U.S. Civil Service Commission. Each agency published its own unique but substantially similar version of the guidelines. These guidelines are referred to as the "Federal Executive Agency Guidelines."

Notably missing was the fact that two agencies did *not* support these new guidelines. Specifically, the Equal Employment Opportunity Commission and the Civil Rights Commission were in opposition to the new version of the guidelines. The following day, the EEOC republished its earlier 1970 guidelines and, in the preamble, noted that "notwithstanding the publication of 'Federal Executive Agency Guidelines on Employee Selection Procedures,' the Equal Employment Opportunity Commission Guidelines on Employee Selection Procedures remain applicable to all employers and other entities subject to the jurisdiction of this commission under Title VII of the Civil Rights Act of 1964. . . . "

Thus a somewhat conflicting situation existed where *two* sets of testing guidelines were available. Sparks (1977) detailed the differences between the two sets of guidelines and also some of the reasons the two agencies failed to affirm the newer version. Basically, the two agencies viewed the new version as being "weaker" than the previous guidelines.

In August 1978, the various agencies resolved their differences and published a new set of guidelines entitled "1978 Uniform Guidelines on Employee Selection Procedures." (See Appendix A of this book.)

The best way to understand the differences between the 1978 Uniform Guidelines and the EEOC 1970 guidelines is, of course, to read both sets. The Uniform Guidelines are considerably longer and contain interpretation and guidance not found in earlier EEOC guidelines. Although the topics covered are much the same, there are some substantial differences. For example:

- The Uniform Guidelines are more specific concerning what adverse impact is. First, they indicate that the *total* selection process of an organization should be examined. If the total process has no adverse impact, the individual components of the selection process generally need not be evaluated separately for adverse impact. This is sometimes referred to as the "bottom-line" approach. (See, however, *Connecticut* v. *Teal* [1982] below.)

- Adverse impact is defined as a situation in which there is a selection rate less than four-fifths (4/5 or 80 percent) of the rate of the group with the highest selection rate (see Chapter 3 for an example). However, the guidelines go on to qualify the definition for situations involving small sample sizes.

- Content and construct validity are given equal status with criterion-related validity as legitimate methodologies. Some courts had interpreted the 1970 EEOC guidelines as not allowing content validity unless criterion-related studies were technically unfeasible.

- "Fairness" is treated in the Uniform Guidelines in the following manner: "When members of one racial, ethnic, or sex group characteristically obtain lower scores on a selection procedure than members of another group, and the differences are not reflected in differences in a measure of job performance, use of the selection procedure may unfairly deny opportunities to members of the group that obtain the lower scores." The definition reflects both a more sophisticated treatment of the fairness issue and avoids any major focus on differential validity.

- The Uniform Guidelines spell out in much more detail the methods needed in order to use "borrowed" studies or to generalize validity results to other jobs.

- The Uniform Guidelines are more specific about the documentation needed in the various validity strategies utilized.

- The Uniform Guidelines indicate a heavier affirmative-action obligation on the part of employers.

- The Uniform Guidelines give greater emphasis to the search for alternative selection procedures that have less adverse impact. The guidelines state, "Where two or more selection procedures are available which serve the user's legitimate interest . . . and which are substantially equally valid for a given purpose, the user should use the procedure which has been demonstrated to have the lesser adverse impact."

Because the Uniform Guidelines were given public scrutiny and also because they were more reflective of statistical concepts of test fairness current at that time, they were frequently used by the courts to help resolve disputes between plaintiffs and defendants regarding testing-related issues.

PROFESSIONAL STANDARDS

Two additional sets of testing "standards" need to be identified. First, in 1966, and again in 1974, the American Psychological Association issued *Standards for Educational and Psychological Tests*. Moreover, in 1975 and 1987, the Society for Industrial-Organizational Psychology of the American Psychological Association published *Principles for the Validation and Use of Personnel Selection Procedures*.*

---

* Division of Industrial-Organizational Psychology, American Psychological Association, *Principles for the Validation and Use of Personnel Selection Procedures*, Washington, D.C., 1987.

In 1985, the American Psychological Association published *Standards for Educational and Psychological Testing*,[†] a revision of the 1974 Standards. As noted by Kleiman and Faley (1985), although not a radical departure from earlier versions, the 1985 Standards will nonetheless be used to help resolve testing-related questions before the courts. Although it tends to take the middle ground on many issues because it is a consensus document, the 1985 Standards does shed additional light on two of the more controversial testing issues before the courts: test fairness and validity generalization.

Regarding test fairness, the 1985 Standards distinguishes between the terms "selection bias" and "test fairness." Selection bias refers to the technical issues related to differential prediction among various groups and is considered an issue separate from test fairness. Test fairness, on the other hand, is considered a nontechnical, moral, issue "subject to different definitions in different social and political circumstances" (p. 14). The 1985 Standards is also quite clear that the regression (Cleary) model is the preferred approach for evaluating selection bias. (See Chapter 5.)

The 1985 Standards also acknowledges the potential usefulness of validity generalization. However, it also states that the credibility of the validity-generalization approach in any instance is primarily a function of accumulated research that should be *extensive*. Thus, although it recognizes the possible extent of the impact of the research on validity generalization, the 1985 Standards does so cautiously.

Like the 1985 Standards, the 1987 Principles does not represent a significant departure from earlier versions but is an attempt to clarify past information as well as incorporate the findings of the more important research of recent years. For example, the Principles, like the Standards, also sheds light on the topic of validity generalization. In fact, it goes into greater detail and appears to be more enthusiastic than Standards about this topic. We strongly suggest that readers familiarize themselves with the information on important issues related to fairness in selecting employees contained in both of these documents.

[†] American Psychological Association, *Standards for Educational and Psychological Testing*, Washington, D.C., 1985.

OTHER LEGAL DEVELOPMENTS AND TRENDS

Since the *Washington* v. *Davis* case, there have been several developments directly relevant to employment testing issues:

1. *Issue of intent*—Recall that in the *Washington* v. *Davis* case, the Supreme Court ruled that discriminatory intent must be proven under a suit charging a violation of a constitutional rule. Such was not the case in Title VII cases, however; statistical evidence of adverse impact was sufficient to indicate possible discrimination. While one or two lower courts have applied the intent rule to a Title VII case (e.g., *Scott* v. *City of Anniston* [1977]), other decisions (e.g., a Supreme Court decision, *Dothard* v. *Rawlinson* [1977]) have reaffirmed the basic *Griggs* principle. Moreover, in *EEOC* v. *Sears, Roebuck and Co.* (1986), the court both reaffirmed the principles in *Griggs* and better defined guidelines to help determine whether statistical evidence was "good"or "bad." Thus the importance of the consequences of employment practices still holds.

2. *EEOC Guidelines*—A December 7, 1976 Supreme Court decision concerning whether the exclusion of pregnancy benefits from disability plans was a violation of Title VII (*General Electric Co.* v. *Gilbert*, 1976) struck a blow against the EEOC. General Electric Company had provided all employees with a disability plan paying 60 percent of weekly earnings to individuals disabled as a result of sickness or accident. Excluded from this plan, however, were disabilities due to pregnancy. The EEOC 1972 guidelines on Sex Discrimination—Part 1604 specifically indicated that pregnancies are, for "all job-related purposes, temporary disabilities and should be treated as such under any health or temporary disability plan. . . . " The Court, in effect, ruled against the EEOC by indicating that this requirement was not entitled to judicial deference because (a) the guidelines contradicted its own earlier (1966) opinion; (b) the guidelines conflicted with intepretations made under the Equal Pay Act; and (c) the guidelines conflicted with statements of the Senate floor manager of Title VII, which made it unmistakably clear that differences in treatment in benefit plans between men and women would continue if the bill became law.

   Within two years, however, Congress passed the Pregnancy Disability Act of 1978, which amended Title VII to change legislatively the ruling in *Gilbert*. This Act made it unlawful to deny to females who were pregnant benefits that males received for other illnesses. It was viewed by the EEOC as a vindication of its earlier position as stated in the 1972 Sex Discrimination guidelines.

Another example of the courts' lack of adherence to part(s) of various sets of EEOC guidelines is the fact that virtually all courts involved with age discrimination cases have ignored the statement in the EEOC-issued guidelines on age discrimination that ADEA adverse impact claims are permissible (e.g., see *Mastie* v. *Great Lakes Steel Corp.*, 1976). Obviously, the Court in *Gilbert* and the overwhelming majority of courts dealing with age discrimination complaints have not given all parts of the EEOC guidelines "great deference."

Other decisions likewise suggest that the testing guidelines have sometimes had a less than tenacious grip on the courts. For example, in *Blake* v. *City of Los Angeles* (1977), the plaintiff argued that the city had not validated its employment practices in the manner recommended in the EEOC regulations. The court, in this instance, simply disregarded the guidelines and stated: "There is no magic in any validating procedure, and the defendants need only supply competent and relevant evidence on this issue" (p. 84). Moreover, in *Connecticut* v. *Teal* (1982), the Supreme Court rejected the bottom-line approach for evaluating adverse impact suggested in the 1978 Uniform Guidelines. Most courts have also rejected the interpretation in the Uniform Guidelines that the defendant is responsible for the search for alternative selection devices (e.g., *I.M.A.G.E.* v. *Bailar*, 1981); others have rejected outright the need for an alternative search at all (e.g., *Commonwealth of Pennsylvania* v. *O'Neill*, 1979). In 1980, a district court (*Pegues* v. *Mississippi State Employment Service*) became the first to reject the well-established principle based on the Uniform Guidelines that validity coefficients are transportable *only* when it can be established that both the job contents *and* job contexts are similar. The judge in *Pegues* based his decision on expert testimony about current meta-analytic validity generalization research findings.

Although it appears that a definite trend has been established to give less attention to the *specifics* of the EEOC testing guidelines, the courts have still relied upon the EEOC guidelines as standards when considering evidence in litigation concerning testing. Thus we predict no great departures from the *general* demands imposed by the guidelines, even though some courts may expressly reject components of the guidelines.

This is not altogether surprising. After all, it should be remembered that the information in the Uniform Guidelines (like that in other EEOC as well as professional guidelines) was not expected to be used as a checklist. For example, as noted in the 1985 APA Standards, assessment of a test's validity "does not rest in the literal satisfaction of every primary standard in this document" (p. 8); such assessments are ultimately based on professional judgment *guided* by the material in such documents. As stated by Kleiman and Faley (1985), "no professionally [or legally] developed document(s) will ever be able to resolve disputes with the clarity and conciseness the courts would like" (p. 42).

Moreover, as noted earlier, the fact that the 1978 Uniform Guidelines and the 1976 APA Principles sometimes were inconsistent with recent research findings led to calls for their revision. Revision of the Uniform Guidelines is still in its preliminary stages; the new Division 14 Principles was published in 1987 (with minor revisions only).

3. *Utility issues*—Although many courts have dealt with the job-relatedness or validity issue, the notion of whether a test demonstrates "practical significance" (utility) in addition to statistical significance was not examined in depth prior to *Ensley Branch* v. *Seibels* (1977).

In this case, tests used in screening police officers and fire fighters were challenged. The tests were demonstrated to have adverse impact, and a validation study was presented to defend the use of the tests. After an intensive analysis of the validation data, the judge indicated that, even though one of the tests demonstrated a "statistically significant relationship of a very low magnitude with a job-relevant criterion measure, (the test) has not been shown to be appropriate for operational use in screening or ranking applicants." The judge used a variety of statistical concepts in arriving at his decision, and the case is well worth reading. Based on the decision in *Ensley Branch* (as well as subsequent decisions—e.g., *Dickerson* v. *U.S. Steel Corp.* [1978] and *Cormier* v. *PPG Industries* [1981]), organizations having tests that demonstrate validity (especially marginal validity) should be aware they may be asked to present evidence that the tests also possess practical and operational value.

It is also interesting to note that utility analysis has played a large part in several cases within employment discrimination areas other than testing. In *Usery* v. *Tamiami Trail Tours, Inc.* (1976), a court of appeals ruled on the use of age as a *bona fide* occupational requirement for use in hiring bus drivers. The court relied largely on a utility analysis to allow age as a legal factor in selection: "The greater the safety factor, measured by the likelihood of harm and the probable severity of that harm in case of an accident, the more stringent may be the job qualifications designed to ensure safe driving." Alternatively, however, the Supreme Court rejected the appeal of McDonnell Douglas Corporation that age was a *bona fide* occupational qualification for the job of testing supersonic jets because of the safety factors involved in the job (*McDonnell Douglas Corp.* v. *Houghty,* 1977). It appears that cases dealing specifically with utility questions and issues have become more routine, and the importance of a test's utility may eventually come to overshadow the importance of its validity.

4. *Alternatives search*—Related to items two and three above is the issue of whether the plaintiff or defendant is responsible for the search for a suitable testing alternative when the test at issue has been shown to have adverse impact yet acceptable validity. The Uniform Guidelines specifies that the employer is responsible for such a search; if two or more procedures have essentially equal validity, the one with the least adverse impact should be used. However, the courts are somewhat divided on this issue.

In earlier cases (e.g., *Chance* v. *Board of Examiners,* [1972]), the courts placed the burden for an alternatives search on the defendant; the 1970 EEOC Guidelines were often deferred to. Eventually, the courts came to the opposite conclusion, even though the 1978 Uniform Guidelines again reinforced the belief that the defendant bore the burden for the alternatives search.

For example, in *Rivera* v. *City of Wichita Falls* (1982) and *I.M.A.G.E.* v. *Bailar* (1981) the court placed the burden on the plaintiff; in *Commonwealth of Pennsylvania* v. *O'Neill* (1979) the court concluded that an alternatives search was "unnecessary." The division in the case law in this area may be somewhat overstated given the conclusions of Reilly and Chao (1982) and Hunter and Hunter (1984) that evidence is unavailable "that traditional alternatives to paper-and-pencil tests have at least equal validity *and* less adverse impact" (Kleiman and Faley, 1985, p. 810–11).

However, should the plaintiff gather appropriate evidence about an alternative selection device, a number of unresolved questions would still remain. One question centers on a comparison of the adverse impact of the original and alternative instruments. How much "less" adverse impact would be sufficient to permit the use of the alternative and what rule(s) should be used to assess differences in adverse impact (e.g., is "less" enough or should there be a "significant" difference in the adverse impact of both instruments). The second issue deals with how the courts should decide whether the validity of the alternative procedure is "at least equal" to that of the original. Given the lack of statistical power found in most validation studies (Sackett and Wade, 1983; Schmidt, Hunter and Urry, 1976), the difference between the two observed validity coefficients would have to be quite sizeable in order to reject the null hypothesis. Conceivably, the situation could arise in which a non-valid selection device is judged to be a suitable alternative to a valid one, simply because the two observed validity coefficients do not significantly differ.

Another issue regarding the alternatives search deals with the concept of utility. For example, should an employer be forced to use an alternative that is "suitable" in the mind of the court, yet has less utility (e.g., costs significantly more to use than the original instrument)? Alternatively, the situation could arise where the use of a less valid test (with less adverse impact) but with *greater* utility might be considered a "suitable" alternative by the courts. "Obviously, there are always less valid tests available to employers, and many of these may potentially have equal or greater utility with similar or less adverse impact" (Kleiman and Faley, 1985, p. 812).

If equal utility *rather* than equal validity should ever become the primary focus of the alternative search, it may create an awesome burden for whomever is judged responsible for the search. However, if utility rather than validity is the ultimate goal of testing, maybe this is the right way for the courts to proceed.

5. *Bottom-line defense*—According to the Uniform Guidelines, employers whose total selection process did not have adverse impact would *not* be expected by federal enforcement agencies to evaluate the individual components of the selection process for adverse impact. Moreover, the Guidelines state that enforcement agencies will not take action against employers whose total selection process did not have adverse impact even though one component of the process did. This is the basis of the so-called "bottom-line" defense. Although the EEOC in comment noted that this policy was the result of a "discretionary" decision on its part, the courts generally have deferred to the Uniform Guidelines in many of their decisions in bottom-line related cases (e.g., see *EEOC* v. *Greyhound Lines* [1980] or *EEOC* v. *Navajo Refining Co.* [1979]).

In *Connecticut* v. *Teal* (1982), the Supreme Court finally provided binding judicial guidance on the use of the bottom-line defense to rebut charges of discrimination by claimants. The case dealt with job candidates who had to participate in a multiple-hurdles selection process that required them to pass a written examination as the first step. Failure to pass the exam meant rejection (i.e., exclusion from further consideration). Many of the black candidates had already served for almost two years as satisfactory provisional employees in the position.

Although the passing rate on the written exam for black candidates was only 68 percent of the passing rate for white candidates, 23 percent of the blacks who entered the selection process were ultimately promoted, compared with 13.5 percent of the whites. Thus, the total selection process did not have adverse impact, although the written test component did. The employer used the promotion (i.e., bottom-line) statistics to support its claim that adverse impact had not been established by the defendant. The district court agreed. On appeal, the Court of Appeals for the Second Circuit overturned the district court's decision.

In arriving at its affirmation of the circuit court's decision, the Supreme Court stated that " . . . Congress never intended to give an employer license to discriminate against some employees on the basis of race or sex merely because he favorably treats other members of the employees' group" (p. 4720). In essence, the Court said it would not sanction an employer policy that protected the rights of groups at the expense of the rights of individuals. Although *Teal* provided guidance to plaintiffs faced with employer defenses based on bottom-line statistics, several issues remained unresolved.

Most important of these issues deals with the use of bottom-line statistical evidence to rebut discrimination claims where a selection process component with adverse impact does not act as an *absolute* barrier to claimants. For example, it is somewhat unclear whether *Teal* applies where multicomponent selection processes allow all candidates to complete all components of the process before the selection decision is made (e.g., a compensatory selection process where the scores obtained from *all* the selection components are combined in some fashion).

Although the Supreme Court did not specifically address this issue in *Teal*, the majority opinion affirmed the circuit court's decision which held, in part, that, "where all of the candidates participate in the entire selection process, and the overall results reveal no significant disparity in impact, scrutinizing individual questions or individual sub-tests would, indeed, conflict with the dictates of common sense" (p. 531). Interestingly, the dissenting opinion also included support for this part of the circuit court decision (see Justice Powell's comments in Footnote 8).

Several more recent district court decisions shed additional light on this matter. In *Williams* v. *City of San Francisco* (1983), for example, the court ruled that the employer's use of the bottom-line defense was not permissible, even though the test in question did not act as an absolute barrier to further considerations for the job. The court was persuaded that even though the test itself did not result in the rejection of candidates, it did have a *major* impact on the final selection decision (see also *Burny* v. *City of Pawtucket*, [1983]).

It seems apparent that if plaintiffs can establish that the component with the adverse impact has decisive consequences in the overall selection decision even though it does not act as an absolute bar to further consideration, the court may likely require the defendant to establish the job relatedness of the offending component even though there is no bottom-line adverse impact. This could be accomplished by having the defendant present evidence about the relative weights placed on each component of the selection process in the final selection decision. Alternatively, policy capturing techniques could be used by plaintiffs to statistically determine the relative weights. At what relative   magnitude a component becomes "decisive," however, will likely be left to the discretion of the courts.

6. *Validity generalization*—The validity generalization research first reported by Schmidt and Hunter in 1977 has had its first direct effect on a court decision. In *Pegues* v. *Mississippi State Employment Service* (1980), the district court ruled that a test developed and validated in one setting could be used to help make selection decisions in another setting. The court's ruling was clearly influenced by the validity generalization research noted in the 1980 Principles and elaborated on extensively by the employer's expert witness.

This is the only case we have been able to find where validity generalization research influenced the court's opinion; most courts still rely heavily on information in the Uniform Guidelines that users may rely on validity studies conducted elsewhere only when there is evidence regarding *both* content and contextual comparability across jobs.

Although we expect more cases to address the issue of transportability of validity evidence from the validity generalization perspective, it is likely that the caution cited in Standards about moving too quickly will prevail.

AFFIRMATIVE ACTION AND FAIRNESS

In many situations, unless employers can either locate or develop alternative selection procedures with less or no adverse impact, they are unlikely to meet affirmative-action pressures related to eliminating discrimination in employment. Under these circumstances, employers are often faced with implementing voluntary or court-imposed employment practices that give some type of outright preferential treatment to members of protected groups.

In terms of selection fairness, an affirmative-action program (AAP) often automatically results in disparate treatment and is susceptible to charges of "reverse discrimination." Differences related to the implementation of the AAP determine to a large degree the extent of the disparate treatment. (For an excellent summary of some of the different ways to implement an AAP, see Ledvinka [1975] or Hunter and Hunter [1984]).

In a legal sense, the disparate treatment related to affirmative action planning will pass court scrutiny if the standards outlined in *U.S. Steelworkers* v. *Weber* (1979) are met by the employer's AAP (i.e., if the plan is "*bona fide*"). In *Steelworkers,* the Supreme Court ruled an AAP is *bona fide* if it met the following four criteria:

1. The purpose of the plan must be remedial in nature. That is, an AAP for its own sake is not legal; it must remedy an imbalance in the employer's work force created by past or present discriminatory policies, procedures, and/or practices;

2. The plan must not unnecessarily trammel the interests of other employees. For example, the AAP must require neither the discharge of employees not covered by the plan nor their replacement with covered employees or new hires;

3. The plan must not exclude all noncovered group members. For example, in the AAP the Supreme Court reviewed in *Steelworkers*, 50 percent of those admitted to the special training program set up as part of the AAP were noncovered employees; the plan did not create an "absolute bar" to the advancement of noncovered employees;

4. The elements of the plan must be reasonable. That is, the plan must be temporary in nature. Once established goals are met, the plan must be dismantled. Many recent Supreme Court decisions have reaffirmed and/or clarified these criteria (e.g., see *Wygant* v. *Jackson Board of Education* [1986] or *Johnson* v. *Transportation Agency, Santa Clara County* [1987]).

The disparate treatment that often results from the implementation of AAPs can affect the utility of organizational selection procedures in several ways. For example, affirmative action planning is likely to open up many more jobs to competition; the exclusion of qualified applicants tends to decrease the overall utility of the organization's selection process since it artificially increases the size of the selection ratio. On the other hand, if the implementation of the AAP involves passing over "more qualified" candidates (i.e., "leapfrogging") to meet affirmative-action goals, there will be a decrease in utility since candidates with predicted lower performance will be selected. Moreover, implementation of an AAP that involves attempts to increase the number of protected group members in the applicant pool can often be costly (Kroeck, Barrett, and Alexander, 1983). Obviously, if the increase in utility due to a reduction in the size of the selection ratio does not compensate for the decrease in utility due to increased recruitment costs and/or the costs of leapfrogging, the AAP will result in a loss of utility.

There have been attempts to resolve the problems inherent in affirmative-action in a psychometric way by basing the plan on one of the various definitions of selection fairness. These attempts may be misguided since each of the various models has an implicit utility related to the employment of various protected groups (e.g., see Hunter, Schmidt, and Rauschenberger, [1977]). Thus a working plan based on the various definitions of selection fairness can result in significant differences in the composition of the flows of employees into and through the organization. For example, when studied over time within the tenets of a stochastic human resources planning model, Ledvinka, Markos, and Ladd (1982) reported that the Cleary model would have the most disadvantageous impact on black employment. This is especially disheartening news because the Cleary model of selection fairness is implicit in the Uniform Guidelines and is explicit in the latest *Standards for Educational and Psychological Testing* (1985) and in several court decisions (e.g., *Cortez* v. *Rosen*, 1974).

Ledvinka *et al.* concluded that a "50 percent quota is the only condition in the present findings that eliminates minority underemployment in all job classes within the period of time anywhere near what the federal government expects . . . " (p. 30). Obviously, affirmative action planning based on the various statistical definitions of selection fairness cannot be relied on to remedy the effects of discriminatory employment practices in a manner "fair" to all. As noted in Kleiman and Faley (1985), fairness is "subject to different definitions in different social and political circumstances" (p. 830). Since fairness issues are ultimately based on political and social circumstances, it is absurd to believe they can be resolved magically with statistical formulas.

Thus, what the courts have legitimized is a system of limited preferential treatment by organizations as long as the organization adheres to the set of standards outlined in *Steelworkers*. Under these standards, some individuals will be treated less favorably and the utility of the organization's selection procedures will likely suffer. However, no statistical procedures that we know of can completely move concerns related to selection fairness and affirmative action planning from the political to the psychometric arena.

SUMMARY

This chapter traced the inception, development, and evolution of major issues related to unfair test discrimination and interlaced the legal evolution with relevant governmental regulations as they emerged as well as some important early research findings that had impact. It appears that unfair test discrimination requires a true interdisciplinary approach.

In addition, we provided our own thoughts about what to expect in the testing arena from a legal perspective. It will be interesting to determine whether these forecasts were truly harbingers of future decisions.

REFERENCES

Albemarle v. Moody Paper Company, 10 FEP 1181 (1975).

American Psychological Association (1985). *Standards for Educational and Psychological Testing*. Washington, D.C.: APA.

Ash, P. (1966). The implications of the Civil Rights Act of 1964 for psychological assessment in industry. *American Psychologist* 21: 797–803.

Association Against Discrimination v. City of Bridgeport, 17 FEP 1308 (1978).

Bartlett, C. J., and B. S. O'Leary (1969). A differential prediction model to moderate the effects of heterogeneous groups in personnel selection and classification. *Personnel Psychology* 22: 1–18.

Blake v. City of Los Angeles, 15 FEP 77 (1977).

Boston Chapter, NAACP v. Beecher, 8 FEP 855 (1974).

Burny v. City of Pawtucket, 34 FEP 1290 (1983).

Byham, W. C., and M. E. Spitzer (1971). *The Law and Personnel Testing*. American Management Association, Inc.

Chance v. Board of Examiners, 4 FEP 596 (1972).

Cohen, S. L. (1974). Issues in the selection of minority group employees. *Human Resource Management* (Spring): 17–18.

Commonwealth of Pennsylvania v. *O'Neill*, 19 FEP 55 (1979).

Connecticut v. *Teal*, 29 FEP 1 (1982).

Cormier v. *PPG Industries*, 26 FEP 652 (1981).

Cortez v. *Rosen*, U. S. District Court, N. D. California, March 11, 1974.

Dickerson v. *U. S. Steel Corp.*, 20 FEP 371 (1978).

Dothard v. *Rawlinson*, 15 FEP 11 (1977).

EEOC v. *Greyhound Lines, Inc.*, 24 FEP 7 (1980).

EEOC v. *Navajo Refining Co.*, 19 FEP 184 (1979).

EEOC v. *Sears, Roebuck and Co.*, 39 FEP 1672 (1986).

Ensley Branch v. *Seibels*, 14 FEP 670 (1977).

Fowler v. *Schwarzwalden*, 5 FEP 270 (1972).

French, R. L. (1965). The Motorola case. *The Industrial Psychologist APA Newsletter*. Division of Industrial Psychology of the American Psychological Association, August.

General Electric Co. v. *Gilbert*, 13 FEP 1657 (1976).

Glazer, N. (1975). *Affirmative Discrimination: Ethinc Inequality and Public Policy*. New York: Basic Books.

Griggs v. *Duke Power Company*, 3 FEP 175 (1971).

Guion, R. M. (1974). Recent EEOC court decisions. *Industrial Psychologist* 2: 21–26.

Holt, T. (1977). A view from Albemarle. *Personnel Psychology* 30: 65–80.

Hunter, J. E., and R. F. Hunter (1984). Validity and utility of alternative predictors of job performance. *Psychological Bulletin* 96: 72–98.

Hunter, J. E.; F. L. Schmidt; and J. M. Rauschenberger (1977). Fairness of psychological tests: Implications of four definitions for selection utility and minority hiring, *Journal of Applied Psychology* **62**: 245–260.

I.M.A.G.E. v. *Bailar,* 28 FEP 770 (1981).

Johnson v. *Transportation Agency, Santa Clara County,* U.S. Supreme Court, March 25, 1987.

Kirkpatrick, J. J.; R. B. Ewen; R. S. Barrett; and R. A Ratzell (1968). *Testing and Fair Employment.* New York: New York University Press.

Kleiman, L. S., and R. H. Faley (1985). The implications of professional and legal guidelines for court decisions involving criterion-related validity: A review and analysis. *Personnel Psychology* **38**: 803–833.

Kroeck, K. G.; G. V. Barrett; and R. A. Alexander (1983). Imposed quotas and personnel selection: A computer simulation study. *Journal of Applied Psychology* **68**: 123–136.

Ledvinka, J. (1975). Technical implications of equal employment law for manpower planning. *Personnel Psychology* **28**: 299–323.

Ledvinka, J., V. H. Markos; and R. T. Ladd (1982). Long-range impact of "fair selection" standards on minority employment, *Journal of Applied Psychology* **67**: 18–36.

Lopez, F. M. (1966). Current problems in test performance of job applicants. *Personnel Psychology* **19**: 10–19.

Mastie v. *Great Lakes Steel Corp.,* 14 FEP 952 (1976).

McDonnell Douglas Corp. v. *Houghty,* 16 FEP 146 (1977).

Myart v. *Motorola,* 110 Cong. Record 5662–64 (1964).

Pegues v. *Mississippi State Employment Service,* 22 FEP 392 (1980).

Reilly, R. R., and G. T. Chao (1982). Validity and fairness of some alternative employee selection procedures. *Personnel Psychology* **35**: 1–62.

Rivera v. *City of Wichita Falls,* 27 FEP 1352 (1982).

Ruch, W. W. (1972). Statistical, legal and moral problems in following the EEOC guidelines. Symposium on Differential Validity and EEOC

Testing Guidelines, Western Psychological Association, Portland, Ore., April 28, 1972.

Russell, J. S. (1984). A review of fair employment cases in the field of training. *Personnel Psychology* 37: 261–276.

Sackett, P. R., and B. E. Wade (1983). On the feasibility of criterion-related validity: The affects of range restriction assumptions on needed sample size. *Journal of Applied Psychology* 68 (3) 374–381.

Sandman, B., and F. Urban (1976). Employment testing and the law. *Labor Law Journal* (Jan.): 38–54.

Schmidt, F. L., and J. E. Hunter (1977). Development of a general solution to the problem of validity generalization. *Journal of Applied Psychology* 62: 529–540.

Schmidt, F. L.; J. E. Hunter; and V. W. Urry (1976). Statistical power in criterion-related validity studies. *Journal of Applied Psychology* 61: 473–485.

Schwartz, D. J. (1976). Implications for personnel measurement. *Personnel Psychology* 29: 521–526.

Scott v. *City of Anniston,* 14 FEP 1099 (1977).

Sparks, C. P. (1977). The not-so-uniform employee selections guidelines. *Personnel Administration* (Feb.): 36–40.

United States v. *Georgia Power Co.,* 5 FEP 587 (1973).

United States v. *Detroit Edison,* 6 FEP 612 (1973).

Usery v. *Tamiami Trial Tours, Inc.,* 12 FEP 1233 (1976).

U.S. Steelworkers v. *Weber,* 20 FEP Cases 1 (1979).

Washington v. *Davis,* 12 FEP 1415 (1976).

Watkins v. *Scott Paper Company,* 12 FEP 1191 (1976).

Williams v. *City of San Francisco* 31 FEP 885 (1983).

Wygant v. *Jackson Board of Education.* U.S. Supreme Court, May 19, 1986.

Unfair Test Discrimination: Statistical Aspects and Research Findings

5

While the courts have examined in detail research studies concerning test validity, they have hardly begun to consider from a psychometric perspective the precise nature of unfair test discrimination or test bias. Early court decisions relied heavily on the concept of *differential validity*, which, while important, is not the entire issue. The nature of test bias is extremely complex from both statistical and conceptual points of view. Not only do there exist a number of definitions and models of unfair test discrimination, but the various models are contradictory under certain conditions and sometimes have differing implications. At present, there is little consensus concerning which definition is the most adequate, and the various models are currently undergoing evaluation. For example, a Spring 1976 issue of the *Journal of Educational Measurement* devoted almost one hundred pages to several articles by well-known experts evaluating different models of test fairness.

The purpose of this chapter is threefold: (1) to expose the reader to some of the basic concepts and models that have been proposed concerning test fairness and bias; (2) to provide a brief discussion of several of the more complex models; and (3) to present some of the research results based on the different models of test fairness. We do not want to overwhelm readers with complex statistical models which are comprehensible to only the more statistically sophisticated individuals, but because it is entirely conceivable that the more complex models will be involved in future court testimony, it would be irresponsible to ignore these models.

MODELS OF TEST FAIRNESS

Model I: Systematic Mean Difference between Subgroups on Tests

One concept often presented in lay circles is that a difference between minority and nonminority group members on a test is an indication of unfair test discrimination, particularly if the minority-group members score consistently *lower* than the nonminority members. For example, if a black group of employees demonstrates an average score of 35 on a verbal aptitude test compared to a score of 47 for a white group and the *t*-test of this difference is statistically significant, some will conclude that the test is biased against blacks. Presumably, the test would be fair only if there exists no statistically significant difference between the average of the two groups.

This definition or model is inadequate, however, for several reasons:

1. It reflects some confusion between discrimination in a legal or moral sense and discrimination in a statistical sense. Tests are designed in such a way as to produce variability among individuals taking the tests; that is, tests are designed to *discriminate* among individuals. Thus some variability among employees is *desired* "discrimination." If everyone received the same score, the test would be useless for making selection decisions. In this light, Guion (1966) has pointed out that *all* employment practices are discriminatory. It is necessary to hire some applicants and to not hire others. Psychological testing is one method of determining the qualifications of individuals prior to actual hiring. Thus tests are discriminatory by nature and are used to identify individuals who are likely to be more qualified for a job than others.

2. *Aggregate* differences between groups will likely occur on *any* reliably measured variable.* It is highly likely that on any particular test, one could detect average differences between men and women, socio-economic groups, or any other groups. In fact, texts by Anastasi

---

* If a test is totally unreliable, essentially no differences will occur between minority- and nonminority-group members.

(1965) and Tyler (1965) detail various differences among the subgroups of the population in aptitude, interest, personality, and other dimensions.

3. Differences in test scores between groups or individuals should not necessarily imply that one or more of the groups (or individuals) are *inferior* to the others. Test differences are intended to be objective in nature with no value judgments involved. What is important, however, is the degree to which the test differentials can be used to predict such job-relevant behavior as performance, absenteeism, or turnover.

A word must be said, however, about a phenomenon that is frequently observed in employment settings. Test differences between blacks and whites on general cognitive tests (e.g., intelligence, aptitude, or reasoning tests) are well substantiated (Shuey, 1966; Dreger and Miller, 1960; 1968). In general, blacks tend to score one to one and a half standard deviations below whites on these particular tests. What is not clear, of course, is the reason(s) behind the observed differences.

Some researchers suggest a hypothesis of "two cultures" or vastly differing environmental factors to account for the differences, others suggest genetic or innate differences (Shuey, 1966; Jensen, 1969), and still others suggest that factors inherent in the test-taking circumstances (e.g., anxiety, or race of examiners) or the test itself (culturally biased items, unfamiliar test content) are responsible for differences observed. For a good review of some of these issues, as well as an excellent review of a variety of statistical models, see Jensen (1980).

It is not necessary to take a position on this issue in order to become familiar with and to understand the issues of unfair testing. The complex issues of race differences on cognitive tests and their causes are, we believe, somewhat independent of issues of test fairness in employment settings.

Model II: Differences in Validity

Another commonly used definition of unfair test discrimination is the difference between groups in the relationships demonstrated between test and criterion scores. If the validity of coefficients computed for each of two groups differs significantly, this is referred to as "differential validity." For example, Einhorn and Bass (1971) indicate: "If a particular employment test shows differences in validity for a given criterion measure between black and white applicants, then the test can be said to be discriminatory in nature with respect to these racial groups if this difference is not taken into account'' (p. 262). Figure 5.1 illustrates a situation where differential validity *may* be occurring. The test demonstrates a relationship to job performance for a white group ($r = .35$), but a nonsignificant correlation ($r = .15$) to job performance for the blacks. This concept of differential validity is used frequently and is, as noted earlier in the text, given considerable recognition in court. In addition, the 1970 EEOC testing guidelines emphasized the importance of assessing the existence of differential validity.

While the notion of differential validity was reasonably clear, it was not clear initially how to conduct the statistical test for its detection. Preliminary research studies conducted the test in the following way: First, the two validity coefficients would be tested to determine if each was significantly different from a *zero* correlation. If one coefficient reached significance and the other did not, differential validity was said to exist. For example, in Fig. 5.1, the validity coefficient for the white group is significantly different from zero at the .05 level given a sample size of 100. The validity of the test for the black group, on the other hand, does

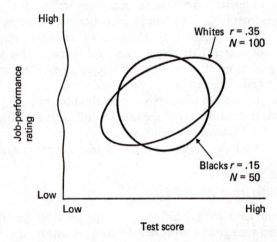

Figure 5.1 *Correlation between test scores and job-performance measure for white and black employees, using different sample sizes.*

not achieve significance. According to this procedure, one might declare this to be evidence of differential validity.

There are two basic problems with this procedure, as Humphreys (1973) pointed out. First, the generally smaller sample size for the black group makes it more difficult to achieve a significant correlation. In general, it is more difficult to achieve significance with samples based on small numbers of subjects than it is with larger samples. This point is exemplified by Fig. 5.2, which shows the relative magnitude of the correlation needed to reach significance (that is, to be considered significantly different from zero) at the .05 level (given no presumption of directionality—that is, a two-tailed test) for samples of various sizes. It

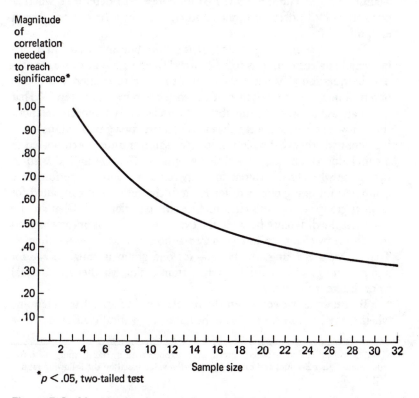

*$p < .05$, two-tailed test

Figure 5.2 *Magnitude of correlation needed to reach significance as a function of sample size.*

may be seen that it takes a higher correlation to be significant with a sample size of 10 ($r = .63$) than with a sample size of 30 ($r = .36$).

In most cases, the minority sample is much smaller than the non-minority sample. In order for the correlations of both samples to be significant, the value of the correlation in the minority group must be larger, frequently much larger, than the corresponding correlation in the non-minority sample. Thus, given a small sample size for the minority group, the odds are relatively high that a test would be valid for the nonminority group and invalid for the minority group.

A second problem is that the more appropriate statistical test is to test for differences *between* the two correlations, not to test each one against zero. As Humphreys (1973) indicates: "To determine whether two correlations differ from one another, they must be compared with each other" (p. 2).

The distinction being made here is subtle, but important. In deciding whether a correlation is significantly different from zero, we are asking the question, "What are the odds that the correlation was of the observed magnitude by chance, if the correlation was really zero?" That is, we are asking whether the observed correlation is a nonzero relationship. However, whether a correlation is nonzero for a group tells us nothing about whether that relationship is the same or different compared to a correlation computed on a different group. We may indeed wish to determine whether the correlation between a test and job performance computed for one group is different from the correlation computed for another group. Under this circumstance, the question is, "What are the odds that the difference between the two correlations was of the observed magnitude by chance, if in fact there was no difference between them?" That is, we are asking whether r_{XY} for one group is equal to r_{XY} for another group. This is quite different from asking whether r_{XY} is equal to or different from zero.

For example, we could test the correlations in Fig. 5.1 to determine whether the two correlations were the same or statistically different.* The

* A test of differences between correlations is accomplished by transforming the correlations into Fisher Z-values and calculating a critical value based on the following ratio (Hayes, 1981):

$$\frac{Z_1 - Z_2}{\sqrt{\dfrac{1}{N_1 - 3} + \dfrac{1}{N_2 - 3}}}.$$

results of this test indicated that the two correlations are *not* significantly different from each other. Thus, using this particular statistical procedure, there is no reason to believe that differential validity occurs.

These data exemplify a common dilemma. Using one kind of statistical test procedure (testing the correlations of the groups to see whether each correlation differs from zero), it is found that the test was valid for one group and not another—an unfair situation, according to some people. Using another statistical procedure (testing whether the correlations differed from each other), an entirely different result is obtained—i.e., that the differences were not significant.

This difference was misunderstood for a number of years. There was a great deal of confusion regarding the appropriate test to determine differential validity. Boehm (1972) clarified the situation considerably when she made explicit the differences between these two concepts, which she labels *differential* validity and *single-group* validity: "A situation where differential validity exists is here defined as one where: (a) there is a significant difference between the correlation obtained for one ethnic group and the correlation of the same device with the same criterion obtained for the other group, and (b) the validity coefficients are significantly different from zero for one or both groups. A related but not identical situation is where a given predictor exhibits validity significantly different from zero from one group only, and there is no significant difference between the two validity coefficients" (p. 33).

It is possible to have four possible outcomes: (1) the test is significantly valid for *whites only;* (2) the test is significantly valid for *blacks only;* (3) the test is significantly valid for both groups; and (4) the test is *not significantly valid for either group*. When a study reveals that at least one correlation of the pair tested is significantly different from zero (outcomes 1, 2, or 3), the next step is to test whether the two correlations differ from each other; that is, to determine whether differential validity is occurring. This, then, represents the proper procedure for ascertaining the existence of differential validity.

Research support for differential validity.   Recent findings have determined that it is quite difficult to detect differential validity in a single study due to low statistical *power.* That is, the probability of finding differences between the validity coefficients for black and white subgroups is relatively low due to small sample sizes and other artifacts. Articles by Trattner and O'Leary (1980) and Drasgow and Kang (1984) illustrate that it is extremely difficult to detect differential validity even when the actual differences in validities are substantial.

In order to increase the statistical power of their methods, researchers began to review a *series* of studies in order to investigate the hypothesis of differential validity. One of the earliest in this regard was conducted by Boehm (1972). She reviewed 13 research studies dealing with black-white differences and similarities in the validity of the employment tests and examined 160 validity coefficients for both black and white samples. A preliminary finding was that 100 of these 160 coefficients were *not* significant, indicating low validity in general. The 60 significant correlations were further examined for differential validity as defined above. Out of the 60 occurrences where some validity was present, only 7 instances of differential validity were observed. In addition, Boehm noted that the findings may have been related to the kinds of job-performance measures utilized. Subjective rating devices appeared to be more frequently associated with observations of single-group validity. She concluded that, in fact, differential validity occurred only rarely.

Several other studies have also cast doubt on the existence of differential validity. For example, Boehm (1977) reviewed a larger set of 31 studies for differential and single-group validity. While not going into great detail about the specifics of the review, her results indicated that studies that appear to demonstrate differential or single-group validity ". . . are largely due to research methodologies that deviate from commonly endorsed professional practices in the area of test validation; that is, that such results are artifactual" (p. 153).

Another review that casts doubt on the existence of differential validity was written by Schmidt, Berner, and Hunter (1973). They summarized the results of 19 studies (most of which were also included by Boehm [1977]) and tested the degree to which the obtained validity outcomes differed from what would be expected if the assumption were made that the validity coefficients for the black and white groups were the same. The results indicated no differences between the groups, and that differential and single-group validity are found only by chance. An additional finding in this review is that studies using subjective criterion measures (e.g., supervisors' ratings, rankings) were no more likely to exhibit differential or single-group validity than studies utilizing more objective criterion measures (e.g., productivity data, absenteeism). Schmidt, *et al.* (1973) concluded that differential validity is illusory in nature and represents a "pseudo problem."

When an article by Katzell and Dyer (1977) criticized prior reviews and suggested that differential validity may exist after all, another string of articles appeared defending particular points of view in this controversy, including those by Hunter and Schmidt (1978) and Katzell and Dyer (1978). Linn (1978) summarized the dialogue by indicating that differential validity will exist under a restrictive definition that the population correlations of the two groups are *precisely* the same. But, he adds, the evidence is *very strong* that the differences between minority and nonminority correlations are very small.

In one other study, Hunter, Schmidt, and Hunter (1979) examined 866 black–white employment-test validity pairs from 39 studies for evidence of differential validity. They looked to see if differential validity existed beyond that which would be expected by chance and other statistical artifacts. Their review indicated no support for the differential validity hypothesis. Thus the research evidence concerning the differential validity hypothesis is not supportive of this phenomenon.

Moreover, Humphreys (1973) indicates that there is a good theoretical reason for adopting the hypothesis of no differences between two groups with regard to their validities. He states, "There is every reason to accept a single biological species for blacks and whites and a high degree of cultural similarity as well. . . . It is much more probable that levels of performance will be affected by the environmental differences than will the size of the correlation between two samples of behavior" (p. 3).

The above literature concerning differential validity dealt exclusively with differences between black and white groups. However, an article by Schmitt, Mellon, and By Lenga (1978) presents evidence indicating that the differential-validity hypothesis may be viable for males and females, especially if academic criteria (e.g., grades, success in school) are used. These researchers examined 6219 pairs of validity coefficients found in both educational and employment contexts. They observed that female validities were slightly, but significantly, higher than male validities for academic criteria. However, when pairs of coefficients that had used *employment* criteria were examined, the findings were not as clear-cut. Studies of male-female validity differences in employment settings showed that the job performance of males was more predictable, but that these data were based on only two studies. The authors indicate that because of small samples, any conclusions regarding differential validity of males and females in employment settings must await the collection of further data. In addition, the differences in validity coefficients could have been artifactual if the females experienced a more homogeneous academic environment.

A more recent study by Hirsh and McDaniel (1987) used meta-analysis procedures to examine whether validity coefficients differed for males and females based on validity information generated for the General Aptitude Test Battery (GATB). Fifty-nine independent pairs of validity coefficients with a total N of 14,945 subjects were used in their analyses. There were 5517 males and 9428 females in the sample. The analysis examined whether validities differed as a function of gender for general cognitive ability, psychomotor ability, and perceptual ability GATB composites. The criterion variable was supervisory ratings. For all three of these predictor composites, females demonstrated slightly higher validities than males. For example, when the cognitive ability composite predicting job performance ratings was used, the estimated mean true validity was .37 for females and .32 for males. There was some evidence that complexity of the job moderated these differential validity findings. For example, the estimated mean true validities for males and females were fairly close for more complex jobs (complexity was measured based on ratings derived from information in the Dictionary of Occupational Title), but the differences increased between males and females for less complex jobs. The authors were somewhat perplexed by this apparent moderating effect and suggested that these findings be viewed cautiously. In sum, however, this study extends the previously mentioned Schmitt, Melon, and By Lenga (1978) results to employment criteria and suggests that some slight differences exist between males and females with regard to their demonstrated validities.

Model III: Differences in Regression Lines

Researchers recognized quite early that test fairness involved something more than differential validity, and that validities "cannot in and of themselves indicate the presence or absence of unfair discrimination" (Kirkpatrick *et al.*, 1968, p. 8). *Mean differences* in job-performance measures and tests must be taken into account. For example, Fig. 5.3 presents the "classic" theoretical case concerning test bias. Although a black and white group have equal validity coefficients, they differ substantially on the employment test, but *no differences are observed on*

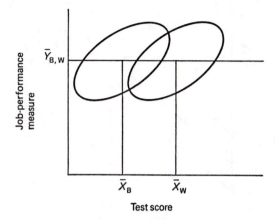

Figure 5.3 *"Classical" case of test bias: mean difference on test scores but no difference in average job performance.*

the criterion measure. Thus, if a particular cutoff score (e.g., the white mean) has been adopted for hiring decisions, almost no blacks would be hired in comparison to whites. However, both groups had essentially the same chances of success on the job!

An alternative way of portraying this circumstance is through the use of regression lines. Figure 5.4 describes the same hypothetical situation, but uses a regression-line format. Also present in this figure is the regression line for the combined, or total, group. Cleary (1968) used this regression-line framework to formalize a more sophisticated approach to test discrimination. She defined it as follows:

> *A test is biased for members of a subgroup of the population if, in the prediction of a criterion for which the test was designed, consistent nonzero errors of prediction are made for members of the subgroup. In other words, the test is biased if the criterion score predicted from the common regression line is consistently too high or too low for members of the subgroup. With this definition of bias, there may be a connotation of "unfair," particularly if the use of the test produces a prediction that is too low (p. 115).*

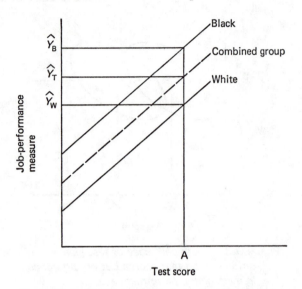

Figure 5.4 *Unfair test discrimination illustrated using regression lines.*

Using this definition, we may apply it to the circumstances shown in Fig. 5.4. For any test score (e.g., point A), we may derive (using the regression equations) three predicted criterion scores: (1) a predicted score based on the regression equation of the combined group ($\hat{Y}_T$); (2) a predicted score for the white group ($\hat{Y}_W$) based on the regression equation of the white sample; and (3) a predicted score for the black group ($\hat{Y}_B$), based on the regression equation for the black sample.

As an example, suppose a situation occurred where the three regression lines had been computed to be as follows:

Combined group $\hat{Y}_T = 3.0 + .50(X)$

Black group $\hat{Y}_B = 4.0 + .50(X)$

White group $\hat{Y}_W = 2.0 + .50(X)$.

Suppose an applicant took a test and scored 10. If the *common* regression equation had been used in deriving his or her predicted criterion score, the result would be 8.0 [$\hat{Y}_T = 3.0 + .50(10)$]. If the applicant were black and the regression equation *based on blacks* had been used to de-

rive the predicted score, the result would be 9.0 [$\hat{Y}_B = 4.0 + .50(10)$].
Thus, the use of the common regression line to make the predictions
would have *under*predicted the applicant's expected job performance (8.0
− 9.0 = −1.0).

If the regression line based solely on the total group had been used,
it would have *underpredicted* the criterion scores of the black group. As
can be seen from Fig. 5.4, the predicted job-performance score for the
black subgroup would be consistently *lower* if based on the regression
line for the total or combined group ($\hat{Y}_T < \hat{Y}_B$). If the selection strategy
adopted was simply to use a common regression and to hire those individuals with the highest *predicted* criterion scores, the blacks would
have had much lower chances of being selected. Put another way, if a
common regression line is used, it will take higher test scores for blacks
to achieve the same level of predicted job performance as whites.

Situations will also vary according to particular regression lines. For
example, overprediction or underprediction may occur, depending on
what specific point on the regression line is being considered. Figure 5.5
presents a situation in which a test is not valid (zero slope) for a white
group, but is valid for a black group. If an employer uses the common
regression equation to make predictions for both black and white em-

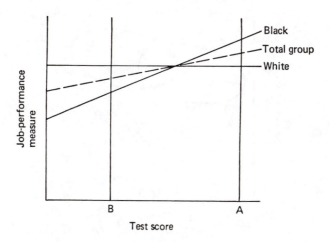

Figure 5.5 *Example of unfair discrimination at different
points on regression lines.*

ployees and adopts a cutoff score at point A on the figure, black subgroup members will be underpredicted. But, if a substantially lower cutoff score is used, e.g., point B, the situation will be reversed—the white subgroup members will be underpredicted. A study by Gael, Grant, and Richie (1975a) gives an example of the effect of adopting different cutoffs on over- and underpredictions.

According to Cleary (1968) fairness may be achieved in two ways:

1. By using a test in which the regression lines do not differ. Figure 5.6 illustrates this situation. The same predicted score is made regardless of which subgroup an individual may be a member.

2. When regression equations differ by subgroup, fairness is achieved by making predictions based on the different regression equations. "Thus, if the regression lines for blacks and whites are not equal, then each person will receive a statistically valid predicted criterion score only if separate regression equations are used for the two races" (Hunter and Schmidt, 1976, p. 1055).

For both alternatives, the selection strategy would be to hire those individuals with the *highest* predicted criterion scores regardless of which equation was used in making the predictions.

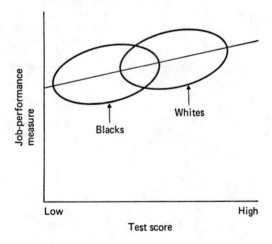

Figure 5.6 *A "fair" test using the Cleary definition.*

Hunter, Schmidt, and Rauschenberger (1977) argue that this model of test bias is the model adopted by the EEOC 1970 guidelines (despite the emphasis on differential validity noted earlier). Moreover, the *Standards for Educational and Psychological Testing* (1985) specifically endorses the Cleary model. More recent court decisions have accepted the Cleary model and rejected the differential validity model (e.g., *Cormier v. PPG Industries, Inc.* [1981]).

It should be pointed out that testing for differential regression lines may be a somewhat tricky endeavor. Although the main thrust is to determine if the slopes and intercept values for the minority and nonminority groups are different, there are different statistical procedures that might be used. One could use analysis of covariance procedures, hierarchical regression procedures, or basic regression techniques. The reader is referred to Schmidt and Hunter (1982), Norberg (1984), and Kleinbaum and Kupper (1978) for more specific commentary on the statistical testing procedures.

Research results: regression-line differences.   What evidence exists that regression lines for minority and nonminority groups differ? One of the earliest tests of regression-line differences between black and white subjects was reported by Gordon (1953). She concluded that the same minimum qualifying scores could be used for blacks and whites in assigning individuals to Air Force technical-training schools.

In 1972, Ruch reported the results of a review of 20 studies in which tests of significance between black and white regression slopes and intercepts were performed. His analyses revealed that across the 20 studies, no evidence was found for differences in regression slopes, but there existed some evidence that the intercept values differed for the various black and white groups. In the 20 studies reviewed, 9 instances were observed where the intercept values were significantly *lower* for blacks than for whites. However, this difference indicates that a common regression line would *overpredict* the expected job performance of the black group members! This is exactly opposite to the thinking of many individuals who believe that tests operate against minorities. Figure 5.7 illustrates a situation in which a black group is overpredicted. The black group demonstrates lower test scores, criterion ratings, and intercept values. If a test score at point A is used for selection and a *common* regression line is used, the black group will be overpredicted, while the white group will

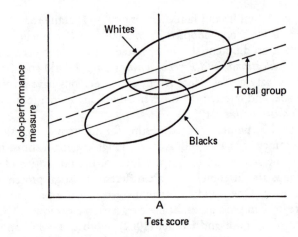

Figure 5.7 *A situation in which a black group is overpredicted when a regression line based on the total sample is used.*

be underpredicted. The use of a common regression line will lead to relatively more black applicants being hired due to their overpredicted criterion scores, compared to a situation in which separate regression lines might be used.

Feild, Bayley, and Bayley (1977) investigated the issue of whether minority-group members (blacks and Mexican-Americans) and majority-group employees would exhibit regression-line differences. Using a criterion measure based on productivity records, no differences were observed. When more subjective ratings were used, a significant difference between the groups on the regression-line intercept values was observed. The minority group had the lower intercept value.

A six-year study was conducted jointly by the Educational Testing Service and the U.S. Civil Service Foundation in order to investigate possible bias in the prediction of job performance and the major findings reported at an Invitational Conference (Campbell *et al.* 1973). The study involved three different job operations (medical technicians, cartographic technicians, and inventory-measurement specialists), three different job-performance measures (ratings, a job-knowledge test, and a work sample), and a number of predictor tests. The evidence indicated relatively few occasions where regression-line differences were found between black and white employee subgroups. Differences, when found, usually indicated that the regression line for whites was above that for the blacks (again signifying lower intercept values for the black group).

Cleary *et al.* (1975) noted several additional instances where tests used to predict academic achievement resulted in relative overprediction for black students. A series of studies conducted at AT&T shed additional information on this issue. Gael and Grant (1972) reported the results of a validation study evaluating the validity of several employment tests in predicting the job performance of minority and nonminority service representatives. Unlike some previous studies, the regression-line slopes and intercepts for the nonminority and minority samples were not significantly different.

Two other studies showed somewhat different results. The first study (Gael, Grant, and Richie, 1975a) covered three telephone-operator jobs that were sufficiently similar to "collapse" across the positions so the sample could be treated as essentially one job. Over 500 black operators and 400 white operators were used, in addition to over 100 Spanish-surnamed individuals. Ten employment tests were administered to these operators prior to their employment and were later correlated with a criterion measure (a composite score based on supervisors' ratings of job proficiency during a standardized one-hour job simulation after the completion of training). A composite test was developed by combining the four best or more predictive tests; subsequently, the regression lines were computed and compared across the various groups. Their analyses indicated that the slopes and intercepts of the two regression lines were significantly *different*. They state: "The common regression equation, it appears, overpredicts black-operator proficiency and underpredicts white- and Spanish-surnamed-operator proficiency at scores below the total sample composite prediction mean" (p. 416). Even though the regression lines differed, the investigators chose a cutoff score on the prediction composite which essentially eliminated any difference in over- or underprediction (i.e., they chose a cutoff score near the point where the regression lines crossed).

A second study reported by Gael, Grant, and Richie (1975b) was based on AT&T clerical jobs. Using a similar test battery and a number of proficiency measures based on work samples, the researchers found evidence that the regression lines for black and white samples differed.

In this case, however, the intercepts were significantly different but the regression slopes were equal. A study by Webster et al. (1978) demonstrated that a common regression line for males and females could not be used for predicting what groups would complete training in hospital corps school. Use of combined equations consistently underpredicted the males (and overpredicted the criterion for the females).

The evidence seems to indicate several findings with respect to possible differences in regression lines for minority and nonminority employee groups:

1. The regression lines generally do *not differ with regard to their slopes.* This confirms several previous reviews concerning the evidence against "differential validity." Employment tests appear to have similar relationships to job performance for both groups.

2. Regression-line *difference in intercept values appears to be a relatively common phenomenon.** However, when observed, the data clearly indicate that minority-group members are usually *overpredicted* rather than underpredicted; that is, the tests tend to predict higher job performance for these members than the job performance that is (or would be) actually observed. Thus, any test bias that operates under this particular model of test fairness appears to be operating *against* majority *white* job candidates and *in favor* of black minority-group members.

3. Some recent evidence suggests that women may also be overpredicted and males underpredicted by a common regression line.

Model IV: Thorndike's "Quota" Model

Another model of test fairness which has received less attention was presented by Thorndike (1971). He examined a situation much like that shown in Fig. 5.8. This situation is "fair" when considered against the Cleary definition: The regression lines of the two groups are essentially the same. However, the situation also reflects a relatively common occurrence: There is, relatively speaking, a greater difference between the two groups on the test than is exhibited on the criterion measure. To

---

* Jensen (1980) suggests that part of this observed intercept differential could be due to less than perfect reliability in the predictors.

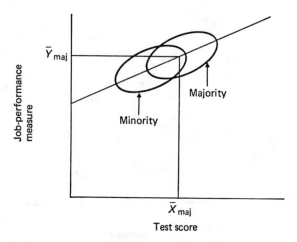

Figure 5.8 *A situation that is "fair" if the Cleary model is used but "unfair" if the Thorndike model is used.*

illustrate, using the example in Fig. 5.8, if the majority test mean were used as a "cutoff," only a small proportion of minority-group members would have been hired (say 10 percent) compared to the majority group (50 percent). However, comparatively more of these minority-group members than would have been hired can actually perform the job adequately. Using the majority mean on the job-performance measure to serve as a standard of adequate job performance, about 25 percent of the blacks can perform (or could perform) the job. The majority group again shows a 50-percent rate. According to this illustration, using the majority mean as a standard, 50 percent of the majority group would have been hired, and 50 percent of the majority-group members could have performed the job adequately. However, while 25 percent of the minority-group members could have done the job, only 10 percent would have been hired. Thorndike argued that this is unfair to the minority-group members. He contended that this situation would have been fair only if 25 percent of the minority-group applicants were hired, since 25 percent could have been successful. To achieve "fairness," *two* cutoff scores would be necessary in order to achieve the desired percentage.

More specifically, Thorndike (1971) proposed that in a fair selection

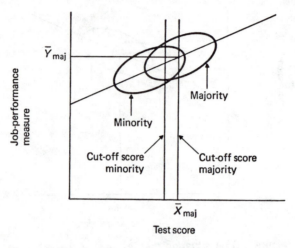

Figure 5.9. *Cutoff points needed to achieve fairness under the Thorndike model.*

procedure, "the qualifying scores on a test should be set at levels that will qualify applicants in the two groups in proportion to the fraction of the two groups reaching a specified level of performance" (p. 63). Figure 5.9 illustrates the cutoff points that would be fair under the Thorndike model using the situation portrayed in Fig. 5.8. In this situation, 50 percent of the majority group exceed a specified criterion level (again using the majority mean as the standard) and 50 percent of the majority group would be selected on the cutoff score for this group (which again would be located at the majority mean on the test). Similarly, 25 percent of the minority group would exceed the specified criterion level, and 25 percent would be selected using a separately developed cutoff score for the minority group located below the majority cutoff.

The Thorndike model involves selecting a certain percentage of minority-group members in order to achieve fairness. The use of a test in this fashion will usually result in a greater number of minorities being selected than when the Cleary model is used. In this illustration, the Cleary model results in 10 percent minorities selected; the Thorndike model results in 25 percent minorities selected.

The implications of this version of test fairness are essentially two-fold:

1. It is sometimes in direct conflict with the Cleary model of fairness. That is, a test that satisfies standards of fairness under the Cleary model may be "unfair" according to the Thorndike model. Only under special circumstances will the models conflict (i.e., the mean difference between the two groups must be the same on *both* the predictor *and* criterion).

2. The Thorndike model is relatively more "liberal" than the Cleary model in that its use would lead to the selection of greater numbers of minority-group members. Because an organization using the Cleary model would be obligated to hire only those individuals with the highest predicted criterion scores, a comparatively small number of minorities would be hired than if the hiring strategy were based on the Thorndike model.

More Complex Models

Even though the preceding models may seem to deal sufficiently with most conceptualizations of unfair test discrimination or bias, several additional models have been advanced. Darlington (1971) and Cole (1973) have presented various models. Petersen and Novick (1976) surveyed earlier models and also introduced several versions of their own. The nine models they surveyed and evaluated were: (1) the regression model (associated with Cleary [1968]); (2) the constant-ratio model (associated with Thorndike [1971]); (3) the conditional-probability model (associated with Cole [1973], and Darlington's [1971] third definition); (4) the equal-probability model (associated with Linn [1973]); (5) the converse constant-ratio model; (6) the converse conditional-probability model; (7) the constant equal-probability model; (8) the equal-risk model (associated with Einhorn and Bass [1971]); and (9) the culture-modified criterion model (associated with Darlington [1971]).

While it is beyond the scope of this text to provide comprehensive expositions and evaluations of these various models (readers are referred to Petersen and Novick [1976], Hunter and Schmidt [1976], and Berk [1982]), several statements may be made regarding them. First, many of the models *are* viable alternatives to the test-bias controversy; as yet, there is no agreement concerning which model is "the correct" model. Instead, the definition of bias depends on the particular researcher or practitioner and his or her choice of the various alternatives. *Principles for the Validation and Use of Personnel Selection Procedures* (1975), published by the APA Division of Industrial-Organizational Psychology, underscored this point by indicating that "the choice of a statistical definition (of test bias) depends on the psychologist's objectives" (p. 2). The choice of a particular definition may also rest with the particular ethical position chosen. Hunter and Schmidt (1976) have spelled out three possible ethical positions that are sometimes taken when making these choices. (These positions will be discussed in a later chapter.)

Second, the various models sometimes conflict in that a test that meets the criteria for being "fair" under one model may very well not be "fair" using the criteria based on a different model of test bias. Only under rare circumstances will a test be fair under two or more models of test bias.

A third point is that the various models may generally be rank ordered with regard to how many minority applicants would be accepted. That is, cutoff scores for minority-group applicants under certain models may be lower than the cutoff scores specified by other models given similar conditions. Thus, more minority applicants may be accepted under one model of test fairness than under other models.

In recent efforts to evaluate the various models, researchers have begun to rely on *utility* analyses. Essentially, the researcher or organization must make *explicit* the perceived *utility* or values associated with different outcomes of selection (e.g., the "cost" of hiring individuals who subsequently fail) for minority and majority applicant populations.

Gross and Su (1975), Petersen and Novick (1976), Hunter, Schmidt, and Rauschenberger (1977), and Cronbach, Yalow, and Schaeffer (1980) provide examples of evaluating various test-bias models by applying utility concepts. Since individuals and institutions may differ in their perceived utilities, it may never be possible to arrive at a test that is "unbiased" for every individual or organization concerned.

In one study, Hunter, Schmidt, and Rauschenberger (1977) showed that selection strategies that generally result in relatively greater minority selection (e.g., the Thorndike model) are not vastly different from the Cleary model in terms of expected productivity for those individuals selected from the applicant pool. The implication of this study is that an organization will suffer relatively little in terms of productivity loss if minority and majority candidates are chosen using a test that is "fair" under models that allow lower cutoff scores for minority candidates, as is the case with the Thorndike model (1971).

Ledvinka, Markos, and Ladd (1982) used a stochastic human resource model to simulate the long-range impact of various models of fairness (e.g., the Cleary model, the Thorndike model) on minority employment. Under varied conditions of validity and selection ratio, these researchers calculated the short- and long-term impact on black representation in the labor force. Their findings revealed that if the test fairness standard implied in the Uniform Guidelines (the Cleary model) were used, it would have a worse impact on blacks in terms of their proportional representation in the labor force than if other models (e.g., the Thorndike model) were used. This is not divergent from what we noted earlier. However, their long-term forecasts indicate a cumulative effect: black representation decreases in a dramatic fashion. One of their conclusions is that "the definition of 'fairness' that seems to be implicit in the federal selection guidelines would, if followed, result in a severe erosion of minority employment. Left to their own devices, employers implicitly choose a definition that is better for minority employment" (p. 30).

This study also points out that different outcomes must be examined in reviewing fairness: the outcomes to the organization in terms of employment of minority members versus the outcomes in terms of expected productivity. In addition, the study illustrates nicely some of our earlier discussion concerning the recent emphasis on the outcomes or utility of selection decisions (see Chapter 2).

INTERNAL MEASURES OF BIAS

It should also be noted that Jensen (1980) has specified a number of test-bias criteria by using the "internal" properties of a test as indicators. That is, in addition to examining the fairness of a test by reviewing its correlational properties with an external criterion (e.g., job performance), one may also review the internal psychometric properties of a test for bias. For example, a test may be examined for such evidence as the following.

1. *Differential reliability*—A test may show greater reliability for one group than for another.

2. *Test-item by race interaction*—If the hypothesis is that a test is biased, one would expect some pattern of differential achievement across the items. That is, on some items, blacks would perform better than whites and on other items the achievement level would be reversed.

3. *Differential factor structures*—If a test is measuring different factors for racial subgroups, one might expect the factor structures to differ if factor-analytic methods are used to probe these potential differences.

4. *Differential item difficulties*—A test may show different levels of item difficulty across the items for blacks and whites.

Jensen (1980) also reviews the evidence for internal test bias and suggests that there is very weak evidence that tests are biased against minorities when these kinds of standards are used. However, his review was based predominantly on non-employment situations, samples, and tests. Nonetheless, the use of internal criteria (or models) of test bias may increase. For example, these kinds of bias standards were used by Madigan (1985) to review job evaluation instruments (a type of measuring device for jobs) for sex bias.

EXAMINATION OF ITEM CONTENT FOR SEX BIAS

A fairly common theme that one encounters is that tests may be biased against females because the item content portrays females in traditionally stereotypic roles and behaviors. An excellent review of the literature in this area is given by Selkow (1984). She reports the results of a study where experts rated the degree of "sexism" for each of 74 psychological and educational instruments. The rating scales that were used (the "Sexism Rating Scale") consisted of 18 different test features (e.g., illustrations, verbal content, instructions). Each feature was examined in terms of the number of males and females included and in which kinds of roles. Moreover, the scales were designed to assess whether the content of the questions or items expressed any stereotypic or demeaning roles or behaviors for females (and males). The results show a wide range of differences among tests in terms of their portrayal of females.

However, whether item content of this nature has any impact on resulting test performance remains a major question. Selkow (1984) reported that there is "remarkably little attention given by publishers and researchers" (p. 25) regarding this issue.

SUMMARY

Where does the preceding leave us with regard to unfair test discrimination or bias? Unfortunately, the answer must be . . . somewhat bewildered. Even among psychometricians and test experts, there is no agreement concerning what constitutes a biased test. Research is currently being conducted that will clarify the situation.

Given this particularly confusing situation, it is *not* clear what to advise practitioners with regard to the model they should adopt as a "standard" to evaluate their tests. Given the present legal climate and state of the art as viewed by the court systems, we recommend adopting the implied EEOC model—the Cleary model. However, it should be noted that this model is clearly one in which relatively fewer minority applicants are selected compared to other models. If an organization wishes to avoid "triggering" the shift in the burden of persuasion, it may desire a selection procedure (e.g., the Thorndike model) that allows the selection of a relatively greater number of minority applicants.

REFERENCES

American Psychological Association (1985). *Standards for Educational and Psychological Testing*. Washington, D.C.: APA.

Anastasi, A. (1965). *Differential Psychology*. New York: MacMillan.

Berk, R. A. ed. (1982). *Handbook of Methods for Detecting Test Bias*. Baltimore, MD.: Johns Hopkins Press.

Block, N. J., and G. Dworkin (eds.) (1976). *The I.Q. Controversy: Critical Readings*. New York: Pantheon Books.

Boehm, V. E. (1972). Negro-white differences in validity of employment and training selection procedures: Summary of research evidence. *Journal of Applied Psychology* 56: 33–39.

—— (1977). Differential prediction: A methodological artifact? *Journal of Applied Psychology* 62: 146–154.

Campbell, J. T.; L. A. Crooks; M. H. Mahoney; and D. A. Rock (1973). *An Investigation of Sources of Bias in the Prediction of Job Performance—A Six Year Study.* (Tech. Rep. PF73-37). Princeton, N.J.: Educational Testing Service.

Cleary, T. A. (1968). Test bias: Prediction of grades of Negro and white students in integrated colleges. *Journal of Educational Measurement* 5: 115–124.

Cleary, T. A.; L. G. Humphreys; S. A. Kendrick; and A. Wesman (1975). Educational uses of tests with disadvantaged students. *American Psychologist* 30: 15–41.

Cole, N. S. (1973). Bias in selection. *Journal of Educational Measurement* 10: 237–255.

Comier v. *PPG Industries, Inc.,* 26, *FEP* 652 (1981).

Cronbach, L. J.; E. Yalow; and G. Schaeffer (1980). A mathematical structure for analyzing fairness in selection. *Personnel Psychology* 33: 693–704.

Darlington, R. B. (1971). Another look at "culture fairness." *Journal of Educational Measurement* 8: 71–82.

Drasgow, F., and T. Kang (1984). Statistical power of differential validity and differential prediction analyses for detecting measurement nonequivalence. *Journal of Applied Psychology* 69: 498–508.

Dreger, R. M., and K. S. Miller (1960). Comparative psychological studies of Negroes and whites in the United States. *Psychological Bulletin* 57: 361–402.

—— (1968). Comparative psychological studies of Negroes and whites in the United States: 1959–1965. *Psychological Bulletin* 70: 1–58.

Einhorn, H. J., and A. R. Bass (1971). Methodological considerations relevant to discrimination in employment testing. *Psychological Bulletin* 75: 261–269.

Feild, H.; G. A. Bayley; and S. Bayley (1977). Employment test validation for minority and nonminority production workers. *Personnel Psychology* 30: 37–46.

Gael, S., and D. L. Grant (1972). Employment test validation for minority and nonminority telephone company service representatives. *Journal of Applied Psychology* 56: 135–139.

Gael, S.; D. L. Grant; and R. J. Richie (1975a). Employment test validation for minority and nonminority telephone operators. *Journal of Applied Psychology* 60: 411–420.

—— (1975b). Employment test validation for minority and nonminority clerks with work sample criteria. *Journal of Applied Psychology* 60: 420–426.

Gordon, M. A. (1953). A study in the applicability of the same minimum qualifying scores for technical schools to white males, WAF and Negro males. (Tech. Rep. 53-34). Lackland AFB, Texas: Human Resources Research Center, November.

Gross, A. L., and W. Su (1975). Defining a "fair" or "unbiased" selection model: A question of utility. *Journal of Applied Psychology* 60: 345–351.

Guion, R. M. (1966). Employment tests and discriminatory hiring. *Industrial Relations* 5: 20–30.

Gulliksen, H., and S. S. Wilks (1950). Regression tests for several samples. *Psychometritia* 15: 91–114.

Haefner, J. E. (1977). Sources of discrimination among employees: A survey investigation. *Journal of Applied Psychology* 62: 265–270.

Hayes, W. L. (1981). *Statistics for the Social Sciences.* New York: Holt, Rinehart, and Winston.

Hirsh, H. R., and M. A. McDaniel (1987). Differential validity by gender in employment settings. Paper presented at Midyear Conference of Society of Industrial/Organizational Psychology, Atlanta, Georgia.

Humphreys, L. G. (1973). Statistical definitions of test validity for minority groups. *Journal of Applied Psychology* 58: 1–4.

Hunter, J. E., and F. L. Schmidt (1976). Critical analysis of the statistical and ethical implications of various definitions of test bias. *Psychological Bulletin* 83: 1053–1071.

—— (1978). Differential and single-group validity of employment tests by race: A critical analysis of three studies. *Journal of Applied Psychology* **63**: 1–11.

Hunter, J. E.; F. L. Schmidt; and J. M. Rauschenberger (1977). Fairness of psychological tests: Implications of four definitions for selection utility and minority hiring. *Journal of Applied Psychology* **62**: 245–260.

Jensen, A. R. (1969). How much can we boost IQ and scholastic achievement? *Harvard Educational Review* **39**: 1–123.

—— (1980). *Bias in Mental Testing*. New York: Free Press.

Katzell, R. A., and F. J. Dyer (1977). Differential validity revived. *Journal of Applied Psychology* **62**: 137–145.

—— (1978). On differential validity and bias. *Journal of Applied Psychology* **68**: 19–21.

Kerlinger, F. N., and E. J. Pedhazur (1973). *Multiple regression behavioral research*. New York: Holt, Rinehart, and Winston.

Kirkpatrick, J. J.; R. B. Ewen; R. S. Barrett; and R. A. Katzell (1968). *Testing and fair employment*. New York: University Press.

Kleinbaum, D. G., and L. L. Kupper (1978). *Applied Regression Analysis and Other Multivariate Methods*. North Scituate, Mass.: Duxbury Press.

Ledvinka, J.; V. H. Markos; and R. T. Ladd (1982). Long-range impact of "fair selection" standards on minority employment. *Journal of Applied Psychology* **67**: 18–36.

Linn, R. L. (1973). Fair test use in selection. *Review of Educational Research* **43**: 139–161.

—— (1978). Single group validity, differential validity, and differential prediction. *Journal of Applied Psychology* **63**: 507–512.

Linn, R. L., and C. E. Werts (1971). Considerations for studies of test bias. *Journal of Educational Measurement* **8**: 1–4.

Madigan, R. M. (1985). Comparable worth judgments: A measurement properties analysis. *Journal of Applied Psychology* 70: 137–147.

Norberg, J. M. (1984). A warning regarding the simplified approach to the evaluation of test fairness in employee selection procedures. *Personnel Psychology* 37: 483–486.

Petersen, N. S., and M. R. Novick (1976). An evaluation of some models for culture-fair selection. *Journal of Educational Measurement* 13: 3–29.

Potthoff, R. F. (1966). *Statistical Aspects of the Problem of Biases in Psychological Tests.* (Institute of Statistics Mimeo Service, No. 479). Chapel Hill, North Carolina: The University of North Carolina.

Ruch, W. W. (1972). A re-analysis of published differential validity studies. Symposium paper presented at American Psychological Association, Honolulu, Hawaii, September.

Schmidt, F. L.; J. G. Berner; and J. E. Hunter (1973). Racial differences in validity of employment tests: Reality or illusion? *Journal of Applied Psychology* 58: 5–9.

Schmidt, F. L., and J. E. Hunter (1982). Two pitfalls in assessing fairness of selection tests using the regression model. *Personnel Psychology* 35: 601–607.

Schmitt, N.; P. M. Mellon; and C. By Lenga (1978). Sex differences in validity for academic and employment criteria, and different types of predictors. *Journal of Applied Psychology* 63: 145–150.

Selkow, P. (1984). *Assessing Sex Bias in Testing: A Review of the Issues and Evaluations of 74 Psychological and Educational Tests.* Westport, Conn.: Greenwood Press.

Shuey, A. M. (1966). *The Testing of Negro Intelligence,* 2d ed. (1966). New York: Social Science Press.

Thorndike, R. L. (1971). Concepts of culture-fairness. *Journal of Educational Measurement* 8: 63–70.

Trattner, M. H., and B. S. O'Leary (1980). Sample sizes for specified statistical power in testing for differential validity. *Journal of Applied Psychology* **65**: 127–134.

Tyler, L. G. (1965). *The Psychology of Human Differences*. New York: Appleton-Century-Crofts.

Webster, E. G.; R. F. Booth; W. K. Graham; and E. F. Alf (1978). A sex comparison of factors related to success in naval hospital corps school. *Personnel Psychology* **31**: 95–106.

Special Issues and Topics in Test Discrimination

6

No book dealing with issues of unfair test discrimination can fail to review some of the particularly thorny problems that are almost intrinsic to test-validation studies. While there are a multitude of questions concerning such issues as test bias, the EEOC guidelines, and specific research methodologies, the objective of this chapter is to review the literature and research concerning nine separate but sometimes related topic areas. The first three concern problems in validation research: (1) problems with the criteria, (2) sample-size problems, and (3) the issue of validity generalization. The next three concern recent validation strategies in selecting employees: (4) content validity, (5) work-sample tests, and (6) the assessment center. The final topics concern the following: (7) developing "culture-fair" tests as a means of achieving test fairness, (8) test bias against the older worker, and (9) test bias in interest inventories.

TOPIC AREA 1: THE CRITERIA PROBLEM

One of the most perplexing research problems is the possibility that there may be "bias" in the job-performance measure chosen as the criterion for validating tests.* For example, if supervisory ratings are used, it is

---

* There are a number of rating errors frequently encountered when using rating scales (e.g., errors of central tendency, errors of leniency). Except where noted, these kinds of

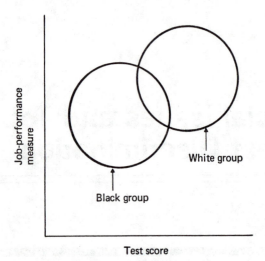

Figure 6.1 *Relationships between test
scores and job performance.*

easy to see how white supervisors may give *lower* job performance ratings
to black employees based on personal stereotypes and prejudices, instead
of basing their ratings on actual job performance.

An example of this phenomenon is shown in Fig. 6.1. Here, the
employment test is *unrelated* to job performance for either the black or
the white group, indicating that the test would not be helpful in predicting job performance *within* either of the two groups. Further, the
blacks do worse on the test and also are rated lower on the job by their
supervisors than the white employees. As some have suggested, this could
be an instance where "bias" in the test predicts "bias" in the criterion.

Giving lower ratings to minority-group members is not the only way
that supervisors display bias. They may also do the following:

1. Inflate their ratings, or "bend over backwards," to show management that there is no prejudice in their ratings.

---

errors are not necessarily associated with "bias." We therefore will not discuss these topics fully here. Further treatment of these errors may be found in the book in this series
entitled *Increasing Productivity Through Performance Appraisal* by Gary P. Latham and
Kenneth N. Wexley.

2. Not make any distinctions among the minority-group employees. That is, supervisors might rate them *all* high, low, or average on a measure of performance. This tendency would be represented by little variation among the ratings given.

3. Rate minority-group employees similarly (e.g., all high or low) on *all* various rating scales, thus creating a "halo" effect. Rater "halo" is the tendency for a rater to give all high or all low ratings to an employee based on an overall general impression. This tendency is usually represented by high intercorrelations among the various categories on the rating scale.

The investigation of possible bias in criterion ratings is important for two reasons:

1. Bias, if it exists, may be a factor which influences the results of a validation study. Remember that some previous investigations have found more evidence for differential validity when relatively poor criterion measures were used.

2. The adequacy of performance measures is also subject to court review, as discussed below.

Legal Review: Performance Measures

One problem indicated by the Supreme Court in its review of the validity study presented in *Albemarle Paper Company* v. *Moody* (1975) was that the supervisory ratings were vague and it was unclear on what basis the supervisors made their judgments. Other challenges to performance measures in the form of supervisory appraisals have been made. Perhaps the first and most-often cited case in this area is *Rowe* v. *General Motors* (1972), decided by the Fifth Circuit Court of Appeals. In this situation, foremen's subjective evaluations of hourly employees' "ability, merit, and capacity" were used in making promotion decisions. After determining that adverse impact had occurred for blacks, the court felt that the performance-appraisal system used for promotions violated Title VII in several ways: First, foremen were given no written instructions about the qualifications necessary for promotion; and second, the standards themselves were vague and subjective. In summarizing the decision, the court added the following:

*All we do today is recognize that promotion/transfer decisions
which depend almost entirely upon the subjective evaluation and
favorable recommendation of the immediate foreman are a ready
mechanism for discrimination against blacks, much of which can
be covertly concealed. . . .*

According to the *Rowe* court, evidence of an appraisal instrument's
appropriateness should include information on both the rating instrument
itself and the rating process. For example, in terms of the rating
instrument, it is important that development of the instrument be based
on a review of job information (i.e., information on the essential elements
of the job derived through job analysis). In terms of the rating
process, it is important that raters operate under specific guidelines (e.g.,
have clear written instructions on how to complete appraisals, rate the
performance of only those subordinates whose job behavior they have
had an opportunity to observe). Moreover, it is clear that a rating process
that includes "safeguards" is preferable. Safeguards include, among
other things, the use of multiple raters, including protected group members
as raters, and the existence of a formal performance appraisal review
and appeal process.

The *Rowe* decision provided the basis for deciding many similar cases.
For example, in *Brito* v. *Zia Company* (1973), a performance-evaluation
form was disallowed as a device for making layoff decisions because it
had not been demonstrated to be valid. Interestingly, the court reviewed
the appraisal form as if it were a "test" and used the EEOC (1970) testing
guidelines as standards against which to evaluate the validity of the form
(see comments in Chapter 3).

In *Wade* v. *Mississippi Cooperative Extension Service* (1974), the
subjective performance-appraisal instrument used in making the promotional
decisions was reviewed carefully by the court. It was used to
assess personal traits such as attitude, personality, temperament, and
habits. The court demanded evidence that the appraisal instrument show
a significant relationship to job performance; this evidence was not provided.
The court ruled as follows in this instance:

*Objective appraisal of performance is based upon scores received
by subordinates rated by supervisors on an evaluation instrument
according to a number of questionable factors. For example, a
substantial portion of the evaluation rating relates to such general*

characteristics as leadership, public acceptance, attitudes toward people, appearance and grooming, personal conduct, outlook on life, ethical habits, resourcefulness, capacity for growth, mental alertness and loyalty to organization. As may be readily observed, these are traits which are susceptible to partiality and to the personal taste, whim or fancy of the evaluator.

The court ruled that this performance appraisal was discriminatory, and was upheld by a court of appeals in 1976.

By now, many courts have reviewed the adequacy of the performance appraisal systems used by organizations. In a study based on many of these decisions, Field and Holley (1982) examined the performance appraisal systems in 66 employment discrimination cases to determine which characteristics seemed to be relevant in deciding the outcome of the cases. Their analysis involved correlating characteristics of the appraisal system (e.g., whether a job analysis was used, the type of appraisal used) with the outcome of the case (whether it went for or against the organization). Of the 66 cases, 46.9 percent went in favor of the defendant (the organization), whereas 53.1 percent went in favor of the plaintiff. Their results were quite revealing. The following performance appraisal variables significantly differentiated the outcomes of the 66 cases:

1. *Provision of written instructions*—Employers seem to lose when there are no specific written instructions for the completion of appraisals. "Apparently, some courts have the view that the provision of such instructions is a prerequisite (though not a guarantee) to systematic, unbiased appraisals" (Holley and Field [1982], p. 400).

2. *Trait versus behavior-oriented appraisals*—Generally, the courts have not been receptive to trait-oriented appraisals and have generally upheld the use of behavior-oriented performance evaluations. For example, such judicial opinions as the following were quoted by Holley and Field (1982):

The operation of an opinion-based appraisal system . . . provides an ideal environment for disparate treatment. Statsny v. Southern Bell Telephone and Telegraph Co. (1978)

. . . The evaluations were based on the best judgment and opinion of the evaluators, but were not based on any definite, identifiable

criteria based on quality or quantity of work or specific performance that were supported by some kind of record. EEOC v. Sandia Corp. (1980)

3. *Use of job analysis*—The data revealed that organizations that used tailor-made and specific job analysis instruments and performed a thorough analysis of the job in question tended to survive court attack.

4. *Review of appraisal results with employees*—The data showed that employers were more successful in discrimination cases when the results of the appraisals were reviewed with the employees.

These results are also consistent with the *Rowe* criteria mentioned above and reviews conducted by Kleiman and Durham (1981), Bernardin and Beatty (1984), and Cascio and Bernardin (1981). One of the themes that emerges from examination of the case law in these areas is that performance appraisal systems are evaluated generally in terms of how fairly they are applied and whether they seem open to subjective biases that can influence the ratings given. Moreover, if an organization has attempted to construct job based appraisal forms, presented training and instructions to raters, examined the rating instruments for reliability (e.g., interrater agreement) and validity (e.g., correlation with other types of evidence such as production records, other forms of ratings), the likelihood is higher that an appraisal instrument will survive court review.

Research Evidence: Bias in Performance Ratings

There are several research articles that investigate the issue of criterion "bias" against minorities. Some early studies, including DeJung and Kaplan (1962) and Cox and Krumboltz (1958), indicated that raters tend to give significantly higher ratings to those of their own race. But Schmidt and Johnson (1973), on the other hand, found no race effect when examining peer ratings of black and white employees.

Bass and Turner (1973) suggested that criterion "bias" may not be particularly strong if present at all. They investigated racial discrimination and bias in criterion measures for black and white bank tellers. Two kinds of criterion data were available—supervisory ratings and more objective measures (e.g., percentage of time worked) of performance. The results of the study indicated the following:

1. The differences between the black and white employees on the various criterion measures were generally small and the differences that were statistically significant were reduced to nonsignificance when the effects of age and tenure were removed.

2. White supervisors based their evaluations of black subordinates on more objective job data, whereas they evaluated white employees more on the basis of subjective job data. If anything, the white supervisors seemed to be leaning over backwards to be objective in rating black subordinates.

A study by Hamner et al. (1974) was quite systematic in its experimental approach to the investigation of criterion bias. They studied rating bias as a function of both sex and race. A total of 36 black and white business students volunteered to be "raters" in this laboratory experiment. They were asked to view films depicting stock workers in a grocery store. Each film showed an individual working at either a high or a low level of performance. The actual levels of performance for "high" performance were identical (48 food cans stocked), as were the performance levels of the "low" performers (24 cans stacked). Thus, "true" levels of performance were established. In addition, the stock workers presented in the films represented black and white groups, as well as male and female workers.

The raters were asked to evaluate the performance of each worker in the films* on their "overall task performance," using a scale which ranged from 1 (weak in overall performance) to 15 (an exceptionally good worker). The data indicated several findings:

1. Not surprisingly, the "high" performers were rated significantly higher than the "low" performers. In other words, actual performance was a major factor in the ratings given.

2. Females were rated significantly *higher* than males. In particular, high-performance females received significantly higher ratings than high-performance males.

3. Black raters tended to rate blacks higher than whites (8.50 versus 7.77). White raters tended to rate blacks lower than whites (7.80

---

* One of the problems with this study is that the stimulus films were not randomly presented to the raters, making the results somewhat clouded by "order" effects.

versus 8.27). While this constituted a significant effect, it was not particularly strong.

4. An additional finding was that high-performing blacks were rated only slightly higher than low-performing blacks. However, high-performing whites were clearly rated higher than low-performing whites.

These findings suggest that criterion bias does appear to operate against blacks. The authors noted that "the fact that blacks received significantly lower ratings than whites from white raters when performance levels were identical indicates a potentially serious problem of racial bias" (p. 709).

A replication of this study was conducted by Bigoness (1976) using 60 male, white undergraduates as raters. Using the same films and experimental methodology in conducting the study, his results indicated that the race of the performer was *not* a significant factor in the ratings given. In fact, there was some evidence that low-performing blacks were rated higher than low-performing whites. As in the first study, females tended to be evaluated more highly than males, even though they performed identically.

Three aspects of these two studies need to be pointed out. (1) The "raters" were undergraduate students, who may differ substantially from their real-world counterparts. (2) The "job" depicted was rather simplistic and straightforward. Perhaps even greater "bias" might occur if the jobs were more complex. (3) The magnitudes of the differences, even though statistically significant, were *not* particularly strong. Actual performance remained the dominant force influencing the ratings. By comparison, the effects due to race and sex were not particularly powerful.

Another study investigating this issue was conducted by Hall and Hall (1976). College students were asked to evaluate a case study concerning how a personnel manager handled a job-vacancy problem. The manager was depicted as either black or white and either male or female. No differences between the evaluations were observed for either the white versus the black managers or the male versus the female managers. However, the *race* of the *rater* proved to be significant when evaluating the white manager. White raters gave significantly higher ratings to the white managers than black raters did.

An interesting study was conducted by Brugnoli, Campion, and Basen (1979). Fifty-six maintenance mechanics evaluated a videotape of a black job applicant and a white job applicant performing a "relevant task" (e.g., laying out, drilling, and tapping) and an "irrelevant task" (e.g., indexing drill bits). Applicants were evaluated by the mechanics, who used either a highly specific behavioral recording form or a global rating form. Race-linked bias was found only when subjects were asked to make global evaluations after observing an applicant's performance on a task representing irrelevant job behavior.

In an effort to "tease" apart the differences between black and white ratees based on *both* objective performance criteria and subjective performance ratings, Ford, Kraiger, and Schechtman (1986) located 53 black-white samples across a wide range of occupations; each sample included at least one objective and one subjective measure of performance for the same group of black and white employees*. The total sample size across the 53 samples was 7405 for whites and 2817 for blacks. Statistical procedures that permitted the aggregation of these data ("meta-analysis procedures") were used. The results showed that there were consistent but small differences between black and white samples on both the subjective and objective performance measures, with whites demonstrating higher performance levels. Moreover, there were slightly greater differences found on the objective measures in contrast to the subjective measures, a finding contrary to what many people believe. If we are to believe that the relatively objective measures used in these 53 samples are uncontaminated by any bias, then these data suggest a slight but consistent performance difference between black and white employees. Ford *et al.* (1986) suggest, however, a number of limiting features of the study, including possible bias in the selection of the samples and possible selection policies on the part of the organizations.

A number of studies have also examined performance appraisal data from the standpoint of gender bias. For example, Norton, Gustafson, and Foster (1977) found evidence that with identical performance levels on several performance-rating scales, females were rated significantly *higher* than males both before and after the raters had been trained in using the rating scales.

In another study, Hagen and Kahn (1975) conducted a laboratory experiment in which it was found that, under conditions of cooperation

---

* The correlation between the subjective and objective measures across the 53 samples was .43.

or observation, raters evaluated a competent woman's performance positively. Yet when competent women were in direct competition with males, the women were evaluated negatively. Thus, conditions of cooperation and competition appear to influence rater evaluation of females.

What might be occurring in some of these studies is that male raters may not have particularly high expectations concerning the performance of women. Thus, when women do perform well, their performance may be overevaluated (Weiner, 1972). A second factor is that males tend to attribute the success of women to luck, or factors outside their control, as opposed to ability and effort (Terborg and Ilgen, 1975).

Nieva and Gutek (1980) provide a good summary of the research concerning sex effects in evaluation. They reported that although most of the studies they reviewed showed a pro-male evaluation bias, contradictory evidence was also found. It was revealed that greater bias occurs when the rater or evaluator is required to make greater leaps of inference (e.g., evaluating reasons for good and poor performance) than when focusing on past performance. Their conclusion: "Without specific and concrete information about the merits of an individual relevant to the demands of particular situations, judges tend to resort to inferences based on what is generally known about the group to which the person belongs" (p. 271). They also reported that a pro-male bias occurs under high sex-role congruency conditions—that is, where females are being evaluated in positions or roles considered typically or stereotypically male. This is a finding we shall discuss later in our chapter on the employment interview.

It is also worth noting a more recent study conducted by Peters *et al.* (1984), who analyzed the performance ratings given to 324 male and 310 female store managers by their supervisors. Females were rated significantly higher by both male and female supervisors, suggesting to these authors that a pro-male bias did not exist, at least for this sample.

A number of studies have also examined performance appraisal and criterion data for bias as a function of age. In a study reported by Schwab and Heneman (1978), 32 personnel specialists evaluated written performance descriptions of four secretaries. The age and job experience of one of the secretaries was manipulated. The results of the study were somewhat mixed. Although there was no significant main effect due to the age of the employee evaluated, a significant interaction revealed that younger raters gave higher evaluations to the older (64-year-old) rather than the younger (24-year-old) target employee. Relatively older raters gave lower evaluations to this same target. In contrast, older raters gave lower evaluations to the 61-year-old target employee. However, this study suffers somewhat because of the use of "pencil-and-paper" stimulus target employees, which means that raters evaluate hypothetical employees without ever seeing an individual or their actual job performance.

Cleveland and Landy (1981) examined the performance ratings of 513 exempt managers from a large manufacturing organization. These data showed significant but small differences on two specific performance measures: self-development and interpersonal skills. Older workers received lower ratings than younger workers on both of these dimensions.

In a later study, Cleveland and Landy (1983) examined the hypothesis that the age stereotype of an occupation interacts with the age-related characteristics of the incumbent to influence rater judgments. In one experiment they conducted to test this hypothesis, 18 employees of a large manufacturing organization reviewed and evaluated information on six target employees who varied in terms of their age (60 or 61, 40 or 41, and 27 or 28), the type of job held (an "older" job represented by the job title of plant manager; an age-neutral job represented by the job title of production planner, and a stereotypically younger job represented by the job title of intermediate programmer). An additional factor—the performance pattern of the target employee—was manipulated: A relatively young or old performance pattern was created by depicting the target employee as having negative evaluation data on several behavioral dimensions believed to reflect an "older" employee performance profile (e.g., lower scores on attention to detail, problem solving, self-development skills) and a "younger" employee performance pattern developed by having relatively higher evaluation data on these same dimensions. The data did not confirm a job by age interaction and only a minor but significant age by performance pattern interaction. Thus, the results of this experiment did not confirm in any major way that older employees receive lower evaluations than younger employees, even in relatively "old" or "young" jobs.

In another study, Ferris et al. (1985) investigated the performance ratings given to 81 registered nurses by supervisors evaluating their performance for a particular day. Their data revealed that supervisors rate relatively older subordinates lower than younger subordinates doing the same job.

There have, in addition, been several reviews that have attempted to summarize the numerous studies exploring the relationship between age and job performance. Rhodes (1983), for example, reported that there are approximately equal numbers of studies reporting that job performance increases with age, decreases with age, or remains the same. She suggested that the relationship between age and performance is a function of other kinds of variables, including the demands of the job, the type of performance measure being used, and sample characteristics.

A recent review of 40 samples using meta-analysis procedures was reported by Waldman and Avolio (1986). Their analysis indicated a pattern of productivity increases at higher ages when using more "objective" job-performance measures, such as number of units produced, patents, publications, etc. On the other hand, when supervisory ratings were used as the measure of performance, the results showed a slight tendency for the ratings to be lower for older employees. Moreover, additional analyses showed that there were differences between professional and nonprofessional employees with regard to the supervisory ratings; older employees were *not* rated more poorly than younger employees for the professional group.

It is apparent that there has been a good deal of research investigating performance appraisal and criterion differences as a function of race, gender, and age. Studies have been conducted in the laboratory, where efforts have been made to "match" minority and nonminority employees to determine if differential ratings occur for these target employees at identical performance levels. Studies have also been conducted in field settings, where differences between relatively objective and subjective job performance measures have been examined. In these studies, a determination of bias has been much less tenable, because the target individuals being rated may have differed on such factors as experience or tenure, which could account for some of the differences observed. In any case, we may identify some trends based on the research evidence:

1. There is some evidence that blacks are given lower ratings than their white counterparts. These data are consistent in both laboratory and field studies. Moreover, studies show that these rating differences occur when either objective or subjective performance measures are used. Some limited research shows that performance differences be-

tween black and white employees diminish when more behaviorally oriented rating procedures are used.

2. There is some evidence that females receive relatively higher ratings than males given identical performance levels. Other studies, however, reveal a "pro-male bias."

3. There is some evidence that older employees receive lower evaluations than relatively younger employees. However, some evidence suggests that these differences are diminished for professional employee subgroups.

4. Actual performance level appears to be the major contributing factor to the ratings individuals receive. Any bias observed is not a particularly powerful effect.

Overall, it appears that bias effects that occur in performance appraisal ratings are likely moderated by a number of other variables.

The criterion problem goes beyond psychometric issues, however. It is generally understood that job performance is a function of other things besides personal effort. Factors such as geographical location, economic fluctuations, and cooperation of coworkers may be major determinants of performance.

If fellow employees reject an individual because of sex, race, or age prejudices, and if their cooperative efforts are necessary to do or to learn a job properly, a lower performance rating might be an accurate reflection of work performance. However, the performance level may have been heavily influenced through these other factors. While it may seem rather old-fashioned to suggest that coworkers express overt animosity toward minority-group workers, underlying negative attitudes do still exist. Haefner (1977) conducted a telephone survey of almost 500 state employees asking with whom they preferred to work. While none of the results indicated that they were unwilling to work with certain minorities, significant differences emerged. Employees prefer working with whites rather than blacks, with males rather than females, with younger rather than older individuals, and with highly competent rather than barely competent individuals. Also, Haefner's results indicated that competent males are significantly preferred to competent females.

Thus, criterion ratings may be influenced by supervisory bias and stereotypes, but in addition, minorities may not be able to reach full potential, due to uncontrollable factors that depress job performance.

Implications

Given that an organization is under suit and adverse impact has been demonstrated, case law strongly implies that any validation study should contain evidence that the criterion measures were investigated for both reliability and possible bias. Again, the 1987 APA Society for Industrial-Organization Psychology's *Principles for the Validation and Use of Personnel Selection Procedures* provides several guidelines. To survive court challenges of criterion measures, organizations must make every effort to do the following: develop criterion measures through carefully developed job analyses; check the reliabilities of these measures; perform statistical tests to detect differences between ratings of minority and majority groups; provide training to raters; and apply any performance-appraisal system uniformly and consistently across all employees.

TOPIC AREA 2: SAMPLE-SIZE PROBLEMS

A particularly vexing problem is that the number of minority-group members who perform a particular job is frequently very much smaller than the number of majority-group members. This problem is compounded in those situations in which the sample size of the majority group is small also.

Organizations are frequently admonished against performing test-validation studies on sample sizes that are too small. In fact, the 1976 Federal Executive Guidelines on selection procedures indicate that test users are not required to perform a validation study if the available sample is less than 30.

There are three basic (but interrelated) problems inherent in the use of small samples:

1. A correlation based on a small sample must be of a *higher* magnitude to reach significance than the magnitude required with a relatively larger sample size. As we saw in Chapter 2, it takes a higher correlation to be significant when based on a small sample.

2. A computed correlation based on a small sample is relatively less *reliable* than a value computed for a larger sample. That is, if one were able to pick independent samples (of the same size) repeatedly and to compute the correlation for each sample, one would find relatively more variation in the correlations computed between two

variables when the samples were small compared to the variation found when the samples were relatively larger.* Thus, when a correlation is computed on a small sample, the true value of the correlation may be considerably different than the value computed.

3. The probability of finding that a test is significantly valid when the test *is actually valid* is considerably lower with small sample sizes. That is, the *power* (see Chapter 2) to detect truly valid tests is considerably less in studies using small samples than in studies using relatively large samples. Schmidt, Hunter, and Urry (1976) called attention to the fact that it may require considerably larger sample sizes than originally thought to detect true validity. For example, they suggest that a sample size of almost 100 is required to find significance (at the .05 level) when the true validity of a test is .35, the selection ratio is near .50, and the reliability of a criterion is .60.

With small samples, there is a higher probability of not finding significance than there is of detecting significance, *even when a test is truly valid.* The article by Schmidt, Hunter, and Urry (1976) is especially noteworthy because it suggests that sample sizes greater than the 30 to 50 usually recommended may be necessary to detect validity, and that samples as small as 30 to 50 may render a validation study "technically unfeasible." A related problem is that given the "usual" sample sizes of minority and majority applicants, there is a relatively low probability of finding a significant difference in validities between the groups (or differential validity).

What should someone investigating the validity of a test do with regard to sample size? Obviously, one should first make every effort to obtain large sample sizes. A strategy which has proven helpful in increasing sample sizes in validation studies is to combine samples from two or more jobs that are substantially similar. These jobs might be "clustered" into relatively "homogeneous" job groupings and a validation study performed as if the various jobs were really just one job. For example, it is commonplace in organizations for clerical and secretarial jobs to share substantially the same job duties and tasks, but they may have different job titles (e.g., clerk typist I, clerk typist II, etc.).

---

* Technically, the standard error of the correlation coefficient is relatively larger given smaller sample sizes.

These jobs might be grouped into one general clerical "job" and treated as one for validation purposes. Mobley and Ramsay (1973) suggested a very useful method of determining job groupings by employing a statistical technique called "cluster analysis."

Another possibility in dealing with small sample sizes is to use a validation strategy known as "synthetic validity." (For a more detailed presentation and review, see Mossholder and Arvey [1984].) This approach involves conducting careful job analyses to isolate dimensions of behavior that are common to several jobs and using the samples in these jobs to validate tests for those behavioral dimensions. For example, suppose an organization wished to validate its tests for employees who were working in five different jobs. Suppose further that careful job analyses revealed that some of these jobs involved identical job requirements and tasks, but the five were sufficiently different to preclude collapsing all five jobs into one. Here, a solution might be to build a matrix to identify the jobs that shared similar behavior requirements. Figure 6.2 shows such a matrix. The job analysis revealed that the behavioral dimensions involved in the various jobs were as follows: direct sales, customer relations, handling details, clerical duties, and supervision. The crosses (X) indicate which dimensions are involved in each job. Given the particular "pattern" displayed, criterion measures might be developed to reflect the various dimensions, and employees from jobs A, C, and E combined

	Direct sales	Customer relations	Handling details	Clerical duties	Supervision
Job A	X	X		X	X
Job B		X		X	
Job C	X		X		
Job D		X			X
Job E	X		X	X	

Figure 6.2 *Example of a synthetic validity matrix.*

(combined sample size = 90) to validate a test, or series of tests, for the criterion reflecting "direct sales," samples from jobs A, B, and D combined to be used to validate tests for the "customer relations" dimension, and so forth. Thus, sufficient sample sizes may be "built up" by breaking jobs into component parts and validating tests against criterion measures reflecting these components—instead of whole jobs. This synthetic-validity approach in an organization is illustrated by Guion (1965). The interested reader is referred to this article for further study.

At this time, the sample-size problem remains essentially unsolved. Technical and statistical methods must be developed in the future allowing organizations to validate tests based on relatively small samples. Until that time, organizations must do what they can, given sample-size contraints. This problem with sample sizes has contributed to the growing shift from criterion-related to content-validation strategies.

Finally, it should be noted that there is nothing statistically impermissible about going ahead and calculating validity coefficients based on small samples. A correlation that reaches significance even though based on a small N is interpreted in *exactly* the same manner as when significance is achieved using a larger sample. Thus, significant correlations obtained using a sample of 15 are, indeed, significant. This fact is sometimes overlooked.

The implications for the researcher using small samples are simply this: It is permissible to calculate validity coefficients, but because of the small samples involved, there is a relatively high probability of *not* finding significant correlations. If significant relationships are found, these correlations are indeed significant and may be interpreted in the same fashion as those obtained using larger samples.

TOPIC AREA 3: VALIDITY GENERALIZATION

Perhaps one of the most important issues in selection research today is the issue of validity generalization. When may a test that has demonstrated adequate validity in one situation and job be used in another situation for a similar, if not identical job, without the necessity of carrying out a full-scale validation study? Industrial psychologists have long believed that validity is situation specific; that is, a test that is valid for a job in one situation may not be valid for the same job in another situation. This belief is based on the fact that different validities appear from study to study, even when the jobs and tests appear to be similar or even essentially identical (Ghiselli, 1966). The usual explanation for this phenomenon is that the nature of the jobs is really different, but the human job analyst just could not detect these subtle but important differences.

Psychologists have had problems resolving technical questions involved in validity generalization. To quote from the 1975 Division of Industrial/Organizational Psychology's *Principles for the Validation and Use of Personnel Selection Procedures*:

> *A pressing problem in employment psychology is that of determining how to generalize validities. Psychologists are strongly urged to engage in cooperative research ventures. . . . Until such time as such cooperative research results in an understanding of the limits of generalization, there will be few principles to observe in this area. (p. 13)*

Several important developments have occurred over the past ten years regarding the major unresolved technical issues related to validity generalization:

1. In a seminal article, Schmidt and Hunter (1977) showed that the patchwork of validity results found across situations was due to the failure to obtain adequate sample sizes, and due, in part, to other statistical artifacts. These researchers present a method of generalizing validity coefficients to new situations without carrying out a validity study of any kind. However, this approach involves compiling the results of all available validation studies pertaining to the particular job, correcting the validity coefficients for statistical artifacts, and reviewing these "corrected" values. If the corrected values prove reasonably high (reflected in the mean of the validity coefficients), Schmidt and Hunter argue that the generalization may be made to a job, provided that job analysis shows the job is similar to those involved in prior research.

    Other impressive evidence has also demonstrated the viability and feasibility of the validity generalization model. Studies conducted by Schmidt, Hunter, and other researchers (e.g., Pearlman, Schmidt, and Hunter [1980]; Schmidt *et al.* [1979]; Schmidt and Hunter, 1984) generally indicate that cognitive ability tests demonstrate considerable transportability. In fact, a study by Schmidt,

Hunter, and Pearlman (1981) indicates that cognitive ability test validities generalize across a wide range of jobs and occupations, even to the point that one might not even need to demonstrate job similarity.

The validity generalization model, however, is not without its critics. A recent article that details some elements needing greater clarification is presented by James, Demaree, and Mulaik (1986); the reader is also referred to an excellent article summarizing the debate over the issues related to validity generalization and meta-analysis presented by Schmidt *et al.* and Sackett *et al.* (1985). We anticipate further developments in this particular domain of employment testing in the next few years.

2. Research has progressed with regard to determining the similarities and differences among jobs; the relative differences across jobs is often a key consideration in validity generalization studies. Several articles (Arvey and Mossholder [1977]; Arvey, Maxwell, and Mossholder [1979], Stutzman [1983], and Harvey [1986]) have reviewed and contrasted different procedures for establishing whether jobs are significantly different from one another. Analysis of variance, cluster analysis, and multivariate analysis of variance procedures seem to be the dominant methods suggested to establish whether jobs differ and the degree of differences among them. As one might imagine, the statistical complexities are quite involved and will not be presented here.

3. The 1987 *Principles for the Validation and Use of Personnel Selection Procedures* and the 1985 *Standards for Educational and Psychological Testing* both have a more positive stance concerning validity generalization. As noted in *Principles:*

> *Current research has shown that the differential effects of numerous variables are not so great as heretofore assumed; much can be attributed to statistical artifacts . . . It now seems well established from both validity generalization studies and cooperative validation efforts that validities generalize far more than once supposed. (p. 26)*

The 1987 *Principles* specify that validity generalization evidence may be used to support the use of a test in a new setting under the following conditions: (1) evidence indicates the testing procedure to be used in the new setting is representative of the procedure(s) on which the validity generalization evidence has been assembled; (2) the two jobs (the one on which the validation study was conducted and the one for which the selection procedure is to be used) involve the same major job behaviors. If these conditions are met, there is support for the notion that situational variables (e.g., different performance standards or working conditions) will have little or no effect on the reported validity coefficient and that the actual validity coefficient will not fall below a specified lower limit in the new setting.

4. The courts have also given the concept of validity generalization limited approval. In *Pegues* v. *Mississippi State Employment Services* (1980) the court's ruling was clearly influenced by the current validity generalization research and the expert witness testimony regarding the viability of the method. In upholding the job-relatedness of the examination in question, the judge stated:

> *Empirical research has demonstrated that validity is not perceptibly changed by differences in location, differences in specific job duties or applicant populations. Plaintiff's allegations that validity is specific to a particular location, a particular set of tasks and to a specific applicant population . . . is not true (p. 254).*

These developments suggest that there will be more use of validity generalization in the future, and that technical solutions to the problem are being worked out.

An example of an early effort to summarize validity-study results for a particular industry is reported by Dunnette (1972). The American Petroleum Institute funded this project as a cooperative effort to determine which tests demonstrated the greatest validity for four kinds of jobs frequently found in oil-refining industries: operating and processing jobs, maintenance jobs, clerical jobs, and testing and quality-control jobs. Dunnette's report summarizes the results of an intensive literature review in which 222 studies and over 1300 validity coefficients were reviewed. An example of the summary data is shown in Table 6.1, where the median and quartile values of the distributions of validity coefficients for maintenance jobs are presented.

Armed with this knowledge, an organization wishing to develop a test battery for maintenance jobs may well want to try out job-knowledge tests and mechanical-ability tests, since they have demonstrated relatively higher validity in past studies. The data reported in Table 6.1 suggest

Table 6.1
Median and quartile values in distributions of validity coefficients for maintenance jobs for different types of predictor instruments.

TYPE OF PREDICTOR	NUMBER OF COEFFICIENTS*	Q1	MEDIAN	Q3	PREDICTOR RANKING†
General intelligence tests	111(8)	0.02	0.20	0.50	10
Quantitative tests	86(6)	0.16	0.35	0.56	4
Verbal tests	16	0.16	0.29	0.42	7
Reading tests	17	0.17	0.38	0.47	2
Mechanical ability tests	76(5)	0.24	0.38	0.53	2
Perceptual speed tests	43	0.07	0.16	0.27	11
Spatial aptitude tests	34	0.15	0.24	0.36	8
Biographical inventories	93(4)	0.19	0.34	0.48	5
Interest inventories	81	-0.10	0.05	0.15	13
Personality inventories	3	—	—	—	—
Motor skill measures	65	0.13	0.22	0.30	9
Job knowledge measures	190	0.31	0.43	0.55	1
Job tryout measures	18	0.28	0.36	0.49	3
Interview ratings	17	0.02	0.08	0.18	12
Chemistry knowledge	38(5)	0.06	0.30	0.49	6
Educational level	3	—	0.03	—	14

* Numbers in parentheses show the number of coefficients that were adjusted for restriction in range.
† Ranked according to magnitude of medians.
Source: Table 8 from Publication 754, *Validity Study Results for Jobs Relevant to the Petroleum Refining Industry,* by Marvin D. Dunnette, First Edition, American Petroleum Institute, 1972. Reprinted courtesy of the American Petroleum Institute.

that organizations may be able to use these tests on the principle of validity generalization without conducting a validation study, provided that job analysis confirms similarities among jobs.

TOPIC AREA 4: CONTENT VALIDITY

With increasing frequency, organizations are turning toward the use of content validity for proving job relatedness. This shift away from criterion-related validation strategies toward the use of content validity is due to several factors:

1. The courts have increasingly acknowledged that content validity is an *equally* acceptable strategy in and of itself, and not just a poor second choice to criterion-related validity.

2. Content validity does not appear to be associated with the thorny psychometric problems of unfair test discrimination or bias that are so much a part of criterion-related studies. Since there is no criterion *per se* in content validity, underprediction and overprediction, differential validity, and other complexities need not be examined.

3. Content validity appears to be a validation strategy that is well accepted by applicants as well as by organizations. The skills, knowledge, and behaviors needed to perform the job are directly tapped; no attempt is made to measure abstract, verbal, and/or qualitative abilities.

4. There have also been changes in the way the various sets of guidelines view the three traditional validity categories. Both the 1985 *Standards* and the 1987 *Principles* look more positively than in the past on content validity evidence; each places greater weight on the quality of validity evidence *regardless* of the category used for validation purposes. As noted in the *Standards,* "An ideal validation includes several types of evidence which span all three of the traditional categories" (p. 11).

For a long time, it appeared as if content validity was not going to be legally accepted as an acceptable validation strategy, unless criterion-related validity was first demonstrated not to be feasible. This early tendency may have been due, in part, to the somewhat confusing way in which the various professional and legal guidelines were initially written and applied (Kleiman and Faley, 1978).

Since content validity has received more positive recognition from the courts as well as the developers of the various sets of guidelines, and because it is perceived by many to be less susceptible to the problems that plague the other validation categories (e.g., small sample sizes, restriction in range), it has been touted as a panacea for the various ills that surround validation. However, it may not be the panacea so many hope it will be. For example, Guion (1978) has long been disturbed about the issue of test bias in content validity. He feels that bias may perhaps occur in content validation procedures through the sampling of the job content domains of minority and majority group members. It is more apparent than many would like that issues of fairness and bias can be associated with content validity (see Hunter [1975] for a theoretical approach to analyzing content valid tests for possible sampling biases).

Legal Review: Content Validity

It is, nonetheless, instructive to review how the courts have dealt with content validity. A perusal of cases involving content validity reveals that courts find content-validity issues far more understandable than the issues involved in criterion-related validation strategies. For example, in *Guardians Association* v. *Civil Service Commission of the City of New York* (1980), the judge noted that "taking the quality of test preparation into account in judging test validity would be useful in lessening the risk that a court would fall into error in umpiring a battle of experts who speak a language it does not fully understand" (p. 243). Similarly, the complexities of criterion-related studies and the psychometric and statistical issues led one judge to comment: "As is common in Title VII litigation, this case has led the Court 'deep' into the jargon of psychological testing." (*Jackson* v. *Nassau County Civil Service* [1976]).

One of the most instructive cases involving content validity was *Kirkland* v. *New York Department of Correctional Services* (1974). The test being litigated was a promotional exam for correctional officers. Whites passed the exam at a rate of 30.9 percent compared to a 7.7 percent rate for blacks. The court ruled that sufficient evidence had been presented to shift the burden of persuasion to the organization to demonstrate that the test was job-related. The organization attempted to establish the job-relatedness of the test based on content-validity evidence. Prior to considering the evidence, the court defined the requirements of "content validity."

While first recognizing that the knowledge, skills, and abilities tested in an exam must coincide with some of the knowledge, skills, and abilities required to perform the job successfully, the court went on to be more specific, indicating that the following criteria must be met for a test to have content validity:

1. The attributes selected for examination must be critical and not merely peripherally related to job performance (see also *Berkman* v. *City of New York* [1982] and *Easley* v. *Anheuser Busch, Inc.* [1983].

2. The various portions of the examination must be accurately weighted to reflect the relative importance to the job of the attributes for which they test (see also *Burney* v. *City of Pawtucket* [1983] and *Easley* v. *Anheuser Busch, Inc.* [1983].

3. The level of difficulty of the exam must match the level of difficulty for the job.

The court indicated that the primary emphasis in content validity is on the validity of the *methods* used in creating the examination, not on the independent validity of the end product. Here the court was clearly saying that adequacy of the procedures and methods by which a test was put together is more important than any final index of validity. The court cited an earlier decision from *Vulcan Society Fire Department, Inc.* v. *Civil Service of the City of New York* (1973) in this regard:

> *Instead of burying himself in a question-by-question analysis of Exam 0159 to determine if the test had construct or content validity, the judge noted that it was critical to each of the validation schemes that the examination be carefully prepared with a keen awareness of the need to design questions to test for particular traits or abilities that had been determined to be relevant to the job.*

In *Kirkland,* the court noted that the cornerstone in the construction of a content-valid examination is the *job analysis.* "Without such an analysis . . . a test constructor is aiming in the dark and can only hope to achieve job relatedness through their importance relative to blind luck."

As might be expected, the test was judged inadequate to meet these standards of content validity. Specifically, the defendants could not prove that they had performed an adequate job analysis. The individuals who constructed the test did so without "intimate knowledge" of the job. Also, after the court carefully scrutinized the six subject-matter experts who had prepared the test to determine how familiar they were with the job, it rejected the notion that they "had in their heads a job analysis sufficient to satisfy legal and professional requirements."

This is an important decision for several reasons:

1. It was one of the first to emphasize the important role of *job analysis* in constructing a test claimed to be content valid.

2. The court's emphasis on the *manner* in which the test was prepared indicated that the *documentation* of the development of content-valid exams would be an important issue in the future.

3. The emphasis on the proper selection and weighting of the test components to reflect *critical* attributes of job performance suggested that future courts would be quite probing of the methods by which exams were prepared and of what was included in the exams. That is, in addition to test preparation issues, test content issues would also be important determinants of the quality of a content-validity study. As noted by the judge in *I.M.A.G.E.* v. *Bailor* (1981), "insufficient spadework usually results in a poor garden" (p. 808).

It appears that evidence of a test's validity based on the content validity strategy can survive court review if the content validity study is reasonably well conducted and carefully documented. As would be expected, much of the focus in such cases is on the adequacy of job-analysis information. However, focusing on job analysis alone without regard to test content issues can have serious negative consequences.

For example, consider *United States* v. *City of St. Louis* (1976). In this case, a written test for promotion to the rank of captain in a city fire department was shown to have adverse impact against blacks. The test had been developed and validated by a professional outside consultant. The consultant conducted two-hour interviews with 27 fire captains to obtain a complete specification of all components of the job and of their importance. Exam items were constructed and distributed in the exam in accordance with this job-analysis information. Further, the items were reviewed by an expert panel of technical advisors from the fire department. While supervisory skills were *not* included in the exam, they were to be evaluated during a conditional work period for applicants who passed the test. The court ruled that the exam was indeed content valid despite the expert witness whose "criticisms of the examination amounted to no more than nit-picking." The job analysis was said to be thorough and the items were distributed among the areas of knowledge required in accordance with the importance given to the area by the individuals interviewed during the job-analysis phase. The court of appeals, however, did not agree. In *Firefighters Institute* v. *City of St. Louis* (1977), the appeals court did not challenge the adequacy of the job analysis that was conducted, but maintained, instead, that the test failed to test the "one major attribute that separates a fire fighter from a fire captain, that of supervisory ability." Because this was such an important aspect of the job (over 40 percent of a fire captain's time was spent in supervision) and was not reflected in the test, the test was ruled *not* content valid. The court indicated as follows:

> *The job analysis here may have appeared impressive in relation to those challenged in other cases, but a good analysis in any situation is of little use when the exam fails to reflect what is found in the job analysis.*

The court was apparently saying here that a content-valid test must contain *all* the critical job components as revealed by a job analysis; it is not enough to perform a job analysis—test content must reflect the important job components revealed by the job analysis. However, the court appeared to also be aware of the fact that measuring something as abstract as supervisory ability would be almost impossible using pencil-and-paper tests, and indicated that one potential technique, the assessment center (to be discussed later under Topic Area 6), might be particularly useful. The court charged the organization with the task of devising a test of supervisory skills which was valid and indicated that the assessment center was "conceivably a good idea," but did not require that particular approach be taken.

In a similar case, *United States* v. *City of Chicago* (1978), the appeals court sent a case back to the district level to determine if a promotional exam was content valid. The appeals court demanded that the lower court determine whether the exam reflected the various functions of the job as shown through a job analysis and that these functions are tested (i.e., weighted) according to their importance in the job. In *Bridgeport Guardians* v. *Police Department* (1977) the court ruled that the content-validity approach was appropriate due to problems of small sample size and the subjectivity of *any* criterion of work performance. In addition, the court pointed out that while the preparation of the exam did not conform completely with the standards recommended by the American Psychological Association, these departures did not establish a "lack of job-relatedness."

In *Detroit Police Officers Association* v. *Young* (1978), a district court ruled that a promotional exam was content valid and in compliance with the standards of content validity indicated by EEOC guidelines. Finally, a district court judge indicated that a civil-service senior accountant's test was content valid in *Contreras* v. *City of Los Angeles* (1978), even though several successful job performers failed the exam. In this situation, 12 senior accountants determined the "match" between the test items and the skills of senior accountants and the court ruled that this validation effort was adequate under the circumstances, even when some items were trivial or nonessential.

In a 1976 article, Scharf suggested several areas of content validity that would be the subject of future litigation. He predicted, for example, that future litigation would focus more closely on the appropriateness or adequacy of the various job-analysis techniques avaliable to job analysts. He also predicted that the courts would further elaborate on what constituted sufficient information from a job analysis to provide a basis for a claim of content validity. Although information contained in many of the cases mentioned above confirm Scharf's second prediction, we do not know of any case that confirms his prediction that the courts will involve themselves in a debate over the "appropriateness" of specific job-analysis techniques used for content-validation purposes. The courts appear to be more interested in the quality of job-analysis evidence than they are in the specific techniques used to generate the evidence. (Interestingly, this is not the case when job-analysis information is used to support job grouping or validity-generalization claims.)

The courts have also questioned other aspects of job analysis. For example, the "subjective" nature of many job analyses have come under attack. Job analyses are typically conducted by one analyst who interviews one job holder for several hours. In this situation, two questions come easily to mind:

1. Is an interview with only *one* job incumbent a *sufficient sample* to fully understand the job? Perhaps more rigorous efforts should be made to sample the employee population in each job systematically to ensure full representation. It is well known that individual workers sometimes "redefine" their jobs to fit their own particular skills and capabilities. Thus, a job for one worker may be a different job for another employee. Further, a job may differ according to where in an organization it is performed. For example, a pipefitter in a boiler room may perform a certain set of tasks and duties which may differ from the tasks performed by a pipefitter working in the maintenance department.

   There also might exist systematic differences between minority- and nonminority-group members in job activities. Thus, any job analysis based on representatives of *only one* group may be excluding aspects of the job performed by the other group. For example, black police officers might be systematically assigned to ghetto neighborhoods which require more caution, exposure to crime, and danger. Borman, Hollenbeck, and Olivero (1977) performed a study comparing female and male stockbrokers working in the same job, and found significant differences in the way the two groups spent their time. Although the courts appear interested in the issues related to selecting a sample of incumbents for job-analysis purposes (e.g., see *Guardians* [1980]), it does not appear that the majority/minority makeup of the sample is important. At least this aspect of the job-analysis sample has not been mentioned in any of the cases we reviewed. Once again, the possible concern is that content-valid tests that adversely impact protected group members may do so because they only sample job behaviors and KSAs that reflect the major components of work performed by majority rather than protected group members. Cascio and Phillips (1979) have shown, however, that a wide variety of performance tests (entry level and promotional, motor and verbal) which were properly content-validated without specifically requiring a job analysis based on minority representation, exhibited no adverse impact.

2. Are the job analysts themselves free from bias? For example, does a white analyst lower his or her evaluation of a job when interviewing a black incumbent? Similarly, is a male analyst's interpretation of the nature of a job influenced in some manner when he is inter-

viewing a female incumbent? Along these lines, Clarenbach (1975) has suggested that sex-role stereotypes by individuals analyzing jobs for the *Dictionary of Occupational Titles* is one of the factors responsible for the underrating of "women's work." In a study investigating this issue, Arvey, Passino, and Lounsbury (1977) found little evidence that job analysts influence their ratings of a job according to whether the incumbent interviewed is male or female. (However, some evidence indicated that male and female *analysts* differed in their description of the same job.)

In any case, it might be desirable in job analyses to sample incumbents more representatively from among the employee population and, also, to use more than one analyst. These points seem somewhat ripe for litigation.

A final caution related to content validation should be mentioned. Both the legal and professional guidelines (original and new versions) note that content validity is an inappropriate strategy for demonstrating the validity of selection procedures that purport to measure traits or constructs (e.g., intelligence, insight, judgment). Thus, in the sense of a general rule, as the inferential leap increases between the content of the selection procedure and the content of the job, the appropriateness of the content approach for validation purposes decreases. That is, the more closely the content of the test approximates tasks to be performed on the job, the more appropriate is the content approach for validation purposes.

TOPIC AREA 5: WORK-SAMPLE TESTS

Work-sample tests are exams with high (or potentially high) content validity. These tests sample the actual work that is performed in the job, such as typing and shorthand for secretarial and clerical jobs. O'Leary (1973) indicates that tests that simulate the job are valuable on two counts: (1) they are directly and logically related to the behavior being predicted; and (2) they allow job candidates to obtain a feel for the job and learn about its potential suitability.

McClelland (1973) sent ripples across the psychological community by hotly challenging the validity of intelligence tests and recommending criterion or work sampling to predict job proficiency. He said: "If you want to test who will be a good policeman, go find out what a policeman does. Follow him around, make a list of his activities, and sample from that list in screening applicants'' (p. 7).

How effective are work-sample testing procedures? Given that many individuals recommend work-sample procedures in favor of pencil-and-paper tests, what evidence exists concerning the usefulness of these types of tests? In one of the first published demonstrations of the usefulness of the work-sampling technique, Campion (1972) described how he built a work sample for maintenance mechanics. Based on a complete job analysis, four tasks were selected as potential predictors or tests of job performance: installing pulleys and belts, disassembling and repairing a gear box, installing and aligning a motor, and pressing a bushing into a sprocket and reaming it to fit a shaft. Thirty-four maintenance employees were asked to perform these tasks while being closely observed and rated by job experts. These employees also took a battery of traditional pencil-and-paper tests for comparison purposes. The supervisors of these employees provided independent ratings of each employee on three criteria: use of tools, accuracy of work, and overall mechanical ability. Finally, the work-sample scores (based on the experts' ratings), the pencil-and-paper tests, and the job-performance ratings were correlated to obtain the validity coefficients for the two types of predictors. The results are shown in Table 6.2. These data clearly demonstrate that the work-sample test was a more accurate predictor of job performance than the traditional pencil-and-paper tests.

In a later study, Asher and Sciarrino (1974) reviewed the research literature to determine the validity of work samples compared to other more traditional tests (e.g., intelligence, personality). Their review indicated that work-sample tests are among the most predictive tests; in almost all the studies reviewed, work-sample tests were in the top half of the tests with the highest validity coefficients.

The Campion (1972) study and the Asher and Sciarrino (1974) review lend strong evidence to the notion that work-sample tests tend to be relatively more valid than other tests.

What might be helpful is to compare minority and majority subgroups on work-sample tests. The work-sampling approach has been criticized because it penalizes those individuals who do not have previous work experience or other opportunities to develop the relevant job skills. Because minority-group members have often been excluded from skilled job lines, they may be apt to perform less well on these tests than others.

Table 6.2

Correlations between predictors and criterion variables.

	CRITERION MEASURES		
PREDICTOR	Use of Tools	Accuracy of Work	Overall Mechanical Ability
Work sample	.66*	.42†	.46*
Bennett Mechanical Comprehensive Test (Form AA)	.08	−.04	−.21
Wonderlic Personnel Test (Form D)	−.23	−.19	−.32
Short employment tests:			
Verbal	−.24	−.02	−.04
Numerical	.07	−.13	−.10
Clerical aptitude	−.03	−.19	−.09

* $p < .01$
† $p < .05$
Source: From J. E. Campion (1972). Copyright 1972 by the American Psychological Association. Reprinted by permission of the author.

One study which compared blacks and whites was reported by Schoenfeldt *et al.* (1976). A test was rigorously constructed and designed to directly reflect job-related reading activities. A job analysis was conducted to determine exactly what materials were read by entry-level employees, as well as the importance of these materials for job performance. Fifteen types of reading (e.g., safety, rules, operating procedures, work agreements) were identified and sample test items were chosen. Two alternative forms of the test were developed with 39 and 36 items, respectively.

The two forms were administered to over 450 individuals and results showed a significant difference between black and white subjects on one of the forms. Fewer blacks failed to pass. Thus, this study suggests that work samples may still be vulnerable to "adverse impact."

Another study investigating the relative adverse impact of work samples and more traditional tests is reported by Schmidt *et al.* (1977). In this study, work samples (based on task analyses of metal-trade jobs) were developed in which each person tested was expected to deliver a finished product, which was subsequently graded according to particular tolerance levels. Twenty-nine minorities (predominantly blacks) and 58 nonminorities completed work samples, several pencil-and-paper knowledge tests, and attitude measures concerning the "fairness" of the tests. A comparison of the differences between the minority and nonminority samples on the two types of tests revealed that the adverse impact of the work samples was considerably less than that of the pencil-and-paper tests. In addition, both minority and majority members saw the job-sample tests as significantly fairer, clearer, and more appropriate in their level of difficulty.

As noted above, Cascio and Phillips (1979) reported that a wide variety of properly validated performance tests exhibited no adverse impact based on either race or sex. They also reported that performance tests tended to have greater face validity and to be more cost efficient and more acceptable to applicants than traditional paper-and-pencil tests.

Thus the work-sample approach has much to recommend it. Because of the *logical relationship* between the tests and the jobs, and because of the *acceptability* of work samples to courts, applicants, and organizations, we can expect more emphasis on these kinds of tests in the future. However, some researchers (e.g., Guion, 1978 and Hamner *et al.*, 1974) have called attention to the fact that individuals who evaluate the performance of applicants during a work-sample test may still be susceptible to bias in the evaluation process. Although this is always a possibility, Cascio and Phillips reported finding no evidence of rater-by-ratee interaction race or sex effects in their study. "Of the 19 comparisons which were possible, not one such difference in ratings was significant" (p. 760). Moreover, the interrater reliabilities they reported were quite high, and although the reliability estimates were based on only a small sample of observations, the convergence of similar results across many studies conducted with subjects from different populations in different situations was quite persuasive.

TOPIC AREA 6: ASSESSMENT CENTERS

One particular type of work sample, or simulation, is known as the *assessment center.* This procedure is typically used in selection for supervisory and managerial positions. Several research studies have evaluated minority and nonminority employee differences in assessment centers.

First, however, what is an assessment center? Supervisory and managerial-level job candidates attending an assessment center participate in two to three days of group and individual exercises, role playing, managerial simulations, and psychological tests. The exercises and techniques involved in an assessment center usually include the following:

1. *In-basket exercise*—This exercise requires a person to deal with a typical set of written materials found in a manager's in-basket. The items range from situations where no action should be taken to very complex problems. Time limits are usually given.

2. *Leaderless group discussion*—The most common procedure is for approximately six candidates to be given a problem on which they must reach a consensus, usually within an hour. No formal leadership roles are assigned.

3. *Business game*—Participants (usually in groups) are asked to engage in some kind of business in which they must purchase materials and manufacture and market a finished product.

4. *Interview*—An intensive one- to two-hour in-depth interview is usually conducted with each participant.

In addition, the participants in an assessment center are administered a battery of pencil-and-paper tests (measuring intelligence, personality, vocational interests). During most of the role-playing and group exercises, each paticipant is closely watched by trained observers. These observers may be trained psychologists, but usually they are higher-level managers from the organization itself who have been trained as assessors. After viewing the assessment-center activities, the assessors meet and reach a consensus rating of each participant for a number of variables considered important for effective management. They also make an overall assessment rating. For example, the assessment ratings generally used by the American Telephone and Telegraph (AT&T) system, which was one of the first organizations to use and evaluate the method, are the following (Bray and Grant, 1966):

1. Organization and planning
2. Decision making
3. Creativity
4. Human relations skills

5. Behavior flexibility
6. Personal impact
7. Tolerance of uncertainty
8. Resistance to stress
9. Scholastic aptitudes
10. Range of interests
11. Inner work standards
12. Primacy of work
13. Oral communication skills
14. Perception of social cues
15. Self-objectivity
16. Energy
17. Realism of expectations
18. Bell system value orientation
19. Social objectivity
20. Need for achievement
21. Ability
22. Need for supervision approval
23. Need for peer approval
24. Goal flexibility

The assessment center represents a form of work sampling and, therefore, has content validity, according to many of its proponents. (However, some researchers—e.g., Dreher and Sackett, 1981 and Sackett, 1987—have serious reservations about the content validity of assessment centers used to predict future job performance.) The main reasons proponents claim that the assessment center is content valid include the following:

1. Many of the exercises, games, and so forth are constructed to reflect *directly* the kinds of problems managers are likely to face. For example, the in-basket exercise is developed from actual memos, letters, and other data obtained from sampling real managers' files.

2. The judgements and evaluations made are based on actual *observed* behaviors instead of those *inferred* from test scores. In addition, the

assessment center offers a lengthy view of each individual, and, thus, evaluations and judgments are based on the "whole person" and not just on isolated instances of behavior.

The research conducted on the assessment center is, nonetheless, based on the criterion-related validation paradigm. Ratings on the assessment-center variables and on the overall assessment rating are usually correlated with current performance (concurrent design). In the original study of this type, however, the participants were followed up eight years later and the assessment ratings compared to their progress in management (predictive design).

The validity data for the assessment-center method are highly ecouraging. Of 23 studies that compared the usefulness of the assessment center to other types of predictors and tests, Byham (1970) reports that the assessment center proved more effective in 22 cases and had equal validity in the one remaining case. In addition, Huck's (1973) review of the validity of the assessment center indicated that judgments made during the center were highly predictive of managerial advancement and progress. That is, individuals who were seen by assessment-center observers as having good potential for advancement did indeed tend to move up higher and more rapidly than individuals seen as having relatively less potential.

Cohen, Moses, and Byham (1974) reported similar findings. Across the 21 studies these authors reviewed, they found a median correlation of .63 predicting potential or promotion. However, they also reported only a "corrected" median correlation of .43 predicting supervisory ratings of actual performance later on the job. Studies by Klimoski and Strickland (1977, 1981) support these later results (although Klimoski and Strickland report lower absolute validities than Cohen et al., the validities are in the same direction). Gaugler et al. (1987) also reported that assessment centers were more valid for predicting an assessee's job potential ($r_{xy} = .53*$) than for predicting job performance ($r_{xy} = .36*$), based on evidence derived from a meta-analysis of published and unpublished studies. Thus it appears that assessment center ratings are better predictors of potential for promotion than future job performance.

Another recent review, however, paints a slightly different picture. Applying meta-analytic techniques to a subset of published validity stud-

---

* Weighted mean validity coefficient corrected for range restriction and unreliability in the criterion.

ies, Schmitt *et al.* (1984) reported that assessment-center validities varied (although not significantly) as a function of the criterion measure used (the number of validities was small; differences in sample size accounted for most of the variation across coefficients). Interestingly, the largest mean validity coefficient (r_{xy} = .43) was reported for assessment-center predictions of future job performance.

The debate over whether assessment-center predictions of future job performance are comparable to assessment-center predictions of promotion or potential may be only marginally important. There appear to be alternative predictors of future job performance that have validities equivalent to those reported for assessment centers. For example, Klimoski and Strickland (1981) reported that preassessment ratings of current job performance were reasonable (r_{xy} = .38) predictors of future job performance. These authors suggest this may mean that assessment-center ratings "trap" aspects of the promotion decison-making process other than previous performance (see Hunter and Hunter [1984] for other explanations). Klimoski and Strickland suggest that future managerial performance can be better predicted by using alternatives to assessment centers, such as current performance appraisal ratings. Brush and Schoenfeldt (1980) agree, based on evidence gathered from an integrated performance appraisal procedure they developed to generate selection information comparable to that available from assessment centers. These authors believe information currently available in many organizations often yields comparable selection data at a lower cost than assessment centers.

In addition to their enviable validity, assessment centers also appear to possess substantial utility in spite of their sometimes large developmental and administrative costs. For example, Cascio and Silbey (1979) used the Brogden-Cronbach-Gleser model to assess the relative utility of an assessment center against an alternative selection procedure (an interview) and random chance. Six model parameters were systematically varied. The results revealed that even assessment centers with very low validity (r_{xy} = .10) showed positive gains over random chance. In general, as the validity of the assessment center and the size of the criterion standard deviation increased, the expected payoffs from the assessment-center selection procedure became substantial.

Hunter and Hunter (1984) also reported on the relative utility of a number of selection alternatives to random chance including the assessment center. Overall, each alternative had a positive utility. Measures of ability showed the greatest utility; compared to measures of ability, assessment-center measures resulted in a *loss* of utility. Nevertheless, this study indicates that assessment centers exhibit substantial utility and fare relatively well compared with other alternative selection procedures.

At the present time, the assessment center is big business. Well over 1000 organizations are using it for the promotion of managers as well as for selecting sales representatives, customer-contact people, and so forth (Parker, 1980). As we have seen earlier, the courts also recognize that the assessment center might be a valuable tool in selecting and promoting minority and majority candidates (*Firefighters Institute* v. *City of St. Louis* [1977]).

Two questions are particularly relevant concerning the use of the assessment center for minority-group candidates:

1. Do minority candidates do as well as nonminority candidates, or are minority-group persons rated lower?
2. Are the assessment-center ratings equally valid for minority and nonminority candidates? Do assessment-center judgments, for example, predict actual job performance equally well for both groups?

Fortunately, several studies have shed some light on these questions. Moses and Boehm (1975) evaluated the assessment-center ratings given to male and female subjects. They examined the ratings of over 4500 women who had been evaluated in an assessment center sometime between 1963 and 1971, compared to a sample of over 8000 men who had been assessed during the same period. The numbers and percentages of men and women who were rated at the various levels on the final or overall rating are shown in Table 6.3.

The distributions of ratings for men and women were quite similar. About the same percentages of men and women were rated as acceptable or more than acceptable. Thus it does not appear as if any "adverse impact" would occur if these ratings were used for making promotional decisions (as they were). Moses and Boehm also found that the overall assessment rating was equally valid for both the males and the females in the study. For women, the final assessment ratings correlated .37 with management progress in the organization; for men, the corresponding correlation was .44. The researchers concluded that the assessment-center process predicts the future performance of women as accurately as it predicts that of men.

Table 6.3
Distribution of final assessment ratings for men and women who participated in AT&T assessment centers.

FINAL RATING	WOMEN		MEN	
	NUMBER	PERCENT	NUMBER	PERCENT
More than acceptable	294	6.1	638	7.2
Acceptable	1,364	28.1	2,279	25.6
Questionable	1,403	29.0	2,902	32.7
Not acceptable	1,785	36.8	3,066	34.5
Total	4,846		8,885	

Source: From Moses and Boehm (1975). Copyright 1975 by the American Psychological
Association. Reprinted by permission of the author.

A study that evaluated the use of the assessment center for both
black and white females was reported by Huck and Bray (1976). The
sample included 126 nonmanagement women (91 white and 35 black)
who had attended an assessment center between 1966 and 1971 and who
were later promoted into supervisory management positions. In addition,
238 black and 241 white women who had been assessed (at the same
time), but not promoted, were studied. These individuals had been rated
on the various assessment-center variables in addition to receiving an
"overall assessment rating." Later, for the 128 women who had been
promoted, supervisory ratings were given on a number of criterion scales,
including an overall job-performance scale and a potential-for-advance-
ment scale.

The results indicated that the black women were evaluated significantly lower than the white women by the assessment-center staff, regardless of whether they were promoted or not. The average overall assessment rating for the white women who had been promoted was 3.4,
compared to 3.0 for the black women. Similarly, the mean value for the
white women *not* promoted was 2.8, compared to the black-group mean
of 2.4. However, the two groups also differed on one criterion measure
where the black women were rated by their supervisors significantly lower
on overall job performance. The difference was not significant, however,
on supervisory ratings of potential for advancement.

Huck and Bray (1976) examined the validity coefficients based on
the correlations between the assessment-center "overall assessment rat-

ing" and the two global criterion ratings of overall job performance and potential for advancement. For whites, the overall assessment rating correlated .41 with overall job performance, while the corresponding value for the black sample was .38. Both these correlations were significant. The correlation between the overall assessment rating and potential for advancement was .59 for whites and .54 for blacks, both significant. In addition, the regression lines for the two groups did not differ, thus satisfying one definition of test fairness.

These results are shown graphically in Fig. 6.3. The two groups differ in both the assessment-center ratings and the criterion measures, with the blacks scoring correspondingly lower in *both* measures. Further, the assessment-center ratings are highly valid for both groups. The regression lines between the assessment-center ratings and job performance are essentially the same for both groups. According to the Cleary (1968) definition of test fairness discussed earlier, the assessment-center technique is a fair strategy for predicting the performance of black women in this particular organization.

A study by Schmitt and Hill (1977) investigated the effects of the composition of the group (by race and sex) on assessment-center evalu-

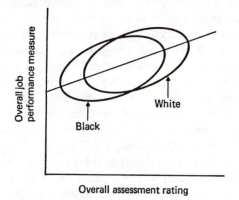

Figure 6.3 *Relationship between job performance and assessment-center ratings. (Based on data given in Huck and Bray, 1976.)*

ations. The question addressed was whether the evaluation of, for example, a black female would change according to the race and sex of the other group members. The results indicated only marginally significant effects, but there was a slight indication that black females are evaluated lower when the other members of an assessment group are predominantly white males. On the other hand, black females were evaluated relatively higher when the group composition was predominantly white females.

After reviewing all the published research findings and many unpublished ones, Byham (1981) concluded that when differences between black and white mean overall assessment-center ratings occur, they seem to be moderated by supervisory level. That is, this pattern of results seems to occur most often among candidates for first-level supervisory positions. He strongly suggests this may not be evidence of discrimination, but rather of the fact that organizations dealing with affirmative-action pressures to increase the number of blacks in managerial positions may be more willing to send marginal blacks to an assessment center in hopes that they will fare well. The fact that the average tenure of black candidates prior to assessment is often lower than white candidates supports this notion.

Finally, some research evidence is available (Thornton and Byham, 1982) that an age bias exists in assessment-center ratings. Older assessees are more likely to receive lower overall assessment ratings. Interestingly, the significant age differences in ratings occur in a pattern similar to the race differences reported above by Byham (1981). That is, significant age differences in overall assessment ratings are usually more likely to occur in programs for first-level supervisors, and like the race differences, the most likely explanation is that the negative correlation between overall assessment rating and age is a function of preassessment selection. Candidates with the highest potential are generally selected early in their careers, whereas marginal or poor candidates are selected later in their careers, possibly as a "consolation prize." The fact that age bias in assessment ratings is much less likely to occur if a self-nomination procedure is used lends support to this explanation. Moreover, there is evidence (Hall, 1976; Neidig *et al.*, 1978; Gaugler *et al.*, 1987) that assessment-center ratings are equally valid for older and younger candidates.

Based on the research literature concerning the assessment center, four preliminary statements may be made:

1. The assessment-center techniques appear to be highly valid and predictive for individuals across a large number of criteria and organizations.

2. The assessment-center techniques also appear to be reasonably "fair" based on race, sex, and age. White women are rated about the same as white males, and, based on overall assessment-center ratings, there is little evidence to suggest that black women are "underpredicted" compared with white women. Black women, though, do receive comparatively lower evaluations than white men when members of the assessment group are predominantly white males. Small age-related differences in assessment-center ratings have been reported; these findings and the reported race-related differences appear to be moderated by supervisory level and not the result of rater biases.

3. The content validity of the assessment center has never been directly assessed, although many have suggested the content approach to validation is especially appropriate for assessment centers (e.g., Byham, 1980 and Norton, 1977). Byham notes that the applicability of the content approach is one of the assessment centers more attractive characteristics. Studies evaluating the validity of assessment centers, however, have relied almost exclusively on criterion-related studies. Thus, although proponents of the assessment center advocate the content validity and work-sampling properties of the procedure, no study has rigorously examined this proposition to date (see Dreher and Sackett [1981] for an analysis of problems with applying content-validity evidence to assessment-center procedures).

4. Since assessment centers appear to be significantly better than other selection procedures when it comes to adverse impact (Byham, 1981), it is not surprising to find they have received positive support from the courts and the EEOC. For example, in the well-publicized sex discrimination case against AT&T, the consent decree included provisions that assessment centers be extensively used to help identify those females most likely to succeed in upper-management positions. Other courts have evaluated the merits of assessment centers relative to more traditional selection procedures and found the assessment-center approach preferable (e.g., *Firefighters Institute* v. *City of St. Louis* [1977]; *James* v. *Stockham Valves and Fittings* [1977]; *U.S.* v. *City of Chicago* [1976]).

TOPIC AREA 7: CULTURE-FAIR TESTS

During the first few years of the controversy concerning test bias against minority-group members, many individuals felt that an answer to this problem was to develop a test or set of tests that were "culture fair," thus limiting the effects of disadvantaged backgrounds. A basic assumption behind this approach was that differences between minority- and majority-group members on traditional pencil-and-paper verbal tests were due to factors associated with the tests themselves.

One factor often suggested is that test items are culturally "loaded" or familiar only to those individuals who share white middle-class experiences. For example, the content on many intelligence tests may not be familiar to the culturally deprived. An item that has the word "umbrella" in one of the questions might be "unfair" because some people in our society may not know what it is. A 100-item test developed by Williams (1975) provides a dramatic example of this "effect" operating in reverse. The test is called the Black Intelligence Test of Cultural Homogeneity (BITCH) and is intended to be a "cultural-specific" test that taps the cultural experiences of blacks living in this country. (Another such test is the Scales Inner City Intelligence Test [Scales, 1973]). When the BITCH is administered to both white and black subjects, there is virtually no overlap between the two distributions—the blacks score considerably higher. However, just because race correlates highly with test scores does not necessarily mean race has anything to do with performance on this test. That is, a middle-class black person raised in suburbia may perform just as poorly on the BITCH as a middle-class white person. Although the BITCH does not correlate well with other traditional measures of intelligence, Matarazzo and Wiens (1977) suggest it may have potential usefulness in selecting white police officers who might need to patrol in predominantly black neighborhoods.

The verbal nature of many tests is another factor that may account for test differences between racial and cultural subgroups. Since the culturally disadvantaged have had relatively less experience with verbal materials, the reading levels of tests may be too high and, consequently, result in substantial test-score differences. In summary, the *test itself* by virtue of its content, instructions, or nature could be the factor depressing the scores of minority-group subjects.

Partly in response to these notions, attempts were made to devise culture-fair tests that would minimize test differentials between racial and cultural groups.* For example, the Davis-Eells games, the Catell Culture Fair Intelligence Test, the Raven's Progressive Matrices, and others were developed. While a precise definition of "culture fair" was never developed, a common theme among culture-fair tests was the decreased emphasis on verbal items (and instructions), and a correspondingly greater emphasis on such psychological processes as visualization, spatial reasoning, and abstract reasoning, with the intent being to minimize or eliminate differences between cultural groups.

How good are these culture-fair tests? Do they indeed reduce the differentials between cultural groups? Are they equally, if not more, valid than traditional verbally oriented tests?

A review by Arvey (1972) suggests that culture-fair tests have not met the expectations of test users. In fact, studies by Moore, MacNaughton, and Osborn (1969), Tenopyr (1967), and Higgins and Silvers (1958) indicate that disadvantaged groups actually perform worse on culture-fair tests than on traditional tests. The implications for selection situations are obvious: Disadvantaged individuals may have even *less* of a chance of being hired for a job or of entering a training program if they are selected on the basis of culture-fair tests rather than on more traditional measures of cognitive abilities.

A second question concerns the validity of culture-fair tests. That is, do they predict job performance in the present social milieu? Campbell *et al.* (1970) compared the validity coefficients of black and white subgroups on culture-fair and nonculture-fair tests. They concluded that there were consistently higher validities for blacks than for whites on tests that might be considered "culture bound," including subtraction-multiplication, necessary arithmetic, and vocabulary; but there were higher validities for whites on tests that might be considered "culture free," including finger dexterity and picture-number tests. This and other studies have not shown consistently higher validity coefficients for culture-fair tests.

---

* In constructing tests that have the objective of minimizing group differences, test developers could cut *out* items that differentiated between groups or *add* items that favor one of the groups (when it was discovered that women performed better on the verbal sections of the Stanford-Binet, more performance items were added to eliminate the differences).

In general, the quest for a culture-fair test seems to have failed. The tests that were developed showed even greater differentials between cultural and racial groups and did not increase predictability. It is also likely that the items differentiating between cultures may also be the most valid items. Thus tests that do *not* show any differences between groups may also *not* be related to *any* relevant criterion in our society.

TOPIC AREA 8: TEST BIAS AGAINST THE OLDER WORKER

While a great deal of interest and research has focused on discrimination against blacks, it is also possible that selection tests might be unfair to older workers. This would most likely occur where there were no significant differences between the job performance of older and younger workers, yet there were significant differences in their test performance. Reviews of the literature on the relationship between age and job performance shed some light on this matter.

After a review of 115 studies, Rhodes (1983) concluded that research results on the age/job performance relationship were inconsistent. Meier and Kerr (1976) reported somewhat more encouraging results, concluding that there is reasonably good evidence that relatively younger and older employees do not differ in their job performance. Both studies note that the stereotype of the older worker as a less proficient worker received little support overall. Where age-related differences were uncovered, it appeared that they depended on the nature of the measure of performance and the demands of the job. Moreover, Rhodes noted that a majority of the research relating age to important organizational variables has been fraught with methodological and conceptual limitations (e.g., poor research designs, questionable analytical strategies, lack of theoretical grounding). Faley, Kleiman and Lengnick-Hall (1984) have also noted that research evidence related to a finding of age discrimination is often misleading. For instance, these authors provide an example where evidence that the mean performance of young police patrol officers was superior to that of older patrol officers was used to defend a BFOQ based on age. In actuality, the difference was most likely due not to age per se but to the fact that effective patrol officers who were older had already been promoted. This would occur "naturally" as a result of the Peter Principle—at any given time a greater number of older as compared to younger workers will have "topped out" at any job level. As noted by

Pritchard, Maxwell, and Jordan (1984), interpreting analyses of the relationship between age and promotions "is made difficult by the fact that one would expect some relationship between age and promotions unfavorable to older employees in the absence of age discrimination" (p. 199).

Rhodes (1983) and Faley et al. (1984) also report that older workers are often able to accommodate the effects of aging that are related to job performance. Interestingly, many of the factors Rhodes suggests may be affected by aging (hearing, vision, speed and accuracy of movement, etc.) are many of the same that older workers are able to make adjustments for after a short time on the job. For example, University of Missouri researchers found that although older typists had slower reaction times than younger ones, their work performances were equivalent because the older typists compensated by looking farther ahead in the text as they typed. Similarly, a University of Michigan study reported that older waiters kept up with younger ones because the older waiters accomplished more during each visit to the table. Heneman (1974) and Faley et al. (1984) provide an excellent overview of many of the issues involved in detecting employment-test discrimination against different age groups. Faley and Kleiman (1985) also provide an excellent cross-cultural overview of the similarities and differences in the way age discrimination is defined and remedied in the United States and other developed countries.

There appears to be a more consistent body of research evidence that older individuals tend to do worse on particular kinds of tests that are often used in employment. For example, older workers tend to do worse on performance (as opposed to verbal) tests and speed tests (Anastasi, 1965). Contrived testing situations also tend to exacerbate these differences. As the circumstances of testing become less similar to the circumstances of work, the results of testing are more likely to produce an underestimate of the true capabilities of older workers. Older people often perform better on the job because the work setting is more familiar to them and they are able to draw from experience (Faley et al., 1984). Some research suggests the ability to distill lessons from experience may actually improve with age, while other researchers contend that the mind actually grows stronger with age in more subjective but no less important tasks such as reaching judgments (see Giniger, Dispenzieri, and Eisenberg, 1983).

In one of the first reported empirical investigations of test discrimination against older workers, Arvey and Mussio (1973) studied 263 female clerical workers who participated in a test-validation project in which several intelligence-oriented tests were administered, including a clerical aptitude test. Also, supervisors were asked to rate these employees on an overall effectiveness scale. The employees were divided into two age groups: One group consisted of those 24 years old or younger ($N = 70$) and the other consisted of those over 50 ($N = 60$). Results of the study indicated *no differences* between the two groups in job performance. On the test of clerical aptitude, the older employees did significantly worse than the younger group. However, this test was differentially valid in that it correlated .47 with performance for the older group and .02 for the younger group. This difference in magnitude of the correlations between the two groups was significant. Fig. 6.4 depicts the situation graphically. Using the Cleary definitions described in the previous chapter, the two groups have different regression lines, with the older group being *under*predicted. If any one particular cutoff score were chosen as a cutoff (e.g., 38), virtually all of the older individuals would be excluded from the work force. However, the authors indicate that the test " . . . would have no usefulness for predicting performance of the younger group. . . . Conversely, the test has potentially great usefulness in selecting older employees" (p. 28).

As the results of this study demonstrate, selection-test bias against the older worker is certainly a possibility. Generally speaking, however, most age-discrimination cases are based on promotional and forced retirement personnel decisions, rather than selection into a job. As far as we know, there has never been a suit directly challenging a particular type of employment test based on its adverse impact against older workers. As noted by Reilly and Chao (1982), little is known about the adverse impact of alternative selection procedures; this is especially true where the adverse impact is based on age. Most information we have about the adverse impact of alternative procedures relates to race and sex. The relative "newness" of age as a characteristic of interest likely contributes to our lack of understanding in this area.

However, as noted above in our discussion of assessment centers, there is some evidence that younger assessees receive higher ratings than older ones. As is also noted above, this difference rarely occurs and is likely the result of job-related and not discriminatory factors.

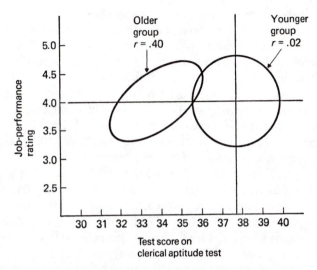

Figure 6.4 *Unfair test discrimination against older employee group. (Based on Arvey and Mussio, 1973.)*

TOPIC AREA 9: TEST BIAS IN INTEREST INVENTORIES

The perceptive reader will have noted that most, if not all, court cases concerning unfair test discrimination have involved *race* (*not sex*) discrimination challenges. The reason that challenges on the basis of sex discrimination are so infrequent is simply that women tend to score as well as, or better than, males. Thus, "adverse impact" against women is seldom shown when more general intellectual tests are given.

There is a particular kind of test, however, used with some frequency in employment settings, that has been criticized because of its possible bias against females. This kind of test is the *interest inventory,* in which individuals indicate their likes, dislikes, or indifference to a number of occupations, activities, school subjects, and other items. These responses are computer scored to indicate the particular occupational areas a person may find satisfying, because there is a match between the person's interests and those of successful individuals already employed in those occupations. Typically, scores on such inventories are used to counsel individuals about career decisions; they have also been used by organizations to make selection decisions. Scores on interest inventories have been found to be moderately predictive of occupational entry, satisfaction with occupational choice, and even changes in occupations (Nunnally, 1967). They have not been found to predict future job performance very well unless a special scoring key (e.g., a key for a specific engineering job as opposed to all engineering jobs) is developed. Under these circumstances chances are enhanced for successfully predicting job performance based on interests (Dunnette, Wernimont, and Abrahams, 1964). Unfortunately, the predictive ability of data derived from interest inventories is somewhat artificially mitigated by two facts: (1) there are likely to be few individual differences in interests within any one occupation, and (2) many inventories are ipsatively scored, which means that person-by-person comparisons are not meaningful (Schneider, 1983). Two of the best-known interest inventories are the Kuder Occupational Interest Inventory and the Strong-Campbell Interest Inventory.

Criticisms of interest inventories with regard to possible sex bias fall into several categories*:

1. Scale "scores" for women are usually available only in "traditional" women's occupational areas. That is, a woman could receive interest-inventory scores in such areas as secretary, teacher, or nurse, but not in more male-dominated areas such as lawyer, physician, or plumber. This has the possible effects of restricting the occupational choices of women to only these areas and encouraging counselors or placement officers to treat women differently from men. The latest Strong-Campbell Interest Inventory represents a shift from the previous format. Currently one form for both sexes is used and scores for both sexes on almost all occupational scales are derived and printed.

2. The fact that men and women typically differ in their responses to the interest items suggests to some that an inventory is biased. For example, a larger proportion of men than women obtain high career-interest scores in the scientific, technical, and business-contact areas. On the other hand, more women than men obtain higher career-interest scores in social service, creative arts, and business clerical-

---

* For an excellent discussion of these issues, see Selkow (1984).

interest areas (Gottfredson, Holland, and Gottfredson, 1975). In addition, some data indicate that males and females within *the same* occupational areas differ on the interest items. For example, Campbell (1976) found a 15-percent difference in the way male and female lawyers responded to 43 of 91 scale items. This has led to efforts by some individuals to build interest inventories that minimize, if not eliminate, sex differences (culture-fair tests?) and to ascertain the validity of these inventories (Hanson and Rayman, 1976).

3. There is confusion concerning how to interpret the results of an interest inventory completed by a member of the opposite sex. Individuals tend to score higher on an opposite-sex scale. For example, most men will obtain a higher score than most women on a mechanically oriented female scale (Hansen, 1976).

4. There are claims that the language used in interest inventories is sexist in that the items and instructions are masculine in tone (Gottfredson, 1976). For example, does asking people whether they would enjoy working as a salesman (instead of a salesperson) influence the choice males and females make on such inventories?

Research efforts are presently under way to clarify these issues and to substantiate or refute the charges. Diamond (1975) has edited and published a book of articles entitled "Issues of Sex Bias and Sex Fairness in Career Interest Measurement" which may help to illuminate and guide interested readers; the *Journal of Vocational Behavior* is an additional source of research studies concerning sex bias in interest inventories.

It is quite possible that future court cases will involve challenges to interest inventories with regard to sex bias. It's almost certain that the shifting burden of persuasion standard applied to other cases involving test discrimination would similarly be applied in a review of interest inventories. Thus two questions are brought immediately to mind:

1. Would "adverse impact" result from the scores women receive on particular scales of the challenged inventory?

2. Would the interest inventories hold up under a review of their job relatedness?

At this point, there are no cases to review that will show how these tests stand up.

SUMMARY

This chapter was intended to review and illuminate several pertinent issues germane to unfair testing and discrimination. Relevant court decisions were reviewed and research results presented where appropriate and/ or available. Obviously, we have not dealt with all the relevant issues in this area or even gone into great depth in any one area. Readers are urged to explore those areas in which they are especially interested by consulting the various sources cited for greater coverage.

Because of the independence of the various topics, it is somewhat difficult to provide an integrated recap. Thus, we will make several summary statements based on each topical area.

- *The criterion problem.* One of the most difficult problem areas facing researchers is defending the validity and reliability of the particular criteria used in test validation or for other personnel decisions such as promotions. A review of the legal literature on performance-appraisal instruments indicated that these forms were vulnerable to attack and that many suits depended on the validity of the appraisal instruments themselves. Courts have tended to view such instruments as tests and evaluated them against the EEOC guidelines. We predict that courts will begin to review appraisal instruments from the standpoint of content validity; i.e., their presumed or demonstrated logical relationship to the job.

- *Sample-size problems and validity generalization.* We discussed in some detail the problem of conducting validation studies with small sample sizes. In fact, larger samples than previously thought necessary may be in order to detect "true" validity coefficients. Several strategies were suggested about how to deal with this problem, including collapsing across jobs, synthetic validity, and validity generalization. It is likely that further technical advancements will be made soon in this area and available to the practitioner.

- *Content validity, work samples, and assessment-center approaches.* The legal and psychological research literature concerning these three related strategies was reviewed. It appears as if all three currently meet court approval. The research data indicate relatively less adverse impact than traditional paper-and-pencil methods of selection, and the methods are reasonably valid for both minority-and majority-group members. We predict greater use of these methods and validation strategy in the future.

- *Culture-fair tests.* The rationale behind the development of culture-fair tests was reviewed as well as the research evidence concerning these tests. It appears as if the search for culture-fair tests is illusory. Data indicate an even greater adverse impact using these tests, with no substantial increase in validity.

- *Test bias against the elderly and females.* We provided a review of the existing literature concerning possible test unfairness to older employees. While there were some indications that test bias may be present, more data are needed. Problems with interest inventories were reviewed with regard to their possible discriminatory effects against females. It was noted that no court cases have yet been brought to bear concerning sex bias in interest inventories and that possible future court cases may involve such challenges.

REFERENCES

Albemarle Paper Company v. *Moody,* 10 FEP 1181 (1975).

American Psychological Association (1985). *Standards for Educational and Psychological Testing.* Washington, D.C.: APA.

Anastasi, A. (1965). *Differential Psychology.* New York: MacMillan.

Arvey, R. D. (1972). Some comments on culture fair tests. *Personnel Psychology* 25: 433–448.

Arvey, R. D., and K. M. Mossholder (1977). A proposed methodology for determining similarities and differences among jobs. *Personnel Psychology* 30: 363–374.

Arvey, R. D.; S. E. Maxwell; and K. M. Mossholder (1979). Even more ideas about methodologies for determining job differences and similarities. *Personnel Psychology* 32: 529–538.

Arvey, R. D., and S. J. Mussio (1973). Test discrimination, job performance and age. *Industrial Gerontology* 16: 22–29.

Arvey, R. D.; E. M. Passino; and J. W. Lounsbury (1977). Job analysis results as influenced by sex of incumbent and sex of analyst. *Journal of Applied Psychology* **62**: 411–416.

Asher, J. J., and J. A. Sciarrino (1974). Realistic work sample tests: A review. *Personnel Psychology* **27**: 519–534.

Bass, A. R., and J. H. Turner (1973). Ethnic group differences in relationships among criteria of job performance. *Journal of Applied Psychology* **57**: 101–109.

Berkman v. *City of New York,* 28 FEP 856 (1982).

Bernardin, H. J., and R. W. Beatty (1984). *Performance Appraisal: Assessing Human Behavior at Work.* Boston: Kent Publishing.

Bigoness, W. J. (1976). Effect of applicant's sex, race and performance on employer's performance ratings: Some additional findings. *Journal of Applied Psychology* **61**: 80–84.

Borman, W. C.; G. P. Hollenbeck; and G. Olivero (1977). Women and men as stockbrokers: a comparison of job approaches. Unpublished paper.

Bray, D. W., and D. L. Grant (1966). The assessment center in the measurement potential for business management. *Psychological Monographs: General and Applied* **80** (17): 53.

Bridgeport Guardians v. *Police Department,* 16 FEP 486 (1977).

Brito v. *Zia Company,* 5 FEP 1207 (1973).

Brugnoli, G. A.; J. E. Campion; and J. A. Basen (1979). Racial bias in the use of work samples for personnel selection. *Journal of Applied Psychology* **64**: 119–123.

Brush, D. H., and L. F. Schoenfeldt (1980). Identifying managerial potential: An alternative to assessment centers. *Personnel* **26**: 68–76.

Burney v. *City of Pawtucket,* 34 FEP 1274 (1983).

Byham, W. C. (1970). Assessment centers for spotting future managers. *Harvard Business Review* **48**: 393–395.

Byham, W. C. (1980). *What Do We Know About Assessment Centers?*

Preliminary Report. The Assessment Center Research Group, Pittsburgh, June.

Byham, W. C. (1981). *Dimensions of Managerial Success*. Pittsburgh: Development Dimensions International.

Campbell, J. (1976). Differential response for female and male law students on the Strong-Campbell Interest Inventory: The question of separate sex norms. *Journal of Counseling Psychology* 23: 130–135.

Campbell, J. T.; L. W. Pike; R. L. Flaugher; and M. H. Mahoney (1970). The prediction of supervisor's ratings from aptitude tests using a cross-ethnic cross-validation procedure. *Educational Testing Service*, PR-70-18, October.

Campion, J. E. (1972). Work sampling for personnel selection. *Journal of Applied Psychology* 56: 40–44.

Cascio, W. F., and H. J. Bernardin (1981). Implications of performance appraisal litigation for personnel decisions. *Personnel Psychology* 34: 211–226.

Cascio, W. F., and N. Phillips (1979). Performance testing: A rose among thorns? *Personnel Psychology* 32: 751–766.

Cascio, W. F., and V. Silbey (1979). Utility of the assessment center as a selection device. *Journal of Applied Psychology* 64: 107–118.

Clarenbach, K. F. (1975). *Women's Work: Up from .878*. Report on D.O.T. research project. Madison: University of Wisconsin, January.

Cleary, T. A. (1968). Test bias: Prediction of grades of negro and white students in integrated colleges. *Journal of Applied Psychology* 5: 115–124.

Cleveland, J. N., and F. J. Landy (1981). The influence of rater and ratee age on two performance judgments. *Personnel Psychology* 34: 19–29.

——— (1983). The effects of person and job stereotypes on two personnel decisions. *Journal of Applied Psychology* 68: 609–619.

Cohen, B.; J. L. Moses; and W. C. Byham (1974). The validity of assessment centers: A literature review. Monograph II. Pittsburgh: Development Dimensions Press.

Cohen, S. L. (1980a). Validity and assessment center technology: One and the same? *Human Resource Management* 19(4): 2–11.

Cohen, S. L. (1980b). The bottom line on assessment center technology. *Personnel Administrator* 25(2): 50–55.

Contreras v. *City of Los Angeles*, 17 FEP 80 (1978).

Cox, J. A., and J. D. Krumboltz (1958). Racial bias in ratings of basic airman. *Sociometry* 21: 292–299.

DeJung, J. E., and H. Kaplan (1962). Some differential effects of race of rater and ratee on early peer ratings of combat aptitude. *Journal of Applied Psychology* 46: 370–374.

Detroit Police Officers Association v. *Young*, 16 FEP 51007 (1978).

Diamond, E. G. (ed.) (1975). *Issues of Sex Bias in Career Interest Measurement.* Department of Health, Education and Welfare, National Institute of Education, Spring.

Division of Industrial-Organizational Psychology, American Psychological Association (1975). *Principles for the Validation and Use of Personnel Selection Procedures.* Dayton, OH: APA.

Dreher, G. F., and P. R. Sackett (1981). Some problems with applying content validity evidence to assessment center procedures. *Academy of Management Review* 6: 551–560.

Dunnette, M. D. (1972). *Validity Study Results for Jobs Relevant to the Petroleum Refining Industry.* Washington, D.C.: American Petroleum Institute.

Dunnette, M. D.; P. Wernimont; and N. Abrahams (1964). Further research on vocational interest differences among several types of engineers. *Personnel and Guidance Journal* 42: 484–493.

Easley v. *Anheuser Busch, Inc.*, 34 FEP 380 (1983).

EEOC v. *Sandia Corp.*, 23 FEP 810 (1980).

Faley, R. H., and L. S. Kleiman (1985). The regulation of employment-related age discrimination in the United States: Implications for other developed countries. *Equal Opportunities International* 4: 14–19.

Faley, R. H.; L. S. Kleiman; and M. L. Lengnick-Hall (1984). Age discrimination and personnel psychology: A review and synthesis of the legal literature with implications for future research. *Personnel Psychology* 37: 327–350.

Ferris, G. R.; V. L. Yates; D. C. Gilmore; and K. M. Rowland (1985). The influence of subordinate age on performance ratings and causal attributions. *Personnel Psychology* 38: 545–557.

Field, H. S., and W. H. Holley (1982). The relationship of performance appraisal system characteristics to verdicts in selected employment discrimination cases. *Academy of Management Journal* 25: 392–406.

Firefighters Institute v. *City of St. Louis,* 14 FEP 1486 (1977).

Ford, J. K.; K. Kraiger; and S. L. Schechtman (1986). Study of race effects in objective indices and subjective evaluations of performance: A meta-analysis of performance criteria. *Psychological Bulletin* 99: 330–337.

Gaugler, B. B.; D. B. Rosenthal; G. C. Thornton III; and C. Bentson (1987). Meta-analysis of assessment center validity. *Journal of Applied Psychology* 72: 493–511.

Ghiselli, E. E. (1966). *The Validity of Occupational Aptitude Testing.* New York: Wiley.

Giniger, S.; A. Dispenzieri; and J. Eisenberg (1983). Age, experience, and performance on speed and skill jobs in an applied setting. *Journal of Applied Psychology* 68: 469–475.

Gottfredson, G. D. (1976). A note on sexist wording in interest measurement. *Measurement and Evaluation in Guidance* 8: 221–223.

Gottfredson, G. D.; J. L. Holland; and L. S. Gottfredson (1975). The relation of vocational aspirations and assessments to employment reality. *Journal of Vocational Behavior* 7: 135–148.

Guardians Association v. *Civil Service Commission of the City of New York,* 23 FEP 677 (1980).

Guion, R. M. (1978). Scoring of content domain samples: The problem of fairness. *Journal of Applied Psychology* 63: 499–506.

—— (1965). Synthetic validity in a small company: A demonstration. *Personnel Psychology* 18: 49–65.

Haefner, J. E. (1977). Sources of discrimination among employees: a survey investigation. *Journal of Applied Psychology* 62: 265–270.

Hagen, R. L., and A. Kahn (1975). Discrimination against competent women. *Journal of Applied Social Psychology* 5: 362–376.

Hall, F. S., and D. T. Hall (1976). Effects of job incumbent's race and sex on evaluations of managerial performance. *Academy of Management Journal* 19: 476–481.

Hall, H. L. An evaluation of the upward mobility assessment center for the Bureau of Engraving and Printing (TM76-6). Washington, D.C.: U.S. Civil Service Commission, July.

Hamner, W. C.; J. S. Kim; L. Baird; and W. J. Bigoness (1974). Race and sex as determinants of ratings by potential employers in a simulated work-sampling task. *Journal of Applied Psychology* 59: 705–711.

Hansen, J. C. (1976). Exploring new directions for Strong-Campbell Interest Inventory occupational scale construction. *Journal of Vocational Behavior* 9: 147–160.

Hanson, G. R., and J. Rayman (1976). Validity of sex-balanced interest inventory scales. *Journal of Vocational Behavior* 9: 279–291.

Harvey, R. J. (1986). Quantitative approaches to job classification: A review and critique. *Personnel Psychology* 39: 267–290.

Heneman, H. G. III (1974). Age discrimination and employment testing. *Industrial Gerontology* 17: 65–71.

Higgins, C., and C. H. Silvers (1958). A comparison of Stanford-Binet and colored raven progressive matrices IQ for children with low socioeconomic status. *Journal of Consulting Psychology* 22: 565–568.

Huck, J. R. (1973). Assessment centers: A review of the external and internal validities. *Personnel Psychology* 26: 191–212.

Huck, J. R., and D. W. Bray (1976). Management assessment center evaluations and subsequent job performance of white and black females. *Personnel Psychology* 29: 13–30.

Hunter, J. E. (1975). The statistical detection of content bias in achievement tests. Paper presented at the National Institute for Education Invitational Conference on Test Bias in Achievement Tests, Annapolis, MD.

Hunter, J. E., and R. F. Hunter (1984). Validity and utility of alternative predictors of job performance. *Psychological Bulletin* 96: 72–98.

I.M.A.G.E. v. *Bailor,* 28 FEP 770 (1981).

Jackson v. *Nassau County Civil Service,* 14 FEP 780 (1976).

James, L. R.; R. G. Demaree; and S. A. Mulaik (1986). A note on validity generalization procedures. *Journal of Applied Psychology* 71: 440–450.

James v. *Stockham Valves and Fittings,* 15 FEP 827 (1977).

Kirkland v. *New York Department of Correctional Services,* 7 FEP 700 (1974).

Kleiman, L. S., and R. S. Durham (1981). Performance appraisal, promotion, and the courts: A critical review. *Personnel Psychology* 34: 103–121.

Kleiman, L. S., and R. H. Faley (1978). Assessing content validity: Standards set by the court. *Personnel Psychology* 31: 701–713.

Klimoski, R. J., and W. J. Strickland (1977). Assessment centers: Valid or merely prescient? *Personnel Psychology* 30: 353–361.

Klimoski, R. J., and W. J. Strickland (1981). The comparative view of assessment centers. Unpublished manuscript, Department of Psychology, Ohio State University.

Matarazzo, J. D., and A. M. Wiens (1977). Black intelligence test of cultural homogeneity and Wechsler Adult Intelligence Scale scores of black and white police applicants. *Journal of Applied Psychology* 62: 57–63.

McClelland, D. (1973). Testing for competence rather than for intelligence. *American Psychologist* 28: 1–14.

Meier, E. L., and E. Kerr (1976). Capabilities of middle-aged and older workers: A survey of the literature. *Industrial Gerontology*, Summer, 147–156.

Mobley, W. H., and R. S. Ramsay (1973). Hierarchical clustering on the basis of inter-job similarity as a tool in validity generalizations. *Personnel Psychology* **26**: 213–226.

Moore, C. L.; J. F. MacNaughton; and H. G. Osburn (1969). Ethnic differences within an industrial selection battery. *Personnel Psychology* **22**: 473–482.

Moses, J., and V. E. Boehm (1975). Relationship of assessment center performance to management progress of women. *Journal of Applied Psychology* **60**: 527–529.

Mossholder, K., and R. D. Arvey (1984). Synthetic validity: A conceptual and comparative review. *Journal of Applied Psychology* **69**: 322–333.

Neidig, R. D.; J. C. Martin; and R. E. Yates (1978). The FBI's Management Aptitude Program Assessment Center: Research Report No. 1 (TM78-3). Washington, D.C.: Applied Psychology Section, Personnel Research and Development Center, U.S. Civil Service Commission, April.

Nieva, V. F., and B. A. Gutek (1980). Sex effects on evaluation. *Academy of Management Review* **5**: 267–276.

Norton, S. D. (1977). The empirical and content validity of assessment centers vs. traditional methods for predicting managerial success. *Academy of Management Review* **2**: 442–453.

Norton, S. D.; D. P. Gustafson; and C. E. Foster (1977). Assessment for management potential: Scale design and development, training effects and rater/ratee sex effects. *Academy of Management Journal* **20**: 117–131.

Nunnaly, J. (1967). *Psychometric Theory*. New York: McGraw-Hill.

O'Leary, L. R. (1973). Fair employment, sound psychometric practice and reality: A dilemma and a partial solution. *American Psychologist* **28**: 147–149.

Parker, T. C. (1980). Assessment Centers: A statistical study. *Personnel Administrator* **25**: 65–67.

Pearlman, K.; F. L. Schmidt; and J. E. Hunter (1980). Validity generalization results for tests used to predict job proficiency and training success in clerical occupations. *Journal of Applied Psychology* 65: 373–406.

Pegues v. *Mississippi State Employment Services,* 22 FEP 392 (1980).

Peters, L.; E. J. O'Connor; J. Weekley; A. Pooyan; B. Frank; and B. Erenkrantz (1984). Sex bias and managerial evaluations: A replication and extension. *Journal of Applied Psychology* 69: 349–352.

Pritchard, R. D.; S. E. Maxwell; and W. C. Jordan (1984). Interpreting relationships between age and promotion in age-discrimination cases. *Journal of Applied Psychology* 69: 199–206.

Reilly, R. R., and G. T. Chao (1982). Validity and fairness of some alternative employee selection procedures. *Personnel Psychology* 35: 1–62.

Rhodes, S. R. (1983). Age-related differences in work attitudes and behavior: A review and conceptual analysis. *Psychological Bulletin* 93: 328–367.

Rowen v. *General Motors,* 4 FEP 445 (1972).

Sackett, P. (1987). Assessment centers and content validity: Some neglected issues. *Personnel Psychology* 40: 13–25.

Sackett, P. R., N. Schmitt; M. L. Tenopyr; J. Kehoe; and S. Zedeck (1985). Commentary on forty questions about validity generalization and meta-analysis. *Personnel Psychology* 38: 697–798.

Scales, R., Jr. (1973). *Scales Inner City Intelligence Test.* Wilmington, NC: Scales.

Schmidt, F. L.; A. L. Greenthal; J. G. Berner; J. E. Hunter; and F. M. Seaton (1977). Job sample vs. pencil-and-paper trades and technical tests: Adverse impact and examinee attitudes. *Personnel Psychology* 30: 187–198.

Schmidt, F. L., and J. E. Hunter (1977). Development of a general solution to the problem of validity generalization. *Journal of Applied Psychology* 62: 529–540.

Schmidt, F. L., and J. E. Hunter (1984). A within setting test of the situational specificity hypothesis in personnel selection. *Personnel Psychology* 37: 317–326.

Schmidt, F. L.; J. E. Hunter; and K. Pearlman (1981). Task differences as moderators of aptitude test validity in selection: A red herring. *Journal of Applied Psychology* 66: 166–185.

Schmidt, F. L.; J. E. Hunter; K. Perlman; and H. Rothstein Hirsh (1985). Forty questions about validity generalization and meta-analysis. *Personnel Psychology* 38: 697–798.

Schmidt, F. L.; J. E. Hunter; K. Pearlman; and G. S. Shane (1979). Further tests of the Schmidt-Hunter Bayesian validity generalization procedure. *Personnel Psychology* 32: 257–281.

Schmidt, F. L.; J. E. Hunter; and V. W. Urry (1976). Statistical power in criterion-related validation studies. *Journal of Applied Psychology* 61: 473–485.

Schmidt, F. L., and R. H. Johnson (1973). Effect of race on peer ratings in an industrial situation. *Journal of Applied Psychology* 57: 237–241.

Schmitt, N.; R. Z. Gooding; R. D. Noe; and M. Kirsch (1984). Metanalyses of validity studies published between 1964 and 1982 and the investigation of study characteristics. *Personnel Psychology* 37: 407–422.

Schmidtt, N., and T. E. Hill (1977). Sex and race composition of assessment center groups as a determinant of peer and assessor ratings. *Journal of Applied Psychology* 62: 261–264.

Schneider, B. (1983). Interactional psychology and organizational behavior. In L. L. Cummings and B. L. Staw (eds.), *Research in Organizational Behavior.* Greenwich, Conn.: JAI Press.

Schoenfeldt, L. F.; B. B. Schoenfeldt; S. R. Acker; and M. R. Perlson (1976). Content validity revisited: The development of a content-oriented test of industrial reading. *Journal of Applied Psychology* 61: 581–588.

Schwab, D. P., and H. G. Heneman III (1978). Age stereotyping in performance appraisal. *Journal of Applied Psychology* 63: 573–578.

Selkow, P. (1984). *Assessing Sex Bias in Testing.* Westport, Conn.: Greenwood Press.

Sharf, J. C. (1976). Legal and technical considerations in the use of content validity. Paper presented at the Second Annual Conference on Equal Employment Opportunity Law, October 28.

Society for Industrial-Organizational Psychology, American Psychological Association (1987). *Principles for the Validation and Use of Personnel Selection Procedures.* College Park, MD: APA.

Statsny v. *Southern Bell Telephone and Telegraph Co.,* 23 FEP 631 (1978).

Stutzman, T. M. (1983). Within classification job differences. *Personnel Psychology* 36: 503–516.

Tenopyr, M. L. (1967). Race and socio-economic status as moderators predicting machine-shop training success. Paper presented at symposium at American Psychological Association Convention, Washington, D.C., September.

Terborg, J. P., and D. R. Ilgen (1975). A theoretical approach to sex discrimination in traditionally masculine occupations. *Organizational Behavior and Human Performance* 13: 352–376.

Thornton, G. C., and W. C. Byham (1982). *Assessment Centers and Managerial Performance.* New York: Academic Press.

U.S. v. *City of Chicago,* 11 FEP 417 (1976).

United States v. *City of Chicago,* 16 FEP 908 (1978).

United States v. *City of St. Louis,* 14 FEP 1473 (1976).

Vulcan Society Fire Department, Inc. v. *Civil Service of the City of New York,* 6 FEP 1045 (1973).

Wade v. *Mississippi Cooperative Extension Service,* 7 FEP 282 (1974), 12 FEP 1041 (1976).

Waldman, D. A., and B. J. Avolio (1986). A meta-analysis of age differences in job performance. *Journal of Applied Psychology* 71, 33–38.

Weiner, B. (1972). From each according to his abilities: The role of effort in a moral society. Paper presented at the 80th annual convention of the American Psychological Association, Honolulu, Hawaii, September.

Williams, R. L. (1975). Black intelligence test of cultural homogeneity: Manual of directions. (Available from Robert L. Williams, Williams & Associates, Inc., 6374 Delmar Boulevard, St. Louis, Missouri 63130).

Discrimination in the Employment Interview

7

Perhaps no other selection technique is used as frequently in business as the personal interview. It is almost unthinkable to many that an applicant could gain entry into an organization without an interview of some sort. Many organizations are dropping the use of employment tests and beginning to rely predominantly on the interview process for evaluating job candidates. For example, an article in the *Wall Street Journal* (September 5, 1975) indicated that: "The use of testing is declining sharply in American business for reasons that have very little to do with its accuracy. . . . Many employers feel that the guidelines applied to testing are so rigorous, expensive, and time-consuming that they have decided to chuck it all and go back to the seat of the pants approach to hiring and promotion."

The interview process is particularly vulnerable to subjective biases, prejudices, and stereotypes on the part of interviewers; that is, interviewers may evaluate minority-group members lower than nonminority candidates, even when the candidates are similarly qualified. As a consequence, it is open to challenge from civil rights litigants. What many employers fail to realize is that the interview is classified as a "test" in the *Uniform Guidelines* and, as such, is subject to the same scrutiny as traditional pencil-and-paper employment tests.

SOURCES OF DIFFERENTIAL INTERVIEWEE EVALUATIONS

Prior to examining case law and research evidence concerning the interview and possible discrimination, it is a good idea to review the possible mechanisms behind differential evaluations given to interviewees. There are several factors that might contribute to bias: (1) factors inherent in the interview itself, (2) stereotyping, and (3) differential behavior of interviewees.

Factors Inherent in the Interview

There is considerable evidence that the interview is neither a reliable nor a valid selection device. Several reviews of research on the interview (Mayfield, 1964; Ulrich and Trumbo, 1965; Wagner, 1949; Wright, 1969; Arvey and Campion, 1982) cast serious doubt on the interview as a process yielding reliable decisions to forecast job behavior and performance. Schmitt (1976) reviewed research on the interview and noted that a large number of factors influence interview decisions. Some of the researchers have found, for example, the following:

1. Interviewers tend to give insufficient weight to favorable information on job candidates. Springbett (in Webster, 1964) found that as little as one unfavorable bit of information on a candidate led to rejection 90 percent of the time for candidates taking an Army personnel interview. Similar findings in other studies indicate that the interview is predominantly a search for reasons to reject candidates.

2. Decisions in the interview occur very early. One study (Webster, 1964) indicated that most personnel interviewers in their sample made their decisions after just 4 minutes of a 15-minute interview.

3. Judgments by interviewers are too often based on superficial characteristics that are unrelated to subsequent job success (Dipboye and Wiley, 1975). Obviously, such variables as sex, race, and age may be used to make the decisions.

4. Interviewers form stereotypes concerning the requisite characteristics necessary for adequate job performance and attempt to "match" the character of job candidates to those perceived characteristics.

To the extent that interviewers have inaccurate knowledge of what is needed in the job or have inaccurate impressions of the characteristics of the candidates, their decisions will also tend to be inaccurate (Webster, 1964).

Stereotyping

Interview decisions are generally subjective in nature, and are thus susceptible to the influence of stereotypes. However, as Brigham (1971) has indicated, there is a good deal of confusion concerning the precise definition of stereotypes and their correlates. Although a widely accepted definition of stereotypes does not exist (Miller, 1982; Hamilton, 1981), most definitions imply that the interview involves making judgments about people on the basis of their group membership (e.g., race, sex, age). When we stereotype an individual, we ascribe to that individual a number of traits based on the traits associated with the group of which he or she is a member. Thus, stereotyping involves basically two processes:

1. The formation of impressions and trait descriptions of particular groups.

2. The assignment of these traits to a particular individual once his or her membership in that group is known. An obvious example of this process is the rejection of a female candidate for the job of "ship foreman" by a male interviewer, because his impression is that women in general are emotional, excitable, and too talkative for the job.

Stereotypical characteristics commonly associated with men and women are shown in Table 7.1. Generally, males are perceived as more aggressive and independent than women, and women are seen as more gentle and nurturant. How these perceptions could possibly influence the decisions made in interviews was illustrated in a study by Schein (1973). She asked 300 male managers to indicate which of 92 adjectives best describe (1) women in general, (2) men in general, or (3) successful middle managers. (Each manager described only one of these three subgroups.)

She found that the relationship between the average description of the middle manager and the average description of the male was much higher ($r = .62$) than between the managers and the females ($r = .06$). In fact, on 60 of the 92 items, the descriptions of the managers were

Table 7.1
Stereotypical characteristics commonly associated
with males and females.

MALES	FEMALES
Adventurous	Appearance-oriented
Aggressive	Artistic
Blunt	Compassionate
Competitive	Dependent
Confident	Emotional, excitable
Crude	Gentle
Decisive	Humanitarian
Dominant	Neat
Enterprising	Needing security
Independent	Passive
Intelligent	Sensitive
Logical	Submissive
Objective	Sympathetic
Rough	Talkative
Worldly	Tender

Reprinted by permission of the Society for The Psychological
Study of Social Issues.

more similar to men than to the descriptions given to women. These
findings suggest that even before an interview or any formal selection
process has begun, the perceived similarity between the characteristics of
successful middle managers and men in general increases the probability
of a male, rather than a female, being selected (or promoted) to a managerial position. These results were replicated with a group of 167 female
managers (Schein, 1975). In this study, 167 female middle managers rated
women in general, men in general, or successful middle managers on the
same 92 adjectives. Like the male managers in the previous study, the
female managers provided descriptions of successful middle managers that
were far more similar to men than to women. The results suggest that
female managers are as likely as males to accept a stereotypical male characteristic as the basis for success in management.

   These two findings confirm the frequent observation that the model
of a successful manager is aggressive, competitive, and firm. The sex typing of management as a male occupation, requiring male traits, poses a

major barrier to women who would otherwise qualify for positions of leadership (Dipboye, 1975).

These kinds of stereotypes operate not only to influence the initial reactions of interviewers, but also to shape their expectations of the job candidates during the interview. For example, interviewers may evaluate female job candidates on a different set of criteria—e.g., beauty, typing skills, or poise—than male candidates. A study by Cecil, Paul, and Olins (1973) attempted to identify the qualities perceived to be important for male and female applicants for the same job. Over 100 subjects indicated the importance of each of 50 variables (e.g., pleasant voice, aggressiveness) to interviewers evaluating either a male or female job candidate. The following variables were significantly more important when *males* were being evaluated:

- Ability to change one's mind on an issue
- Ability to persuade
- Ability to withstand a great deal of pressure
- Exceptional motivation
- Aggressiveness

For *females,* on the other hand, the following variables were considered more important:

- Pleasant voice
- Excellent clerical skills
- High school graduate
- Excellent computational skills
- Immaculate appearance
- Ability to express self well.

The standards used to evaluate the females basically involved clerical and cosmetic concerns, where the standards for males had aggressive and persuasive dimensions.

Besides these stereotypical traits, "myths" abound concerning women which may also serve to influence an interviewer's judgment. In a study conducted in 1975 by Dipboye, some of these widely held beliefs included the following:

- American women work primarily for "pin money."
- Women are less concerned than men with advancement and promotion on the job.
- Women are more concerned with socio-technical aspects of their jobs.
- Women are more content than men with intellectually undemanding jobs.

Although some of the research reported above may seem dated, more recent articles suggest that progress in dispelling sexual myths has moved slowly (e.g., see articles in Stead, 1985). What seems to have changed most is the nature of the sexual myths that plague women in the workplace. While in the past, sexual myths mitigated against women entering the business world (e.g., "women belong in the home and not in the workplace"), today's sexual myths mitigate more so against women making progress in the workplace (e.g., "it is better to select a male for a job that involves extensive travel since male allegiance is to the job and female allegiance is to family and home").

Several research studies have also shown that many of the stereotypes associated with women are false. Considerable overlapping of the distribution of males and females on any trait make statements concerning *all* or *most* women clearly erroneous. For example, Fig. 7.1 presents two hypothetical distributions for males and females on the trait "dominance." As may be seen from this figure, while there may be a difference between the two averages (which might reach statistical significance), the two distributions overlap considerably. There are a number of females

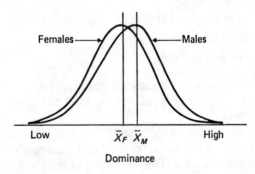

Fig. 7.1 *Illustration of distribution overlap.*

whose scores exceed the average score of males. Similarly, there are a number of males who score lower than the average female on this trait.

In general, there are many similarities between males and females on the majority of psychological variables (Dipboye, 1975; Crowely *et al.*, 1973; Rosen and Jerdee, 1976a). Likewise, considerable overlapping occurs with regard to distributions based on white and black groups, old and young employees, and other stereotyped groups.

Stereotypes are also associated, obviously, with race. For example, Karlins, Coffman, and Walters (1969) compared the racial stereotypes of undergraduate students in 1967 with stereotypes reported in 1933 and 1951. Subjects in all three studies indicated those traits thought to be typical of blacks. Table 7.2 presents the results of the study where the percentage of subjects checking the various traits is indicated. While these

Table 7.2
Stereotyping of blacks over 25-year period.

TRAIT	PERCENT CHECKING TRAIT		
	1933	1951	1967
Superstitious	84	41	13
Lazy	75	31	26
Happy-go-lucky	38	17	27
Ignorant	38	24	11
Musical	26	33	47
Ostentatious	26	11	25
Very religious	24	17	8
Stupid	22	10	4
Physically dirty	17	—	3
Naive	14	—	4
Slovenly	13	—	5
Unreliable	12	—	6
Pleasure-loving	—	19	26
Sensitive	—	—	17
Gregarious	—	—	17
Talkative	—	—	14
Imitative	—	—	13

From M. Karlins, T. L. Coffman, and G. Walters (1969). Copyright 1969 by the American Psychological Association. Reprinted by permission of the author.

data indicate a consistent trend over the 25-year period to characterize blacks more favorably, there was still a considerable amount of stereotyping that existed. More than 25 percent of a mid-1960s sample of college students still described blacks as lazy, superstitious, musical, ostentatious, and pleasure-loving. Considerably more information concerning the nature of racial and ethnic stereotypes may be found in Jones (1972) and Brigham (1971). Moreover, several stereotypes that have plagued blacks in the workplace probably have changed. However, the pattern of change in black stereotypes probably is similar to that noted above associated with sexual stereotyping.

The nature of age stereotypes and how they relate to the job has also received some research attention. Rosen and Jerdee (1976c) asked over 100 business students and realtors to imagine that they were going to meet two individuals for the first time and that the only information they had about the two people is that one was 30 years old and the other 60. The participants in the study then considered 65 characteristics and indicated the degree to which each characteristic described the average 60-year-old male and the average 30-year-old male. Significant differences were found on several characteristics and are summarized below:

30-year-old male described as significantly:	60-year-old male described as significantly:
More productive, efficient, motivated	More accident-prone
More capable of working under pressure	More rigid and dogmatic
More ambitious, eager, and future-oriented	
More receptive to new ideas, adaptable, and versatile	

Clearly many of the traits and characteristics ascribed to the older group are unfavorable.* Moreover, it seems that black students hold even more unfavorable stereotypes about older workers than do white students (Crew, 1984). Rosen and Jerdee (1976a) note that these stereotypes are

---

* Not all clichés used in connection with older individuals are negative (e.g., "aging like fine wine," "the wisdom of age").

inconsistent with objective research findings and changes associated with aging. For example some data indicate that older workers are *better* accident risks than younger workers (McCormick and Tiffin, 1974). Shaie (1974) concluded that age differences in intellectual performance, while statistically significant, may be so small as to have virtually no practical significance.

Stereotypes, however, are not always "bad." They provide us with ways in which to order our lives and give a sense of predictablity to the world. Katz (1960) has delineated several useful functions that stereotypes fulfill for different people:

1. *Instrumental function*—People hold particular attributes and stereotypes about others (regardless of whether they are accurate), if holding these viewpoints is associated with gaining rewards or avoiding punishment. For example, holding an opinion that a "wife's work is in the home" also implies that males should not have to cook or do housework.

2. *Ego-defense function*—Occasionally, stereotypes are held because of their protective security. Some men who are competing for jobs in the marketplace may find women, especially competent women who are also looking for jobs, threatening. One study (Bowman, Worthy, and Greyer, 1965) showed that young male executives and managers tended to hold negative attitudes toward female executives. Perhaps they were trying to protect their own self-confidence by adopting those opinions.

3. *Value-expressive function*—In this instance, the expression of a stereotype may reflect a cherished value. We have all grown up in a particular culture, where our socialization pattern has emphasized the differences between boys and girls, masculine and feminine, and what is considered appropriate sex-role behavior. In short, these stereotypes are a product of a deep-rooted cultural history with no maliciousness intended by individuals who hold these opinions and values.

4. *Order functions*—Stereotypes provide a means by which we make sense out of everyday life. They provide an "ordered, more or less consistent picture of the world, to which our habits, our tasks, our capacities, our comforts, and our hopes have adjusted themselves" (Lippman, 1922, p. 81).

To sum up, the specific nature of stereotypes may well influence interviewer evaluation of job candidates. To the extent that the stereotypes are basically negative, deviate from the perception of what is needed for the job, or translate into different expectations and standards to be evaluated for minority-group members, then stereotypes may well have the effect of lowering the evaluations of interviewers, even when the candidates are equally qualified for the job.

Terborg (1977) has sounded a warning against the too-quick acceptance of the notion that the pervasive effects of stereotypes explain or account for all differences in treatment between men and women managers. One alternative he poses is that many women are truly not yet qualified for managerial positions. "This is not meant to suggest that women lack potential for the job, but that the cumulative effects of past discrimination have prevented women from gaining necessary skills and experience" (p. 649).

Differential Behavior of Interviewees

One additional explanation for different evaluations of minority-group candidates as a result of interviews is that minority applicants may behave in a manner that is unfamiliar to interviewers. Hall (1966) specifically argues that subcultural differences in nonverbal behavior have resulted in whites misreading black applicants and in blacks, therefore, failing to get jobs. That is, it is possible that blacks emit verbal and nonverbal behavior (e.g., "jive talk") that is acceptable or even desirable in their subculture, but this same behavior may be misinterpreted or confused by a white interviewer.

An interesting study was conducted in this regard by Fugita, Wexley, and Hillery (1974). Twenty white and 20 black female undergraduate students were asked to participate in an employment interview. Two black and two white males acted as interviewers and eight questions were asked of the interviewees. Results of the study showed that the black interviewees maintained significantly less eye contact with both white and black interviewers. The least amount of visual interaction occurred when a black interviewee was interviewed by a black. Black interviewers were also given shorter glances than were given white interviewers by both black and white interviewees. In sum, the race of the interviewee and the interviewer appeared to be a significant factor in the kind and amount of behavior that occurred during the interview. What would have also been of great interest is whether these differences in behavior also produced differences in evaluations by the interviewers.

It is also possible that women, older workers, and handicapped individuals also *differ* in their reactions while taking interviews which could contribute to lower evaluations. For example, older job candidates may be more thoughtful and cautious in their interview responses than younger candidates.

An interesting review of male and female speech patterns (Hass, 1979) revealed that "men may be more loquacious and directive; . . . talk more about sports, money, and business; and more frequently refer to time, space, quantity, destructive action, perceptual attributes, physical movements, and objects. Women are often more supportive, polite, and expressive, and they talk more about home and family, and use more words implying feeling, evaluation, interpretation, and psychological state" (p. 616). Such differences in verbal behavior between males and females within the context of the interview could obviously influence interviewer judgments.

LEGAL ASPECTS: THE INTERVIEW

To a certain extent, the litigation involving the interview and the performance appraisal (see Chapter 5) overlaps, has common authorities, and is difficult to separate. Both decision-making processes are considered "subjective" in the sense that they involve the collecting, processing, and integration of information by humans—one in the form of interviews and the other usually in the form of an immediate supervisor. Also, there are no quantitative scores which automatically emerge from an interview or appraisal (although the judgments of an interviewer and supervisor may be quantified and often are). This is in contrast to more "objective" standards (such as psychological test scores and height and weight requirements) used in making employment decisions. Essentially, no judgmental factors are involved at arriving at these kinds of "scores." Although the interview is widely recognized as an inherently more subjective employment selection device, the courts have expressly declined to suggest that an employer may not properly include interviews in its employment process (e.g., *Hamilton* v. *General Motors Corp* [1979]). Thus the use of informal and unscored selection procedures such as interviews have not been found to be *automatically* unlawful.* However, the courts have also been quick to point out that reliance on subjective selection procedures is likely to encourage discrimination, or at least offer a convenient pretext for it, leaving ample room for bias to operate (e.g., *Stallings* v. *Container Corp.* [1977] or *EEOC* v. *Detroit Edison* [1975].

A frequently cited case in litigation involving interviews is *Rowe* v. *General Motors* (1972). This case, reviewed in Chapter 6, involved a foreman's subjective evaluation of an employee for promotional purposes. Because there were no written guidelines for the promotional qualifications and the existing standards were vague, the court ruled against the appraisal system.

In a 1971 decision, the EEOC (EEOC Decision No. 72-0703, 1971) ruled that an employer's decision not to hire a black woman because of her "poor attitude" during an interview was in violation of Title VII. In this administrative ruling, the EEOC cited a number of court decisions (including *Rowe* v. *General Motors*) in establishing that, if discriminatory impact of a hiring system is shown, "it is essential that the system be objective in nature and be such as to permit review."

However, unless adverse impact is established, the courts (as suggested in *Hamilton* and noted in *Rogers*) will not automatically rule against the use of even very subjective employment procedures. For example, in *Hester* v. *Southern Railway Company* (1974), a black female applicant was denied a clerical job partly as a result of the interview process. The district court ruled that adverse impact had been demonstrated and that the interviewing procedure was faulty because of its subjective nature and because it was based on "no formal guidelines, standards and instructions." The court of appeals, however, overturned the decision because it could not find clear proof that these selection procedures (tests, interviews, etc.) had resulted in adverse impact even though they were subjective in nature.

Another case involved a court decision that struck down an interview used in hiring teachers which had adverse impact. In *United States* v. *Hazelwood School District* (1976), the court noted that the criteria for

---

* As noted in *Rogers* v. *International Paper Co.* (1975), "Subjective criteria are not to be condemned as unlawful per se, for in all fairness to applicants and employers alike, decisions about hiring and promotion in supervisory and managerial jobs cannot realistically be made using objective standards alone."

hiring used in the interview process were similar to the vague criteria used in *Rowe* v. *General Motors*. It is instructive to read what the court said in this instance:

> *Principals are free to give whatever weight they desire to subjective factors in making their hiring decisions. Indeed, one principal testified that interviewing an applicant was "like dating a girl, some of them impress you, some of them don't . . . " No evidence was presented which would indicate that any two principals apply the same criteria—objective or subjective—to evaluate applicants.*

In another case, *King* v. *New Hampshire Department of Resources and Economic Development* (1977), the court indicated that questions asked during the interview may be used to help establish inferentially discriminatory intent (i.e., disparate treatment). In this case, the court of appeals upheld a lower court decision that the questions put to a female applicant had discriminatory intent since they did not relate to a *bona fide* occupational qualification. A woman applying for a job with the meter patrol was asked during her interview whether she could wield a sledgehammer, had any construction experience, or could "run somebody in." None of these queries, the judge noted, had anything to do with the job in question.

Weiner v. *County of Oakland* (1976) also dealt with the kinds of questions asked in the interview and their possible bias. Mrs. Weiner applied for the position of "Intermediate Planner" and was given an oral interview. While Mrs. Weiner was ranked third on the list of eligible applicants, four men were hired to fill the available positions. As grounds for not hiring Mrs. Weiner, the county was only able to suggest some doubt about the flexibility of her approach to planning.

The court ruled that Mrs. Weiner had made out a *prima facie* case of sex discrimination. She was able to demonstrate that she was a woman rejected in favor of men no better qualified than she and that Oakland County continued to seek applications from persons of her qualifications after her rejection.

At this point, the burden of persuasion shifted to the county to establish that it had valid business requirements justifying its conduct. The county apparently attempted to defend the use of the interview by asserting that the decision reached was based on subjective evaluations made during the interview which were in no way the product of sex discrimination.

The court, however, reviewed the kinds of questions asked of Mrs. Weiner and found that they were suggestive of bias against women. Questions such as the following were asked: Does your husband approve of your working? Will your family suffer if you are not home to prepare dinner? Are you able to work compatibly with young, aggressive men? The court ruled that these kinds of questions during the interview, along with other facts, were sufficient to substantiate the charge of discrimination, and awarded her back pay.

It is obvious from these cases that organizations might have a difficult time demonstrating that the interview process is valid. In *Harless* v. *Duck* (1977), however, an organization was able to provide sufficient evidence to the court regarding the interview to survive a challenge. In this case, a woman brought a class-action suit against a midwestern police department charging discrimination in hiring because of sex. The department used three testing devices to make hiring decisions: (1) a written mental abilities test (which was not challenged), (2) a physical agility test (to be reviewed in a later chapter), and (3) a structured oral interview. The interview consisted of approximately 30 questions posed to each candidate apparently by a team of interviewers. The questions were designed to determine an "applicant's communication skills, decision-making and problem-solving skills, and reactions to stress situations." It was determined that 43 percent of the females failed the oral interview, compared to 15 percent of the males. After some discussion of proper sample sizes to detect significant differences, the court determined that the discrepancy in pass rates was significant and that the interview did indeed have a discriminatory or adverse effect. In defending the validity of the interview, the organization relied on two sources of evidence:

1. That the oral interview had construct and content validity. The expert witness for the organization testified as follows:

   The structured oral interview portions of the exam, which consisted of hypothetical questions simulating situations likely to be encountered by patrolmen, measured several dimensions identified through the job analysis that would differentiate between persons who would be better patrol officers, if put in a position to perform patrol functions.

Apparently the court did not get into the details of the differences between construct and content validity, nor question the adequacy of the job analysis.

2. A significant relationship between performance in the interview and performance at the police academy was shown. The *Harless* court relied on the decision in *Washington* v. *Davis* (1976, see Chapter 4) to justify the use of training success as a legitimate criterion for validating a selection procedure.

The court found this evidence sufficient in demonstrating the validity of the interview.

In a more recent case (*Reynolds* v. *Sheet Metal Workers,* 1981), the circuit court ruled that the use of subjective interview procedures without formal guidelines and standards was illegal when the procedures resulted in adverse impact. Since blacks seeking admittance to skilled apprenticeship programs were adversely impacted by the unions use of a highly subjective interview, the court ruled for the plaintiffs. The court urged the defendant union to develop evaluation procedures that reflected the specific characteristics needed for the job the apprenticeship program prepared people, and to apply these standards uniformly to all applicants.

It is somewhat surprising that more cases dealing with the interview have not been litigated. It seems apparent that one direction the courts are moving in is to explore in depth the nature of the questions asked and the information elicited in the interviews. In other words, the courts will more fully examine the *content* of the interview. For example, inquiries during the interview that might convey to the applicant the impression that persons in a protected class will be discriminated against will be viewed as discriminatory. In one case, the EEOC and the New York Human Rights Commission concluded that a New York law firm had violated Title VII when interviewers emphasized to female applicants that the firm had only one woman lawyer and that she was assigned to an area of work traditionally performed by women. Thus, "the interviews are conducted in such a manner as to express a preference for men and to discourage women from pursuing employment with respondent firm" (Babcock *et al.*, 1975, p. 380).

In addition, specific questions on application blanks and other preemployment inquiries are being litigated. Managers have expressed a good deal of confusion concerning what they may or may not ask, either on an application form or during an interview. (This will be discussed in more detail in the next chapter.)

Overall, it seems that the use of the interview will have greater legal risk under certain circumstances. These include the following:

1. If particular kinds of questions convey an impression of an underlying discriminatory attitude or intent, the interview is at high risk. That is, reference to "girls" and inquiries to females about non–job-related areas, such as marital status, parenthood, or child care, may be sufficient to convince a court that discriminatory "animus" or intent was operating.

2. If particular kinds of questions operate in such a fashion as to have a differential impact or adverse impact on protected groups, the interview is at risk. For example, questions that revolve around such matters as financial status or place of residence may have an adverse impact on protected minorities and thus need to be specifically validated.

3. If interviews are conducted differently for various candidates, the interview is at risk. That is, if candidates receive differential treatment (e.g., through different questions), then the interview is vulnerable to charges of discrimination.

4. Interviews and the subjective nature of the interview may be more vulnerable when used in entry level or lower level jobs compared to higher level and/or more complex jobs. The courts tend to more readily accept subjective selection procedures when the job or jobs at issue are white collar—particularly professional and supervisory jobs (Waintroob, 1979). It appears that judges tend to believe that upper level jobs are more complex and thus often involve job characteristics that cannot be easily measured objectively (e.g., the ability to get along with others). The legal literature suggests that the criteria reviewed for bias and discrimination changes slightly as one moves up the organizational hierarchy. Courts seem to review not so much the content of the specific instrument used in the selection procedure, but whether the instrument was applied fairly and uniformly in the context of selecting for higher level and complex jobs.

RESEARCH FINDINGS:
DISCRIMINATORY EFFECTS OF THE INTERVIEW

A number of studies have been published reporting the results of investigations concerning whether equally qualified minority-group members receive lower evaluations on the basis of the interview. These studies have generally employed one of three kinds of research strategies:

1. *Resume studies*—In this kind of study, subjects (such as students, managers, or recruiters) are asked to review a series of job resumes to determine the suitability of each candidate for employability and/or the starting wage they might offer. Each resume usually contains information about the subject's educational background and past experience, with a glossy photograph attached. In the typical study the race, sex, age, or handicapped status of the job candidates can be manipulated through the photograph and names which are also printed on each resume. Thus half of the interviewers may be asked to make evaluations concerning, for example, five males and five females. The other half of the interviewers may be asked to evaluate five males and five females, with the only change being that the names and photographs have been switched so that no change whatsoever has occurred with regard to the qualifications of the candidates; the only changes are in sex, race, age, or handicapped status. Obviously, the interviewers are unaware that the resumes they are evaluating may differ from those being evaluated by other interviewers. In addition, some studies have added several other variables such as attractiveness of applicant, or type of job to determine whether these characteristics might interact with minority status and influence the evaluations given. It should also be noted that these "resume" studies obviously do not involve a face-to-face interview, and thus one must infer that any discriminatory effects found in these studies would generalize to actual interview circumstances.

2. *In-basket study*—In this design, participants are asked to *assume the role* of a personnel director or manager working through an in-basket requiring action on a number of items. Typically, each in-basket provides information about the various departments in the organization, information about the members of the organization (e.g., per-

formance-appraisal data and attendance information). Also contained in each participant's in-basket are a series of different types of personnel problems, and the participants are asked to make decisions based on the information given. One of the decisions typically presented is to hire or promote an individual. The problems are written in two or more versions so as to change the sex, race, age, or handicapped status of one or more of the characters in the problem. For example, one participant may receive an in-basket set in which the problem involves whether a male should be hired or promoted, while another participant receives the very same information, but the sex of the person being considered is female.

Additional kinds of problems are presented besides hiring and promotion. For example, training and development opportunities, leaves of absence, job assignments, and so forth are investigated with regard to whether participants make different kinds of decisions based on stereotyped information concerning the individuals depicted in the in-basket materials.

3. *Videotape studies or field experiments*—Less frequently studies employ designs where actual minority and nonminority interviewees are observed by interviewers either in person or by videotape presentations. Typically, the subjects in the study interview (or observe) only one job candidate, who is either a minority or a nonminority job candidate, and evaluate the suitability of the candidate for hiring. Efforts are made to control the content of the interview to ensure that the same questions are asked and similar responses are delivered by the interviewees.

In a 1979 review, Arvey summarized the research literature concerning evidence of bias in the employment interview with regard to blacks, females, the handicapped, and the older applicant. Below we review these earlier findings and provide an update of more recent literature and research trends.

APPLICANT SEX

Many of the preliminary studies in this area indicated that females were generally given lower evaluations than men who had identical qualifications. While there were several studies which did not demonstrate any significant effects, the previous edition of this text suggested that, on the whole, differential evaluations as a function of applicant sex were likely in interview situations and that they were not confined to only male interviewers. Some more recent studies are consistent with this earlier statement. For example, Simas and McCarrey (1979) conducted a study where 84 male and female personnel officers who were classified into either high, moderate, or low authoritarian groups, evaluated male and female applicants in simulated videotaped recruitment interviews. The "high authoritarian" personnel officers of both sexes rated the male applicants more favorably than female applicants and indicated that they would make more job offers to the male applicants. Similarly, a study conducted by McIntyre, Moberg, and Posner (1980) showed preferential treatment in favor of males over females when resumes of fictitious applicants for entry-level professional positions were mailed to 458 potential employers. McDonald and Hakel (1985) also showed that females were given lower evaluations than males, but that this effect was quite small.

In addition, evidence has been strong that the type of job interacts with gender to influence the evaluations given. For example, earlier studies by Cohen and Bunker (1976), Cash, Gillen, and Burns (1977), and Muchinsky and Harris (1977) support the contention that when females apply for jobs that are considered traditional male jobs, they receive lower evaluations. Similarly, males applying for stereotypically female type jobs also receive lower evaluations compared to females. Thus the contextual situation is an important factor in evaluating the likelihood of bias in the employment interview. This finding is given further support by several recent studies. Hodgins and Kalin (1985) showed that the type of occupation was an important determinant of male and female evaluations. However, their study also demonstrated that when specific information about a candidate becomes available, this information tends to diminish the sex stereotyping processes. Parsons and Liden (1984) found that females were given higher evaluations when being evaluated for relatively low-level jobs in an amusement park. A recent study conducted by Arvey et al. (1987) investigated whether females would receive relatively higher evaluations than males when being considered for a retail sales clerk position in shopping mall store outlets. This hypothesis was confirmed.

An additional variable that has been investigated in several studies has been the *attractiveness* of the job candidates. Dipboye, Fromkin, and Wiback (1975) and Dipboye, Arvey, and Terpstra (1977) investigated the notion that physical attractiveness may be a more important variable in influencing interview evaluations for females than for males. While these two studies tended to support this proposition, studies by Cash, Gillen, and Burns (1977) and Heilman and Saruwatari (1979) must be considered. For example, Heilman and Saruwatari hypothesized that because attractive women are regarded as more feminine than unattractive women and attractive men are regarded as more masculine than unattractive men, attractive women would be at a disadvantage when being considered for stereotypically "male" jobs or jobs believed to require predominantly masculine talents for successful job performance. In this study, 45 male and female college students evaluated application forms and photos of male and female candidates who had been judged to be attractive or unattractive. These candidates were evaluated for either a clerical or management position on a number of dependent variables, such as qualifications, hiring recommendation, and starting salary. Analyses revealed that attractive females were given higher evaluations than unattractive females when being considered for the clerical job, but attractive females were rated lower when considered for the management job. In contrast, for male candidates attractiveness always led to higher evaluations regardless of the job.

Cann, Siegfried, and Pearce (1981) conducted a study investigating whether sex and physical attractiveness would be less potent variables in influencing interviewers' decisions if the interviewers postponed an overall judgment and rated specific qualifications first. However, their results indicated that both sex and physical attractiveness variables were still significant even after the specific qualifications had been evaluated.

Another variable investigated has been applicant *qualifications* or competence. Investigators have tried to determine whether interviewers evaluate highly competent females lower than highly competent males, compared to the differences in evaluations occurring when the candidates are less qualified. It has been suggested that highly competent or qualified females are unusually threatening to male interviewers. Several studies bear directly on this issue. The Dipboye, Fromkin, and Wiback (1975) study found that highly qualified job candidates were preferred over less qualified candidates, but there was no indication of an interaction between this variable and applicant sex. Similar results were obtained by Dipboye, Arvey, and Terpstra (1977) with the exception of some evidence indicating that the qualifications of candidates interacted with applicant attractiveness, but not with sex.

The study by Muchinsky and Harris (1977) found significant differences between males and females of *average* ability (as indicated by scholastic standing), but no differences between male and female applicants at *high* or *low* ability levels.

Heneman (1977) reported a study where college students evaluated hypothetical applicants for the job of life-insurance agent. The qualifications of applicants were manipulated through the use of test scores. In this study, highly qualified females were evaluated as being much *less* suitable for hiring than highly qualified males.

Finally, the resume study conducted by Haefner (1977) found that, while highly competent individuals were preferred over less competent candidates, preference was clearly given to highly competent males over highly competent females. Thus the studies to date show mixed results regarding the possible threat to men of competent women.

It should be noted, however, that those studies that *include* qualifications find that qualifications play the *major* role in the evaluations given. That is, interviewers base their evaluations primarily on the qualifications of candidates and only secondarily on other factors such as sex or race.

Several additional variables have been investigated in this context. One variable is the predominant *sex of the subordinates*. Rose and Andiappan (1978) hypothesized that the differences between evaluations of male and female job candidates would be greatest when interviewers evaluated such candidates for managerial jobs which involved a work force that was primarily either male or female. The results of their resume study indicated that female candidates are evaluated more favorably when the subordinate is also female. Likewise, male candidates were given high evaluations when their potential subordinate work force was male. These authors suggest that whenever evaluators are aware of the specific work context for comparable male and female applicants, " . . . their evaluations are likely to be strongly affected by whether or not the applicant's and subordinate's sexes match, not by the applicant's sex alone" (p. 109).

Rosen and Mericle (1979) investigated the effects of applicant sex in selection decisions under conditions of strong or weak fair employment policy statements. Seventy-eight municipal administrators evaluated resumes of male and female applicants under conditions in which an organization indicated either strong emphasis or only lip service to fair employment practices. Results indicated that preference for male or female applicants was not influenced by strength of the policy statements. However, interviewers recommended lower starting salaries for females under the strong fair employment condition. The authors interpreted this finding as perhaps due to greater resistance on the part of managers or a reaction against hiring-constraints imposed by strong affirmative-action policies. This may represent a subtle attempt to undermine the career prospects for recently hired females.

As Arvey and Campion (1982) noted, the recent studies dealing with applicant sex as it influences interviewers' decisions reflect a growing awareness that contextual and other personal variables need to be considered in combination with the sex variables. The phenonenon may be more complex than realized. An example of this thinking is reflected in a study by Heilman (1980). She suggests "that situational factors can preclude, or at least reduce, the likelihood of discriminatory personnel decisions, although they leave the decision-maker's stereotypic belief system intact" (p. 387). As support for this proposition, Heilman (1980) reports the results of an investigation in which interviewers evaluated a female candidate's application form along with interviewing seven additional candidates. The sex of the applicant pool was manipulated so that the percent of females in the pool was either 12.5, 25, 37.5, 50, or 100. Results indicated that when women represented 25 percent or less of the total pool, the female applicant was evaluated more unfavorably than if the pool reflected a larger percentage of female applicants.

It should be noted that not all studies demonstrate sex bias in the employment interview situation. For example, Renwick and Tosi (1978) suggested that when more information about job candidates is available, interviewers will rely less on their stereotypes when making evaluations and judgments. Tosi and Einbender (1985) reviewed 21 studies investigating gender bias and showed that judges faced with limited information about candidate competence or job requirements tended to make biased or stereotyped judgments; those with more information did not. This hypothesis was given additional support by a recent study by Heilman (1984), in which highly job-relevant information was found to produce less differential treatment of male and female applicants than did information of low job relevance or no information at all.

It is important to note here the implications of research that focuses on gender rather than sex. Unger (1979) refers to differences between men and women as "sex differences" and beliefs about the differences between men and women as "gender differences." According to an extensive review of the psychological research on gender and sex by Deaux (1984), sex effects are less evident (and, as noted above, usually situationally dependent), while gender effects appear to be pervasive. On the other hand, Powell (1987) found that sex effects rarely were reported in the recruitment literature while the effects of gender on recruiters' responses to applicants were inconsistent. Whatever the true effect(s), the distinction between sex and gender may be meaningful and provide better answers to questions related to the research on bias in the interview process.

APPLICANT RACE

Surprisingly, only a few studies have dealt with the race of the applicant in interview evaluations. Even more surprising is the lack of evidence of racial bias in interviews.

Wexley and Nemeroff (1974) presented resumes of a black or a white applicant to 120 students who had been asked to evaluate *either* the black *or* the white candidate for suitability as a mechanical-engineer technician. In addition, each resume contained information indicating whether the candidate was relatively similar in background to the interviewer (e.g., father was an office worker, mother was a schoolteacher) or dissimilar to the interviewer (e.g., father was a laborer, mother was a domestic worker). The students were also divided into two groups based on scores on an attitude measure of prejudice: one group was relatively high in racial prejudice, the other relatively low in racial prejudice. They found that race of the applicant had no effect on the employability ratings given. However, similarity of biographical background did prove to be a major determinant of the evaluations of job candidates. Candidates similar to the interviewer were given high evaluations. Moreover, the prejudiced interviewers gave lower ratings to *both* white *and* black applicants.

Haefner (1977) also used a resume design and found that race interacted with both sex and age to influence interviewers' evaluations, but the effects were very small.

Rand and Wexley (1975) used videotaped employment interviews of both white and black applicants. Again, the race of the applicant did *not* significantly affect the evaluations. As before, the biographical similarity and racial prejudice of the interviewers influenced the evaluations, but affected the ratings of *both* black *and* white applicants.

In a study involving a design where fictitious but realistic resumes were mailed to actual employers, McIntyre, Moberg, and Posner (1980) examined the pattern of responses made by organizations. Resumes of minority (black or female) and nonminority job candidates were sent to 458 companies. The data indicated that males were given preferential treatment compared to females. In addition, results indicated that the black applicants were given more favorable treatment than white applicants.

A study conducted by Newman (1978) discussed the results of sending bogus resumes for black and white applicants to 240 companies. The data indicated a definite trend for larger companies to discriminate in favor of blacks. However, Newman and Krzystofiak (1979) found that this tendency did not generalize to situations where employment managers were aware of their role in the study. It should be noted, however, that these studies are of the recruitment process rather than of employment interviews.

Mullins (1982) used videotaped stimulus materials to examine interviewer ratings of high and low quality candidates role-played by black and white males. The study used 176 white business administration students who viewed the videotaped interviews. Results indicated that the most important variable influencing the interview ratings was applicant quality, but that the black applicant was significantly favored over the white applicant.

In a field study examining actual interviewer ratings of candidates for positions in an amusement park, Parsons and Liden (1984) found that blacks were rated significantly lower than white applicants on a number of interview dimensions.

The data from these studies are mixed. It appears as if black applicants receive higher ratings than whites in interview circumstances. However, in a "field" setting, some limited evidence indicates that blacks receive lower evaluations. One must be careful, however, because the

black and white candidates evaluated under the actual job interview situations may not have the same qualifications. That is, the control of the
qualifications for the candidates is not held constant as they are in the
resume or videotape conditions.

One possible factor that accounts for higher evaluations given to black
candidates is that "interviewers" (either students or managers) may have
been sensitive to EEO and legal issues as well as to the affirmative-action
requirements of their organizations.

APPLICANT AGE

Only a few studies have investigated the effects of the age of candidates
on interviewers' evaluations. Haefner (1977) found that age significantly
affected interviewers' evaluations and that age also interacted with race
(as noted above) and with competence. While age played no role in the
evaluation of barely competent candidates, younger, highly competent
individuals were preferred to older individuals who were equally competent.

Using the in-basket methodology, Rosen and Jerdee (1976b) found
that older employees were evaluated as less suitable for a job than younger
employees. In addition, the older employees were evaluated as being (1)
less promotable, (2) more resistant to change, (3) less capable physically,
and (4) less likely to have organizational support for retraining opportunities.

Conner et al. (1978) used pencil-and-paper stimulus materials and
showed that older job candidates received lower evaluations than younger
candidates.

Most of the research focusing on this target population is limited
because of the use of pencil-and-paper job candidates, which tells us very
little about judgments about older job candidates based on actual face-
to-face interviews. An exception to the past research is presented by Gordon (1984). Using videotaped mock employment interviews where the
age level of the candidate was manipulated (25, 40, and 55 years), Gordon's data revealed lower evaluations for the older candidates. This research, however, was also limited by using students as judges and by
using a very short interview (three to four minutes). As Arvey and Campion (1982) have indicated, more realistic interview situations need to be

used and "real" interviewers and normal working adults should be asked to make judgments instead of undergraduate college students.

A recent article by Avolio and Barrett (1987) outlined a number of methodological confounds that could conceivably influence subjects' evaluations of older and younger job candidates in research of this type. They indicated that many studies do not control for differential experiences of younger versus older job candidates. That is, subjects evaluating older job candidates may infer that these candidates have relatively more experience simply because of their age. In addition, there may be the inference that older individuals applying for the same position as a younger candidate may be somewhat "slow" or less advanced because of the greater opportunities they may have encountered over the years. Another confound mentioned by Avolio and Barrett is that subjects may form differential attributions concerning the cause of unemployment for older versus younger job candidates. "Specifically, the cause of an older worker's unemployment status, if not specified, may be viewed negatively by raters as attributable to poor prior job performance, technological obsolescence, or an organization's attempt to get rid of 'dead wood'" (Avolio and Barrett [1987], p. 57). Another factor that needs to be controlled is the "nearness to retirement" factor. Individuals who are perceived as having a relatively shorter time to contribute to the organization may be viewed as less attractive applicants regardless of age. However, older candidates may be presented as being near retirement age, which would trigger this kind of response.

In an effort to provide controls for these potential variables, Avolio and Barrett (1987) presented a study that investigated ratings of interviewee potential by using a simulated auditory interview. One hundred fifty six male and female participants listened to a 12-minute interview of a candidate applying for a temporary supervisory position. Results indicated that participants gave significantly lower evaluations to an older candidate (59 years old) with similar qualifications to a younger candidate (32 years old).

The literature is sparse on whether older females represent a particularly vulnerable subgroup for unfair bias in the employment interview. The studies by Persell and Torrence (1980) and Haefner (1977) found some limited support for sex by age interactions. Given the changing demographics and lifestyles in our society and the growing need for employment on the part of older females, it is especially important to conduct more research in this area.

One intriguing issue concerns whether bias against older workers might also be a function of the job. Just as occupational sex typing may operate in conjunction with sex stereotypes in creating the perception that one sex is more appropriate for a given occupation, occupational age typing may operate in a similar manner. Some indirect evidence suggests that there does exist some kind of age typing of jobs. Gordon and Arvey (1985) had 150 respondents give their perceived average age of people employed across 59 different occupations. Their results showed a clear rank-ordering of jobs from relatively "older" to "younger" jobs based on these age perceptions. Moreover, the rank-ordering was highly related to the median age levels of occupants based on census data. To date, however, we found no studies that investigated age bias as a function of job type in the employment interview.

Taken as a whole, this literature seems to present a fairly pervasive bias against older job candidates in the employment interview. Much more research needs to be conducted in order to determine the conditions under which more or less bias occurs and the kinds of interventions and training programs that could serve to diminish such bias.

APPLICANT HANDICAP

There is a dearth of studies investigating the effects of handicapped status on interview evaluations.

Krefting and Brief (1977) report the results of a study in which 145 college students evaluated a packet of resumes and other materials necessary for determining whether or not an applicant should be hired for a typist position. The applicant in the resume was depicted as either healthy or confined to a wheelchair, and as either experienced or inexperienced.

The individuals reviewing the resume materials gave estimates of the applicant's health, motivation, and potential for staying, in addition to an overall rating. The disabled applicants were seen as significantly *more* motivated and as more likely to become long-term employees than non-disabled applicants. However, a puzzling interaction also occurred. The inexperienced disabled applicant was evaluated higher overall than the experienced disabled applicant. The authors suggest that the results of the study were relatively encouraging for qualified disabled applicants, but argued that the evaluations elicited in the selection process are in large part a function of the fit between the disability and the nature of the job.

In a second study along these lines, Rose and Brief (1977) assessed the impact of applicant disability (epilepsy) and job type on evaluation judgments. One hundred forty-five students evaluated a resume and other data which portrayed the applicant as either healthy or epileptic (although the seizures were currently under control). Moreover, the applicants were portrayed as applying for a job that involved either a great deal of public contact and supervisory responsibilities, or no public contact and supervisory responsibilities. Subjects gave evaluations along several dimensions. Results indicated that epileptic and normal applicants were rated equally in overall performance, time with the firm, work effort, and amount of salary. There was, however, a significant interaction between disability and type of job on several evaluations. Epileptics seeking nonpublic jobs were rated more likely to satisfy clients than normal applicants.

A third study was less encouraging. Johnson and Heal (1976) compared a wheelchair job applicant with a healthy applicant. Fifty actual employment agencies were visited by one of the researchers who indicated interest in finding a job. However, in half of the interviews the same researcher who rated the agency responses appeared in a wheelchair. Handicapped applicants were offered significantly fewer future job interviews and were given a more pessimistic estimate of the job market by the agency representatives. In addition, the representatives told the handicapped applicants that the chances for getting the sought-after job were low and they discouraged them from seeking a position with normal public exposure. While the results of this study may have been influenced by the fact that the researcher did the ratings herself, the results certainly suggest that lower evaluations are given by interviewers to an individual with a handicap.

Stone and Sawatzki (1980) conducted a study where 90 MBA students observed one of six taped interviews which portrayed three conditions of disability (psychiatric, physical, and no disability) and two levels of work history (good or bad). Results indicated that applicants who were described as having two hospitalizations for nervous breakdowns had a lower probabilty of being hired. More obvious was the finding that applicants with good work histories were given significantly higher evaluations.

A study by Hastorf, Wildfogel, and Cassman (1979) reviewed acknowledgment of handicap as a tactic in social interaction. Subjects observed two videotapes of handicapped individuals being interviewed and then chose the one with whom they would prefer to work on a cooperative task. The results suggested that subjects prefer to work with interviewees who acknowledged their handicap.

In another study, Snyder *et al.* (1979) found that subjects avoided a person wearing a metal leg brace and chose to view movies with normal subjects, when avoiding the handicapped person could masquerade as a moving preference.

An excellent review of the literature involving employment decisions regarding the handicapped was provided by Rose (1980). In his review, Rose indicates that there are four classes of variables potentially related to discrimination against the handicapped. These are: (1) the nature of the handicap, (2) other personal attributes of the applicant or worker, (3) the nature of the job or occupation being considered, and (4) characteristics of the potential employing organizations, particularly the characteristics of the hiring and assessment procedures used by the organization. In addition, Rose delineates the methodological limitations of the research published in this area.

SUMMARY

It seems reasonably clear from the foregoing discussion that the selection interview is not *immune* to employment-discrimination litigation. Organizations that drop their employment-testing programs and rely solely on the interview as a basis on which to hire their employees may find themselves in later difficulties for several reasons:

1. The number of cases involving the interview appear to be increasing. Lawyers for plaintiffs are becoming more knowledgeable and sophisticated in building successful cases against the employment interview.

2. The research evidence, as well as data associated with court cases, indicates that the interview process will possibly result in disproportionate rates of selection between minority and nonminority members.

3. Validity evidence based on the interview is notoriously poor. In addition, the interview has not yet been scrutinized as carefully as tests. That is, research concerning whether evaluations made during the

interview and the resulting predictions of performance are equally accurate for minority and nonminority groups has rarely been conducted (e.g., Arvey *et al.*, 1987). Predictions based on the interview may be also reviewed for under- and overprediction or bias as defined by other statistical models of fairness (e.g., Arvey *et al.*, 1987).

Thus, if an organization is charged with a violation of Title VII based on the interview, and "adverse impact" is shown, evidence for the criterion-related validity of the interview may be difficult to muster. One possible strategy is for organizations to build a defense based on *content* validity, e.g., *Harless* v. *Duck* (1977), but it is probable that strict standards of review for content validity evidence would likely be applied. Thus, job analyses, expert consensus, and other parts of the content-validity procedures will eventually need to be demonstrated.

An alternative strategy organizations might adopt is to make efforts to ensure that interviewer stereotypes and prejudicial attitudes are minimized during the interview process. This requires that upper management be sensitive to these matters and not tolerate unfair discrimination against qualified minorities.

Another way to minimize interviewer bias is to instruct interviewers in the kinds of questions tainted with biases. For example, the United States Civil Service Commission offers the following suggestions concerning interviewing women:*

- *Use correct words. A woman is not a "girl," "honey," "dear," etc. Address her by her own name.*

- *Don't inquire into non–job-related areas. Questions about marital status, parenthood, childcare, and her husband's job are not relevant to the job for which she is being interviewed. The fact that sexism has been prevalent in so many job situations will put a woman candidate on the defensive when such questions are asked.*

- *Don't bring up your own prejudices. As a manager, your job is to carry out your company's commitment to equal employment opportunity.*

- *Don't flirt with or patronize a woman candidate.*

---

* Abstracted and published in *Fair Employment Practices*, No. 328, September 15, 1977.

- *Don't joke, even if you are uncomfortable. The woman candidate has the same serious interest in applying for a job as a male applicant.*

- *Don't insult a woman candidate by indicating that your interest in her stems from your desire to improve the department's EEO image. A woman wants to be considered on the same terms as a man, i.e., on the basis of her competence and potential for the job. She does not want to be hired simply because she is a woman.*

Perhaps one of the best approaches to minimizing the influence of racial and sex stereotypes is to provide interviewers with thorough job descriptions and a statement of job specifications. A study by Langsdale and Weitz (1973) indicated that interviewers are more apt to agree about job candidates when there is a good deal of information concerning the job than are interviewers who did not have as much information about the job. Wiener and Schneiderman (1974) conducted two experiments showing that complete and unambiguous job information reduces the effect of irrelevant stereotypes on interviewer decisions.

Another approach is to urge that interviewers validate their own judgments on several quantitative scales and follow up on the individuals hired to determine the relationship between their judgments and the performance of those hired. There is nothing as sobering as learning that your own judgments about people were completely inaccurate. This may sensitize interviewers to the fallibility of their judgments and alert interviewers to biases and stereotypes.

REFERENCES

Arvey, R. D. (1979). Unfair discrimination in the employment interview: Legal and psychological aspects. *Psychological Bulletin* 86: 736–765.

Arvey, R. D., and J. E. Campion (1982). The employment interview: A summary and review of recent research. *Personnel Psychology* 35: 281–322.

Arvey, R. D.; H. Miller; R. Gould; and P. Birch (1987). Interview validity for selecting sales clerks. *Personnel Psychology* 40: 1–12.

Avolio, B. J., and G. V. Barrett (1987). Effects of age stereotyping in a simulated interview. *Psychology and Aging* 2: 56–63.

Babcock, B.; A. Freedman; E. Norton; and A. Ross (1975). *Sex Discrimination and the Law: Causes and Remedies.* Toronto: Little, Brown.

Bowman, G.; B. Worthy; and S. Greyer (1965) Are women executives people? *Harvard Business Review* 43: 14.

Brigham, J. C. (1971). Ethnic stereotypes. *Psychological Bulletin* 76: 15–38.

Broverman, I. K.; S. R. Vogel; D. M. Broverman; F. E. Clarkson; and P. S. Rosenkrantz (1972). Sex role stereotypes: A current appraisal. *Journal of Social Issues* 28: 59–78.

Cann, E.; W. D. Siegfried; and L. Pearce (1981). Forced attention to specific applicant qualification: Impact on physical attractiveness and sex of applicant biases. *Personnel Psychology* 34: 65–76.

Cash, T. E.; B. Gillen; and D. S. Burns (1977). Sexism and "Beautyism" in personnel consultants' decision making. *Journal of Applied Psychology* 62: 301–370.

Cecil, E. A.; R. J. Paul; and R. A. Olins (1973). Perceived importance of selected variables used to evaluate male and female job applicants. *Personnel Psychology* 26: 397–404.

Cohen, S. L., and K. A. Bunker (1975). Subtle effects of sex role stereotypes on recruiters' hiring decisions. *Journal of Applied Psychology* 60: 566–572.

Conner, C. L.; P. Walsh; D. H. Litzelman; and M. G. Alvarez (1978). Evaluation of job candidates: The effects of age versus success. *Journal of Gerontology* 33: 246–252.

Crew, J. C. (1984). Age stereotypes as a function of race. *Academy of Management Journal* 27: 431–435.

Crowley, J.; T. Levitin; and R. Quinn (1973). Seven deadly half-truths about women. *Psychology Today,* March, 94–96.

Deaux, K. (1984). From individual differences to social categories: Analysis of a decade's research on gender. *American Psychologist* 39: 105–116.

Dipboye, R. L. (1975). Women as managers and stereotypes and realities.

Survey of Business, Center for Business and Economic Research, The University of Tennessee, May/June, **10**: 22–25.

Dipboye, R. L.; R. D. Arvey; and D. E. Terpstra (1977). Sex and physical attractiveness of raters and applicants as determinants of resume evaluations. *Journal of Applied Psychology* **62**: 288–294.

Dipboye, R. L.; H. L. Fromkin; and K. Wiback (1975). Relative importance of applicant sex, attractiveness and scholastic standing in evaluation of job applicant resumes. *Journal of Applied Psychology* **60**: 39–43.

——— (1977). Reactions of college recruiters to interviewer sex and self-presentation style. *Journal of Vocational Behavior* **10**: 1–12.

EEOC Decision No 72-0703, 4 FEP 435 (1971).

EEOC v. *Detroit Edison,* 10 FEP 239 (1975).

Fugita, S. S.; K. N. Wexley; and J. M. Hillery (1974). Black-white differences in nonverbal behavior in an interview setting. *Journal of Applied Social Psychology* **4**: 343–350.

Gordon, R. A. (1984). *The effect of accountability on age discrimination.* Doctoral dissertation, University of Houston.

Gordon, R. A., and R. D. Arvey (1985). Perceived and actual ages of workers. *Journal of Vocational Behavior* **28**: 21–28.

Haefner, J. E. (1977). Race, age, sex and competence as factors in employer selection of the disadvantaged. *Journal of Applied Psychology* **62**: 199–202.

Hall, E. T. (1966). *The Hidden Dimensions.* New York: Doubleday.

Hamilton, D. L. (ed.) (1981). *Cognitive Processes in Stereotyping and Intergroup Behavior.* Hillsdale, NJ: Lawrence Earlbaum.

Hamilton v. *General Motors Corp.*, 21 FEP 521 (1979).

Harless v. *Duck,* 14 FEP 1616 (1977).

Hass, A. (1979). Male and female spoken language differences: Stereotypes and evidence. *Psychological Bulletin* **86**: 616–626.

Hastorf, A. H.; J. Wildfogel; and T. Cassman (1979). Acknowledgement of handicap as a tactic in social interaction. *Journal of Personality and Social Psychology* 37: 1790–1797.

Heilman, M. E. (1980). The impact of situational factors on personnel decisions concerning women: Varying the sex composition of the applicant pool. *Organizational Behavior and Human Performance* 26: 386–395.

Heilman, M. E. (1984). Information as a deterrent against sex discrimination: The effects of applicant sex and information type on preliminary employment decisions. *Organizational Behavior and Human Performance* 33: 174–186.

Heilman, M. E., and L. R. Saruwatari (1979). When beauty is beastly: The effects of appearance and sex on evaluations of job applicants for managerial and nonmanagerial jobs. *Organizational Behavior and Human Performance* 23: 360–372.

Heneman, H. G., III (1977). Impact of test information and applicant sex on applicant evaluations in a selection simulation. *Journal of Applied Psychology* 62: 524–527.

Hester v. *Southern Railway Co.,* 8 FEP 646 (1974).

Hodgins, D. C., and R. Kalin (1985). Reducing sex bias in judgements of occupational suitability by the provision of sextyped personality information. *Canadian Journal of Behavioral Science* 17: 346–357.

Johnson, R., and L. W. Heal (1976). Private employment agency responses to the physically handicapped applicant in a wheelchair. *Journal of Applied Rehabilitation Counseling* 7: 12–21.

Jones, J. M. (1972). *Prejudice and Racism*. Reading, Mass.: Addison-Wesley.

Karlins, M.; T. L. Coffman; and G. Walters (1969). On the fading of social stereotypes: Studies in three generations of college students. *Journal of Personality and Social Psychology* 13: 1–16.

Katz, D. (1960). The functional approach to the study of attitudes. *Public Opinion Quarterly* 24: 163–177.

King v. *New Hampshire Department of Resources and Economic Development,* 15 FEP 669 (1977).

Krefting, L. A., and A. P. Brief (1977). The impact of applicant disability on evaluative judgments in the selection process. *Academy of Management Journal* 19: 675–680.

Langsdale, J., and J. Weitz (1973). Estimating the influence of job information on interviewer agreement. *Journal of Applied Psychology* 57: 23–27.

Lippman, W. (1922). *Public Opinion.* New York: Harcourt-Brace-Jovanovich.

Mayfield, E. C. (1964). The selection interview: A reevaluation of published research. *Personnel Psychology* 17: 239–260.

McCormick, E. J., and J. Tiffin (1974). *Industrial Psychology,* 6th ed. Englewood Cliffs, N.J.: Prentice-Hall.

McDonald, T., and M. D. Hakel (1985). Effects of applicant race, sex, suitability, and answers on interviewer's questioning strategy and ratings. *Personnel Psychology* 38: 321–334.

McIntyre, S.; D. J. Moberg; and B. Z. Posner (1980). Preferential treatment in preselection decisions according to sex and race. *Academy of Management Journal* 23: 738–749.

Miller, A. G. (1982). Historical and contemporary perspectives on stereotyping. In A. G. Miller (ed.). *In the Eye of the Beholder: Contemporary Issues in Stereotyping.* New York: Praeger.

Muchinsky, P. M., and S. L. Harris (1977). The effect of applicant sex and scholastic standing on the evaluation of job applicant resumes in sex-typed occupations. *Journal of Vocational Behavior* 11: 95–108.

Mullins, T. (1982). Interviewer decisions as a function of applicant race, applicant quality and interviewer prejudice. *Personnel Psychology* 35: 163–173.

Newman, J. M. (1978). Discrimination in recruitment: An empirical analysis. *Industrial and Labor Relations Review* 23: 15–23.

Newman, J. M., and F. Krzystofiak (1979). Self-reports versus unobtrusive measures: Balancing method variable and ethical concerns in employment discrimination research. *Journal of Applied Psychology* 64: 82–85.

Parsons, C. K., and R. C. Liden (1984). Interviewer perceptions of applicant qualifications: A multivariate field study of demographic characteristics and nonverbal cues. *Journal of Applied Psychology* 69: 557–568.

Persell, D. E., and W. W. Torrance (1980). The older woman and her search for employment. *Aging and Work* 3: 121–138.

Powell, G. N. (1987). The effects of sex and gender on recruitment. *Academy of Management Review* 12: 731–743.

Rand, T. M., and K. N. Wexley (1975). Demonstration of the effect, "Similar to me," in simulated employment interviews. *Psychological Reports* 36: 535–544.

Renwick, P. A., and H. Tosi (1978). The effects of sex, marital status, and educational background on selection decisions. *Academy of Management Journal* 21: 93–103.

Reynolds v. *Sheet Metal Workers,* 25 *FEP* 837 (1981).

Rogers v. *International Paper Co.,* 10 *FEP* 404 (1975).

Rose, G. L. (1980). *Employment decisions regarding the handicapped: Experimental evidence.* Presentation at American Psychological Association, Montreal, September.

Rose, G. L., and P. Andiappan (1978). Sex effects on managerial hiring decisions. *Academy of Management Journal* 21: 104–112.

Rose, G. L., and A. Brief (1977). The impact of job type and applicant disability on judgment in the selection process. Paper delivered at Academy of Management Conference, Orlando, Florida, August.

Rosen, B., and T. H. Jerdee (1976a). *Becoming Aware.* Chicago: Science Research Associates.

——— (1976b). The influence of age stereotypes on managerial decisions. *Journal of Applied Psychology* 61: 428–432.

—— (1976c). The nature of job-related age stereotypes. *Journal of Applied Psychology* 61: 180–183.

Rosen, B., and M. F. Mericle (1979). Influence of strong versus weak fair employment policies and applicant's sex on selection decisions and salary recommendations in a management simulation. *Journal of Applied Psychology* 64: 435–439.

Rowe v. *General Motors,* 4 FEP 445 (1972).

Schein, V. E. (1973). The relationship between sex role stereotypes and requisite management characteristics. *Journal of Applied Psychology* 57: 95–100.

—— (1975). Relationships between sex role stereotypes and requisite management characteristics among female managers. *Journal of Applied Psychology* 60: 340–344.

Schmitt, N. (1976). Social and situational determinants of interview decisions: Implications for the employment interview. *Personnel Psychology* 29: 79–102.

Shaie, K. W. (1974). Translations in gerontology—from lab to life: Intellectual functioning. *American Psychologist* 29: 802–807.

Simas, K., and M. McCarrey (1979). Impact of recruiter authoritarianism and applicant sex on evaluation and selection decisions in a recruitment interview analogue study. *Journal of Applied Psychology* 64: 483–491.

Snyder, M.; R. Kleck; A. Strenta; and S. Mentzer (1979). Avoidance of the handicapped: An attributional ambiguity analysis. *Journal of Personality and Social Psychology* 37: 2297–2306.

Stallings v. *Container Corp.,* 17 FEP 321 (1977).

Stead, B. A. (ed.) (1985). *Women in Management.* Englewood Cliffs, NJ: Prentice-Hall.

Stone, C. I., and B. Sawatzki (1980). Hiring bias and the disabled interview: Effects of manipulating work history and disability information of the disabled job applicant. *Journal of Vocational Behavior* 16: 96–104.

Terborg, J. R. (1977). Women in management: A research view. *Journal of Applied Psychology* 62: 647–664.

Tosi, H. L., and S. W. Einbender (1985). The effects of the type and amount of information in sex discrimination research: A meta-analysis. *Academy of Management Review* 28: 712–723.

Ulrich, L., and D. Trumbo (1965). The selection interview since 1949. *Psychological Bulletin* 63: 100–116.

Unger, R. E. (1979). Toward a redefinition of sex and gender. *American Psychologist* 34: 1085–1094.

United States v. *Hazelwood School District,* 11 EPD 10854 (1976).

Wagner, R. (1949). The employment interview: A critical review. *Personnel Psychology* 2: 17–46.

Waintroob, A. R. (1979). The developing laws of equal employment opportunity at the white collar and professional level. 21 *William and Mary Law Review* 45.

Webster, E. C. (1964). *Decision making in the employment interview.* Montreal, Industrial Relations Center, McGill University.

Weiner v. *County of Oakland,* 14 FEP 380 (1976).

Wexley, R. N., and W. F. Nemeroff (1974). The effects of racial prejudice, race of applicant and biographical similarity on interviewer evaluation of job applicants. *Journal of Social and Behavioral Sciences* 20: 66–78.

Wiener, Y., and M. L. Schneiderman (1974). Use of job information as a criterion in employment decisions of interviewers. *Journal of Applied Psychology* 59: 699–704.

Wright, O. R., Jr. (1969). Summary of research on the selection interview since 1964. *Personnel Psychology* 22: 391–413.

Preemployment Inquiries and Other Components of the Selection Process

8

In the previous chapters, we focused primarily on two kinds of selection mechanisms—employment tests and the interview. But what about the other criteria—such as application blanks, reference checks, and so forth—that employers commonly use to help them select people for jobs? This chapter deals with these other preemployment selection devices. Those preemployment inquiries most vulnerable to legal attack will be identified and reviewed from both legal and research perspectives. The specific topic areas include the following: education and experience requirements, physical requirements (height and weight requirements, agility testing, physical factors, handicaps and disabilities), physiologically based screening procedures, arrests and convictions, recruitment, reference checks, and time lags between selection hurdles.

GUIDELINES ON PREEMPLOYMENT INQUIRIES

Guidelines concerning preemployment inquiries have been set forth by a variety of state human rights commissions in addition to the proposed set of guidelines EEOC issued in October 1976. Most of the guidelines issued by the states urge employers to review their present application forms and the content of their interviews to determine the following:

1. If the questions asked result in a disparate impact in screening out minorities;

2. If the information gleaned from the questions is really needed to judge an applicant's competence or qualifications for the job.

An example of the type of published guidelines that concern preemployment inquiries is shown in Table 8.1. These are the guidelines that were issued in 1975 by the Washington State Human Rights Commission and are representative of more current guidelines. While these guidelines are also representative of many states, differences do exist from state to state. The reader may want to consult the human rights commission in his or her own state to obtain a set of their guidelines, if available.

EDUCATION AND EXPERIENCE REQUIREMENTS

Education and experience requirements have been used by organizations for years as a part of their hiring practices. Thus it is not surprising they were included as "selection procedures" in the EEOC testing guidelines (1970) and in later guideline revisions.

Education Requirements

Historically, education requirements have been reviewed by the courts with the same detail as employment tests. It is widely known that education requirements have an adverse impact on blacks and other minorities. (Thus the use of a high school education requirement, as a prerequisite for hiring, tends to screen out greater numbers of blacks than whites.) The classic court case *Griggs* v. *Duke Power* (see Chapter 5) partially focused on this requirement. Demonstrating the validity of a particular degree is quite difficult, because usually there are no employees in the position with *less* than the educational level specified. Thus there is little variability on this "predictor," and it is impossible to conduct a criterion-related validity study.

Civil rights advocates believe the use of education requirements is discriminatory for several reasons:

1. Many minority members do not have the same kind of opportunities as nonminorities to complete high school, college, or other degree programs because of the high costs of education and inferior schools and teachers.

TABLE 8.1
Preemployment inquiry guidelines issued by Washington State Human Rights Commission.

SUBJECT	FAIR PREEMPLOYMENT INQUIRIES	UNFAIR PREEMPLOYMENT INQUIRIES
Age	Inquiries as to birth date and proof of true age are permitted.	Any inquiry which implies a preference for persons under 40 years of age.
Arrests (see also Convictions)	None.	All inquiries relating to arrests.
Citizenship	Whether applicant is prevented from lawfully becoming employed in this country because of visa or immigration status. Whether applicant can provide proof of citizenship, visa, or alien registration number after being hired.	Whether applicant is citizen. Requirement before hiring that applicant present birth certificate, naturalization or baptismal record. *Any inquiry into citizenship which would tend to divulge applicant's lineage, ancestry, national origin, descent, or birthplace.*
Convictions (see also Arrests)	(1) Inquiries concerning specified convictions which relate reasonably to fitness to perform the particular job(s) being applied for, PROVIDED that such inquiries be limited to convictions for which the date of conviction or prison release is within 7 years of the date of the job application. (2) Where the employer believes, after careful consideration, that it is not practicable to inquire about specified convictions, the employer may inquire generally about all convictions for which the date of the conviction or prison release, whichever is more recent, is within 7	Inquiries which would divulge convictions which (a) do not relate reasonably to fitness to perform the particular job or (b) do not relate solely to convictions for which the date of conviction or prison release is within 7 years of the date of the job application.

(cont.)

TABLE 8.1 (Cont.)

SUBJECT	FAIR PREEMPLOYMENT INQUIRIES	UNFAIR PREEMPLOYMENT INQUIRIES
	years of the date of the job application, PROVIDED that such general inquiries be accompanied by a disclaimer informing the applicant that a conviction record will not necessarily bar him or her from employment. (Law enforcement agencies are exempt from this rule. See WAC 162-16-060 for further guidance on proper use of conviction records.)	
Family	Whether applicant can meet specified work schedules or has activities, commitments, or responsibilities that may prevent him or her from meeting work attendance requirements.	Specific inquiries concerning spouse, spouse's employment or salary, children, child care arrangements, or dependents.
Handicap	Whether applicant has certain specific sensory, mental, or physical handicaps which relate reasonably to fitness to perform the particular job. Whether applicant has any handicaps or health problems which may affect work performance or which the employer should take into account in determining job placement.	Overgeneral inquiries (e.g., "Do you have any handicaps?") which would tend to divulge handicaps or health conditions which do not relate reasonably to fitness to perform the job.
Height and weight	Inquiries as to ability to perform actual job requirements. Being of a certain height or weight will not be considered to be a job requirement unless the employer can	Any inquiry which is not based on actual job requirements.

	show that no employee with the ineligible height or weight could do the work.	
Marital status (see also Name and Family)	None.	Whether the applicant is married, single, divorced, separated, engaged, widowed, etc. ( ) Mr. ( ) Mrs. ( ) Miss ( ) Ms.
Military	Inquiries concerning education, training, or work experience in the armed forces of the United States.	Type or condition of military discharge. Applicant's experience in other than U.S. armed forces. Request for discharge papers.
Name	Whether applicant has worked for this company or a competitor under a different name and, if so, what name. Name under which applicant is known to references if different from present name.	Inquiry into original name where it has been changed by court order or marriage. Inquiries about a name which would divulge marital status, lineage, ancestry, national origin, or descent.
National origin	Inquiries into applicant's ability to read, write, and speak foreign languages, when such inquiries are based on job requirements.	Inquiries into applicant's lineage, ancestry, national origin, descent, birthplace, or mother tongue. National origin of applicant's parents or spouse.
Organizations	Inquiry into organization memberships, excluding any organization the name or character of which indicates the race, color, creed, sex, marital status,	Requirement that applicant list all organizations, clubs, societies, and lodges to which he or she belongs.

(cont.)

TABLE 8.1 (Cont.)

SUBJECT	FAIR PREEMPLOYMENT INQUIRIES	UNFAIR PREEMPLOYMENT INQUIRIES
	religion, or national origin or ancestry of its members.	
Photographs	May be requested after hiring for identification purposes.	Request that applicant submit a photograph, mandatorily or optionally, at any time before hiring.
Pregnancy (see also Handicap)	Inquiries as to a duration of stay on job or anticipated absences which are made to males and females alike.	All questions as to pregnancy, and medical history concerning pregnancy and related matters.
Race or color	None.	Any inquiry concerning race or color of skin, hair, eyes, etc.
Relatives	Names of applicant's relatives already employed by this company or by any competitor.	Names and addresses of any relative other than those listed as proper.

(While the law does not directly prohibit policies governing the employment of relatives, any policy which has the effect of disadvantaging minorities, women, married couples, or other protected classes, would be a violation of the law unless it is shown to serve a necessary business purpose.)

SUBJECT	FAIR PREEMPLOYMENT INQUIRIES	UNFAIR PREEMPLOYMENT INQUIRIES
Religion or creed	None.	Inquiries concerning applicant's religious denomination, religious affiliations, church, parish, pastor, or religious holidays observed.
Residence	Inquiries about address to the extent needed to facilitate contacting the applicant.	Names or relationship of persons with whom applicant resides. Whether applicant owns or rents own home.
Sex	None.	Any inquiry.

(*Source:* Employment Practices, 1975)

2. A high school diploma requirement is excessively broad. The skills supposedly attained by diploma holders may not be the skills needed in certain jobs. For example, knowledge of United States history (a required course in some states) is probably not needed in a crafts job.

3. Possession of a high school diploma is not a guarantee that the individual has absorbed the basic skills taught in high school. Thus, a diploma may not be an accurate "measure" of who actually has particular skills and knowledge.

Virtually every kind of education requirement has met legal challenges. The most frequently attacked requirement is that of a high school education. Case law has progressed to the point where it is fairly clear that education requirements will *not* survive challenge, given adverse impact and the absence of validity evidence. In *Johnson* v. *Goodyear Tire and Rubber Co.* (1974), for example, a high school diploma requirement was disallowed at the court of appeals level.

Another court of appeals in *Pettway* v. *American Cast Iron Pipe Co.* (1974) reviewed the high school requirement for entrance into an apprentice program. Quoting from the lower court, the appeals court indicated the following:

> *This is not to say that such requirements are not desirable . . . it simply means that the "diploma" test cannot be used to measure the qualities. Many high school courses needed for a diploma (history, literature, physical education, etc.) are not necessary for these abilities . . . a high school diploma or equivalent criterion does not effectively measure the reading and study skills necessary for the course work required by the apprenticeship.*

However, there have been exceptions. In *League of United Latin American Citizens* v. *City of Santa Ana* (1976) the court gave a somewhat odd interpretation of the *Griggs* decision and indicated that it was "reluctant to accept the idea that educational requirements must be empirically validated" and applied a different standard to review the requirement for a patrolman's job. Instead, the court relied on the task force report of the President's Commission on Law Enforcement and the Administration of Justice, which both recommend a high school education requirement.

Postsecondary education requirements (e.g., advanced degrees) have also been litigated. These decisions involve other types of employment practices besides hiring: promotion, classification, and professional licensing. Table 8.2, taken from Zultowski, Arvey, and Dawson (1978), summarizes the court cases involving postsecondary educational requirements.

Perhaps one of the best known cases in this area is *Spurlock* v. *United Airlines* (1972). In 1969, United Airlines adopted several requirements for admission to its flight-officer training program, which included (1) a college degree, preferably in the "hard" sciences, and (2) a minimum of 500 hours of flight time. A suit was filed by a black male who was denied admission under the new college and flight-time requirements.

United Airlines first provided data showing a direct and substantial correlation between successful completion of the flight-officer training program and possession of a college degree—especially when the degree was in a science-related area. This was an attempt to show "business necessity." Second, United showed that it had uniformly applied its rules concerning flight officers' qualifications without regard to race throughout the years. Finally, United said that the requirement for a college degree was the least important of its flight-officer requirements, and could be waived in light of considerable flight time.

Given this information, the district court ruled that United's flight-officer qualifications were job-related, fair, and reasonable. Further, the court stated that "a line had to be drawn somewhere," and if the plaintiff's complaint in this case were upheld, a situation could develop whereby United would not be able to eliminate unqualified flight officers at any stage of the training program.

Approximately a year later, the plaintiff's case was again heard by a United States circuit court of appeals. Having once again to defend the business necessity of its college degree requirements, United repeated that the college degree requirement was the least important of its requirements for the flight-officer training program and that the applicant could compensate for it by having a substantial amount of flying time. United then pointed out that once flight officers are hired, they go through a rigorous training program and are required to attend intensive refresher courses every six months to maintain optimal performance ability. Possession of a college degree, then, points to the individual's ability to understand and retain information and concepts presented in the classroom atmosphere of the training program and the refresher course.

The court of appeals ruled that United had shown that its college degree requirement for flight officers was sufficiently job-related to warrant its use as a lawful preemployment standard. This court, however, gave special attention to the human and economic risks involved in the selection of unqualified flight officers. Since public interest clearly lies in having highly qualified flight officers, and since this college degree requirement has been shown to be job-related, this circuit court ruled that the lower trial court had correctly decided in favor of United Airlines. It is important to note the following:

1. This early decision did *not* rely on the EEOC guidelines or demand criterion-related validity.

2. The defense of the requirement rested on the fact that a college education was an "indicator" of individuals' ability to abstract and conceptualize and, thus, to deal with the requirements of the organization's training program.

3. The court gave attention to the utility aspects of the case and the risks involved in making poor selection decisions.

A recent review of court cases and EEOC decisions that involved consideration of education requirements was presented by Meritt-Haston and Wexley (1983). They reviewed 83 court cases and EEOC decisions and found that education requirements were likely to withstand court scrutiny under the following circumstances:

1. A relatively high educational degree was being challenged. That is, Master's and Ph.D. degrees were more likely to be given court approval than lower level degrees (e.g., a Bachelor's degree or a high school degree).

2. A highly technical job, a job that involves risk to the safety of the public, or a job that requires advance knowledge was being challenged.

3. The organization offers some rational assertion of validity, evidence of criterion-related validity, or an effective affirmative-action program. The converse of this, obviously, is that organizations will likely

TABLE 8.2
A summary of court cases involving postsecondary educational requirements in employment decisions.

	ADVANCED DEGREES	BACHELOR'S DEGREE	SPECIFIC COLLEGE COURSEWORK	SOME COLLEGE EXPERIENCE
Hiring	*Armstead* v. *Starkville Municipal Separate School District*[a] (1972)	*Payne* v. *Travenol Laboratories, Inc.* (1976)	*Morgan* v. *Kerrigan* (1976)	EEOC Decision No. 71-2237 (1971)
		Spurlock v. *United Airlines*[b] (1972)	*Holliman* v. *Price* (1975)	EEOC Decision No. 71-1447[c] (1971)
	Wade v. *Mississippi Cooperative Extension Service* (1974)	*U.S.* v. *Lee Way Motor Freight, Inc.* (1973)	*King* v. *Civil Service Commission* (1974)	
		EEOC Decision No. 70-402		
		Goodloe v. *Martin Marietta Corp.* (1974)		
		Jackson v. *Sargent* (1974)		

Promotion and classification	
	Townsend v. *Nassau County Medical Center* (1976, 1977)
	Richardson v. *Civil Service Commission* (1973)
	Strain v. *Philpott*[c] (1971)
	EEOC Decision No. 72-0697 (1972)
	EEOC Decision No. 75-040[d] (1975)
Professional licensing	*Dent* v. *State of West Virginia* (1889)
	Watson v. *State of Maryland* (1910)
	Berger v. *Board of Psychologist Examiners* (1976)
	Taylor v. *Hays* (1970)

[a] Also involves employee retention.
[b] College degree preferred in the "hard" sciences.
[c] College degree must be from specific institution.
[d] College degree must include study in electronics.
[e] Concerns college students for summer employment.

Source: Zultowski (1978). Copyright 1978 by the American Psychological Association. Adapted by permission of the author.

be unable to defend their use of education requirements for lower level jobs when they fail to present any validation evidence or convincing rationale.

As noted by Schlei and Grossman (1985), "Decisions continue to follow the trend of relaxing stringent validation requirements for highly skilled and professional jobs while maintaining such requirements for relatively low skilled positions" (p. 21).

Education requirements: Validity. It is difficult to establish the validity of education requirements. Since they have been *assumed* to be valid, education requirements are among the most frequently used, but the least formally validated, selection devices.

Two strategies may be used to validate such requirements. Criterion-related validation studies may be attempted when sufficient variability exists in a sample to permit the analyses. However, a particular education requirement (e.g., a high school education) may have been in effect for a number of years. Thus, there may be no employees holding the position with *less* than the required degree. This lack of variability results in "restriction of range" (see Chapter 2), and in some instances a correlation cannot even be calculated because there is no variability. (Recall that in calculating a correlation, it is necessary for the variables being correlated to exhibit some variability; the standard deviations are used in the denominator of the equation.)

Content validity represents a second strategy, especially when setting postsecondary and/or specialized training requirements. In many jobs, determination of content validity is rather straightforward. For example, a bachelor's degree in architecture may be a reasonable requirement for employment as an architect.

The published research literature has only a few reports of the relationship between education and job performance. Robinson (1972), Kavanagh and Yale (1972), McClelland and Rhodes (1969), and Cascio (1976) indicate that education (and other demographic variables) is positively related to job performance.

The review by Meritt-Haston and Wexley (1983) cited earlier also summarized the results of 12 studies that involved some kind of validation effort. After weighting the correlations by sample size and with a combined total sample size of over 71,000 subjects across the 12 studies, the average correlation between education and tenure was .27. The correlation between education level and ratings of job performance was .15; the correlation with number of promotions was .23. Although these correlations would probably be much higher if proper corrections for restriction in range and unreliability were made, they are comparable to corrected coefficients reported by Hunter and Hunter (1984). Thus there appears to be some good evidence for the validity of education requirements.

Experience Requirements

Experience requirements are often used in the selection of employees. In applying for jobs, applicants will frequently learn that in order to even apply they need to have a certain number of years of experience in a particular content or job area. The rationale behind using and applying experience requirements are well known. First, it is assumed that direct experience with a particular job or content area (e.g., accounting or computer programming) has resulted in an accumulation of the needed stock of knowledge, skills, abilities, and other characteristics necessary for successful job performance. A second assumption concerns motivation. It is presumed that individuals with past experience have been drawn to and are satisfied with the particular occupational activities involved and are "motivated" to continue to perform them. Finally, there is the assumption based on the "behavioral consistency" model: The best predictor of future behavior is past behavior.

From a fairness perspective, however, there are certain kinds of considerations that need to be understood about the use of experience requirements. A major concern is that subgroups within some protected classifications often have not had the opportunities to obtain the necessary job experiences. That is, because of past discrimination and fewer educational opportunities, minorities may not have the same level of job and content experiences. Similarly, females may not have the same experience levels due to childbearing and child-rearing periods.

Another concern is that the experience requirements imposed by organizations may simply be artificial barriers and really have nothing to do with job performance. A more glaring issue involves *the amount* of experience needed to perform the job. It may be that a certain amount or level of experience may be necessary to successfully perform a job, but some organizations impose what seems to be inordinate requirements (e.g., five or more years of experience). Whether these requirements are really necessary or simply represent tradition or whim is an important consideration. Unfortunately, it is quite difficult to substantiate particular experience requirements. Most organizations rely on the "face validity" of these requirements. Yet there has been considerable litigation focusing on experience requirements as selection (and promotion) criteria. Arvey and McGowen (1983) summarized 39 legal cases dealing directly or indirectly with experience requirements. Their review of these cases revealed a number of "themes":

1. Experience requirements have been upheld, but not always. Of the cases reviewed, experience requirements were upheld in 17 cases, not upheld in 16, and in 6 cases the authors were not able to determine the disposition.

2. Once a *prima facie* case is established, courts review experience requirements for evidence of business necessity. In some cases, the courts appeared to review the experience requirements on the basis of the face validity of the requirement. In other cases, the courts appear to look for stronger and/or empirical evidence. For example, in *Bradshaw* v. *Associated Transport* (1975), the court ruled that the experience requirements were subjective and arbitrary.

3. Experience requirements are more likely to be upheld when there are greater economic and human risks involved with failure to perform adequately. An example of this theme was illustrated in *Spurlock* v. *United Air Lines, Inc.* (1972), where the court articulated that there was a lighter burden to show job relatedness when there was a high degree of risk and costs involved in hiring unqualified people.

4. Requirements tend to fail if court scrutiny reveals or suggests that the experience requirement is arbitrary and tends to perpetuate the effects of past discrimination, especially in cases where minorities are less likely to have achieved the required experience.

5. Experience requirements tend to be upheld for higher level jobs that are more complex. It appears that the courts review experience requirements for lower level jobs with greater suspicion. There is some indication that experience requirements will not be upheld if (1) candidates can perform the job with relatively short on-the-job training, or (2) candidates might have been able to attain the requisite

skills, abilities, knowledge, and so forth through a variety of other experiences.

6. Experience requirements are not upheld if they are applied differentially.

Experience requirements: Validity. How valid are experience requirements? There are very few studies investigating this issue. Gordon and Fitzgibbons (1982) found a significant correlation of .15 between output and experience on the present job for 162 sewing machine operators.

One of the more recent and rigorously conducted studies is reported by Schmidt, Hunter, and Outerbridge (1986). These authors advanced two hypotheses: (1) Job experience has a greater impact on job knowledge than on direct work-sample performance. That is, they suggest that the experience individuals accumulate has more impact on the stock of individual knowledges than on immediate work performance as reflected by work samples. (2) Job experience does not affect job performance criterion ratings directly, but rather has an indirect impact via job knowledge. Thus they suggest a rather complex path relationship where job experience is related to job performance primarily through its impact on job knowledge. Using data from four military studies with a combined total sample size of 1474, these hypotheses were generally confirmed.

The problem with this study is that it dealt with job experience in a present or current job. The issue we are most interested in concerns the validity of past experience on present or future job performance. Using conventional ratings of previous experience on related jobs and tasks, McDaniel and Schmidt (1985) found a mean correlation of .14 with supervisory ratings of job performance. This was based on a meta-analysis of 89 studies with a total N of 6816. These results are similar to those reported by Hunter and Hunter (1984). Moreover, Hunter & Hunter have reported that the use of experience requirements for hiring, promotion, and certification purposes has resulted in substantial utility for the federal government.

Although there is not an overabundance of research investigating this issue, the available data appear to support the proposition that experience demonstrates a small but significant relationship with job performance. We were unable to locate any studies examining the issue of whether or not experience might demonstrate any differential relationship with performance.

PHYSICAL REQUIREMENTS IN SELECTION

Perhaps one of the more hotly contested areas in selection has been the merit of adopting physical requirements in selection. This debate has focused on two issues in selecting employees:

1. Requiring that applicants *meet or surpass* particular physical requirements (e.g., height, weight, or agility) to be considered for employment.
2. *Not* hiring individuals for a job because of a particular physical handicap or disability (e.g., blindness or confinement to a wheelchair).

In general, the adoption of physical requirements such as height and weight has the natural effect of screening out proportionally greater numbers of females and some ethnic-group members other than white males. An excellent recent article providing a comprehensive review of these issues is provided by Hogan and Quigley (1986).

Height and Weight

Height requirements have been commonly applied in police and fire departments across this country. It is a widely held belief that a patrol officer's height has an important effect on the officer's job performance. As a result of this belief, one study (Eisenberg, Kent, and Wall, 1973) showed that in 1973, 97 percent of a large sample of the nation's police departments had adopted some minimum height requirement, with the average minimum requirement being 5 ft 8 in.

However, height and weight requirements have the natural effect of screening out proportionally greater numbers of females and some ethnic-group members (Spanish-American, Orientals) than white males. For example, based on data published by the U.S. Department of Health and Human Services, *any* height requirement would serve to exclude greater proportions of women than men applying for a job. For example,* if an organization specified a 5 ft. 8 in. height requirement, greater than 90 percent of females would fail to reach this level, compared to less than 45 percent of males. If plaintiffs are able to demonstrate that these kinds of requirements operate in an adverse fashion, as they generally are able to do, the burden of persuasion shifts to the organization to demonstrate the validity of the requirements—which is relatively more difficult to do.

The reasons given for the adoption of such standards vary, but several "themes" are relatively commonplace. It is said that body size (height and weight) is related to physical strength, and strength is associated with effective job performance in an officer's job. There might be several reasons for this relationship: Shorter officers might be injured more by people trying to take advantage of them; shorter officers may simply not be able to subdue criminals as effectively as taller officers; or shorter officers may somehow invite more frequent attacks, resulting in their experiencing greater injuries than taller officers.

White and Block (1975) point out that these arguments are by no means conclusive. One of the problems with these arguments, they note, is that the relationship between physical strength and officer effectiveness simply has not been established, but is, rather, a widely held belief, yet to be demonstrated. "For example, over 95 percent of police deaths in the past decade have been the result of the use of firearms by the assailant. No study has established that physical strength would have been effective in preventing these deaths. . . . " (White and Block, 1975, p. 3). Physical strength is but one of several "tools" that an officer has to help him or her to perform effectively. Other factors such as following proper arrest procedures or knowing how to deal with people may reduce the need to resort to physical force.

---

* Obviously, a particular applicant pool may make these norms inappropriate; the particular men and women applying for the position may be taller or shorter on the average than the average general adult population. For example, in *National Airlines, Inc., In re* (1977), the court indicated it ". . . must discount heavily such studies . . . because they are not restricted to young, healthy, good-looking men and women who are employed to be in close contact with customers under sometimes trying conditions. . . . " However, the Supreme Court in *Dothard* v. *Rawlinson* (1977) indicated the usefulness of such statistics when there was no reason to suppose that the physical height and weight characteristics of the applicants differ markedly from those of the national population.

Height and weight requirements: Legal aspects. The most important case in this area was decided in June 1977 by the Supreme Court. In *Dothard* v. *Rawlinson* (1977) a female who was refused employment as a correctional-counselor trainee because she had not met the minimum weight (120 lb) and height (5 ft 2 in.) requirements established by an Alabama statute brought suit.

The height requirement was found to exclude 33.3 percent of women between the ages of 18 and 70 in the United States, compared to only 1.3 percent of men this age. Similar statistics were found for the weight restriction. The defendants argued that these minimum requirements did not involve any purposeful discriminating motives. The Supreme Court indicated that the principles outlined in *Griggs* v. *Duke Power* (1971) and *Albemarle Paper Co.* v. *Moody* (1975) were applicable here. That is, for a plaintiff to establish a *prima facie* case of discrimination, the plaintiff

> . . *need only to show that the facially neutral standards in question select applicants for hire in a significantly discriminatory pattern. Once it has shown that the employment standards are discriminatory in effect, the employer must meet "the burden of showing that any given requirement [has] . . . a manifest relation to the employment in question."*

The defendants then argued that the height and weight requirements were job-related because they have a relationship to strength, which is needed in the performance of the job. However, they did not produce any evidence demonstrating this presumed relationship.* The Supreme Court indicated that if strength is a real job requirement, then a test that measures strength directly should have been adopted. In sum, the requirements were not shown to be job-related, and the Supreme Court ruled against their use.

This case is important for two reasons: First, it indicates that height and weight requirements, *if* they exclude greater proportions of minority-group members, must be job-related. Second, the Court reiterated the notion that the *consequences* of an employment practice trigger the *shift-*

---

* A concurring opinion written by Justice Rehnquist indicates that the defendants may have legitimately argued that these minimum standards gave the prison guards the *appearance* of strength.

ing burden of persuasion. The *Washington* v. *Davis* (1976) case had concerned some civil rights advocates because it appeared to indicate a shift in the Supreme Court's position toward the need to demonstrate *intentional discrimination.*

Another aspect of the *Dothard* v. *Rawlinson* decision worth mention is that the Court held that it was legal to assign only males to close contact security systems when there would be considerable exposure to danger, exposure to sex offenders, or a climate of violence. The Court said: "A woman's relative ability to maintain order in a male, maximum security, unclassified penitentiary of the type Alabama now runs could be directly reduced by her womanhood." This part of the decision runs clearly contrary to prior decisions that allowed distinctions of this sort between men and women to be made only on very rare occasions. Justices Marshall and Brennan cast dissenting opinions concerning this part of the decision. They indicated that "there is simply no evidence in the record to show that women guards would create any danger to security in Alabama prisons significantly greater than already exists."

Organizations have on occasion successfully defended the use of height and weight requirements. In *Blake* v. *City of Los Angeles* (1977), a case was filed claiming that a 5 ft. 6 in. height requirement imposed by the city police department was discriminatory against females. The district court ruled that the city had supplied competent and reliable evidence regarding the job-relatedness of the requirement. It is not clear from the court record what specific evidence was used in making this judgment, but it appears to have been based on expert opinion and testimony. The court indicated: "The affadavits, for the most part, merely point out what is obvious and needs little proof. The affidavits suggest that a stronger and taller officer can more quickly and effectively control another person in event of a confrontation." However, on appeal the district court's decision was overturned and the police department developed a physical abilities test to replace the height requirement.

Height requirements: Research evidence. Perhaps the best review of both published and unpublished studies on the relationship between height and police officers' performance is White and Block's (1975) review of eight studies. In some instances, they used more appropriate statistics to reanalyze data. They concluded that the evidence for a significant relationship between height and officer effectiveness was practically nonexistent.

White and Block (1975) asked several police departments to cooperate in a study to examine this relationship. Eventually, five major departments participated in one phase or another. Two significant problems
were inherent in the concurrent-validity study. First, many of the departments had been using height requirements in their hiring procedures
for years and, thus, the samples suffered from restriction of range. Second, many departments had lowered these standards. Thus seniority was
confounded with height, since the newer officers tended to be shorter.

In general, the data from these five departments indicate essentially
no relationship between officer height and performance. Findings from
two departments (Nassau County and Dallas) in which officer experience
was controlled showed that, with only one exception, height differences
had no statistically significant effects on performance. Specifically:

1. No statistically significant relationship with height was found in
   either department for assaults on officers, auto accidents, department complaints, injuries on duty, or department commendations.
2. The one significant finding (in one department) was that shorter
   officers received a greater number of citizen complaints than taller
   officers.

Based on this study and on their review of the literature, White and
Block (1975) recommended that police departments eliminate the height
requirement and develop a selection system based on the overall potential
of the applicant. This important study has been used by several courts
in their review of height and weight requirements.

Another study, cited by various courts, indicates that women perform
as well as men in patrol-officer jobs, and that physical size may be un-
important (Block and Anderson, 1974). Eighty-six women were hired as
new patrol officers in the District of Columbia and were assigned to traditional male territories. A comparison group of males was hired at the
same time and also given patrol assignments. The average height of the
women was 5 ft. 7 in. versus 5 ft. 10 in. for the men. The average weight
of the women was 138 lb. compared to 170 lb. for the men. The men
and women performed patrol work in a generally similar manner, with
no indication that the women could not perform the job, or would be
victimized more often. While the performance ratings of the two groups
were about the same, women, as a group, made fewer arrests and gave
fewer traffic citations. Also, men were more likely to engage in serious

"unbecoming conduct." One unexpected finding in this study was that the performance ratings of taller officers (both male and female) tended to be *lower*.

In sum, the results of this study suggest that women perform equally to men in a traditionally male-oriented job. The study casts serious doubt on the viability of practices that exclude total classes of individuals from jobs based on untested presumptions.

Strength and Agility Factors

A strategy adopted by many organizations is to use strength and agility exams instead of height and weight to test job candidates. For example, candidates might be asked to lift heavy weights in order to determine their suitability for employment as garbage collectors or fire fighters.

A problem with these tests, however, is that women perform less well on these kinds of physical ability tests than men do. For example, Snook and Ciriello (1974) compared the performance levels of 31 women on six standardized basic handling tasks (e.g., lifting, lowering, pushing). The individuals were instructed to adjust their work load to the maximum amount they could handle without strain or discomfort; then their performance levels were compared to those of a sample of males from an earlier study. Results of the study indicated that the women handled significantly less weight and work load than industrial men on almost every task. However, the evidence did indicate that the performance differences beween the sexes were greater for certain tasks. The authors concluded that there are significant differences between men and women in ability to perform manual-handling tasks, and that these results were consistent with other experimental research.

How have these kinds of tests fared in the courts?

Strength and agility tests: Legal aspects. Hogan and Quigley (1986) summarized a number of court cases that involved the review of physical-ability testing programs. A summary of these court cases is presented in Table 8.3. In general, physical ability tests have been subject to the same standards of legal scrutiny as other selection devices where the courts recognize a number of validation techniques that are professionally acceptable. Table 8.3 reveals that organizations have not fared too well in defending the validity of their physical-ability tests. There appear to be several common problem areas or themes that cut across many of these cases.

TABLE 8.3
Cases litigated involving physical tests for employee selection.

CASE	CLAIM/JOB	SELECTION BATTERY	DEFENSE	DECISION
Hail v. White	Sex discrimination Title VII Police officer	Physical agility tests: Squat thrusts (25 in 1 min) Sit-ups (25 required) Push-ups (22 required) Squat jumps (27 required) Pull-ups (6 required)	"Synthetic validation" claimed No empirical evidence given	Tests upheld as "not unreasonable" and not non-job related" (8 Empl. Prac. Dec. [CCH] (9637)
Officers for Justice v. *Civil Service Commission*	Sex discrimination and national origin discrimination Title VII Fourteenth Amendment Police officer	Physical agility tests: Primarily upper-body strength Sandbag lift Wall test Dynamometer strength test 63% of men passed 1.2% of women passed	Concurrent study attempted	Job performance not predicted Tests in violation of Title VII Job analysis "not careful" and not done in accordance with guidelines No search for alternatives with less adverse impact Defendants enjoined from further use of tests

Hardy v. Stumpf	Sex discrimination Title VII Fourteenth Amendment Police officer	Physical agility tests: Run 300 ft. scale 6 ft wall Run 300 ft register 75 lb on grip dynamometer, drag 140 lb dummy 50 ft, and raise it to a 2 ft high platform Complete above in 2.5 min 15% of women passed 85% of men passed	Content validity claimed based on job analysis and concurrent study	Tests found reasonable and supported by job analysis Tests therefore upheld and not in violation of Title VII or Fourteenth Amendment
United States v. City of Buffalo	Sex discrimination Title VII Police officer	MPTC* standards score based on weighted sum of (a) numerical score for height/weight and (b) agility, strength, speed, and endurance test scores	MPTC* standards adopted after abandoning height requirement	Undue advantage given to taller persons Defendants enjoined from further use of tests

(cont.)

TABLE 8.3 (Cont.)

CASE	CLAIM/JOB	SELECTION BATTERY	DEFENSE	DECISION
Hull v. Cason	Race discrimination Title VII Fourteenth Amendment Fire fighter	Physical agility tests: Dummy carry (up a ladder) Pull-ups (2 required)	No defense presented in text decision	Use of tests upheld: "That an occupational function consumes a *de minimus* proportion of one's workday . . . does not necessarily diminish the need for selecting one who can best perform that function" (18 Fair Empl. Prac. Dec. [BNA] 1930)
Blake v. City of Los Angeles	Sex discrimination Title VII Fourteenth Amendment Police officer	Physical abilities tests: Run 50 yd, scale 6 ft wall Run 50 yd, 1 min overhand hang from chinning bar Run 50 ft, drag 140 lb dead weight 50 ft	Concurrent and content validation attempted	Job-relatedness not established Validation studies flawed Prediction of training success insufficient Defendants enjoined from further use of tests

Case	Issue / Job	Tests	Validity	Outcome
United States v. *City of Philadelphia*	Sex discrimination Police officer	"Tremor" test—holding a stylus steady for 17 s Endurance run—12 min run on 1/8 mi track—scored on number of laps Physical performance tests: 1/2 mi shuttle run Obstacle course Jump reaction time Hand grip 30.9% of women passed 97.2% of men passed	Concurrent validity claimed	Defendants enjoined from further use of tests No showing of job-relatedness
United States v. *New York*	Race discrimination Sex discrimination Title VII Fourteenth Amendment State trooper	Physical performance test Phase I P/F test: Shotgun aiming Tire change Portable scale life Pull deer off roadway Physical coordination course	Content validity claimed	Defendants enjoined from further use of tests Job analysis inappropriate for content validation Different scoring could have reduced adverse impact

(cont.)

TABLE 8.3 (Cont.)

CASE	CLAIM/JOB	SELECTION BATTERY	DEFENSE	DECISION
		Phase II: Competitive combative v. noncombative Attic opening Mile run Police pursuit course Nonweapon physical contact Drag person from vehicle 40.3% of men scored higher than highest scoring woman		
Harless v. Duck	Sex discrimination Title VII Fourteenth Amendment Police officer	Physical agility tests: 15 push-ups 25 sit-ups 6 ft standard broad jump 25 ft obstacle course (complete 3 or 4 to pass)	Developed through an "intuitive process"	Tests in violation of Title VII Tests not proved valid or job-related Job did not specify amount of strength or exertion required Test used elsewhere but never validated

| Berkman v. City of New York | Sex discrimination
Title VII
Fourteenth Amendment
Fire fighter | Physical agility tests:
Dummy carry
Hand grip
Free-style broad jump
Flexed arm hang
Agility test
Ledge walk
Mile run
0% of women passed
46% of men passed | Content validity claimed
Criterion-related by validity generalization | No justification for tests chosen or scoring used
Tests deleted in 1975 with apparently no detrimental effect on police department
Defendants enjoined from further test use
Validation strategy inappropriate—should have conducted construct or criterion-related validation
Job analysis results contradictory
"Ex post facto" rationalization of test selection
Tests used from other study declared "irrelevant" |

*MPTC = Municipal Police Training Council.

Source: From J. Hogan and A. M. Quigley (1986). Copyright 1986 by the American Psychological Association. Reprinted by permission of the publisher and author.

Many of the decisions have hinged on *adequacy of the job analysis* component. There are several related questions that usually arise in these cases. The first simply involves whether a job analysis was completed. Organizations that utilize physical-ability tests without conducting job analyses to determine the degree to which these tests are rooted in actual job requirements are quite exposed legally when such tests produce adverse impact.

A second problem that commonly occurs in these cases involves the material adequacy of the job analysis performed. Often courts will immerse themselves in an examination of the specific task-based items involved in the job-analysis procedures (for example, see *Officers for Justice v. Civil Service Commission* [1975]). In addition, courts will address rater agreement or reliability concerns of the job analysis as well as who the raters were and how the job-analysis data were collected. According to Hogan and Quigley (1986):

> *The courts clearly recommend that data be collected from qualified, appropriate respondents chosen on either a random or systematic basis. . . . The choice of raters might include job incumbents, first-line supervisors, subject-matter experts or job analysts. . . . Rater experience is central to the courts' evaluation of reliability; it has been noted that the significance of tasks may be quite different for someone who has performed than for someone who has not (p. 1201).*

The third question revolves around the correspondence between the job-analysis information collected and the particular validation strategy performed. A job-analysis that is designed to collect information about the knowledge, skills, abilities, and other characteristics needed to perform a job (KSAOs) may not be sufficiently rich in terms of information concerning the specific important tasks and behaviors that are performed. This latter type of behavioral or task information is much more amenable to constructing work samples that involve tests of physical abilities. This issue was highlighted in *United States* v. *New York* (1979), where the job analysis identified the KSAOs necessary for successful job performance. However, the court found this type of job analysis deficient because job tasks and duties were not defined, and the relative frequency, importance, and skill level of job tasks or duties were not identified. There was no discussion of the relative criticality or relative importance of the subelements identified in the job analysis.

Another theme that emerges from a review of the court cases in this area is that physical-ability tests that are "signs" (see Wernimont and Campbell, 1968) and measure more "abstract" indices of physical ability such as push-ups, squats, pull-ups, and so forth are much less likely to withstand court scrutiny than tests that are "samples" of actual work behavior. Although physical ability tests that measure these more abstract indices are designed to tap constructs such as upper-body strength, stamina, and so forth, it is much more difficult to establish the construct validity of these particular types of testing instruments. Certainly, if such tests are developed and used, they should be buttressed by information gleaned from other types of validation strategies.

One of the most instructive cases in this area is *Berkman* v. *City of New York* (1982), where the court ruled that the use of a content-validation defense was an "after the fact" rationalization. This complex case involved a number of thorny testing and job-analysis issues, and it is informative to read what the court said about the use of construct-oriented tests that measure abstract indices of physical ability:

> *Nothing in the concepts of dynamic strength, gross body equilibrium, stamina, and the like has such a grounding in observable behavior or the way firefighters operate that one could say with confidence that a person who possesses a high degree of these abilities as opposed to others will perform well on the job.*

We believe that physical ability tests that directly reflect actual work behaviors are more likely to survive court scrutiny. However, the adequacy of the job analysis on which these tests are developed will be an important determinant of court approval.

Strength and agility tests: Research evidence.   There is little published research showing differential performance on these tests, or reporting the validity of such tests to predict job performance. One of the best reviews of the research evidence in this area is given by Campion (1983). Hubbard, Hunt, and Krause (1975) have detailed a method of developing job-related strength and agility tests with firm roots in the content-validity strategy. Their five-step procedure included:

1. Task identification through detailed job analysis;
2. Ratings of the tasks by experts familiar with the job for strength and agility factors;
3. Review of possible tests to be recommended;
4. Preliminary choice and try-out of tests;
5. Preparation of report detailing the logic and rationale behind the choice of the tests.

However, they present no data or validity evidence concerning the soundness of their methodology.

One study (Gunderson, Rahe, and Arthur, 1972) used a concurrent validation design to investigate the relationship between physical-fitness tests and success in a rigorous training program for Navy underwater demolition team members. The participants in the study were 299 Navy enlisted men and 94 officers who had volunteered for the program. Physical-fitness measures as well as other data were collected before training and were correlated with success in training. Success was defined as completion of the program (49 percent of the enlisted trainees and 64 percent of the officers completed the program). Physical-fitness tests contributed to prediction of success in both groups. These results are not very surprising, given the arduous physical activity required during training.

Misner, Boileau, and Considine (1977) describe the results of their efforts to develop a physical-performance test for Chicago fire fighter applicants. After several pilot studies, they developed a test consisting of five physical components: stair climb, hose couple, flexed arm hang, body lift and carry, and obstacle run. They administered these tests to over 9000 applicants and reviewed the data for differences between black and white applicants as well as between other ethnic groups. In addition, they compared the test results of 34 women with a male group. Their analyses revealed only slight differences in physical performance between the various racial/ethnic groups, but there were major differences between the male and female applicant samples. The females scored well below the males.

Bernauer and Bonanno (1975) described their efforts to develop a series of physical-fitness tests to distinguish between effective and ineffective employees, using factor-analysis techniques. The seven tests they developed (reaction time, grip strength, percent body fat, step test, heart-rate, balance test, and sit-ups) differentiated between individuals who did or did not successfully complete a pole climbing school.

A study reported by Reilly, Zedeck, and Tenopyr (1979) demonstrated the criterion-related validity of several physical-ability tests for predicting performance in craft jobs. A job analysis was performed on several outdoor telephone craft jobs. Trainees for these positions were evaluated on a number of physical-ability measures based in part on the work of Fleishman (1964); these measures reflected the physical abilities outlined in the job analysis. These measures included such predictors as dynamic trunk strength, reaction time, balance, grip, and arm reach. Two years later, scores on these measures were correlated against a training criterion as well as against turnover. Using multiple regression procedures, these authors reported that the dynamic arm strength measure, the reaction time measure, and step-up time (a measure of stamina) were the best combination of predictors of training performance ($R = .45$). Although significant differences were observed between males and females on these predictors and the two criteria (with females demonstrating significantly lower scores on both sets of measures), further analyses revealed no differences between the regression lines for the male and female subgroups. These findings were replicated in another experiment reported in the same study. However, in this second experiment the final three predictors chosen were body density, balance, and static strength.

In a recent study involving steelworkers, Arnold *et al.* (1982) used an arm dynamometer to measure static strength. They found that this measure of static strength was strongly correlated with a work-sample measure of performance for 168 men and 81 women. Further analyses indicated that although females scored significantly lower on both the dynamometer and the criterion work-sample measures, regression results indicated that there was a slight bias against males. That is, the regression line for males was lower than that obtained for females, such that if a common regression line were used, males would be slightly underpredicted compared to females at any given predictor cutoff point.

Handicaps and Disabilities

Frequently, organizations will not have any formal rules or regulations about hiring individuals with handicaps or disabilities, but these individuals are often denied employment. As noted in Chapter 3, the handicapped are turning to legal remedies in the face of this kind of discrimination and are filing suits under the Vocational Rehabilitation Act of 1973 and/or the Due Process clause of the Fourteenth Amendment.

The affirmative-action obligation imposed by the Labor Department includes a paragraph that parallels the shifting burden of persuasion principle common in Title VII litigation. It states that contractors should review

> *. . . all physical and mental job qualification requirements to insure that, to the extent qualification requirements tend to screen out qualified handicapped individuals, they are job-related and are consistent with business necessity and the safe performance of the job. [60-741.6(C)(1)]*

Definition of handicapped.   It appears as if the definition of handicapped is rather broad. As defined by the Rehabilitation Act, a handicapped individual is a person who:

1. Has a physical or mental impairment that substantially limits one or more of such person's major life activities;

2. Has a record of such impairment; or

3. Is regarded as having such an impairment.

Thus, under this definition, the term "handicapped" includes not only groups traditionally categorized as handicapped (e.g., blind or paraplegic), but also individuals with such conditions as diabetes, epilepsy, or hypertension; coverage under the Rehabilitation Act is *not* limited to traditionally recognizable disabilities. Also included are people with a history of disability or illness (such as cancer), who are presently *not* suffering from the disability or illness, or whose present condition is stabilized (Schlei and Grossman, 1983). As noted in Chapter 3, the courts have also extended the term "handicapped" to include those who have suffered from alcoholism and drug abuse, and may eventually extend it to cover those suffering from acquired immune deficiency syndrome (AIDS).

Some court decisions: Selection of handicapped.   Courts have considered various factors in deciding whether discrimination exists against a handicapped individual. These include:

1. Whether an employee is presently able to do the job;
2. Whether the individual's disease is degenerative and will prevent him or her from performing in the future; and
3. Whether an employer is required to hire or maintain handicapped workers who are unable to meet company performance standards.

In *Gurmankin* v. *Costanzo* (1977), a U.S. court of appeals judge upheld a district court judgment that a school district violated the rights of a blind teacher who was refused consideration as a secondary school English teacher, based on misconceptions and stereotypes about the blind.

In *Montgomery Ward* v. *Bureau of Labor* (1977), an Oregon court of appeals indicated that it was an acceptable practice for an employer to refuse to hire a job applicant who had a history of heart problems, acting in accord with a physician's statement that the applicant might experience another heart injury as a result of employment.

Hoffman v. *Ohio Youth Commission* (1975) involved a man denied employment as a youth counselor on the basis of his blindness. The commission claimed that a blind person suffered from impaired mobility, had less capacity for observing and making diagnostic judgments, and was in greater physical danger. The plaintiff called in a blind person from a similar job who testified that his blindness did *not* represent an undue hardship. The court indicated that the denial of employment was premature and that the organization could have accommodated him.

It seems reasonably clear that courts look for evidence indicating whether the handicap influences job performance. Organizations must present clear rational *or* empirical evidence that a relationship exists, instead of relying on presumptions and stereotypes about the handicapped.

Two strategies can be followed by organizations to review the relationship between handicapped status and job performance:

1. Gather job-performance data from handicapped and nonhandicapped individuals to determine whether statistical differences exist between the two groups. Problems with small sample size and restriction of range will occur, however, since a restriction on hiring handicapped individuals may have preexisted.
2. Conduct a detailed job analysis of the particular job to ascertain the critical job duties involved. Judgment should then be made (usually through the use of expert witnesses such as physicians and psychol-

ogists) concerning the likelihood that individuals with a particular handicap could perform these duties. For example, if a job analysis of an air-traffic controller job reveals that good eyesight is required in order to observe and direct air traffic, it is not difficult to draw the logical conclusion that blind individuals would be unable to perform the job.

A factor to keep in mind, however, is that organizations are asked to make reasonable accommodations to handicapped individuals. Thus, *peripheral* job duties (and informal job qualifications) that adversely affect hiring of the handicapped will probably be rejected by courts.

Employment and the handicapped: Research results. A review of the research literature is limited for two reasons: First, the broad scope of the term "handicap" would necessitate a review of each possible disability. For example, research dealing with employment of the blind, the mentally retarded, the mentally ill, people with heart diseases, and so forth would need to be reviewed. Due to limited space, this literature is *not* comprehensively summarized.

A second reason is the basic scarcity of research dealing with employment and selection of the handicapped. Much of the literature concerning employment issues and the handicapped consists of such material as case studies or descriptions of special training programs for the handicapped, employment problems unique to handicapped individuals, and citations of instances of successful employment of handicapped persons. Very little thorough research is available that documents adverse impact or that examines the relationship between handicapped status and job performance.

An early study by Warshaw (1960) surveyed 174 firms about their outlook on handicapped individuals as job applicants. Personnel officers had various rationales for not hiring workers with physical impairments. The four major reasons given were (1) it makes for bad public and client relations, (2) they are not as effective as normal workers, (3) they need more sick leave, and (4) their coworkers are negatively affected. They concluded that there was no single reason that consistently shaped the attitudes and policies of personnel officers, either for or against the employment of workers with disabilities.

Levitan and Taggart (1977) discussed the employment problems faced by disabled and handicapped individuals, but introduced no data concerning job-performance differences between disabled and nondisabled employees. One problem of interpreting any study comparing relative job-performance levels of disabled versus nondisabled individuals is that employers may be apt to hire only those who have superior potential or who are the least disabled. Thus, there would be restriction in range and a correspondingly suppressed validity coefficient. Another factor is that supervisors may overrate the job performance of the disabled because they exceed expectations. For example, Baker, DiMarco, and Scott (1975) found that blind workers were rewarded significantly more by supervisors than sighted workers for identical performance.

Nagi, McBroom, and Colletts (1972) cited several studies showing that disabled workers compare well with regular production workers. They also indicated that the attitudes of employers toward the handicapped depend on the following:

1. *The type of disability.* Former mental patients seem to be the most negatively affected disability. Perhaps employers express more negative attitudes toward those disabilities that are the least understandable.

2. *Past and present experience with the performance of workers with impairments.* If employers have had generally positive experiences with past or present employees who are disabled, they are more likely to be receptive to hiring other such workers.

There have also been several studies focusing on the employer's physician and the preemployment examination. Physicians differ in judging which disabilities preclude employment, and therefore vary widely in the employment recommendations given. Further, physicians typically have very little information about the *jobs* themselves. Thus, they tend to maintain rather broad perspectives about who are acceptable job candidates.

In one study (cited by Nagi *et al.*, 1972) members of an industrial medical society were mailed the medical descriptions of a number of disabled individuals and asked for their recommendations concerning hiring suitability. However, they were not informed that the disabled individuals were already employed. Only 20 percent of the society members recommended jobs for the disabled individuals already employed.

Summary: Physical Requirements

A "theme" emerging from both the legal and the psychological literature is that physical requirements in selection may represent both a bless-
ing and a curse. When carefully applied, physical tests may be particularly useful in predicting job performance. Situations in which these
requirements may be most useful are where careful job analyses indicate
these particular physical factors are frequently called upon and are important factors in job performance.

Arbitrary physical factors established without job analyses and on the
basis of presumptions of needed physical prowess for a job can, indeed,
be a curse. These factors screen out substantial proportions of some minority groups who could do the job, if given the opportunity. Similarly,
presumptions and stereotypes concerning the capacity of handicapped
and disabled individuals may be equally arbitrary and discriminatory.
One implication of this literature review is that more research should
concern the relationship between physical factors and job performance.

PHYSIOLOGICALLY BASED SCREENING PROCEDURES

As many are aware, employers are beginning to more often use such
devices as genetic screens, polygraph tests, drug tests, and other
physiologically related testing procedures in the selection of employees.
The question of fairness arises if any of these types of testing procedures
have adverse impact against protected groups or if only certain groups
are tested and others are not. For example, some genetic anomalies are
more likely indigenous to specific geographical areas and races; medical
screening devices will obviously result in adverse impact based on national origin and race in these instances. In terms of disparate treatment,
females might not be considered for particular kinds of jobs (e.g., jobs
dealing with toxins or radiation) because of potentially harmful genetic
effects related to pregnancy and fertility, while only blacks may be tested
for genetic anomalies related to sickle cell anemia. Interestingly, it could
be argued that individuals suffering from various conditions these screening devices might uncover (e.g., medical procedures that screen for AIDS)
fit the definition of "handicapped." As such, any adverse employment-
related treatment (selection or otherwise) of these individuals might be
illegal under the Vocational Rehabilitation Act.

An excellent presentation of some of the issues associated with medical screening procedures is presented by Rothstein (1984). He indicates that in situations where medical, genetic, or biologically based screening procedures have adverse impact against protected groups, the courts would likely require an employer to include proof of the following:

1. *There is a valid basis for excluding workers who are presently capable of performing the required work but who may become physically unable or impaired at some point in the future.*

2. *It is essential to the business that employees not suffer or be suffering from an illness.*

3. *There is a high correlation between a specific genetic, cytogenetic, biological, or behavioral trait and the individual's increased risk of disease.*

4. *The specific screening procedure used to determine the presence of the trait has a high predictive value.*

5. *No other medical procedure work rule can achieve the desired goal with less discriminatory impact (Rothstein, 1984, p. 135).*

It appears that the kind of evidence needed in these situations to defend the use of the screening procedure is the kind of evidence relied on for a defense in more traditional testing contexts: Job relatedness and business necessity are the two defenses most likely to be put forth by organizations when such screening devices have any kind of adverse impact against protected groups.

Genetic Screening

Because of the rapid changes in chemical technologies over the last 30 years, many employees have been or will be exposed to chemical pollutants in the work environment. Evidence exists (e.g., Harsanyi and Hutton, 1981; Office of Technology and Assessment, 1983) that many of these employees are, to various degrees, susceptible to these pollutants, which may increase the likelihood of their contracting occupational diseases.

As a response to the potential harm to employees due to such exposure and because of recent extraordinary advances in medical technology related to genetic engineering, genetic employment screening will likely be an important selection-related issue of the future. As noted by Olian (1984), job applicants or present employees who are diagnosed through genetic screening tests as possessing genetic syndromes that may be "hypersusceptible" to harmful pollutants would "be screened out of chemically dangerous jobs and placed only in positions where environmental toxins do not present special hazards" (p. 424). Unfortunately, because of the many difficulties of doing research in this area (e.g., low base rates, long latency periods), there is little *direct* evidence to support the relationship between differences in genetic predisposition to chemical pollutants and the incidence of occupational diseases.

In light of the fact that there is little research that directly assesses the relationship between genetic deficiencies and occupational diseases, the most important fairness issue related to genetic employment testing concerns the existing evidence that many underlying genetic deficiencies are distributed unequally across groups within legally protected classifications. For example, glucose-6-phosphate-dehydrogenase (G–6–P–D) is a genetic deficiency that occurs only among men. Moreover, it is much more likely to occur among black, Filipino, or Mediterranean Jewish men. Genetic screening for this deficiency, thus, will likely result in disparate impact under Title VII based on sex, as well as race, national origin, and/ or religion. Moreover, since the costs of genetic testing are presently high and because the incidence of genetic aberrations in the general population is low, disparate treatment under Title VII will also likely occur. This will happen because it is unlikely that *all* applicants or present employees will be required to take a screening test; members of groups with a known "hypersusceptibility" will likely be the only ones tested. Disparate treatment is also likely to occur since many employers may not use the tests at all but rely simply on information about the occurrence of genetic syndromes in various groups. Thus some employers will automatically screen members of protected subgroups away from jobs where exposure to chemical hazards may affect the related underlying genetic syndrome (e.g., steering black men away from jobs where chemicals may trigger the G–6–P–D syndrome or women from jobs where chemical exposure may cause genetic damage to an unborn fetus).

Once a *prima facie* case of disparate impact or treatment is established, employers bear the responsibility of demonstrating the job-relatedness of the testing procedure. As noted above, however, research evidence concerning the job-relatedness of genetic screening devices that could withstand legal scrutiny does not yet exist. Therefore under the job-relatedness standard, employers are not likely to prevail, unless they can persuade the courts that something less than the strict job-relatedness standard should be applied.

For example, in the age discrimination case law, the courts have determined that employment decisions based solely on age are "reasonable" when the likelihood of harm to other employees or the public can be established and evidence of job-relatedness (i.e., that age is a BFOQ) is not available. However, there is little likelihood that anyone other than the employee will suffer direct physical harm from exposure to workplace pollutants. Moreover, the Supreme Court in *Dothard* v. *Rawlinson* (1977) interpreted Title VII to allow individuals to make their own choices about the workplace health dangers they are willing to accept. Thus even though genetic testing devices may successfully screen individuals who are highly sensitive to workplace pollutants, it may be the individual's right to ignore the test results. Considering these circumstances, as well as the fact that genetic screening will likely result in disparate impact and/or treatment, it may be a better strategy for organizations to seek alternatives to genetic screening.

The most obvious alternative to genetic screening is for employers to introduce engineering controls that minimize or eliminate the effects of workplace pollutants. It is very likely that plaintiffs in a Title VII suit would suggest such controls as a suitable alternative since engineering controls would substantially mitigate against disparate impact or treatment and also would "elevate the environmental safety level for the total work force" (Olian, 1984, p. 435). Unfortunately, engineering controls are generally quite costly and may be only marginally effective for some pollutants.

With the great strides in genetic engineering being made today, genetic screening for employment purposes is a very likely reality in the near future. It will be interesting to see how the legal and professional guidelines used to help resolve other discrimination complaints are applied in this instance.

Drug Testing

Presently, about 35 percent of Fortune 500 companies require indiscriminate drug testing of present or future employees. Federal, state, and local governments are moving in the direction of requiring such testing for many "sensitive" occupations (e.g., airline pilot, fire fighter, police officer). The primary force behind these programs is the perception that drug-related problems have a significant and direct relationship to on-the-job behavior (e.g., eroded performance, increased accidents). Although there are estimates that drug abuse costs businesses approximately $33 billion annually in lost productivity, most of these estimates are based on tenuous assumptions about the relationship between productivity and salary, and thus "are extrapolations and projections that have no convincing data base" (Morgan, 1984, p. 305).

Aside from the fact that we do not yet have an accurate picture of the true costs of drug use directly related to on-the-job performance, the two most important focal points in the debate over indiscriminate drug testing involve the technical and legal issues important to an understanding of this rather complex phenomenon.

The technical issues include concerns related to the reliability of drug tests themselves as well as concerns related to the reliability of drug testing laboratories and technicians. Although such tests rarely miss an illegal drug user, they do produce many false positives. It has been estimated that the inexpensive types of urine tests most frequently used by employers have a 5 to 20 percent error rate (Rust, 1986). Many of these false positives result from the fact that other *legal* substances produce the same results as illegal ones (this phenomenon is called "cross-reactivity"). For example, therapeutic cold medicines, such as Contac and Sudafed, can indicate amphetamine use, and cough medicines that contain dextromethorphan can create a false positive for morphine use. Even assuming perfect accuracy of the tests themselves, testing for drugs where "contact highs" are possible (as is the case with marijuana) involves the problem of the "passive inhaler"—the person who tests positive because of exposure to the drug use of others (see Zeidenberg, Bourbon, and Nahas, 1977).

Related to the above problems is the often overlooked fact that most tests are extremely imprecise. For example, a urinalysis does not measure the amount of a drug taken or indicate when the drug was taken. It thus cannot be used to determine the degree to which a drug has affected someone nor can it distinguish between off-the-job recreational use and on-the-job impairment. Because of these factors, it has been argued that indiscriminate drug testing is more likely to punish the casual pot user rather than workers with serious drug and alcohol problems. Moreover, the rapid increase in the number of companies involved in mandatory drug testing has spawned underground information on how to beat the tests as well as a black market for "drug-free" urine.

Although more sophisticated, less error-prone urine tests are available, they are also markedly more expensive to use and are just as imprecise as the cheaper tests. A possible solution to the imprecision problem would be to require employers to do confirmatory blood testing. Unlike urine tests, blood tests can yield information specific to both current use and degree of exposure; they are, however, as intrusive, if not more intrusive in a legal sense, than urine tests. Unfortunately, many small to medium size employers are likely to rely on the cheaper urine tests alone to make their hiring decisions and to thus avoid the added time and expense and potential legal hassles involved in confirmatory testing.

Compounding the error-rate problems associated with the tests is the unreliability of drug testing laboratories and technicians. For example, samples can get contaminated, sabotaged, or mislabeled, and tests bungled by poorly trained or inattentive technicians. As noted by Rust (1986), a well-publicized, well-controlled, ten-year study conducted by the Federal Centers for Disease Control reported that all but two of the 13 "established" independent laboratories investigated in the study had unacceptably high error rates (i.e., greater than 20 percent).

One way employers may avoid the technical problems associated with physiologically based drug testing would be to use paper-and-pencil drug testing procedures (see Alvord, 1985 or Jones, 1980). Similar to paper-and-pencil honesty tests (discussed below), paper-and-pencil drug testing procedures apparently are intended to measure an individual's attitudes toward drug use/abuse. The logic is that attitudes predict future behavior(s). However, the technical problems associated with paper-and-pencil honesty tests probably also apply to paper-and-pencil drug testing procedures, and they may mitigate against their use as the principle method for employment-related drug screening. Nonetheless, they may be somewhat useful as "prescreening" devices used prior to physiologically based drug testing procedures. If employers feel they must drug screen job applicants or present employees, this type of selection paradigm may help lower the number of false positives associated with physiologically based drug testing procedures.

The most important legal issue related to drug testing deals with the *means it is permissible to come by evidence of drug use*. What the courts have said regarding this matter is that the methods used must be implemented within constitutional limits. Thus the bottom-line legal issue involves the proper balance between the constitutional rights of employees and the business interests of employers.

Case law suggests that different legal standards apply depending on whether the employer is involved in a private or public sector business; this may change in the future. Currently, the prohibitions contained in the Fourth Amendment against unreasonable intrusion by the federal government into the privacy rights of individuals have been interpreted by the overwhelming majority of courts to include the taking of urine or blood samples from government employees without reasonable cause. For example, when drug testing of a government employee is *required* and there is no evidence to suggest that the employee's work performance has suffered, the testing violates the employee's constitutional protections against unreasonable search and seizure. These prohibitions have been extended to employees of state and local governments (as well as a small number of private sector employers whose actions are closely connected with state or local governments) based on court interpretations of the Fourteenth Amendment. However, the Fourth and Fourteenth Amendments do not prohibit the vast majority of private sector employers from requiring job applicants or present employees to submit to unreasonable searches and seizures.

The relief that private sector employers may feel based on the case law that supports their right to mandate indiscriminate drug testing may be short-lived. Assuming no major changes in the current case law, once private sector employees realize they are not afforded the same protections as their public sector counterparts, they are very likely to aggressively petition their elected representatives to extend legislatively the same provisions that now protect employees in the public sector. Thus the major significance of privacy regulations in the debate over drug testing may not involve existing regulations as much as laws that may be passed in the near future. For example, there are already municipalities (e.g., San Francisco) and states (e.g., California) as well as government regulatory agencies (e.g., the Federal Railroad Administration) that have their own privacy regulations that prohibit or restrict the use of drug testing by private sector employers.

Even if the prohibitions contained in other regulations are not more widely extended to the private sector, private sector employers are still subject to civil lawsuits for "wrongful action," as well as lawsuits based on provisions of Title VII of the Civil Rights Act of 1964. For example, there is evidence that drug use is not uniform across all race/sex groupings and therefore indiscriminate drug testing is likely to result in adverse impact under Title VII against some protected groups. If adverse impact is established, employers would bear the burden of proving the job-relatedness of drug testing programs. As noted above, drug testing is not a good job performance test since it cannot tell us anything meaningful about work performance. That is, even if an employee tests positive, it does not necessarily mean the employee is impaired at the time. Thus employers will not be able to establish the job-relatedness of their testing programs without supplemental evidence based on reasonable cause (e.g., a serious erosion of performance, an accident at work, behavioral manifestations such as noticeable problems in speaking, walking, staying awake).

The multitude of serious problems related to indiscriminate drug testing programs leads one to believe that once employers become more aware of these shortcomings, there will be somewhat of a retreat from the rush to institute mandatory indiscriminate testing programs. What employers are likely to fall back upon are testing programs that rely on well-trained supervisors as indicators of whether there is reasonable cause to suspect that an employee has a work-related drug use problem that warrants confirmatory compulsory drug testing.

Honesty Testing

As the estimated cost of employee theft has skyrocketed, employers have increasingly turned to the use of testing procedures that purport to predict the truthfulness or honesty of job applicants or current employees. These tests can be classified into two major types: the polygraph and the paper-and-pencil honesty test.

The polygraph (more commonly known as the "lie detector") primarily assesses changes in an examinee's galvanic skin response, cardiac cycle, and respiration during a monitored interview. The assumption is that lying can be detected by an analysis of observable changes in an examinee's physiological response pattern during questioning. In addition to the polygraph results themselves, examiners usually also take into account ancillary information about the examinee (e.g., past history, demeanor, admissions prior to testing) when arriving at an overall judgment.

Although there is evidence to suggest that the polygraph is reliable and valid, the research this evidence is based on is fraught with methodological limitations and other problems. For example, the validity of the polygraph has been brought into question since reactions besides guilt can trigger changes in an examinee's physiological response pattern (Saxe, Dougherty, and Cross, 1985). It is a fact that people differ in terms of their autonomic arousal levels (called lability) as well as their fear of the consequences of being found guilty, both of which can affect their physiological response patterns. Moreover, countermeasures such as the use of drugs or concealed physical activities can also help a candidate avoid detection; prior polygraph experience has also been shown to affect polygraph results. It is thus no surprise that evidence about the accuracy of the polygraph for employment purposes varies considerably from study to study (Sackett and Decker, 1979).

In addition to concerns about the polygraph's validity, there are concerns related to the frequency of false positives associated with polygraph usage. Since the base rate of theft in most organizations is considered small, it is likely that many innocent people will be misidentified; unless a polygraph has near perfect validity, a large number of false positives will occur. Moreover, since the accuracy of polygraph results are heavily influenced by the characteristics and behaviors of both the examiner and the examinee (Saxe, Dougherty, and Cross, 1985), the potential for disparate treatment or impact against protected classifications is increased.

In response to the highly intrusive nature of polygraph testing as well as the questionable nature of the research on the polygraph's validity and the potential serious harm to misclassified examinees, more than 20 states have either completely banned or heavily regulated the use of polygraphs for employment testing purposes. Consequently, the use of polygraph testing for employment purposes is fast becoming a non-issue.

However, the use of paper-and-pencil honesty tests has increased in popularity, partly as a response to present regulatory prohibitions on the employment use of the polygraph. Moreover, there are two bills before the Congress which would either ban outright or severely restrict the employment-related use of the polygraph in the future.

In this type of test, respondents are usually asked various sets of questions designed to solicit information bearing on an individual's honesty. For example, the questions may solicit information related to the respondent's attitudes toward theft or attitudes about punishment for crimes of theft. Moreover, biodata may be solicited as well as admissions of previous theft or other deviant behavior.

Despite reporting that the reliabilities of paper-and-pencil honesty tests were consistently high and that their validities were comparable to those of ability tests without adversely impacting blacks or women, Sackett and Harris (1984) did not enthusiastically endorse their use. Like the research related to the polygraph, research on the validity of paper-and-pencil honesty tests is plagued with methodological limitations, especially with the criterion measures used. For example, many paper-and-pencil honesty tests have been validated against polygraph results or admissions of past theft behavior, both of which are seriously flawed measures. Correlations in some studies are inflated by social desirability; others are based on more than the scores derived from the honesty test itself, making it difficult to assess the contribution of each to the reported results. Moreover, Sackett and Harris note that much of the research on paper-and-pencil honesty tests has occurred outside the mainstream of psychological testing and, thus, has not often been subjected to careful analysis.

Paper-and-pencil honesty tests are also likely to produce many false positives. As noted by Sackett and Harris (1984), ". . . depending on which test cutoff an organization chooses to use, anywhere from 25 to 75 percent of job applicants will fail an honesty test" (p. 242). Thus the same ethical concerns associated with the polygraph—that many innocent people will suffer negative employment repercussions as a result of being misidentified—also applies here. However, since paper-and-pencil honesty tests are far less physically intrusive than polygraph tests, it is unlikely that governmental regulation, such as that applied to the use of the polygraph for employment purposes will be extended to the use of paper-and-pencil honesty tests. Since other devices used to detect theft behavior at work have not been perceived by employers to be as effective as the polygraph or paper-and-pencil honesty tests, and because paper-and-pencil honesty tests are one of the least costly alternatives, we would expect to see a rise in their use as the use of the polygraph declines.

Moreover, as noted above about paper-and-pencil drug testing procedures, paper-and-pencil honesty tests may be somewhat useful as "pre-screening" devices to help lower the number of false positives that result from the subsequent use of the polygraph.

ARRESTS AND CONVICTIONS

It is well established through case law that an organization may *not* hire or fire employees on the basis of their arrest records. Because blacks tend to be arrested at higher rates than whites, a policy of denying employment for prior arrests would adversely affect them. At the same time, virtually no data exist to support the contention that those individuals who have been arrested perform less efficiently or less honestly than other employees (*Gregory* v. *Litton Systems, Inc.* [1972]).

In addition, EEOC takes the position that asking applicants about their arrest records will have a "chilling effect" upon the willingness of blacks to apply for employment, and that such requests may also induce applicants to falsify their application forms (an act for which they may later be fired).

Whether an employer may refuse to hire an employee on the basis of prior *convictions* is a more complex matter. In situations where there is economic and human risk, the courts have been flexible in requiring a demonstration of the business necessity of the conviction factor. For example, in *Richardson* v. *Hotel Corporation of America* (1972), a hotel was allowed to reject applicants for positions that are "security sensitive" (e.g., have access to room keys, access to rooms without inquiry), if they had been convicted of a serious crime. But, on the other hand, an organization that rejects applicants for jobs that do not involve possible economic loss or safety risks may be prevented from using a conviction record for making hiring decisions (*Green* v. *Missouri Pacific Railroad Company* [1975]).

Due to legal ambiguities, employers who want information about convictions would be well advised to state on their application blank: "Conviction of a crime is not an automatic bar to employment—all circumstances will be considered" (Schlei and Grossman [1976], p. 159).

Some recent legal developments have suggested that if organizations do ask for conviction information yet fail to use this information for screening purposes, they may be liable for subsequent consequences. This rationale falls within the legal doctrine of "negligent hiring" under which an employer may be liable for the wrongful acts of employees even though the acts committed were *outside* the actual scope of the employee's job duties. For example, in *Ponticas et al.* v. *K.M.S. Investments et al.* (1983), the owner and operator of an apartment complex was ruled negligent in failing to make reasonable investigation of an apartment manager's background. In this case, an individual applied for resident manager of an apartment complex and indicated that although he had been convicted of a crime, the crime consisted of "traffic tickets." The owner failed to investigate this information more thoroughly and hired the individual, who subsequently raped one of the tenants. Further investigation would have revealed numerous prior convictions and employment problems.

ADDITIONAL COMPONENTS OF THE SELECTION PROCESS

There are several phases of the selection process that were not covered in previous chapters. In this chapter, only a limited perspective on these components is presented because the legal principles are substantially the same as those involved in other components. Also, the available scientific research is very sparse, indeed.

Recruitment

Efforts to find qualified minority job candidates and solicit their applications for job openings are a requirement of most affirmative-action programs. The recruitment practices of prospective employers range all the way from word-of-mouth mechanisms to advertising in national newspapers. However, it is becoming clear to many affirmative-action coordinators that more active recruiting efforts need to be implemented to attract qualified minority applicants. In spite of this, few research studies are available to help organizations plan recruiting efforts; most have been testimonials. For example, the following suggestions were provided by the *Fair Employment Compliance Newsletter* (1976):*

- *Get out in the field.* Employers must visit schools, employment agencies, etc. to build friendly working relationships from potential

---

* Published by Management Resources, Inc., New York.

sources of minority candidates. Also, invite recruiting sources to an open-house briefing session at the organization.

- *Set up referral arrangements with other employers.* Contact other friendly employers and ask for resumés in their files which might meet the particular qualifications needed.

- *Develop future employees.* Cooperate with universities and other schools in sponsoring work-study programs in predominantly black and female institutions.

- *Make it easy for potential applicants to learn about job openings.* Attempt to reach potential applicants through newspapers and magazines aimed at minority and female audiences. Place spots on local television and radio stations and use telephone recruitment systems.

Byham and Spitzer (1971) emphasized that effective recruiting is really a marketing task as well as a personnel task. The recruitment process must include a marketing orientation because prospective applicants must be sold on the desirability of working for the company.

One study that did investigate the effectiveness of various recruitment mechanisms was reported by Hunt and Cohen (1971). Two hundred interviews were conducted with young adult male blacks and Puerto Ricans to determine whether they were aware of job openings at the New York City Police Department and, if so, how they had learned about them. Seventy-six percent of the 200 interviewees knew the openings existed. The five most frequently mentioned sources of knowledge of openings were (1) newspapers, (2) the police department's mobile recruiting team, (3) radio stations, (4) subway posters, and (5) friends or family members who were policemen. In addition, the study reported the features of a patrol officer's job that were viewed as unusually desirable or undesirable.

This study, one of the few that systematically explored responses to different recruitment efforts by minority members, makes recommendations directed at changing the current recruitment practices based on these findings.

Recruitment: Legal aspects.   An excellent review of the legal aspects in recruitment is provided by Mansfield (1973). Recruitment procedures are subject to the same kind of court review as are other "neutral" factors used in the selection of job candidates. It is quite possible that organizations that rely on traditional avenues of recruitment may not receive a particularly large number of minority applicants. Minority-group members may be shut out from these jobs because recruitment notices never reach them. "Since job information tends to be transmitted among people on the same social level, customary methods of communicating job openings primarily reach members of the majority and the information circulates among their peers" (Mansfield, 1973, p. 134). However, the legal issues concerning whether adverse impact has been shown are particularly complex due to such factors as the recruitment locale or area in question and to alternative explanations for any observed effects (e.g., worker job performance, employer reputation).

Nonetheless, courts have found that the recruitment practices of many organizations are in violation of Title VII. For example:

- The practice of relying on referrals by a predominantly white worker rather than seeking new employees in the market force was ruled discriminatory (*EEOC* v. *Detroit Edison* [1975]).

- Word-of-mouth recruitment served only to perpetuate an all-white work force and thus violates Title VII (*Long* v. *Sapp* [1974]).

- A company can violate Title VII by only recruiting from stations under same ownership (*EEOC* v. *New York Times Broadcasting Service* [1976]).

- Recruitment practices favoring friends and relatives of union members were judged unlawful (*EEOC* v. *Local 14, International Union of Operating Engineers* [1976]).

Once adverse impact has been demonstrated, it becomes necessary for the company to defend its recruitment practices by showing a "business necessity." At present, it is not clear what evidence will suffice to meet this burden. Mansfield (1973) suggests that additional costs to the company in increased recruitment may not be an adequate defense.

One recruitment technique that has drawn legal fire is job advertising. Title VII addressed this issue directly in Sec. 704(6):

> It shall be an unlawful employment practice for an employer . . . to print . . . any notice of advertisement relating to employment . . . indicating any preference, limitation, specification, or discrimination, based on race, color, religion, or national origin ex-

cept . . . when religion, race or national origin is a bona fide *occupational qualification for employment.*

In the context of this provision, advertisements that have referred to an "attractive lady,"* "career-minded men,"† and a "real sharp girl"‡ have been ruled discriminatory. One issued raised in the suit against AT&T was whether AT&T's recruitment advertising included sex-stereotyped ads. The EEOC asked two Stanford professors, Dr. Sandra Bem and Dr. Daryl Bem, to study the AT&T practice. High school seniors were asked to read a booklet including various kinds of advertisements and indicate their interest in applying for the AT&T jobs presented. However, for a number of the advertisements, the wordings had been changed to reflect a sex-typed ad. For instance, where a traditional male job (e.g., lineman) was described in typical male terms and a traditional female job (e.g., telephone operator) was also designated as such, they substituted sex-neutral ads in which no sex-typing language was allowed, and also sex-reversed ads in which the sex-typing language was reversed. The results of this experiment indicated that substantially more women would apply for a traditionally male job, if recruited through neutral or sex-reversed advertisements (Babcock *et al.,* 1975, p. 299).

In addition, the Age Discrimination in Employment Act of 1967 (as amended in 1986) prohibits any advertisement indicating preference, limitations, specification, or discrimination, based on an individual's age.

Reference Check

The reference check is a reasonably common practice among employers in selecting employees. While some organizations have forms and check-lists that previous employers are asked to complete, many times the reference check takes the form of an informal telephone call.

There has been little litigation concerning reference checks. In *EEOC* v. *National Academy of Sciences* (1976), an applicant was denied a position on the basis of an unfavorable employment reference provided by her former supervisor. The individual applying for the position charged a vi-

---

* CCH EEOC December 6005 (1969).
† CCH EEOC December 6296 (1971).
‡ Cited in Schlei and Grossman, 1976, p. 450.

olation of Title VII because the reference check had a disproportionate impact on blacks, and was not job-related. The court found otherwise, however. Data presented at the trial indicated (1) that a disproportionate impact did not occur, and (2) a validation study was presented (the details of the study were not included in the decision), which indicated a significant relationship between the reference check and work behavior.

In *Rutherford* v. *American Bank of Commerce* (1976) an employee won a judgment against an organization that had, in the letter of recommendation, mentioned that the former employee had filed a sex-discrimination charge against the firm. The employee was unable to secure later employment. The court ruled that the employer had unlawfully retaliated against the former employee because she had sought to exercise her rights under Title VII.

In terms of validity, the published research on the reference check is not particularly encouraging. Browning (1968) correlated reference-check ratings after one year on the job for 508 elementary school teachers, and found that none of the various factors in the rating form had any value in predicting end-of-year ratings. Mosel and Goheen conducted a series of studies in the late 1950s (Mosel and Goheen, 1958; Goheen and Mosel, 1959; Mosel and Goheen, 1959) which showed relatively little evidence for the validity of the reference-check procedure. More encouraging evidence for the reference check has been presented by Nash (1971) and Carroll and Nash (1972). However, little evidence is available concerning differences between minority- and nonminority-group members on reference-check information or subgroup validity differences.

Time Lags between Selection Hurdles

One problem ignored in the recruitment and selection of minority candidates is that the *time lag* between the initial application and subsequent psychological testing (interview, or other formal selection procedure) may represent a significant barrier in their hiring. Minority (and majority) applicants may withdraw simply because of the great time lapse between selection procedures. This time lapse may be of particular importance in large organizations and civil service operations where individuals complete application forms several months, or longer, prior to undergoing the next phase of the selection process.

This view is supported by the research of Hunt and Cohen (1971) who reported that over half of the white candidates for a patrolman's job who passed the first written exam did not continue to the point of completing all the selection procedures, even though they had not been officially eliminated. Black candidates exhibited an even higher dropout rate. These authors attributed this to the long duration (17 months) of the selection process.

A study that addressed this issue directly was reported by Arvey *et al.* (1975). Seventy jobs were identified for which minority-group members (predominantly blacks or Indians) had applied. The number of days between the closing date for application and the first formal selection procedure (usually an oral exam or a pencil-and-paper test) was measured. Thirty jobs had short time delays (mean delay was 14.1 days) and 39 jobs had relatively long "time lags" (mean delay was 76.0 days).

The percentage of minority candidates who failed to appear after a *long* time delay was almost double the percentage found for the majority group. The difference was statistically significant. Several factors may have accounted for this phenomenon (e.g., minority members needing to take other jobs immediately), but the fact still remains that such organizations might be able to improve track records of hiring minorities by decreasing the length of time between the application and the next phase of the selection process.

SUMMARY

This chapter has reviewed a wide range of topic areas. Again, it is difficult to provide a general summary of all the specific areas covered. What is clear, however, is that a majority of the "components" of the selection process have been subject to legal review. Thus, it is not only testing and the interview which organizations must carefully review for evidence of possible unfair discrimination.

The present chapter called attention to the fact that many states have issued guidelines on permissible preemployment inquiries. It also reviewed the legal status of the use of educational requirements in hiring employees and found that the use of such requirements—particularly the use of a high school requirement—is vulnerable to attack. There has been very little published research that establishes the validity of such requirements.

The chapter paid particular attention to the use of physical requirements in selection systems. Many cases have dealt with the legality of imposing height and weight requirements. Most organizations have failed to establish the validity of these requirements, even when it has been shown that such standards impose a severe adverse impact against women.

The chapter also reviewed the legal and research data concerning strength and agility requirements. There are reasonably good indications that organizations will survive legal review if they can gather data to support their contention (either through empirical or logical analysis) that the physical skills they require match those the particular job requires.

A major concern of the chapter was the impact of imposing physical requirements on the selection of disabled and handicapped applicants. It provided a legal and research review and noted the lack of research on the selection of handicapped and disabled workers.

In addition, it focused on the use of arrests and convictions as factors in employing individuals and noted that while there was some legal justification for the use of *convictions* in not hiring into high-risk jobs, the use of arrest records for not hiring has less justification.

Finally, the chapter concluded by reviewing aspects of recruitment and advertising, reference checking, and also the delay process involved in selecting employees. Organizations may wish to take advantage of more aggressive recruiting mechanisms in searching out minority members in addition to shortening the time required to go through the application process.

REFERENCES

Albemarle Paper Co. v. *Moody,* 10 FEP 1181 (1975).

Arnold, J. D.; J. M. Rauschenberger; W. G. Soubel; and R. M. Guion (1982). *Journal of Applied Psychology* 67: 588–604.

Alvord, G. (1985). Validation of the personnel selection inventory as a screening test for bus operators. *Journal of Security Administration* 8: 37–47.

Armstead v. *Starkville Municipal Separate School District,* 461 F.2d 276, 4 FEP 864 (1972).

Arvey, R. D.; M. E. Gordon; D. P. Massengill; and S. J. Mussio (1975). Differential dropout rates of minority and majority job candidates due to "time lags" between selection procedures. *Personnel Psychology* **28**: 175–180.

Arvey, R. D., and S. L. McGowen (1983). The use of experience requirements in selecting employees: A legal review. *Personnel Selection and Training Bulletin* 4, 28–41. (Published by Memphis State University, Center for Nuclear Studies, Advancement and Continuing Education.)

Babcock, B. A.; A. E. Freedman; E. H. Norton; and S. C. Ross (1975). *Sex Discrimination and the Law: Causes and Remedies.* Boston: Little, Brown.

Baker, L. D.; N. DiMarco; and W. E. Scott (1975). Effects of supervisor's sex and level of authoritarianism on evaluating and reinforcement of blind and sighted workers. *Journal of Applied Psychology* **60**: 28–32.

Berger v. *Board of Psychologist Examiners,* 521 F.2d 1056, 44 L.W. 2235 (1976).

Berkman v. *City of New York,* 536 F. *Suppl.* 177 (1982).

Bernauer, E. M., and J. Bonanno (1975). Development of physical profiles for specific jobs. *Journal of Occupational Medicine* **17**: 27–33.

Blake v. *City of Los Angeles,* 15 FEP 77 (1977).

Blake v. *City of Los Angeles,* 19 FEP 1441 (1979).

Block, P. B., and D. J. Anderson (1974). *Policewomen on Patrol: Final Report,* Police Foundation, May.

Bradshaw v. *Associated Transport, Inc.,* 12 FEP 859 (1975).

Browning, R. C. (1968). Validity of reference ratings from previous employees. *Personnel Psychology* **21**: 389–393.

Byham, W. C., and M. E. Spitzer (1971). *The Law and Personnel Testing.* American Management Association.

Campion, M. A. (1983). Personnel selection for physically demanding jobs: Review and recommendations. *Personnel Psychology* **36**: 527–550.

Carroll, S. J., and A. N. Nash (1972). Effectiveness of a forced-choice reference check. *Personnel Administration* 35: 42–146.

Cascio, W. (1976). Turnover, biographical data and fair employment practices. *Journal of Applied Psychology* 61: 576–580.

Connecticut General Life Insurance v. DILHR, 13 FEP 1811 (1976).

Dent v. *State of West Virginia*, 129 U.S. 114, 9 S.CT. 231, 32 L.ED. 623 (1889).

Dothard v. *Rawlinson*, 15 FEP 11 (1977).

EEOC Decision No. 70-402, 2 FEP 427 (1970).

EEOC Decision No. 71-1447, 3 FEP 391 (1971).

EEOC Decision No. 71-2237, 3 FEP 1200 (1971).

EEOC Decision No. 72-0697, 4 FEP 44 (1972).

EEOC Decision No. 75-040, 10 FEP 287 (1975).

EEOC v. *Detroit Edison*, 10 FEP 239, 247 and 1063 (1975).

EEOC v. *Local 14, International Union of Operating Engineers*, 11 EPD 10190 (1976).

EEOC v. *National Academy of Sciences*, 12 FEP 1690 (1976).

EEOC v. *New York Times Broadcasting Service*, 14 FEP 802 (1976).

Eisenberg, T.; D. A. Kent; and C. R. Wall (1973). *Police Personnel Practices in State and Local Governments.* International Association of Chiefs of Police *et al.*, Washington, D.C.

Fleishman, E. A. (1964). *The Structure and Measurement of Physical Abilities.* Englewood Cliffs, N.J.: Prentice-Hall.

Goheen, H. W., and J. N. Mosel (1959). Validity of the employment recommendation: II. Comparison with field investigations. *Personnel Psychology* 12: 297–301.

Goodloe v. *Martin Marietta Corp.*, 5 FEP 1046 (1972), 10 FEP 1176 (1974).

Gordon, M. E., and W. J. Fitzgibbons (1982). An empirical test of the validity of seniority as a factor in staffing decisions. *Journal of Applied Psychology* 67: 311–319.

Green v. *Missouri Pacific Railroad Company,* 10 FEP 1409 (1975).

Gregory v. *Litton Systems,* 5 FEP 267 (1972).

Griggs v. *Duke Power,* 3 FEP 175 (1971).

Gunderson, G. H.; R. H. Rahe; and R. T. Arthur (1972). Prediction of performance in stressful underwater demolition training. *Journal of Applied Psychology* 56: 430–432.

Gurmankin v. *Costanzo,* 14 FEP 1359 (1977).

Hail v. *White,* 8 Emp. Prac. Dec. 9637 (1973).

Hardy v. *Stumpf,* 27 FEP (1978).

Harless v. *Duck,* 22 FEP 1073 (1980).

Harsanyi, Z., and R. Hutton (1981). *Genetic Prophecy: Beyond the Double Helix.* New York: Bantam Books.

Hoffman v. *Ohio Youth Commission,* 13 FEP 30 (1975).

Hogan, J., and A. M. Quigley (1986). Physical standards for employment and the courts. *American Psychologist* 41: 1193–1217.

Holliman v. *Price,* 9 FEP 1363(1975).

Hubbard, H. F.; T. Hunt; and R. D. Krause (1975). Job related strength and agility tests—a methodology. *Public Personnel Management,* Sept–Oct.

Hull v. *Cason,* 18 FEP 1379 (1978).

Hunt, I. C., and B. Cohen (1971). *Minority recruiting in the New York City Police Department.* The New York City Rand Institute, May.

Hunter, J. E., and R. F. Hunter (1984). Validity and utility of alternative predictors of job performance. *Psychological Bulletin* 96: 72, 98.

Jackson v. *Sargent,* 10 FEP 178 (1975).

Johnson v. *Goodyear Tire and Rubber Company,* 7 FEP 627 (1974).

Jones, J. W. (1980). Attitudinal correlates of employees' deviance: Theft, alcohol use, and nonprescribed drug use. *Psychological Reports* 47: 71–77.

Kavanagh, M. J., and D. R. Yale (1972). Biographical correlates of middle managers' performance. *Personnel Psychology* 25: 319–332.

King v. Civil Service Commission, 7 FEP 348 (1973).

King v. Civil Service Commission, 14 FEP 315 (1974).

League of United Latin American Citizens v. City of Santa Ana, 12 FEP 651 (1976).

Levitan, S. A., and R. Taggart (1977). *Jobs for the Disabled.* Baltimore: Johns Hopkins University Press.

Long v. Sapp, 8 FEP 1079 and 1084 (1974).

Mansfield, D. K. (1973). The recruitment of job applicants under Title VII and the Civil Rights Act of 1964. *The Columbia Journal of Law and Social Problems* 9: 131–165.

McClelland, J. N., and F. Rhodes (1969). Prediction of job success for hospital aides and orderlies from MMPI scores and personal history data. *Journal of Applied Psychology* 53: 49–54.

McDaniel, M. A., and F. L. Schmidt (1985). *A meta-analysis of the validity of training and experience ratings in personnel selection.* Washington, D.C.: Office of Staffing Policy, U.S. Office of Personnel Management.

Meritt-Haston, R. and K. N. Wexley (1983). Educational requirements: Legality and validity. *Personnel Psychology* 36: 743–753.

Misner, J. E.; R. A. Boileau; and W. J. Considine (1977). Development of a physical performance test for Chicago firefighter applicants. Technical report submitted to Department of Personnel, City of Chicago, Room 1100 City Hall, Chicago, Illinois, 60602, March 14.

Montgomery Ward v. Bureau of Labor, 14 FEP 1091 (1977).

Morgan, J. (1984). Problems of mass urine screening for misused drugs. *Journal of Psychoactive Drugs* 16: 305–317.

Morgan v. *Kerrigan*, 11 EPD 6671 (1976).

Mosel, J. N., and H. W. Goheen (1958). The validity of the employment recommendation questionnaire in personnel selection: I. Skilled trades. *Personnel Psychology* 11: 481–490.

——— (1959). The employment recommendation questionnaire: III. Validity of different types of references. *Personnel Psychology* 12: 469–477.

Nagi, S.; W. H. McBroom; and J. Colletts (1972). Work, employment and the disabled. *The American Journal of Economics and Society* 31: 20–34.

Nash, A. M. (1971). Modifications of a forced-choice format for use in personnel selection and appraisal. *Psychological Reports* 28: 108–110.

National Airlines, Inc., In re, 14 FEP 1806 (1972).

Office of Technology and Assessment. (1983). *The Role of Genetic Testing in the Prevention of Occupational Disease.* Washington, D.C.: Government Printing Office.

Officers for Justice v. *Civil Service Commission,* 11 FEP 815 (1975).

Olian, J. D. (1984). Genetic screening for employment purposes. *Personnel Psychology* 37: 423–438.

Payne v. *Travenol Laboratories, Inc.,* 12 FEP 770, 11 CCH EPD 7289 (1976).

Pettway v. *American Cast Iron Pipe Co.,* 7 FEP 1115 (1974).

Ponticas et al. v. *K.M.S. Investments et al.,* 331 *N.W. 2d* 907 (Minn. 1983).

Reilly, R. R.; S. Zedeck; and M. Tenopyr (1979). Validity and fairness of physical ability tests for predicting performance in craft jobs. *Journal of Applied Psychology* 64: 262–274.

Richardson v. *Civil Service Commission,* 387 F. Supp. 1267, 7 FEP 425 (1973).

Richardson v. *Hotel Corporation of America,* 5 FEP 23 (1972).

Robinson, D. D. (1972). Predictions of clerical turnover in banks by means of a weighted application blank. *Journal of Applied Psychology* **56**: 282.

Rothstein, M. A. (1984). *Medical screening of workers.* Washington, D.C.: Bureau of National Affairs.

Rust, M. (1986). The legal dilemma. *American Bar Association Journal* **3**: 51–54.

Rutherford v. *American Bank of Commerce,* 12 FEP 1184 (1976).

Sackett, P. R., and P. J. Decker (1979). Detection of deception in the employment context: A review and critical analysis. *Personnel Psychology* **32**: 487–506.

Sackett, P. R., and M. M. Harris (1984). Honesty testing for personnel selection: A review and critique. *Personnel Psychology* **37**: 221–246.

Saxe, L.; D. Dougherty; and T. Cross (1985). The validity of polygraph testing: Scientific analysis and public scrutiny. *American Psychologist* **40**: 355–366.

Schlei, B. L., and P. Grossman (1976). *Employment Discrimination Law.* Washington, D.C.: Bureau of National Affairs, Inc.

Schlei, B. L., and P. Grossman (1985). *Employment Discrimination Law: 1983–1984 Cumulative Supplement.* M. Dichter and D. Cathart (eds.) Washington, D.C.: Bureau of National Affairs, Inc.

Schmidt, F. L.; J. E. Hunter; and A. N. Outerbridge (1986). Impact of job experience and ability on job knowledge, work sample performance, and supervisory ratings of job performance. *Journal of Applied Psychology* **71**: 432–439.

Snook, S. H., and M. S. Ciriello (1974). Maximum weights and work loads acceptable to female workers. *Occupational Health Nursing* **22**: 11–20.

Spurlock v. *United Airlines, Inc.,* 475 F.2d 216, 3 FEP 839 (1971), 5 FEP 17 (1972).

Strain v. *Philpott,* 3 FEP 922 (1971).

Taylor v. *Hays,* 131 ILL. App. 2d 305, 264 N.E. 2d 814 (1970).

Townsend v. *Nassau County Medical Center,* 11 EPD 7564 (1976), 14 EPD 5306 (1977).

United States v. *City of Buffalo,* 37 FEP 628 (1985).

United States v. *City of Philadelphia,* 21 FEP 30277 (1979).

United States v. *Lee Way Motor Freight, Inc.,* 7 FEP 710 (1973).

United States v. *New York,* 21 *Empl. Prac. Dec.* 30314 (1979).

Wade v. *Mississippi Cooperative Extension Service,* 372 F. Supp. 126, 7 FEP 282 (1974).

Warshaw, L. J. (1960). Employment of the handicapped. *New York State Journal of Medicine* 60: 2426–2433.

Washington v. *Davis,* 12 FEP 1415 (1976).

Watson v. *State of Maryland,* 218 U.S. 173, 30 S. Ct. 644, 54 L.ED. 987 (1910).

Wernimont, P., and J. Campbell (1968). Signs, samples, and criteria. *Journal of Applied Psychology* 52: 372–73.

White, T. W., and P. B. Block (1975). *Police officer height and selected aspects of performance.* Police Foundation and International Association of Chiefs of Police, October.

Zeidenberg, J.; C. L. Bourbon; and R. Nahas (1977). Marijuana intoxication by passive inhalation: Documentation by detection of urinary metabolites. *American Journal of Psychiatry* 134: 76–89.

Zultowski, W. H.; R. D. Arvey; and B. L. Dawson (1978). Post-secondary educational requirements in employment decisions: A legal perspective. *Professional Psychology.* Aug: 507–525.

Summary, Trends, and Recommendations

9

Since the first edition of this book was published in 1979, hundreds of Title VII cases have been litigated in the selection domain. It has been an almost impossible task to keep track of the legal swings in this arena and to also stay abreast of the technical and research developments. Case law has developed progressively and many research developments have made the field of selection a far more sophisticated profession than it was ten years ago. In fact, we are convinced that the driving force behind many of the technical developments in staffing and selection has been due largely to the pressure exerted by Title VII and court interpretations of the *Uniform Guidelines*. We believe that we are far better off, as a profession, as a consequence of the legal pressure exerted over the years; this legal pressure has often resulted in the implementation of better business practices by organizations.

However, while many developments have occurred, it is somewhat surprising that little of the basic legal framework presented earlier has changed. For example, when adverse impact against a protected group occurs, organizations still must demonstrate the validity of their selection device. Moreover, the Uniform Guidelines still play a major role in helping judges better assess the credibility of the employer's validity evidence.

This chapter summarizes some of the themes abstracted from both the legal and research literatures that we believe indicate recent trends and potential directions. As in previous chapters, a summary of the legal literature is presented first.

LEGAL ASPECTS: SUMMARY, RECENT DEVELOPMENTS, AND TRENDS

The courts have become fully involved in almost every aspect of the selection process. Charges of discrimination have been levied against the full range of procedures, including recruitment, employment testing, and preemployment inquiries. In these cases, the "shifting burden of persuasion" principle is typically applied. Once the plaintiff establishes adverse impact, the burden of persuasion passes to the organization, which must demonstrate job-relatedness; if disparate treatment is established, the organization must articulate a non-discriminatory reason for its actions (see again Figure 3.3).

The EEOC and other governmental agencies issued guidelines in 1970 and 1978 that appeared to be the major standards by which the courts would review the adequacy of validation studies. For a time it appeared that organizations would always lose test-bias cases, because most validation studies could not pass review by these standards. The *Albemarle* v. *Moody* (1975) case seems to be a "high-water mark" in the selection area. In this case, the Supreme Court exhibited a willingness to give in-depth review to both the validation strategy and the deficiencies of the validation study. The Court used the 1970 EEOC testing guidelines as a "checklist" to evaluate the merits of the employer's validation study.

However, as noted in the first edition, the overall trend has shifted in a somewhat more conservative direction. Court decisions have moved more in favor of organizations than plaintiffs, especially as events that have taken place *outside* the court system have affected court decisions. In keeping with this conservative trend, the EEOC has begun the process of revising the 1978 Uniform Guidelines; revisions are likely in the near future.

Below is a summary of some of the more important legal trends that will likely affect the future of fairness issues:

1. *The existing case law indicates that the various sets of EEOC-issued guidelines will not be automatically accorded "great deference."* Several important Supreme Court decisions have not been in accord

with the information contained in the various EEOC guidelines, which indicates that the courts take other factors into account. Consider the following cases.

In *General Electric* v. *Gilbert* (1976), a case concerned with whether pregnancy of an employee was to be considered a temporary disability (see Chapter 4), the Court decided that the EEOC 1972 guidelines on sex discrimination were not entitled to judicial deference. If Congress had not enacted the Pregnancy Disability Act of 1978, the Court's ruling in *Gilbert* would stand today. Or in *Trans World Airlines* v. *Hardison* (1977), the Court did not explicitly reject any specific EEOC guidelines, but the decision was contrary to the viewpoint of the EEOC as expressed in their brief submitted to the Court. Finally, in *Connecticut* v. *Teal* (1982), the Court rejected the EEOC's approach to the use of "bottom-line" statistics for establishing adverse impact contained in the Uniform Guidelines. As the Court noted about the Uniform Guidelines in *Blake* v. *City of Los Angeles* (1977), "There is no magic in any validating procedure, and the defendants need only supply competent and relevant evidence on this issue" (p. 84).

We continue to believe that future court decisions will vary somewhat from EEOC opinions and guidelines, and the application of these guidelines will continue to be less "automatic" than in earlier court decisions. It should be noted, however, that the courts will still rely on the various sets of guidelines for substantial *guidance* in interpreting whether a selection device is valid. Thus deviance from the guideines issued by the various governmental administrative agencies does *not* mean total rejection of them, merely that they should not be viewed as *more* than guidelines. Moreover, if the Uniform Guidelines (or other guidelines) are revised as planned and the revisions reflect the conservative direction the EEOC and other agencies have come to take, court decisions based on these various sets of guidelines may be more in keeping with the "new" information they contain.

2. *The courts will begin to shift toward using utility losses and gains in reviewing selection procedures.* In the first edition of this book, it was suggested that the courts would begin to use utility evidence in reviewing the adequacy of selection procedures. This has occurred and is likely to continue. For example, in *Spurlock* v. *United Air-*

lines, Inc. (1972), the Supreme Court opened the door to the use of other than empirical evidence to support a defendant's rebuttal to a *prima facie* case of discrimination—especially in cases where the human or economic risks of hiring unqualified applicants were great. Applying the *Spurlock* principle in *Hodgson* v. *Greyhound Bus Lines, Inc.* (1974), the circuit court ruled that the defendant did not have to present evidence that bus driver applicants over 40 could not perform safely to support its use of age as a BFOQ. The court ruled that the defendant had to demonstrate only a "rational basis in fact to believe that elimination of its maximum hiring age would increase the likelihood of risk or harm to its passengers" (p. 819).

Moreover, in several cases where evidence of validity was marginal, the courts have looked to utility evidence to help formulate a ruling. For example, in *Pegues* v. *Mississippi State Employment Service* (1980), the judge considered the tests under review to have practical value (even though the reported validities were low) because of the considerable dollar value associated with the reported levels of validity and the grave consequences associated with false positives. Similarly, while low validity coefficients were reported in *Commonwealth of Pennsylvania* v. *O'Neill* (1979), the tests were nonetheless judged useful since the selection ratio was low and the risk of selecting applicants who were unqualified, as in *Pegues,* was high.

Alternatively, the judge in *Ensley Branch, NAACP,* v. *Seibels* (1977) ruled against the defendant even though the validity coefficient that the defendant introduced as evidence was statistically significant. The judge based his ruling on the fact that the validity coefficient was barely significant and the utility of the test was only marginal, especially in light of the amount of adverse impact reported.

It appears that validity evidence can often influence the court's ruling. Employers would be wise to consider utility in addition to validity evidence as they attempt to defend their employment procedures before the courts.

3. *The amount of litigation involving the handicapped and elderly will continue to increase substantially.* Since the Rehabilitation Act has been interpreted to include drug and alcohol abuse as handicaps that substantially limit an individual's ability to obtain employment, lawsuits involving these issues will increase. This is especially true as

organizations institute substance-abuse testing programs that selectively screen these individuals. Moreover, some suggest that individuals with AIDS should also be protected under the act; individuals with predispositions to genetic anomalies screened through genetic testing may also be covered. At the present time, it is unclear what the rights of employers and employees will be under these circumstances.

Age discrimination lawsuits are also appearing with greater frequency than in the distant past, especially in an economy where significant numbers of terminations and layoffs are occurring. This is likely to continue now that congressional action has done away with mandatory retirement as we have known it in the private sector. As a consequence, the actual physical and mental requirements for job performance will be scrutinized to assess how disabilities and age affect job performance (an excellent review of the relationship between age and job performance is contained in Rhodes, 1983).

4. *The courts will continue to exhibit an increased statistical knowledge and sophistication.* The "numbers game," as some people have called it, continues to gain more focused attention. For example, the *Hazelwood School District* v. *United States* (1977) decision addressed the proper statistics to be used in determining whether adverse impact occurred. In its decision, the Supreme Court considered percentages and standard deviations, as well as expected values, in reviewing whether the percentage of minority teachers in a school was disproportionately low. The Court was also heavily involved in statistical comparisons in *Teamsters* v. *United States* (1977), but sounded a voice of healthy caution:

> *Statistics are equally competent in proving employment discrimination. We caution only that statistics are not irrefutable; they come in infinite variety and, like any other kind of evidence, they may be rebutted. In short, their usefulness depends on all the surrounding facts and circumstances.*

More recently, in *EEOC* v. *Sears, Roebuck and Co.* (1986), the district court judge exhibited a remarkable level of sophistication as he sifted through reams of statistical evidence presented to establish and rebut a *prima facie* case of adverse impact. The judge reviewed the results of studies based on univariate and multivariate, least squares and logit multiple regression analyses. The judge's decision to reject the plaintiff's case rested on his analysis that many of the assumptions underlying the statistical procedures used by the plaintiff had not been met.

5. *Content validity will be used more frequently.* While unpopular several years ago, the courts have now recognized that it may be equal to criterion-related studies. Nevertheless, as courts become more sophisticated, it also seems likely that job-analysis procedures and methods will undergo close review. For example, the method of building content-valid tests and/or work samples based on job analysis has already been challenged. In addition, professional researchers will become more acquainted with the procedures and steps required to develop tests having "content validity." An article by Guion (1978) was one of the first to discuss issues of test fairness and content validity.

Content validity has also received greater recognition as a "legitimate" validation strategy in the latest *Standards for Educational and Psychological Testing* (1985). As noted by Kleiman and Faley (1985), "the Standards place great weight on the quality of validity evidence, regardless of the validation category used. An ideal validation includes several types of evidence, which span all three of the traditional categories. . . . Inferences about content are linked to test construction as well as to establishing evidence of validity after a test has been developed and chosen for use" (p. 831).

6. *Reverse discrimination lawsuits will likely decrease now that the Supreme Court has reaffirmed and further clarified the standards for affirmative-action–related preferential treatment.* In *U.S. Steelworkers* v. *Weber* (1979), the Supreme Court delineated a set of critera by which the courts could better determine the legality of organizational procedures that give preferential treatment to members of protected classifications based on Title VII standards. Recent Supreme Court decisions have affirmed and clarified these Title VII criteria as well as provided guidance about how they differ from constitutionally-based standards.

In the first edition of this book, it was suggested that organizations would turn to the development and administration of valid selection, classification, and placement devices in order to avoid the lawsuits that would likely accompany charges of reverse discrimination that result from the implementation of affirmative-action programs. This has occurred to some degree.

For example, in *Reeves* v. *Eaves* (1977), the court cooperated with the various parties to develop objective tests that would permit the selection of employees based on qualifications rather than affirmative-action–related preferential treatment that took race into consideration. Moreover, in *U.S.* v. *Paradise* (1987), rather than immediately imposing a strict hiring quota system, the court approved a consent decree giving the employer time to develop a set of selection procedures that would comply with the Uniform Guidelines.

What the courts appear to be saying is that even selection systems based on the implementation of programs that result in preferential treatment are much less likely to increase the flow of protected group members into and through the organization if the underlying organizational policies, procedures, and/or practices that created the problem in the first place are not identified and remedied. Selection procedures that involve voluntary or involuntary affirmative-action-related preferential treatment are *not* to be preferred over those that are valid and mitigate adverse impact in a more proactive fashion. However, if some type of proactive approach is not implemented where adverse impact exists, the courts will not shy away from the use of remedies that permit preferential treatment.

A very interesting and still pertinent discussion of the legal and technical issues involved in "benign discrimination" and compensatory treatment based on racial and ethnic characteristics is provided by Novick and Ellis (1977). One suggestion they make is that, instead of accepting group membership (e.g., race) as a surrogate for "disadvantage," future research efforts should focus instead on the identification and measurement of those factors that constitute "disadvantage."

SUMMARY, DIRECTIONS, AND TRENDS SUGGESTED BY RESEARCH

Beginning first with employment tests, the literature reviewed here suggests the following.

1. Many employment tests, especially those testing abstract processes (e.g., intelligence, cognitive reasoning) exhibit a sizeable mean difference in test scores between black and white employees and ap-

plicants. Thus the use of such tests almost always results in a finding of "adverse impact" against blacks when these tests are used in hiring.

2. The use of physical ability tests and standards results in a sizeable mean difference between males and females. This finding is not unusual or surprising.

3. There is increasing evidence that employment tests that measure cognitive abilities (after correction for statistical artifacts and small sample fluctuations), exhibit reasonably high validities across a large number of jobs and organizations. Thus there is increasingly strong evidence that cognitive test validities generalize to new situations or are "transportable." However, as noted above, these tests are also likely to adversely impact black minorities.

4. Although earlier research suggested that tests that might be valid for majority group members might not be valid for minority group members, data now indicate that findings of "differential validity" occur only rarely; thus a test that is valid for one group tends to be valid for the other group.

5. Models of test "fairness" have been developed and evaluated. The most widely used model at present is the "Cleary" model of test fairness (differential regression lines). Research studies show that tests do not appear to be unfair to blacks according to this model of fairness, as was previously believed. On the contrary, some evidence suggests that tests are unfair to white applicants or employees based on the Cleary model.

6. Research models that emphasize the relative utility of selection models have gained considerable acceptance and respect over the last ten years. Organizations are able to defend the use of selection devices (sometimes even those with marginal validity) by relying on utility analyses that demonstrate (1) considerable dollar value increments in productivity gained through the use of tests or (2) considerable economic and/or safety losses suffered when particular selection devices or alternative devices with lower validity were used.

7. Content validity methods and models have continued to receive a good deal of attention and development. Professional standards have evolved and continue to receive elaboration. Job analysis again con-

tinues to be a critical component of the content validity test development strategy.

Research concerning the employment interview can be summarized as follows:

1. Evidence concerning whether interviewers are unfair to female applicants continues to be accumulated. Although evidence indicates that females tend to receive lower interviewer evaluations than males, these differences are moderated by the type of job for which the applicants are being reviewed, the amount of information concerning the candidates, the qualifications of the candidates, and other important variables. We are less definite today in stating that the employment interview is discriminatory against females. Although the evidence points in this direction, other situational factors may provide the mechanisms under which such bias becomes manifested.

2. The limited studies regarding race bias in the employment interview show mixed findings. Although most studies demonstrate that blacks do *not* receive lower evaluations than whites in interview rating circumstances, these studies tended to be for "research only" purposes. Some studies show that in more real "field" settings, blacks receive lower evaluations.

3. There continues to be essentially no evidence supporting the notion that interview validities vary as a function of race, gender, etc. Only one study has examined whether differential regression lines occur as a function of age or gender (Arvey *et al.*, 1987). No differences were observed here, which indicates that, at least under one model of fairness (the Cleary model), the employment interview was not biased for these groups.

4. Taken as a whole, the research evidence indicates that older job candidates receive lower evaluations than younger candidates. Methodological confounds that potentially influence interviewer ratings of older candidates (e.g., nearness to retirement) are being identified and investigated. However, the evidence is mounting that older candidates may be particularly vulnerable targets of bias in the context of the employment interview.

5. Although there is not a great deal of literature dealing with bias against the handicapped in the interview, some research suggests that

these individuals receive lower evaluations compared to the non-handicapped. Moreover, some of the available data suggest that handicapped individuals are evaluated equally or even higher on some dimensions (e.g., motivation to work) but lower on others (e.g., acceptability as coworkers). No research has been conducted that examines the validity of the interview for predicting the job performance of individuals who have various handicaps.

The following conclusions about different preemployment inquiries can be drawn:

1. Recent research summarizing the few studies that have been published substantiates the validity of educational requirements. However, the use of educational requirements is likely to have a disproportionate impact on minority-group members, and organizations tend to have little data substantiating the validity of these requirements. The use of experience requirements has received slightly more research attention since the first edition of this text. The meager amount of available evidence indicates that experience requirements demonstrate a small but significant relationship with job performance and have been shown to have substantial utility when used for hiring, promotion, or certification purposes by the federal government.

2. Height and weight requirements have fairly clear adverse impact against some protected group members, especially females. Little research has been conducted evaluating the validity of these requirements, and the few studies performed show sparse relationships in predicting job performance.

3. Physical-ability tests are almost certain to have an adverse effect against females. There is mounting evidence, however, that when based on careful job-analysis procedures, physical-ability tests that directly reflect aspects of the job will be received more favorably by courts than tests of the underlying physical-ability constructs that must be defended via criterion- and construct-validity strategies.

4. Physiologically based screening tests that are used for selection purposes are likely to be reviewed much like other kinds of selection devices. That is, such tests will be examined in terms of their accuracy, reliability, and validity in predicting job performance. At this

time, no major issues of fairness have been raised regarding these tests, but it is interesting to speculate about this possibility in the future. It is quite possible that practices that incorporate drug testing, polygraph testing, genetic screening, and so forth will be reviewed from a Title VII perspective in the future.

FUTURE TRENDS

We predict that greater attention will be given to methodological and statistical concepts as they relate to selection issues and that the following areas will be given more attention:

1. The issue of the statistical power of validation designs to detect true validity will continue to receive research attention.

2. The problems associated with *small sample sizes* will be studied even more. Selection specialists and practitioners will become more aware of the problems of detecting significance and making proper inferences based on small sample sizes.

3. The area of validity generalization will begin to receive more attention by researchers; the implications of this model with regard to fairness issues will be more fully explored.

4. More sophisticated models of employee flow and recruitment will be studied. Very little research has been conducted concerning the flow of individuals through the organization and the impact of selection systems in these recursive models.

5. More attention will be given to utility models and their implications regarding the relative ''costs'' of different selection strategies.

6. Greater attention will be given to job analyses and the role of job analysis in content-validity paradigms. Researchers will begin to explore the limits of generalizing across jobs as well as across tests.

We also predict that selection specialists will become more acquainted with some of the *ethical* issues associated with discrimination. For example, Hunter and Schmidt (1976) identified three distinct ethical positions that could be adopted. The first position is that of ''unqualified individualism.'' This means that organizations are ethically bound to use whatever information yields the most predictive information about job performance (even if it means using such factors as race or sex as predictors), and to always select those individuals with the highest predicted performance level. This position is paramount to the classic American philosophy of hiring on the basis of merit. If such factors as sex or race were actually related to job performance, a person holding this ethical position would feel bound to use them in selection.

A second position identified by Hunter and Schmidt is "qualified individualism." Those who hold this position *refuse* to use such factors as race or sex as predictors even if they increase the accuracy of predictions about job performance. Thus a qualified individualist will use only traditional measures of ability and motivation in selection.

Finally, Hunter and Schmidt (1976) identified a "quota" mechanism. This position is based on selecting individuals in proportion to their population percentage; i.e., minorities should receive their "fair share" of any desirable job. For example, in a city of 60 percent whites and 30 percent blacks, an individual who holds a "quota" position would feel obligated to hire according to these percentages. An implicit assumption in this last definition is that subgroup differences are completely irrelevant for practically all jobs. Hunter and Schmidt examined these three ethical positions and detailed how particular statistical models of test bias have their origin in one or another of the ethical positions.

CHOOSING A SELECTION PROCEDURE

One way to review the various procedures is to evaluate the potential adverse impact on various minority groups. Figure 9.1 summarizes the various selection procedures and their likelihood of adverse impact on the four groups considered in this book.

A selection procedure likely to have adverse impact against one minority group is *not* likely to have such an impact against another group. Put another way, there is probably no single selection procedure that will not have disproportionate impact against some group. In short, there is no perfect selection device.

One strategy a personnel manager might employ is to differentiate the selection procedure used, depending on the types of candidates applying for a job. For example, if a large number of women are expected to apply for a job, a manager may decide to avoid the job interview as the major selection device and adopt some form of testing instead. Or

	Blacks	Females	Elderly	Handicapped
Cognitive ability tests	√√	+	√	?
Work – sample tests	+	NE	NE	NE
Interview	NE	√	√	√
Educational requirements	√√	+	√	?
Physical ability tests (height, weight, etc.)	+	√√	?	√√

√√ = Fairly established evidence of adverse impact

√ = Some evidence of adverse impact

? = No data that bear direct evidence, but adverse impact seems likely depending on type of handicap or type of test

NE = Little or no evidence to indicate one way or the other

+ = Evidence indicates that particular minority group does as well or even better than majority members

Fig. 9.1 *Several selection procedures and their possible adverse impact against different minority groups.*

if, on the other hand, a larger number of black applicants are expected, then the interview may prove useful in minimizing adverse impact. (However, this strategy is admittedly not helpful when it comes to choosing a strategy for selecting black females.)

Below are some guidelines for the practitioner concerning the selection of job candidates:

1. Keep ongoing, accurate records of the applicant flow. Monitor the numbers of minority and nonminority job candidates hired compared to the numbers applying for positions, in order to identify which particular selection procedures might have adverse impact.

2. Determine the job-relatedness of those particular selection procedures that exhibit an adverse impact, or seem likely to have an ad-

verse impact based on past research. Thus instead of attempting to validate *all* selection procedures used, it may be desirable to focus on those procedures most likely to be challenged.

3. Consider the use of work samples or other content-based selection procedures. If carefully developed, they are less likely to have adverse impact than more traditional tests. They have equal or greater validity than traditional tests, and are favorably accepted by the courts and employees themselves.

4. When choosing a selection test, rely on research findings and professional recommendations. Do not rely on test titles or testimonials about their validity.

5. If your validation strategy requires the use of performance ratings as criteria, be sure to examine the reliability and validity of them. Further, make sure that the scales reflect the critical components of work behavior as reflected in careful job analyses.

6. Consider the use of the validity-generalization strategy and/or synthetic validity paradigms as outlined in Chapter 6.

7. Conduct careful job analyses of the various jobs to determine the physical requirements of these jobs. As we have seen, denial of jobs to handicapped applicants is likely to be challenged unless evidence is presented that the job truly involves certain physical components.

8. If your organization requires a physical exam prior to hiring candidates, make sure the physician is well aware of the physical components of the job. Further, alert physicians to the litigation and suits being filed and the role they may have in helping your organization be "fair" in selecting employees.

9. Be particularly careful of height and weight requirements that may have been in existence for a long time. If these requirements have not been validated, consider eliminating them.

10. Conduct a careful audit of the current educational requirements specified for the jobs in your organization. Determine if these requirements are unrealistically high and/or whether the specific knowledges and skills involved in the jobs correspond to those same knowledges and skills derived from the educational experience. If the requirements cannot be justified, consider dropping them.

11. Begin to build careful and thorough documentary evidence concern-

ing the validity (criterion-related or content) of the selection devices used in your organization. Read the 1978 Uniform Guidelines concerning what documentation evidence is necessary, and follow these guidelines.

12. Begin to systematically quantify and record the evaluations made by your interviewers. Ask interviewers to correlate their judgments with later indices of job performance of those individuals hired. Interviewers will likely be surprised to learn that their evaluations are not as accurate as they might have believed.

13. Distribute to interviewers available state guidelines concerning allowable preemployment inquiries. If not available, hold workshops concerning the kinds of questions often asked during interviews that are potentially discriminatory in nature.

14. Alert all individuals in the organization about the various myths/ stereotypes concerning minority employees. Consider holding workshops on the topic of discrimination in employment.

15. Begin an active recruitment program. Make positive efforts (which may be costly) to use the best methods of advertising jobs to minorities.

16. Stay up-to-date with court developments. Consider subscribing to *Fair Employment Practices* or some other updating service. Make sure that relevant decisions are summarized and circulated widely throughout the organization, whether the decision was, in your opinion, a favorable or unfavorable one.

REFERENCES

Albemarle v. *Moody,* 10 FEP 1181 (1975).

American Psychological Association (1985). *Standards for Educational and Psychological Testing.* Washington, D.C.: APA.

Arvey, R. D.; H. Miller, R. Gould; and P. Birch (1987). Interview validity for selecting sales clerks. *Personnel Psychology* **40:** 1–12.

Blake v. *City of Los Angeles,* 15 FEP 76 (1977).

Commonwealth of Pennsylvania v. *O'Neill,* 465 F. Suppl. 451 (E.D. Penn.) (1979).

Connecticut v. *Teal,* 24 FEP Cases 1 (1982).

EEOC v. *Sears, Roebuck and Co.,* 39 FEP Cases 1672 (1986).

General Electric v. *Gilbert,* 13 FEP 1657 (1976).

Guion, R. M. (1978). Scoring of content domain samples: The problem of fairness. *Journal of Applied Psychology* 63: 499–506.

Hazelwood School District v. *United States,* 15 FEP 1 (1977).

Hodgson v. *Greyhound Bus Lines, Inc.,* 7 FEP Cases 817 (1974).

Hunter, J. E., and F. L. Schmidt (1976). Critical analysis of the statistical and ethical implications of various definitions of test bias. *Psychological Bulletin* 83: 1053–1071.

Kleiman, L. S., and R. H. Faley (1985). The implications of professional and legal guidelines for court decisions involving criterion-related validity: A review and analysis. *Personnel Psychology* 38: 803–833.

Novick, M. R., and D. D. Ellis, Jr. (1977). Equal opportunity in educational and employment selection. *American Psychologist* 32: 306–320.

Pegues v. *Mississippi State Employment Service,* 22 FEP Cases 392 (1980).

Reeves v. *Eaves,* 15 FEP 441 (1977).

Rhodes, S. R. (1983). Age-related differences in work attitudes and behavior: A review and conceptual analysis. *Psychological Bulletin* 93: 328–367.

Spurlock v. *United Airlines, Inc.,* 5 FEP Cases 17 (1972).

Teamsters v. *United States,* 14 FEP 1514 (1977).

Trans World Airlines v. *Hardison,* 14 FEP 1704 (1977).

United States v. *Paradise,* U.S. Supreme Court, No. 85-999, February 25 (1987).

U.S. Steelworkers v. *Weber,* 20 FEP Cases 1 (1979).

1978 Uniform Guidelines on Employee Selection Procedures

Appendix

General Principles

SECTION 1. *Statement of purpose.—A. Need for uniformity—Issuing agencies.* The Federal government's need for a uniform set of principles on the question of the use of tests and other selection procedures has long been recognized. The Equal Employment Opportunity Commission, the Civil Service Commission, the Department of Labor, and the Department of Justice jointly have adopted these uniform guidelines to meet that need, and to apply the same principles to the Federal Government as are applied to other employers.

B. *Purpose of guidelines.* These guidelines incorporate a single set of principles which are designed to assist employers, labor organizations, employment agencies, and licensing and certification boards to comply with requirements of Federal law prohibiting employment practices which discriminate on grounds of race, color, religion, sex, and national origin. They are designed to provide a framework for determining the proper use of tests and other selection procedures. These guidelines do not require a user to conduct validity studies of selection proce-dures where no adverse impact results. However, all users are encouraged to use selection procedures which are valid, especially users operating under merit principles.

C. *Relation to prior guidelines.* These guidelines are based upon and supersede previously issued guidelines on employee selection procedures. These guidelines have been built upon court decisions, the previously issued guidelines of the agencies, and the practical experience of the agencies, as well as the standards of the psychological profession. These guidelines are intended to be consistent with existing law.

SEC. 2. *Scope.—A. Application of guidelines.* These guidelines will be applied by the Equal Employment Opportunity Commission in the enforcement of title VII of the Civil Rights Act of 1964, as amended by the Equal Employment Opportunity Act of 1972 (hereinafter "Title VII"); by the Department of Labor, and the contract compliance agencies until the transfer of authority contemplated by the President's Reorganization Plan No. 1 of 1978, in the administration and enforcement of Executive Order 11246, as amended by Executive Order 11375 (hereinafter "Executive Order 11246"); by the Civil Service Commission and other Federal agencies subject to section 717 of Title VII; by the Civil Service Commission in exercising its responsibilities toward State and local governments under section 208(b)(1) of the Intergovernmental-Personnel Act; by the Department of Justice in exercising its responsibilities under Federal law; by the Office of Revenue Sharing of the Department of the Treasury under the State and Local Fiscal Assistance Act of 1972, as amended; and by any other Federal agency which adopts them.

B. *Employment decisions.* These guidelines apply to tests and other selection procedures which are used as a basis for any employment decision. Employment decisions include but are not limited to hiring, promotion, demotion, membership (for example, in a labor organization), referral, retention, and licensing and certification, to the extent that licensing and certification may be covered by Federal equal employment opportunity law. Other selection decisions, such as selection for training or transfer, may also be considered employment decisions if they lead to any of the decisions listed above.

C. *Selection procedures.* These guidelines apply only to selection procedures which are used as a basis for making employment decisions. For example, the use of recruiting procedures designed to attract members of a particular race, sex, or ethnic group, which were previously denied employment opportunities or which are currently underutilized, may be necessary to bring an employer into compliance with Federal law, and is frequently an essential element of any effective affirmative action program; but recruitment practices are not considered by these guidelines to be selection procedures. Similarly, these guidelines do not pertain to the question of the lawfulness of a seniority system within the meaning of section 703(h), Executive Order 11246 or other provisions of Federal law or regulation, except to the extent that such systems utilize selection procedures to determine qualifications or abilities to perform the job. Nothing in these guidelines is intended or should be interpreted as discouraging the use of a selection procedure for the purpose of determining qualifications or for the purpose of selection on the basis of relative qualifications, if the selection procedure had been validated in accord with these guidelines for each such purpose for which it is to be used.

D. *Limitations.* These guidelines apply only to persons subject to Title VII, Executive Order 11246, or other equal employment opportunity requirements of Federal law. These guidelines do not apply to responsibilities under the Age Discrimination in Employment Act of 1967, as amended, not to discriminate on the basis of age, or under sections 501, 503, and 504 of the Rehabilitation Act of 1973, not to discriminate on the basis of handicap.

E. *Indian preference not affected.* These guidelines do not restrict any obligation imposed or right granted by Federal law to users to extend a preference in employment to Indians living on or near an Indian reservation in connection with employment opportunities on or near an Indian reservation.

SEC. 3. *Discrimination defined: Relationship between use of selection procedures and discrimination.*—A. *Procedure having adverse impact constitutes discrimination unless justified.* The use of any selection procedure which has an adverse impact on the hiring, promotion, or other employment or membership opportunities of members of any race, sex, or ethnic group will be considered to be discriminatory and inconsistent with these guidelines, unless the procedure has been validated in accordance with these guidelines, or the provisions of section 6 below are satisfied.

B. *Consideration of suitable alternative selection procedures.* Where two or more selection procedures are available which serve the user's legitimate interest in efficient and trustworthy workmanship, and which are substantially equally valid for a given purpose, the user should use the procedure which has been demonstrated to have the lesser adverse impact. Accordingly, whenever a validity study is called for by these guidelines, the user should include, as a part of the validity study, an investigation of suitable alternative selection procedures and suitable alternative methods of using the selection procedure which have as little adverse impact as possible, to determine the appropriateness of using or validating them in accord with these guidelines. If a user has made a reasonable effort to become aware of such alternative procedures and validity has been demonstrated in accord with these guidelines, the use of the test or other selection procedure may continue until such time as it should reasonably be reviewed for currency. Whenever the user is shown an alternative selection procedure with evidence of less adverse impact and substantial evidence of validity for the same job in similar circumstances, the user should investigate it to determine the appropriateness of using or validating it in accord with these guidelines. This subsection is not intended to preclude the combination of procedures into a significantly more valid procedure, if the use of such a combination has been shown to be in compliance with the guidelines.

SEC. 4. *Information on impact.*—A. *Records concerning impact.* Each user should maintain and have available for inspection records or other information which will disclose the impact which its tests and other selection procedures have upon employment opportunities of persons by identifiable race, sex, or ethnic group as set forth in subparagraph B below in order to determine compliance with these guidelines. Where there are large numbers of applicants and procedures are administered frequently, such information may be retained on a sample basis, provided that the sample is appropriate in terms of the applicant population and adequate in size.

B. *Applicable race, sex, and ethnic groups for recordkeeping.* The records called for by this section are to be maintained by sex, and the following races and ethnic groups: Blacks (Negroes), American Indians (including Alaskan Natives), Asians (including Pacific Islanders), Hispanic (including persons of Mexican, Puerto Rican, Cuban, Central or South American, or other Spanish origin or culture regardless of race), whites (Caucasians) other than Hispanic, and totals. The race, sex, and ethnic classifications called for by this section are consistent with the Equal Employment Opportunity Standard Form 100, Employer Information Report EEO-1 series of reports. The user should adopt safeguards to insure that the records required by this paragraph are used for appropriate purposes such as determining adverse impact, or (where required) for developing and monitoring

affirmative action programs, and that such records are not used improperly. See sections 4E and 17(4), below.

C. *Evaluation of selection rates. The "bottom line."* If the information called for by sections 4A and B above shows that the total selection process for a job has an adverse impact, the individual components of the selection process should be evaluated for adverse impact. If this information shows that the total selection process does not have an adverse impact, the Federal enforcement agencies, in the exercise of their administrative and prosecutorial discretion, in usual circumstances, will not expect a user to evaluate the individual components for adverse impact, or to validate such individual components, and will not take enforcement action based upon adverse impact of any component of that process, including the separate parts of a multipart selection procedure or any separate procedure that is used as an alternative method of selection. However, in the following circumstances the Federal enforcement agencies will expect a user to evaluate the individual components for adverse impact and may, where appropriate, take enforcement action with respect to the individual components: (1) where the selection procedure is a significant factor in the continuation of patterns of assignments of incumbent employees caused by prior discriminatory employment practices, (2) where the weight of court decisions or administrative interpretations hold that a specific procedure (such as height or weight requirements or no-arrest records) is not job related in the same or similar circumstances. In unusual circumstances, other than those listed in (1) and (2) above, the Federal enforcement agencies may request a user to evaluate the individual components for adverse impact and may, where appropriate, take enforcement action with respect to the individual component.

D. *Adverse impact and the "four-fifths rule."* A selection rate for any race, sex, or ethnic group which is less than four-fifths (⅘) (or eighty percent) of the rate for the group with the highest rate will generally be regarded by the Federal enforcement agencies as evidence of adverse impact, while a greater than four-fifths rate will generally not be regarded by Federal enforcement agencies as evidence of adverse impact. Smaller differences in selection rate may nevertheless constitute adverse impact, where they are significant in both statistical and practical terms or where a user's actions have discouraged applicants disproportionately on grounds of race, sex, or ethnic group. Greater differences in selection rate may not constitute adverse impact where the differences are based on small numbers and are not statistically significant, or where special recruiting or other programs cause the pool of minority or female candidates to be atypical of the normal pool of applicants from that group. Where the user's evidence concerning the impact of a selection procedure indicates adverse impact but is based upon numbers which are too small to be reliable, evidence concerning the impact of the procedure over a longer period of time and/or evidence concerning the impact which the selection procedure had when used in the same manner in similar circumstances elsewhere may be considered in determining adverse impact. Where the user has not maintained data on adverse impact as required by the documentation section of applicable guidelines, the Federal enforcement agencies may draw an inference of adverse impact of the selection process from the failure of the user to maintain such data, if the user has an underutilization of a group in the job category, as compared to the group's representation in the relevant labor market or, in the case of jobs filled from within, the applicable work force.

E. *Consideration of user's equal employment opportunity posture.* In carrying out their obligations, the Federal enforcement agencies will consider the general posture of the user with respect to equal employment opportunity for the job or group of jobs in question. Where a user has adopted an affirmative action program, the Federal enforcement agencies will consider the provisions of that program, including the goals and timetables which the user has adopted and the progress which the user has made in carrying out that program and in meeting the goals and timetables. While such affirmative action programs may in design and execution be race, color, sex, or ethnic conscious, selection procedures under such programs should be based upon the ability or relative ability to do the work.

SEC. 5. *General standards for validity studies.*—A. *Acceptable types of validity studies.* For the purposes of satisfying these guidelines, users may rely upon criterion-related validity studies, content validity studies or construct validity studies, in accordance with the standards set forth in the technical standards of these guidelines, section 14 below. New strategies for showing the validity of selection procedures will be evaluated as they become accepted by the psychological profession.

B. *Criterion-related, content, and construct validity.* Evidence of the validity of a test or other selection procedure by a criterion-related validity study should consist of empirical data demonstrating that the selection procedure is predictive of or significantly correlated with important elements of job performance. See section 14B below. Evidence of the validity of a test or other selection procedure by a content validity study should consist of data showing that the content of the selection procedure is representative of important aspects of performance on the job for which the candidates are to be evaluated. See section 14C below. Evidence of the validity of a test or other selection procedure through a construct ˍvalidity study should consist of data showing that the procedure measures the degree to which candidates have identifiable characteristics which have been determined to be important in successful performance in the job for which the candidates are to be evaluated. See section 14D below.

C. *Guidelines are consistent with professional standards.* The provisions of these guidelines relating to validation of selection procedures are intended to be consistent with generally accepted professional standards for evaluating standardized tests and other selection procedures, such as those described in the Standards for Educational and Psychological Tests prepared by a joint committee of the American Psychological Association, the American Educational Research Association, and the National Council on Measurement in Education (American Psychological Association, Washington, D.C., 1974) (hereinafter "A.P.A. Standards") and standard textbooks and journals in the field of personnel selection.

D. *Need for documentation of valid-*

ity. For any selection procedure which is part of a selection process which has an adverse impact and which selection procedure has an adverse impact, each user should maintain and have available such documentation as is described in section 15 below.

E. *Accuracy and standardization.* Validity studies should be carried out under conditions which assure insofar as possible the adequacy and accuracy of the research and the report. Selection procedures should be administered and scored under standardized conditions.

F. *Caution against selection on basis of knowledges, skills, or ability learned in brief orientation period.* In general, users should avoid making employment decisions on the basis of measures of knowledges, skills, or abilities which are normally learned in a brief orientation period, and which have an adverse impact.

G. *Method of use of selection procedures.* The evidence of both the validity and utility of a selection procedure should support the method the user chooses for operational use of the procedure, if that method of use has a greater adverse impact than another method of use. Evidence which may be sufficient to support the use of a selection procedure on a pass/fail (screening) basis may be insufficient to support the use of the same procedure on a ranking basis under these guidelines. Thus, if a user decides to use a selection procedure on a ranking basis, and that method of use has a greater adverse impact than use on an appropriate pass/fail basis (see section 5H below), the user should have sufficient evidence of validity and utility to support the use on a ranking basis. See sections 3B, 14B (5) and (6), and 14C (8) and (9).

H. *Cutoff scores.* Where cutoff scores are used, they should normally be set so as to be reasonable and consistent with normal expectations of acceptable proficiency within the work force. Where applicants are ranked on the basis of properly validated selection procedures and those applicants scoring below a higher cutoff score than appropriate in light of such expectations have little or no chance of being selected for employment, the higher cutoff score may be appropriate, but the degree of adverse impact should be considered.

I. *Use of selection procedures for higher level jobs.* If job progression structures are so established that employees will probably, within a reasonable period of time and in a majority of cases, progress to a higher level, it may be considered that the applicants are being evaluated for a job or jobs at the higher level. However, where job progression is not so nearly automatic, or the time span is such that higher level jobs or employees' potential may be expected to change in significant ways, it should be considered that applicants are being evaluated for a job at or near the entry level. A "reasonable period of time" will vary for different jobs and employment situations but will seldom be more than 5 years. Use of selection procedures to evaluate applicants for a higher level job would not be appropriate:

(1) If the majority of those remaining employed do not progress to the higher level job;

(2) If there is a reason to doubt that the higher level job will continue to require essentially similar skills during the progression period; or

(3) If the selection procedures measure knowledges, skills, or abilities required for advancement which would be expected to develop principally from the training or experience on the job.

J. *Interim use of selection procedures.* Users may continue the use of a selection procedure which is not at the moment fully supported by the required evidence of validity, provided: (1) The user has available substantial evidence of validity, and (2) the user has in progress, when technically feasible, a study which is designed to produce the additional evidence required by these guidelines within a reasonable time. If such a study is not technically feasible, see section 6B. If the study does not demonstrate validity, this provision of these guidelines for interim use shall not constitute a defense in any action, nor shall it relieve the user of any obligations arising under Federal law.

K. *Review of validity studies for currency.* Whenever validity has been shown in accord with these guidelines for the use of a particular selection procedure for a job or group of jobs, additional studies need not be performed until such time as the validity study is subject to review as provided in section 3B above. There are no absolutes in the area of determining the currency of a validity study. All circumstances concerning the study, including the validation strategy used, and changes in the relevant labor market and the job should be considered in the determination of when a validity study is outdated.

SEC. 6. *Use of selection procedures which have not been validated.*—A. *Use of alternate selection procedures to eliminate adverse impact.* A user may choose to utilize alternative selection procedures in order to eliminate adverse impact or as part of an affirmative action program. See section 13 below. Such alternative procedures should eliminate the adverse impact in the total selection process, should be lawful and should be as job related as possible.

B. *Where validity studies cannot or need not be performed.* There are circumstances in which a user cannot or need not utilize the validation techniques contemplated by these guidelines. In such circumstances, the user should utilize selection procedures which are as job related as possible and which will minimize or eliminate adverse impact, as set forth below.

(1) *Where informal or unscored procedures are used.* When an informal or unscored selection procedure which has an adverse impact is utilized, the user should eliminate the adverse impact, or modify the procedure to one which is a formal, scored or quantified measure or combination of measures and then validate the procedure in accord with these guidelines, or otherwise justify continued use of the procedure in accord with Federal law.

(2) *Where formal and scored procedures are used.* When a formal and scored selection procedure is used which has an adverse impact, the validation techniques contemplated by these guidelines usually should be followed if technically feasible. Where the user cannot or need not follow the validation techniques anticipated by these guidelines, the user should either modify the procedure to eliminate adverse impact or otherwise justify continued use of the procedure in accord with Federal law.

SEC. 7. *Use of other validity studies.*—A. *Validity studies not conducted by the user.* Users may, under certain circumstances, support the use of selection procedures by validity studies conducted by other users or conducted by test publishers or distributors and described in test manuals. While publishers of selection procedures have a professional obligation to provide evidence of validity which meets generally accepted professional standards (see section 5C above), users are cautioned that they are responsible for compliance with these guidelines. Accordingly, users seeking to obtain selection procedures from publishers and distributors should be careful to determine that, in the event the user becomes subject to the validity requirements of these guidelines, the necessary information to support validity has been determined and will be made available to the user.

B. *Use of criterion-related validity evidence from other sources.* Criterion-related validity studies conducted by one test user, or described in test manuals and the professional literature, will be considered acceptable for use by another user when the following requirements are met:

(1) *Validity evidence.* Evidence from the available studies meeting the standards of section 14B below clearly demonstrates that the selection procedure is valid;

(2) *Job similarity.* The incumbents in the user's job and the incumbents in the job or group of jobs on which the validity study was conducted perform substantially the same major work behaviors, as shown by appropriate job analyses both on the job or group of jobs on which the validity study was performed and on the job for which the selection procedure is to be used; and

(3) *Fairness evidence.* The studies include a study of test fairness for each race, sex, and ethnic group which constitutes a significant factor in the borrowing user's relevant labor market for the job or jobs in question. If the studies under consideration satisfy (1) and (2) above but do not contain an investigation of test fairness, and it is not technically feasible for the borrowing user to conduct an internal study of test fairness, the borrowing user may utilize the study until studies conducted elsewhere meeting the requirements of these guidelines show test unfairness, or until such time as it becomes technically feasible to conduct an internal study of test fairness and the results of that study can be acted upon. Users obtaining selection procedures from publishers should

consider, as one factor in the decision to purchase a particular selection procedure, the availability of evidence concerning test fairness.

C. *Validity evidence from multiunit study.* if validity evidence from a study covering more than one unit within an organization statisfies the requirements of section 14B below, evidence of validity specific to each unit will not be required unless there are variables which are likely to affect validity significantly.

D. *Other significant variables.* If there are variables in the other studies which are likely to affect validity significantly, the user may not rely upon such studies, but will be expected either to conduct an internal validity study or to comply with section 6 above.

SEC. 8. *Cooperative studies.*—A. *Encouragement of cooperative studies.* The agencies issuing these guidelines encourage employers, labor organizations, and employment agencies to cooperate in research, development, search for lawful alternatives, and validity studies in order to achieve procedures which are consistent with these guidelines.

B. *Standards for use of cooperative studies.* If validity evidence from a cooperative study satisfies the requirements of section 14 below, evidence of validity specific to each user will not be required unless there are variables in the user's situation which are likely to affect validity significantly.

SEC. 9. *No assumption of validity.*—A. *Unacceptable substitutes for evidence of validity.* Under no circumstances will the general reputation of a test or other selection procedures, its author or its publisher, or casual reports of it's validity be accepted in lieu of evidence of validity. Specifically ruled out are: assumptions of validity based on a procedure's name or descriptive labels; all forms of promotional literature; data bearing on the frequency of a procedure's usage; testimonial statements and credentials of sellers, users, or consultants; and other nonempirical or anecdotal accounts of selection practices or selection outcomes.

B. *Encouragement of professional supervision.* Professional supervision of selection activities is encouraged but is not a substitute for documented evidence of validity. The enforcement agencies will take into account the fact that a thorough job analysis was conducted and that careful development and use of a selection procedure in accordance with professional standards enhance the probability that the selection procedure is valid for the job.

SEC. 10. *Employment agencies and employment services.*—A. *Where selection procedures are devised by agency.* An employment agency, including private employment agencies and State employment agencies, which agrees to a request by an employer or labor organization to device and utilize a selection procedure should follow the standards in these guidelines for determining adverse impact. If adverse impact exists the agency should comply with these guidelines. An employment agency is not relieved of its obligation herein because the user did not request such validation or has requested the use of some lesser standard of validation than is provided in these guidelines. The use of an employment agency does not relieve an employer or labor organization or other user of its responsibilities under Federal law to provide equal employment opportunity or its obligations as a user under these guidelines.

B. *Where selection procedures are devised elsewhere.* Where an employment agency or service is requested to administer a selection procedure which has been devised elsewhere and to make referrals pursuant to the results, the employment agency or service should maintain and have available evidence of the impact of the selection and referral procedures which it administers. If adverse impact results the agency or service should comply with these guidelines. If the agency or service seeks to comply with these guidelines by reliance upon validity studies or other data in the possession of the employer, it should obtain and have available such information.

SEC. 11. *Disparate treatment.* The principles of disparate or unequal treatment must be distinguished from the concepts of validation. A selection procedure—even though validated against job performance in accordance with these guidelines—cannot be imposed upon members of a race, sex, or ethnic group where other employees, applicants, or members have not been subjected to that standard. Disparate treatment occurs where members of a race, sex, or ethnic group have been denied the same employment, promotion, membership, or other employment opportunities as have been available to other employees or applicants. Those employees or applicants who have been denied equal treatment, because of prior discriminatory practices or policies, must at least be afforded the same opportunities as had existed for other employees or applicants during the period of discrimination. Thus, the persons who were in the class of persons discriminated against during the period the user followed the discriminatory practices should be allowed the opportunity to qualify under less stringent selection procedures previously followed, unless the user demonstrates that the increased standards are required by business necessity. This section does not prohibit a user who has not previously followed merit standards from adopting merit standards which are in compliance with these guidelines; nor does it preclude a user who has previously used invalid or unvalidated selection procedures from developing and using procedures which are in accord with these guidelines.

SEC. 12. *Retesting of applicants.* Users should provide a reasonable opportunity for retesting and reconsideration. Where examinations are administered periodically with public notice, such reasonable opportunity exists, unless persons who have previously been tested are precluded from retesting. The user may however take reasonable steps to preserve the security of its procedures.

SEC. 13. *Affirmative action.*—A. *Affirmative action obligations.* The use of selection procedures which have been validated pursuant to these guidelines does not relieve users of any obligations they may have to undertake affirmative action to assure equal employment opportunity. Nothing in these guidelines is intended to preclude the use of lawful selection procedures which assist in remedying the effects of prior discriminatory practices, or the achievement of affirmative action objectives.

B. *Encouragement of voluntary affirmative action programs.* These guidelines are also intended to encourage the adoption and implementation of voluntary affirmative action programs by users who have no obligation under Federal law to adopt them; but are not intended to impose any new obligations in that regard. The agen-

cies issuing and endorsing these guidelines endorse for all private employers and reaffirm for all governmental employers the Equal Employment Opportunity Coordinating Council's "Policy Statement on Affirmative Action Programs for State and Local Government Agencies" (41 FR 38814, September 13, 1976). That policy statement is attached hereto as appendix, section 17.

TECHNICAL STANDARDS

SEC. 14. *Technical standards for validity studies.* The following minimum standards, as applicable, should be met in conducting a validity study. Nothing in these guidelines is intended to preclude the development and use of other professionally acceptable techniques with respect to validation of selection procedures. Where it is not technically feasible for a user to conduct a validity study, the user has the obligation otherwise to comply with these guidelines. See sections 6 and 7 above.

A. *Validity studies should be based on review of information about the job.* Any validity study should be based upon a review of information about the job for which the selection procedure is to be used. The review should include a job analysis except as provided in section 14B(3) below with respect to criterion-related validity. Any method of job analysis may be used if it provides the information required for the specific validation strategy used.

B. *Technical standards for criterion-related validity studies.*—(1) *Technical feasibility.* Users choosing to validate a selection procedure by a criterion-related validity strategy should determine whether it is technically feasible (as defined in section 16) to conduct such a study in the particular employment context. The determination of the number of persons necessary to permit the conduct of a meaningful criterion-related study should be made by the user on the basis of all relevant information concerning the selection procedure, the potential sample and the employment situation. Where appropriate, jobs with substantially the same major work behaviors may be grouped together for validity studies, in order to obtain an adequate sample. These guidelines do not require a user to hire or promote persons for the purpose of making it possible to conduct a criterion-related study.

(2) *Analysis of the job.* There should be a review of job information to determine measures of work behavior(s) or performance that are relevant to the job or group of jobs in question. These measures or criteria are relevant to the extent that they represent critical or important job duties, work behaviors or work outcomes as developed from the review of job information. The possibility of bias should be considered both in selection of the criterion measures and their application. In view of the possibility of bias in subjective evaluations, supervisory rating techniques and instructions to raters should be carefully developed. All criterion measures and the methods for gathering data need to be examined for freedom from factors which would unfairly alter scores of members of any group. The relevance of criteria and their freedom from bias are of particular concern when there are significant differences in measures of job performance for different groups.

(3) *Criterion measures.* Proper safeguards should be taken to insure that scores on selection procedures do not enter into any judgments of employee adequacy that are to be used as criterion measures. Whatever criteria are used should represent important or critical work behavior(s) or work outcomes. Certain criteria may be used without a full job analysis if the user can show the importance of the criteria to the particular employment context. These criteria include but are not limited to production rate, error rate, tardiness, absenteeism, and length of service. A standardized rating of overall work performance may be used where a study of the job shows that it is an appropriate criterion. Where performance in training is used as a criterion, success in training should be properly measured and the relevance of the training should be shown either through a comparsion of the content of the training program with the critical or important work behavior(s) of the job(s), or through a demonstration of the relationship between measures of performance in training and measures of job performance. Measures of relative success in training include but are not limited to instructor evaluations, performance samples, or tests. Criterion measures consisting of paper and pencil tests will be closely reviewed for job relevance.

(4) *Representativeness of the sample.* Whether the study is predictive or concurrent, the sample subjects should insofar as feasible be representative of the candidates normally available in the relevant labor market for the job or group of jobs in question, and should insofar as feasible include the races, sexes, and ethnic groups normally available in the relevant job market. In determining the representativeness of the sample in a concurrent validity study, the user should take into account the extent to which the specific knowledges or skills which are the primary focus of the test are those which employees learn on the job.

Where samples are combined or compared, attention should be given to see that such samples are comparable in terms of the actual job they perform, the length of time on the job where time on the job is likely to affect performance, and other relevant factors likely to affect validity differences; or that these factors are included in the design of the study and their effects identified.

(5) *Statistical relationships.* The degree of relationship between selection procedure scores and criterion measures should be examined and computed, using professionally acceptable statistical procedures. Generally, a selection procedure is considered related to the criterion, for the purposes of these guidelines, when the relationship between performance on the procedure and performance on the criterion measure is statistically significant at the 0.05 level of significance, which means that it is sufficiently high as to have a probability of no more than one (1) in twenty (20) to have occurred by chance. Absence of a statistically significant relationship between a selection procedure and job performance should not necessarily discourage other investigations of the validity of that selection procedure.

(6) *Operational use of selection procedures.* Users should evaluate each selection procedure to assure that it is appropriate for operational use, including establishment of cutoff scores or rank ordering. Generally, if other factors reman the same, the greater the magnitude of the relationship (e.g., coorelation coefficient) between performance on a selection procedure

and one or more criteria of performance on the job, and the greater the importance and number of aspects of job performance covered by the criteria, the more likely it is that the procedure will be appropriate for use. Reliance upon a selection procedure which is significantly related to a criterion measure, but which is based upon a study involving a large number of subjects and has a low correlation coefficient will be subject to close review if it has a large adverse impact. Sole reliance upon a single selection instrument which is related to only one of many job duties or aspects of job performance will also be subject to close review. The appropriateness of a selection procedure is best evaluated in each particular situation and there are no minimum correlation coefficients applicable to all employment situations. In determining whether a selection procedure is appropriate for operational use the following considerations should also be taken into account: The degree of adverse impact of the procedure, the availability of other selection procedures of greater or substantially equal validity.

(7) *Overstatement of validity findings.* Users should avoid reliance upon techniques which tend to overestimate validity findings as a result of capitalization on chance unless an appropriate safeguard is taken. Reliance upon a few selection procedures or criteria of successful job performance when many selection procedures or criteria of performance have been studied, or the use of optimal statistical weights for selection procedures computed in one sample, are techniques which tend to inflate validity estimates as a result of chance. Use of a large sample is one safeguard: cross-validation is another.

(8) *Fairness.* This section generally calls for studies of unfairness where technically feasible. The concept of fairness or unfairness of selection procedures is a developing concept. In addition, fairness studies generally require substantial numbers of employees in the job or group of jobs being studied. For these reasons, the Federal enforcement agencies recognize that the obligation to conduct studies of fairness imposed by the guidelines generally will be upon users or groups of users with a large number of persons in a a job class, or test developers; and that small users utilizing their own selection procedures will generally not be obligated to conduct such studies because it will be technically infeasible for them to do so.

(a) *Unfairness defined.* When members of one race, sex, or ethnic group characteristically obtain lower scores on a selection procedure than members of another group, and the differences in scores are not reflected in differences in a measure of job performance, use of the selection procedure may unfairly deny opportunities to members of the group that obtains the lower scores.

(b) *Investigation of fairness.* Where a selection procedure results in an adverse impact on a race, sex, or ethnic group identified in accordance with the classifications set forth in section 4 above and that group is a significant factor in the relevant labor market, the user generally should investigate the possible existence of unfairness for that group if it is technically feasible to do so. The greater the severity of the adverse impact on a group, the greater the need to investigate the possible existence of unfairness. Where the weight of evidence from other studies shows that the selection procedure predicts fairly for the group in question and for the same or similar jobs, such evidence may be relied on in connection with the selection procedure at issue.

(c) *General considerations in fairness investigations.* Users conducting a study of fairness should review the A.P.A. Standards regarding investigation of possible bias in testing. An investigation of fairness of a selection procedure depends on both evidence of validity and the manner in which the selection procedure is to be used in a particular employment context. Fairness of a selection procedure cannot necessarily be specified in advance without investigating these factors. Investigation of fairness of a selection procedure in samples where the range of scores on selection procedures or criterion measures is severely restricted for any subgroup sample (as compared to other subgroup samples) may produce misleading evidence of unfairness. That factor should accordingly be taken into account in conducting such studies and before reliance is placed on the results.

(d) *When unfairness is shown.* If unfairness is demonstrated through a showing that members of a particular group perform better or poorer on the job than their scores on the selection procedure would indicate through comparison with how members of other groups perform, the user may either revise or replace the selection instrument in accordance with these guidelines, or may continue to use the selection instrument operationally with appropriate revisions in its use to assure compatibility between the probability of successful job performance and the probability of being selected.

(e) *Technical feasibility of fairness studies.* In addition to the general conditions needed for technical feasibility for the conduct of a criterion-related study (see section 16, below) an investigation of fairness requires the following:

(i) An adequate sample of persons in each group available for the study to achieve findings of statistical significance. Guidelines do not require a user to hire or promote persons on the basis of group classifications for the purpose of making it possible to conduct a study of fairness; but the user has the obligation otherwise to comply with these guidelines.

(ii) The samples for each group should be comparable in terms of the actual job they perform, length of time on the job where time on the job is likely to affect performance, and other relevant factors likely to affect validity differences; or such factors should be included in the design of the study and their effects identified.

(f) *Continued use of selection procedures when fairness studies not feasible.* If a study of fairness should otherwise be performed, but is not technically feasible, a selection procedure may be used which has otherwise met the validity standards of these guidelines, unless the technical infeasibility resulted from discriminatory employment practices which are demonstrated by facts other than past failure to conform with requirements for validation of selection procedures. However, when it becomes technically feasible for the user to perform a study of fairness and such a study is otherwise called for, the user should conduct the study of fairness.

C. *Technical standards for content validity studies.*—(1) *Appropriateness of content validity studies.* Users choosing to validate a selection procedure by a content validity strategy should determine whether it is appropriate to conduct such a study in the particular employment context. A selection procedure can be supported by a content validity strategy to the extent that it is a representative sample of the content of the job. Selection procedures which purport to measure knowledges, skills, or abilities may in certain circumstances be justified by content validity, although they may not be representative samples, if the knowledge, skill, or ability measured by the selection procedure can be operationally defined as provided in section 14C(4) below, and if that knowledge, skill, or ability is a necessary prerequisite to successful job performance.

A selection procedure based upon inferences about mental processes cannot be supported solely or primarily on the basis of content validity. Thus, a content strategy is not appropriate for demonstrating the validity of selection procedures which purport to measure traits or constructs, such as intelligence, aptitude, personality, commonsense, judgment, leadership, and spatial ability. Content validity is also not an appropriate strategy when the selection procedure involves knowledges, skills, or abilities which an employee will be expected to learn on the job.

(2) *Job analysis for content validity.* There should be a job analysis which includes an analysis of the important work behavior(s) required for successful performance and their relative importance and, if the behavior results in work product(s), an analysis of the work product(s). Any job analysis should focus on the work behavior(s) and the tasks associated with them. If work behavior(s) are not observable, the job analysis should identify and analyze those aspects of the behavior(s) that can be observed and the observed work products. The work behavior(s) selected for measurement should be critical work behavior(s) and/or important work behavior(s) constituting most of the job.

(3) *Development of selection procedures.* A selection procedure designed to measure the work behavior may be developed specifically from the job and job analysis in question, or may have been previously developed by the user, or by other users or by a test publisher.

(4) *Standards for demonstrating content validity.* To demonstrate the content validity of a selection procedure,

a user should show that the behavior(s) demonstrated in the selection procedure are a representative sample of the behavior(s) of the job in question or that the selection procedure provides a representative sample of the work product of the job. In the case of a selection procedure measuring a knowledge, skill, or ability, the knowledge, skill, or ability being measured should be operationally defined. In the case of a selection procedure measuring a knowledge, the knowledge being measured should be operationally defined as that body of learned information which is used in and is a necessary prerequisite for observable aspects of work behavior of the job. In the case of skills or abilities, the skill or ability being measured should be operationally defined in terms of observable aspects of work behavior of the job. For any selection procedure measuring a knowledge, skill, or ability the user should show that (a) the selection procedure measures and is a representative sample of that knowledge, skill, or ability; and (b) that knowledge, skill, or ability is used in and is a necessary prerequisite to performance of critical or important work behavior(s). In addition, to be content valid, a selection procedure measuring a skill or ability should either closely approximate an observable work behavior, or its product should closely approximate an observable work product. If a test purports to sample a work behavior or to provide a sample of a work product, the manner and setting of the selection procedure and its level and complexity should closely approximate the work situation. The closer the content and the context of the selection procedure are to work samples or work behaviors, the stronger is the basis for showing content validity. As the content of the selection procedure less resembles a work behavior, or the setting and manner of the administration of the selection procedure less resemble the work situation, or the result less resembles a work product, the less likely the selection procedure is to be content valid, and the greater the need for other evidence of validity.

(5) *Reliability.* The reliability of selection procedures justified on the basis of content validity should be a matter of concern to the user. Whenever it is feasible, appropriate statisti-

cal estimates should be made of the reliability of the selection procedure.

(6) *Prior training or experience.* A requirement for or evaluation of specific prior training or experience based on content validity, including a specification of level or amount of training or experience, should be justified on the basis of the relationship between the content of the training or experience and the content of the job for which the training or experience is to be required or evaluated. The critical consideration is the resemblance between the specific behaviors, products, knowledges, skills, or abilities in the experience or training and the specific behaviors, products, knowledges, skills, or abilities required on the job, whether or not there is close resemblance between the experience or training as a whole and the job as a whole.

(7) *Content validity of training success.* Where a measure of success in a training program is used as a selection procedure and the content of a training program is justified on the basis of content validity, the use should be justified on the relationship between the content of the training program and the content of the job.

(8) *Operational use.* A selection procedure which is supported on the basis of content validity may be used for a job if it represents a critical work behavior (i.e., a behavior which is necessary for performance of the job) or work behaviors which constitute most of the important parts of the job.

(9) *Ranking based on content validity studies.* If a user can show, by a job analysis or otherwise, that a higher score on a content valid selection procedure is likely to result in better job performance, the results may be used to rank persons who score above minimum levels. Where a selection procedure supported solely or primarily by content validity is used to rank job candidates, the selection procedure should measure those aspects of performance which differentiate among levels of job performance.

D. *Technical standards for construct validity studies.*— (1) *Appropriateness of construct validity studies.* Construct validity is a more complex strategy than either criterion-related or content validity. Construct validation is a relatively new and developing procedure in the employment field, and there is at present a lack of substantial literature extending the concept to employment practices. The user should be aware that the effort to obtain sufficient empirical support for construct validity is both an extensive and arduous effort involving a series of research studies, which include criterion related validity studies and which may include content validity studies. Users choosing to justify use of a selection procedure by this strategy should therefore take particular care to assure that the validity study meets the standards set forth below.

(2) *Job analysis for construct validity studies.* There should be a job analysis. This job analysis should show the work behavior(s) required for successful performance of the job, or the groups of jobs being studied, the critical or important work behavior(s) in the job or group of jobs being studied, and an identification of the construct(s) believed to underlie successful performance of these critical or important work behaviors in the job or jobs in question. Each construct should be named and defined, so as to distinguish it from other constructs. If a group of jobs is being studied the jobs should have in common one or more critical or important work behaviors at a comparable level of complexity.

(3) *Relationship to the job.* A selection procedure should then be identified or developed which measures the construct identified in accord with subparagraph (2) above. The user should show by empirical evidence that the selection procedure is validly related to the construct and that the construct is validly related to the performance of critical or important work behavior(s). The relationship between the construct as measured by the selection procedure and the related work behavior(s) should be supported by empirical evidence from one or more criterion-related studies involving the job or jobs in question which satisfy the provisions of section 14B above.

(4) *Use of construct validity study without new criterion-related evidence.*—(a) *Standards for use.* Until such time as professional literature provides more guidance on the use of construct validity in employment situations, the Federal agencies will accept a claim of construct validity without a criterion-related study which satisfies section 14B above only

when the selection procedure has been used elsewhere in a situation in which a criterion-related study has been conducted and the use of a criterion-related validity study in this context meets the standards for transportability of criterion-related validity studies as set forth above in section 7. However, if a study pertains to a number of jobs having common critical or important work behaviors at a comparable level of complexity, and the evidence satisfies subparagraphs 14B (2) and (3) above for those jobs with criterion-related validity evidence for those jobs, the selection procedure may be used for all the jobs to which the study pertains. If construct validity is to be generalized to other jobs or groups of jobs not in the group studied, the Federal enforcement agencies will expect at a minimum additional empirical research evidence meeting the standards of subparagraphs section 14B (2) and (3) above for the additional jobs or groups of jobs.

(b) *Determination of common work behaviors.* In determining whether two or more jobs have one or more work behavior(s) in common, the user should compare the observed work behavior(s) in each of the jobs and should compare the observed work product(s) in each of the jobs. If neither the observed work behavior(s) in each of the jobs nor the observed work product(s) in each of the jobs are the same, the Federal enforcement agencies will presume that the work behavior(s) in each job are different. If the work behaviors are not observable, then evidence of similarity of work products and any other relevant research evidence will be considered in determining whether the work behavior(s) in the two jobs are the same.

DOCUMENTATION OF IMPACT AND
VALIDITY EVIDENCE

SEC. 15. *Documentation of impact and validity evidence.*—A. *Required information.* Users of selection procedures other than those users complying with section 15A(1) below should maintain and have available for each job information on adverse impact of the selection process for that job and, where it is determined a selection process has an adverse impact, evidence of validity as set forth below.

339

(1) *Simplified recordkeeping for users with less than 100 employees.* In order to minimize recordkeeping burdens on employers who employ one hundred (100) or fewer employees, and other users not required to file EEO-1, et seq., reports, such users may satisfy the requirements of this section 15 if they maintain and have available records showing, for each year:

(a) The number of persons hired, promoted, and terminated for each job, by sex, and where appropriate by race and national origin;

(b) The number of applicants for hire and promotion by sex and where appropriate by race and national origin; and

(c) The selection procedures utilized (either standardized or not standardized).

These records should be maintained for each race or national origin group (see section 4 above) constituting more than two percent (2%) of the labor force in the relevant labor area. However, it is not necessary to maintain records by race and/or national origin (see § 4 above) if one race or national origin group in the relevant labor area constitutes more than ninety-eight percent (98%) of the labor force in the area. If the user has reason to believe that a selection procedure has an adverse impact, the user should maintain any available evidence of validity for that procedure (see sections 7A and 8).

(2) *Information on impact.—(a) Collection of information on impact.* Users of selection procedures other than those complying with section 15A(1) above should maintain and have available for each job records or other information showing whether the total selection process for that job has an adverse impact on any of the groups for which records are called for by sections 4B above. Adverse impact determinations should be made at least annually for each such group which constitutes at least 2 percent of the labor force in the relevant labor area or 2 percent of the applicable workforce. Where a total selection process for a job has an adverse impact, the user should maintain and have available records or other information showing which components have an adverse impact. Where the total selection process for a job does not have an adverse impact, information need not be maintained for indi-

vidual components except in circumstance the procedure used to determine adverse impact should be available.

(b) *When adverse impact has been eliminated in the total selection process.* Whenever the total selection process for a particular job has had an adverse impact, as defined in section 4 above, in any year, but no longer has an adverse impact, the user should maintain and have available the information on individual components of the selection process required in the preceding paragraph for the period in which there was adverse impact. In addition, the user should continue to collect such information for at least two (2) years after the adverse impact has been eliminated.

(c) *When data insufficient to determine impact.* Where there has been an insufficient number of selections to determine whether there is an adverse impact of the total selection process for a particular job, the user should continue to collect, maintain and have available the information on individual components of the selection process required in section 15(A)(2)(a) above until the information is sufficient to determine that the overall selection process does not have an adverse impact as defined in section 4 above, or until the job has changed substantially.

(3) *Documentation of validity evidence.—(a) Types of evidence.* Where a total selection process has an adverse impact (see section 4 above) the user should maintain and have available for each component of that process which has an adverse impact, one or more of the following types of documentation evidence:

(i) Documentation evidence showing criterion-related validity of the selection procedure (see section 15B, below).

(ii) Documentation evidence showing content validity of the selection procedure (see section 15C, below).

(iii) Documentation evidence showing construct validity of the selection procedure (see section 15D, below).

(iv) Documentation evidence from other studies showing validity of the stances set forth in subsection 15A(2)(b) below. If the determination of adverse impact is made using a procedure other than the "four-fifths rule," as defined in the first sentence of section 4D above, a justification, consistent with section 4D above, for selection procedure in the user's facility (see section 15E, below).

(v) Documentation evidence showing why a validity study cannot or need not be performed and why continued use of the procedure is consistent with Federal law.

(b) *Form of report.* This evidence should be compiled in a reasonably complete and organized manner to permit direct evaluation of the validity of the selection procedure. Previously written employer or consultant reports of validity, or reports describing validity studies completed before the issuance of these guidelines are acceptable if they are complete in regard to the documentation requirements contained in this section, or if they satisfied requirements of guidelines which were in effect when the validity study was completed. If they are not complete, the required additional documentation should be appended. If necessary information is not available the report of the validity study may still be used as documentation, but its adequacy will be evaluated in terms of compliance with the requirements of these guidelines.

(c) *Completeness.* In the event that evidence of validity is reviewed by an enforcement agency, the validation reports completed after the effective date of these guidelines are expected to contain the information set forth below. Evidence denoted by use of the word "(Essential)" is considered critical. If information denoted essential is not included, the report will be considered incomplete unless the user affirmatively demonstrates either its unavailability due to circumstances beyond the user's control or special circumstances of the user's study which make the information irrelevant. Evidence not so denoted is desirable but its absence will not be a basis for considering a report incomplete. The user should maintain and have available the information called for under the heading "Source Data" in sections 15B(11) and 15D(11). While it is a necessary part of the study, it need not be submitted with the report. All statistical results should be organized and presented in tabular or graphic form to the extent feasible.

B. *Criterion-related validity studies.* Reports of criterion-related validity for a selection procedure should include the following information:

(1) *User(s), location(s), and date(s) of study.* Dates and location(s) of the job analysis or review of job information, the date(s) and location(s) of the administration of the selection procedures and collection of criterion data, and the time between collection of data on selection procedures and criterion measures should be provided (Essential). If the study was conducted at several locations, the address of each location, including city and State, should be shown.

(2) *Problem and setting.* An explicit definition of the purpose(s) of the study and the circumstances in which the study was conducted should be provided. A description of existing selection procedures and cutoff scores, if any, should be provided.

(3) *Job anlysis or review of job information.* A description of the procedure used to analyze the job or group of jobs, or to review the job information should be provided (Essential). Where a review of job information results in criteria which may be used without a full job analysis (see section 14B(3)), the basis for the selection of these criteria should be reported (Essential). Where a job analysis is required a complete description of the work behavior(s) or work outcome(s), and measures of their criticality or importance should be provided (Essential). The report should describe the basis on which the behavior(s) or outcome(s) were determined to be critical or important, such as the proportion of time spent on the respective behaviors, their level of difficulty, their frequency of performance, the consequences of error, or other appropriate factors (Essential). Where two or more jobs are grouped for a validity study, the information called for in this subsection should be provided for each of the jobs, and the justification for the grouping (see section 14B(1)) should be provided (Essential).

(4) *Job titles and codes.* It is desirable to provide the user's job title(s) for the job(s) in question and the corresponding job title(s) and code(s) from U.S. Employment Service's Dictionary of Occupational Titles.

(5) *Criterion measures.* The bases for the selection of the criterion measures should be provided, together with references to the evidence considered in making the selection of criterion measures (essential). A full description of all criteria on which data were col-

lected and means by which they were observed, recorded, evaluated, and quantified, should be provided (essential). If rating techniques are used as criterion measures, the appraisal form(s) and instructions to the rater(s) should be included as part of the validation evidence, or should be explicitly described and available (essential). All steps taken to insure that criterion measures are free from factors which would unfairly alter the scores of members of any group should be described (essential).

(6) *Sample description.* A description of how the research sample was identified and selected should be included (essential). The race, sex, and ethnic composition of the sample, including those groups set forth in section 4A above, should be described (essential). This description should include the size of each subgroup (essential). A description of how the research sample compares with the relevant labor market or work force, the method by which the relevant labor market or work force was defined, and a discussion of the likely effects on validity of differences between the sample and the relevant labor market or work force, are also desirable. Descriptions of educational levels, length of service, and age are also desirable.

(7) *Description of selection procedures.* Any measure, combination of measures, or procedure studied should be completely and explicitly described or attached (essential). If commercially available selection procedures are studied, they should be described by title, form, and publisher (essential). Reports of reliability estimates and how they were established are desirable.

(8) *Techniques and results.* Methods used in analyzing data should be described (essential). Measures of central tendency (e.g., means) and measures of dispersion (e.g., standard deviations and ranges) for all selection procedures and all criteria should be reported for each race, sex, and ethnic group which constitutes a significant factor in the relevant labor market (essential). The magnitude and direction of all relationships between selection procedures and criterion measures investigated should be reported for each relevant race, sex, and ethnic group and for the total group (essential). Where groups are too small to obtain reliable evidence of the magnitude of

the relationship, need not be reported separately. Statements regarding the statistical significance of results should be made (essential). Any statistical adjustments, such as for less then perfect reliability or for restriction of score range in the selection procedure or criterion should be described and explained; and uncorrected correlation coefficients should also be shown (essential). Where the statistical technique categorizes continuous data, such as biserial correlation and the phi coefficient, the categories and the bases on which they were determined should be described and explained (essential). Studies of test fairness should be included where called for by the requirements of section 14B(8) (essential). These studies should include the rationale by which a selection procedure was determined to be fair to the group(s) in question. Where test fairness or unfairness has been demonstrated on the basis of other studies, a bibliography of the relevant studies should be included (essential). If the bibliography includes unpublished studies, copies of these studies, or adequate abstracts or summaries, should be attached (essential). Where revisions have been made in a selection procedure to assure compatability between successful job performance and the probability of being selected, the studies underlying such revisions should be included (essential). All statistical results should be organized and presented by relevant race, sex, and ethnic group (essential).

(9) *Alternative procedures investigated.* The selection procedures investigated and available evidence of their impact should be identified (essential). The scope, method, and findings of the investigation, and the conclusions reached in light of the findings, should be fully described (essential).

(10) *Uses and applications.* T... methods considered for use of the selection procedure (e.g., as a screening device with a cutoff score, for grouping or ranking, or combined with other procedures in a battery) and available evidence of their impact should be described (essential). This description should include the rationale for choosing the method for operational use, and the evidence of the validity and utility of the procedure as it is to be used (essential). The purpose for which the procedure is to be used (e.g., hiring, transfer, promotion) should be

described (essential). If weights are assigned to different parts of the selection procedure, these weights and the validity of the weighted composite should be reported (essential). If the selection procedure is used with a cutoff score, the user should describe the way in which normal expectations of proficiency within the work force were determined and the way in which the cutoff score was determined (essential).

(11) *Source data.* Each user should maintain records showing all pertinent information about individual sample members and raters where they are used, in studies involving the validation of selection procedures. These records should be made available upon request of a compliance agency. In the case of individual sample members these data should include scores on the selection procedure(s), scores on criterion measures, age, sex, race, or ethnic group status, and experience on the specific job on which the validation study was conducted, and may also include such things as education, training, and prior job experience, but should not include names and social security numbers. Records should be maintained which show the ratings given to each sample member by each rater.

(12) *Contact person.* The name, mailing address, and telephone number of the person who may be contacted for further information about the validity study should be provided (essential).

(13) *Accuracy and completeness.* The report should describe the steps taken to assure the accuracy and completeness of the collection, analysis, and report of data and results.

C. *Content validity studies.* Reports of content validity for a selection procedure should include the following information:

(1) *User(s), location(s) and date(s) of study.* Dates and location(s) of the job analysis should be shown (essential).

(2) *Problem and setting.* An explicit definition of the purpose(s) of the study and the circumstances in which the study was conducted should be provided. A description of existing selection procedures and cutoff scores, if any, should be provided.

(3) *Job analysis—Content of the job.* A description of the method used to analyze the job should be provided (essential). The work behavior(s), the associated tasks, and, if the behavior re-

sults in a work product, the work products should be completely described (essential). Measures of criticality and/or importance of the work behavior(s) and the method of determining these measures should be provided (essential). Where the job analysis also identified the knowledges, skills, and abilities used in work behavior(s), an operational definition for each knowledge in terms of a body of learned information and for each skill and ability in terms of observable behaviors and outcomes, and the relationship between each knowledge, skill, or ability and each work behavior, as well as the method used to determine this relationship, should be provided (essential). The work situation should be described, including the setting in which work behavior(s) are performed, and where appropriate, the manner in which knowledges, skills, or abilities are used, and the complexity and difficulty of the knowledge, skill, or ability as used in the work behavior(s).

(4) *Selection procedure and its content.* Selection procedures, including those constructed by or for the user, specific training requirements, composites of selection procedures, and any other procedure supported by content validity, should be completely and explicitly described or attached (essential). If commercially available selection procedures are used, they should be described by title, form, and publisher (essential). The behaviors measured or sampled by the selection procedure should be explicitly described (essential). Where the selection procedure purports to measure a knowledge, skill, or ability, evidence that the selection procedure measures and is a representative sample of the knowledge, skill, or ability should be provided (essential).

(5) *Relationship between the selection procedure and the job.* The evidence demonstrating that the selection procedure is a representative work sample, a representative sample of the work behavior(s), or a representative sample of a knowledge, skill, or ability as used as a part of a work behavior and necessary for that behavior should be provided (essential). The user should identify the work behavior(s) which each item or part of the selection procedure is intended to sample or measure (essential). Where the selection procedure purports to

sample a work behavior or to provide a sample of a work product, a comparison should be provided of the manner, setting, and the level of complexity of the selection procedure with those of the work situation (essential). If any steps were taken to reduce adverse impact on a race, sex, or ethnic group in the content of the procedure or in its administration, these steps should be described. Establishment of time limits, if any, and how these limits are related to the speed with which duties must be performed on the job, should be explained. Measures of central tend- ency (e.g., means) and measures of dispersion (e.g., standard deviations) and estimates of realibility should be reported for all selection procedures if available. Such reports should be made for relevant race, sex, and ethnic subgroups, at least on a statistically reliable sample basis.

(6) *Alternative procedures investigated.* The alternative selection procedures investigated and available evidence of their impact should be identified (essential). The scope, method, and findings of the investigation, and the conclusions reached in light of the findings, should be fully described (essential).

(7) *Uses and applications.* The methods considered for use of the selection procedure (e.g., as a screening device with a cutoff score, for grouping or ranking, or combined with other procedures in a battery) and available evidence of their impact should be described (essential). This description should include the rationale for choosing the method for operational use, and the evidence of the validity and utility of the procedure as it is to be used (essential). The purpose for which the procedure is to be used (e.g., hiring, transfer, promotion) should be described (essential). If the selection procedure is used with a cutoff score, the user should describe the way in which normal expectations of proficiency within the work force were determined and the way in which the cutoff score was determined (essential). In addition, if the selection procedure is to be used for ranking, the user should specify the evidence showing that a higher score on the selection procedure is likely to result in better job performance.

(8) *Contact person.* The name, mailing address, and telephone number of the person who may be contacted for

further information about the validity study should be provided (essential).

(9) *Accuracy and completeness.* The report should describe the steps taken to assure the accuracy and completeness of the collection, analysis, and report of data and results.

D. *Construct validity studies.* Reports of construct validity for a selection procedure should include the following information:

(1) *User(s), location(s), and date(s) of study.* Date(s) and location(s) of the job analysis and the gathering of other evidence called for by these guidelines should be provided (essential).

(2) *Problem and setting.* An explicit definition of the purpose(s) of the study and the circumstances in which the study was conducted should be provided. A description of existing selection procedures and cutoff scores, if any, should be provided.

(3) *Construct definition.* A clear definition of the construct(s) which are believed to underlie successful performance of the critical or important work behavior(s) should be provided (essential). This definition should include the levels of construct performance relevant to the job(s) for which the selection procedure is to be used (essential). There should be a summary of the position of the construct in the psychological literature, or in the absence of such a position, a description of the way in which the definition and measurement of the construct was developed and the psychological theory underlying it (essential). Any quantitative data which identify or define the job constructs, such as factor analyses, should be provided (essential).

(4) *Job analysis.* A description of the method used to analyze the job should be provided (essential). A complete description of the work behavior(s) and, to the extent appropriate, work outcomes and measures of their criticality and/or importance should be provided (essential). The report should also describe the basis on which the behavior(s) or outcomes were determined to be important, such as their level of difficulty, their frequency of performance, the consequences of error or other appropriate factors (essential). Where jobs are grouped or compared for the purposes of generalizing validity evidence, the work behavior(s) and work product(s) for

each of the jobs should be described, and conclusions concerning the similarity of the jobs in terms of observable work behaviors or work products should be made (essential).

(5) *Job titles and codes.* It is desirable to provide the selection procedure user's job title(s) for the job(s) in question and the corresponding job title(s) and code(s) from the United States Employment Service's dictionary of occupational titles.

(6) *Selection procedure.* The selection procedure used as a measure of the construct should be completely and explicitly described or attached (essential). If commercially available selection procedures are used, they should be identified by title, form and publisher (essential). The research evidence of the relationship between the selection procedure and the construct, such as factor structure, should be included (essential). Measures of central tendency, variability and reliability of the selection procedure should be provided (essential). Whenever feasible, these measures should be provided separately for each relevant race, sex and ethnic group.

(7) *Relationship to job performance.* The criterion-related study(ies) and other empirical evidence of the relationship between the construct measured by the selection procedure and the related work behavior(s) for the job or jobs in question should be provided (essential). Documentation of the criterion-related study(ies) should satisfy the provisions of section 15B above or section 15E(1) below, except for studies conducted prior to the effective date of these guidelines (essential). Where a study pertains to a group of jobs, and, on the basis of the study, validity is asserted for a job in the group, the observed work behaviors and the observed work products for each of the jobs should be described (essential). Any other evidence used in determining whether the work behavior(s) in each of the jobs is the same should be fully described (essential).

(8) *Alternative procedures investigated.* The alternative selection procedures investigated and available evidence of their impact should be identified (essential). The scope, method, and findings of the investigation, and the conclusions reached in light of the findings should be fully described (essential).

(9) *Uses and applications.* The methods considered for use of the selection procedure (e.g., as a screening device with a cutoff score, for grouping or ranking, or combined with other procedures in a battery) and available evidence of their impact should be described (essential). This description should include the rationale for choosing the method for operational use, and the evidence of the validity and utility of the procedure as it is to be used (essential). The purpose for which the procedure is to be used (e.g., hiring, transfer, promotion) should be described (essential). If weights are assigned to different parts of the selection procedure, these weights and the validity of the weighted composite should be reported (essential). If the selection procedure is used with a cutoff score, the user should describe the way in which normal expectations of proficiency within the work force were determined and the way in which the cutoff score was determined (essential).

(10) *Accuracy and completeness.* The report should describe the steps taken to assure the accuracy and completeness of the collection, analysis, and report of data and results.

(11) *Source data.* Each user should maintain records showing all pertinent information relating to its study of construct validity.

(12) *Contact person.* The name, mailing address, and telephone number of the individual who may be contacted for further information about the validity study should be provided (essential).

E. *Evidence of validity from other studies.* When validity of a selection procedure is supported by studies not done by the user, the evidence from the original study or studies should be compiled in a manner similar to that required in the appropriate section of this section 15 above. In addition, the following evidence should be supplied:

(1) *Evidence from criterion-related validity studies.—a. Job information.* A description of the important job behavior(s) of the user's job and the basis on which the behaviors were determined to be important should be provided (essential). A full description of the basis for determining that these important work behaviors are the same as those of the job in the original study (or studies) should be provided (essential).

b. *Relevance of criteria.* A full description of the basis on which the criteria used in the original studies are determined to be relevant for the user should be provided (essential).

c. *Other variables.* The similarity of important applicant pool or sample characteristics reported in the original studies to those of the user should be described (essential). A description of the comparison between the race, sex and ethnic composition of the user's relevant labor market and the sample in the original validity studies should be provided (essential).

d. *Use of the selection procedure.* A full description should be provided showing that the use to be made of the selection procedure is consistent with the findings of the original validity studies (essential).

e. *Bibliography.* A bibliography of reports of validity of the selection procedure for the job or jobs in question should be provided (essential). Where any of the studies included an investigation of test fairness, the results of this investigation should be provided (essential). Copies of reports published in journals that are not commonly available should be described in detail or attached (essential). Where a user is relying upon unpublished studies, a reasonable effort should be made to obtain these studies. If these unpublished studies are the sole source of validity evidence they should be described in detail or attached (essential). If these studies are not available, the name and address of the source, an adequate abstract or summary of the validity study and data, and a contact person in the source organization should be provided (essential).

(2) *Evidence from content validity studies.* See section 14C(3) and section 15C above.

(3) *Evidence from construct validity studies.* See sections 14D(2) and 15D above.

F. *Evidence of validity from cooperative studies.* Where a selection procedure has been validated through a cooperative study, evidence that the study satisfies the requirements of sections 7, 8 and 15E should be provided (essential).

G. *Selection for higher level job.* If a selection procedure is used to evaluate candidates for jobs at a higher level than those for which they will initially be employed, the validity evidence should satisfy the documentation provisions of this section 15 for the higher level job or jobs, and in addition, the user should provide: (1) a description of the job progression structure, formal or informal; (2) the data showing how many employees progress to the higher level job and the length of time needed to make this progression; and (3) an identification of any anticipated changes in the higher level job. In addition, if the test measures a knowledge, skill or ability, the user should provide evidence that the knowledge, skill or ability is required for the higher level job and the basis for the conclusion that the knowledge, skill or ability is not expected to develop from the training or experience on the job.

H. *Interim use of selection procedures.* If a selection procedure is being used on an interim basis because the procedure is not fully supported by the required evidence of validity, the user should maintain and have available (1) substantial evidence of validity for the procedure, and (2) a report showing the date on which the study to gather the additional evidence commenced, the estimated completion date of the study, and a description of the data to be collected (essential).

DEFINITIONS

SEC. 16. *Definitions.* The following definitions shall apply throughout these guidelines:

A. *Ability.* A present competence to perform an observable behavior or a behavior which results in an observable product.

B. *Adverse impact.* A substantially different rate of selection in hiring, promotion, or other employment decision which works to the disadvantage of members of a race, sex, or ethnic group. See section 4 of these guidelines.

C. *Compliance with these guidelines.* Use of a selection procedure is in compliance with these guidelines if such use has been validated in accord with these guidelines (as defined below), or if such use does not result in adverse impact on any race, sex, or ethnic group (see section 4, above), or, in unusual circumstances, if use of the procedure is otherwise justified in accord with Federal law. See section 6B, above.

D. *Content validity.* Demonstrated by data showing that the content of a selection procedure is representative of important aspects of performance on the job. See section 5B and section 14C.

E. *Construct validity.* Demonstrated by data showing that the selection procedure measures the degree to which candidates have identifiable characteristics which have been determined to be important for successful job performance. See section 5B and section 14D.

F. *Criterion-related validity.* Demonstrated by empirical data showing that the selection procedure is predictive of or significantly correlated with important elements of work behavior. See sections 5B and 14B.

G. *Employer.* Any employer subject to the provisions of the Civil Rights Act of 1964, as amended, including State or local governments and any Federal agency subject to the provisions of section 717 of the Civil Rights Act of 1964, as amended, and any Federal contractor or subcontractor or federally assisted construction contractor or subcontractor covered by Executive Order 11246, as amended.

H. *Employment agency.* Any employment agency subject to the provisions of the Civil Rights Act of 1964, as amended.

I. *Enforcement action.* For the purposes of section 4 a proceeding by a Federal enforcement agency such as a lawsuit or an administrative proceeding leading to debarment from or withholding, suspension, or termination of Federal Government contracts or the suspension or withholding of Federal Government funds; but not a finding of reasonable cause or a conciliation process or the issuance of right to sue letters under title VII or under Executive Order 11246 where such finding, conciliation, or issuance of notice of right to sue is based upon an individual complaint.

J. *Enforcement agency.* Any agency of the executive branch of the Federal Government which adopts these guidelines for purposes of the enforcement of the equal employment opportunity laws or which has responsibility for securing compliance with them.

K. *Job analysis.* A detailed statement of work behaviors and other information relevant to the job.

L. *Job description.* A general statement of job duties and responsibilities.

M. *Knowledge.* A body of information applied directly to the performance of a function.

N. *Labor organization.* Any labor organization subject to the provisions of the Civil Rights Act of 1964, as amended, and any committee subject thereto controlling apprenticeship or other training.

O. *Observable.* Able to be seen, heard, or otherwise perceived by a person other than the person performing the action.

P. *Race, sex, or ethnic group.* Any group of persons identifiable on the grounds of race, color, religion, sex, or national origin.

Q. *Selection procedure.* Any measure, combination of measures, or procedure used as a basis for any employment decision. Selection procedures include the full range of assessment techniques from traditional paper and pencil tests, performance tests, training programs, or probationary periods and physical, educational, and work experience requirements through informal or casual interviews and unscored application forms.

R. *Selection rate.* The proportion of applicants or candidates who are hired, promoted, or otherwise selected.

S. *Should.* The term "should" as used in these guidelines is intended to connote action which is necessary to achieve compliance with the guidelines, while recognizing that there are circumstances where alternative courses of action are open to users.

T. *Skill.* A present, observable competence to perform a learned psychomoter act.

U. *Technical feasibility.* The existence of conditions permitting the conduct of meaningful criterion-related validity studies. These conditions include: (1) An adequate sample of persons available for the study to achieve findings of statistical significance; (2) having or being able to obtain a sufficient range of scores on the selection procedure and job performance measures to produce validity results which can be expected to be representative of the results if the ranges normally expected were utilized; and (3) having or being able to devise unbiased, reliable and relevant measures of job performance or other criteria of employee adequacy. See section 14B(2). With respect to investigation of possible unfairness, the same considerations are applicable to each group for which the study is made. See section 14B(8).

V. *Unfairness of selection procedure.* A condition in which members of one race, sex, or ethnic group characteristically obtain lower scores on a selection procedure than members of another group, and the differences are not reflected in differences in measures of job performance. See section 14B(7).

W. *User.* Any employer, labor organization, employment agency, or licensing or certification board, to the extent it may be covered by Federal equal employment opportunity law, which uses a selection procedure as a basis for any employment decision. Whenever an employer, labor organization, or employment agency is required by law to restrict recruitment for any occupation to those applicants who have met licensing or certification requirements, the licensing or certifying authority to the extent it may be covered by Federal equal employment opportunity law will be considered the user with respect to those licensing or certification requirements. Whenever a State employment agency or service does no more than administer or monitor a procedure as permitted by Department of Labor regulations, and does so without making referrals or taking any other action on the basis of the results, the State employment agency will not be deemed to be a user.

X. *Validated in accord with these guidelines or properly validated.* A demonstration that one or more validity study or studies meeting the standards of these guidelines has been conducted, including investigation and, where appropriate, use of suitable alternative selection procedures as contemplated by section 3B, and has produced evidence of validity sufficient to warrant use of the procedure for the intended purpose under the standards of these guidelines.

Y. *Work behavior.* An activity performed to achieve the objectives of the job. Work behaviors involve observable (physical) components and unobservable (mental) components. A work behavior consists of the performance of one or more tasks. Knowledges, skills, and abilities are not behaviors, although they may be applied in work behaviors.

APPENDIX

17. *Policy statement on affirmative action* (see section 13B). The Equal Employment Opportunity Coordinating Council was established by act of Congress in 1972, and charged with responsibility for developing and implementing agreements and policies designed, among other things, to eliminate conflict and inconsistency among the agencies of the Federal Government responsible for administering Federal law prohibiting discrimination on grounds of race, color, sex, religion, and national origin. This statement is issued as an initial response to the requests of a number of State and local officials for clarification of the Government's policies concerning the role of affirmative action in the overall equal employment opportunity program. While the Coordinating Council's adoption of this statement expresses only the views of the signatory agencies concerning this important subject, the principles set forth below should serve as policy guidance for other Federal agencies as well.

(1) Equal employment opportunity is the law of the land. In the public sector of our society this means that all persons, regardless of race, color, religion, sex, or national origin shall have equal access to positions in the public service limited only by their ability to do the job. There is ample evidence in all sectors of our society that such equal access frequently has been denied to members of certain groups because of their sex, racial, or ethnic characteristics. The remedy for such past and present discrimination is twofold.

On the one hand, vigorous enforcement of the laws against discrimination is essential. But equally, and perhaps even more important are affirmative, voluntary efforts on the part of public employers to assure that positions in the public service are genuinely and equally accessible to qualified persons, without regard to their sex, racial, or ethnic characteristics. Without such efforts equal employment opportunity is no more than a wish. The importance of voluntary affirmative action on the part of employers is underscored by title VII of the Civil Rights Act of 1964, Executive Order 11246, and related laws and regulations—all of which emphasize voluntary action to achieve equal employment opportunity.

As with most management objectives, a systematic plan based on sound organizational analysis and problem identification is crucial to the accomplishment of affirmative action objectives. For this reason, the Council urges all State and local governments to develop and implement results oriented affirmative action plans which deal with the problems so identified.

The following paragraphs are intended to assist State and local governments by illustrating the kinds of analyses and activities which may be appropriate for a public employer's voluntary affirmative action plan. This statement does not address remedies imposed after a finding of unlawful discrimination.

(2) Voluntary affirmative action to assure equal employment opportunity is appropriate at any stage of the employment process. The first step in the construction of any affirmative action plan should be an analysis of the employer's work force to determine whether precentages of sex, race, or ethnic groups in individual job classifications are substantially similar to the precentages of those groups available in the relevant job market who possess the basic job-related qualifications.

When substantial disparities are found through such analyses, each element of the overall selection process should be examined to determine which elements operate to exclude persons on the basis of sex, race, or ethnic group. Such elements include, but are not limited to, recruitment, testing, ranking certification, interview, recommendations for selection, hiring, promotion, etc. The examination of each element of the selection process should at a minimum include a determination of its validity in predicting job performance.

(3) When an employer has reason to believe that its selection procedures have the exclusionary effect described in paragraph 2 above, it should initiate affirmative steps to remedy the situation. Such steps, which in design and execution may be race, color, sex, or ethnic "conscious," include, but are not limited to the following:

(a) The establishment of a long-term goal, and short-range, interim goals and timetables for the specific job classifications, all of which should take into account the availability of basically qualified persons in the relevant job market;

(b) A recruitment program designed to attract qualified members of the group in question;

(c) A systematic effort to organize work and redesign jobs in ways that provide opportunities for persons lacking "journeyman" level knowledge or skills to enter and, with appropriate training, to progress in a career field;

(d) Revamping selection instruments or procedures which have not yet been validated in order to reduce or eliminate exclusionary effects on particular groups in particular job classifications;

(e) The initiation of measures designed to assure that members of the affected group who are qualified to perform the job are included within the pool of persons from which the selecting official makes the selection;

(f) A systematic effort to provide career advancement training, both classroom and on-the-job, to employees locked into dead end jobs; and

(g) The establishment of a system for regularly monitoring the effectiveness of the particular affirmative action program, and procedures for making timely adjustments in this program where effectiveness is not demonstrated.

(4) The goal of any affirmative action plan should be achievement of genuine equal employment opportunity for all qualified persons. Selection under such plans should be based upon the ability of the applicant(s) to do the work. Such plans should not require the selection of the unqualified, or the unneeded, nor should they require the selection of persons on the basis of race, color, sex, religion, or national origin. Moreover, while the Council believes that this statement should serve to assist State and local employers, as well as Federal agencies, it recognizes that affirmative action cannot be viewed as a standardized program which must be accomplished in the same way at all times in all places.

Accordingly, the Council has not attempted to set forth here either the minimum or maximum voluntary steps that employers may take to deal with their respective situations. Rather, the Council recognizes that under applicable authorities, State and local employers have flexibility to formulate affirmative action plans that are best suited to their particular situations. In this manner, the Council believes that affirmative action programs will best serve the goal of equal employment opportunity. ■

Author Index

Subject Index